犬夜叉

INUYASHA

ANI-MANGA Vol.24

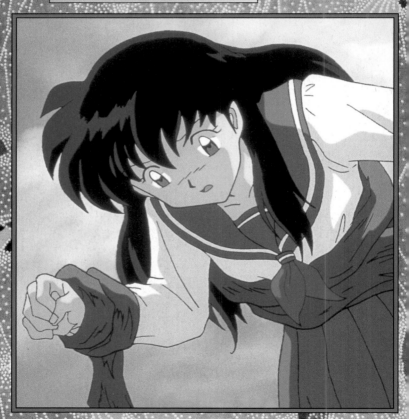

CREATED BY
RUMIKO TAKAHASHI

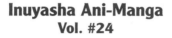

Inuyasha Ani-Manga
Vol. #24

Created by
Rumiko Takahashi

Translation based on the VIZ anime TV series
Translation Assistance/Katy Bridges
Lettering & Editorial Assistance/John Clark
Cover Design & Graphics/Hidemi Sahara
Editor/Ian Robertson

Editor in Chief, Books/Alvin Lu
Editor in Chief, Magazines/Marc Weidenbaum
VP of Publishing Licensing/Rika Inouye
VP of Sales/Gonzalo Ferreyra
Sr. VP of Marketing/Liza Coppola
Publisher/Hyoe Narita

© 2003 Rumiko TAKAHASHI/Shogakukan Inc.
© Rumiko TAKAHASHI/Shogakukan, Yomiuri TV, Sunrise 2000.
First published by Shogakukan Inc. in Japan as "TV Anime-ban Inuyasha."
Ani-Manga is a trademark of VIZ Media, LLC. All rights reserved.
The stories, characters, and incidents mentioned in this publication are entirely fictional.

Printed in the U.S.A.

Published by VIZ Media, LLC
P.O. Box 77010
San Francisco, CA 94107

10 9 8 7 6 5 4 3 2 1
First printing, December 2007

www.viz.com
store.viz.com

PARENTAL ADVISORY
INUYASHA ANI-MANGA is rated T+
for Older Teen and is recommended for
ages 16 and up. This volume contains
realistic and fantasy violence.
ratings.viz.com

Story thus far

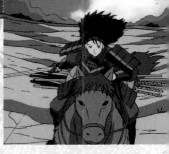

Kagome's mundane teenage existence was turned upside down when she was transported into a mythical version of Japan's medieval past! Kagome is the reincarnation of Lady Kikyo, a great warrior and the defender of the Shikon Jewel, or the Jewel of Four Souls. Kikyo was in love with Inuyasha, a dog-like half-demon who wishes to possess the jewel in order to transform himself into a full-fledged demon. But 50 years earlier, the evil shape-shifting Naraku tricked Kikyo and Inuyasha into betraying one another. The betrayal led to Kikyo's death and Inuyasha's imprisonment under a binding spell...and Inuyasha remained trapped by the spell until Kagome appeared in feudal Japan and unwittingly released him!

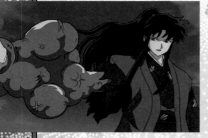

In a skirmish for its possession, the Shikon Jewel accidentally shatters and is strewn across the land. Only Kagome has the power to find the jewel shards, and only Inuyasha has the strength to defeat the demons that now hold them, so the two unlikely partners are bound together in the quest to reclaim all the pieces of the sacred jewel. To prevent Inuyasha from stealing the jewel, Kikyo's sister, Lady Kaede, puts a magical necklace around Inuyasha's neck that allows Kagome to make him "sit" on command. Inuyasha's greatest tool in the fight to recover the sacred jewel shards is his father's sword, the Tetsusaiga, but Inuyasha's half-brother Sesshomaru covets the mighty blade and has tried to steal it more than once.

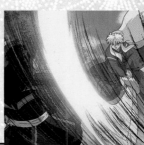

The fight against the mysterious Muso continues! Although he seems to be an incarnation of Naraku like Kagura and Kanna, he doesn't seem to be under Naraku's control. After seeing Kagome, something awakens within Muso—memories of a past that involves Inuyasha and Kikyo. Meanwhile, Inuyasha seeks Totosai in order to find a way to increase the power of the Tetsusaiga.

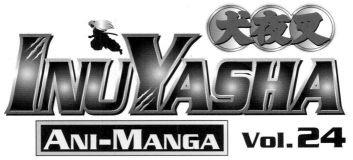

INUYASHA

ANI-MANGA Vol. 24

Contents

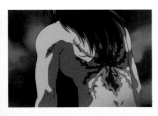

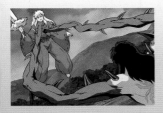

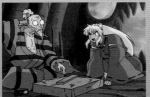

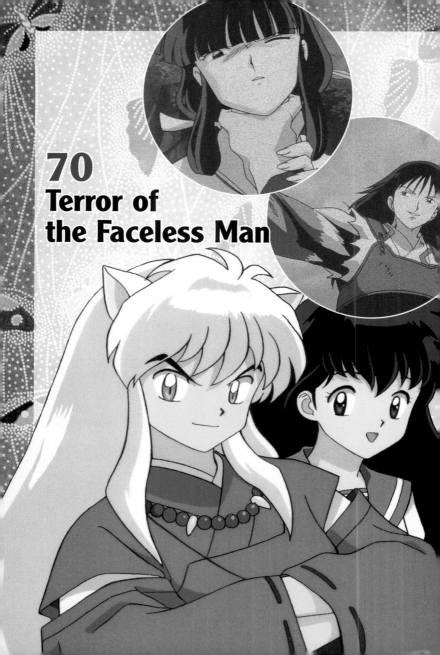

70
Terror of
the Faceless Man

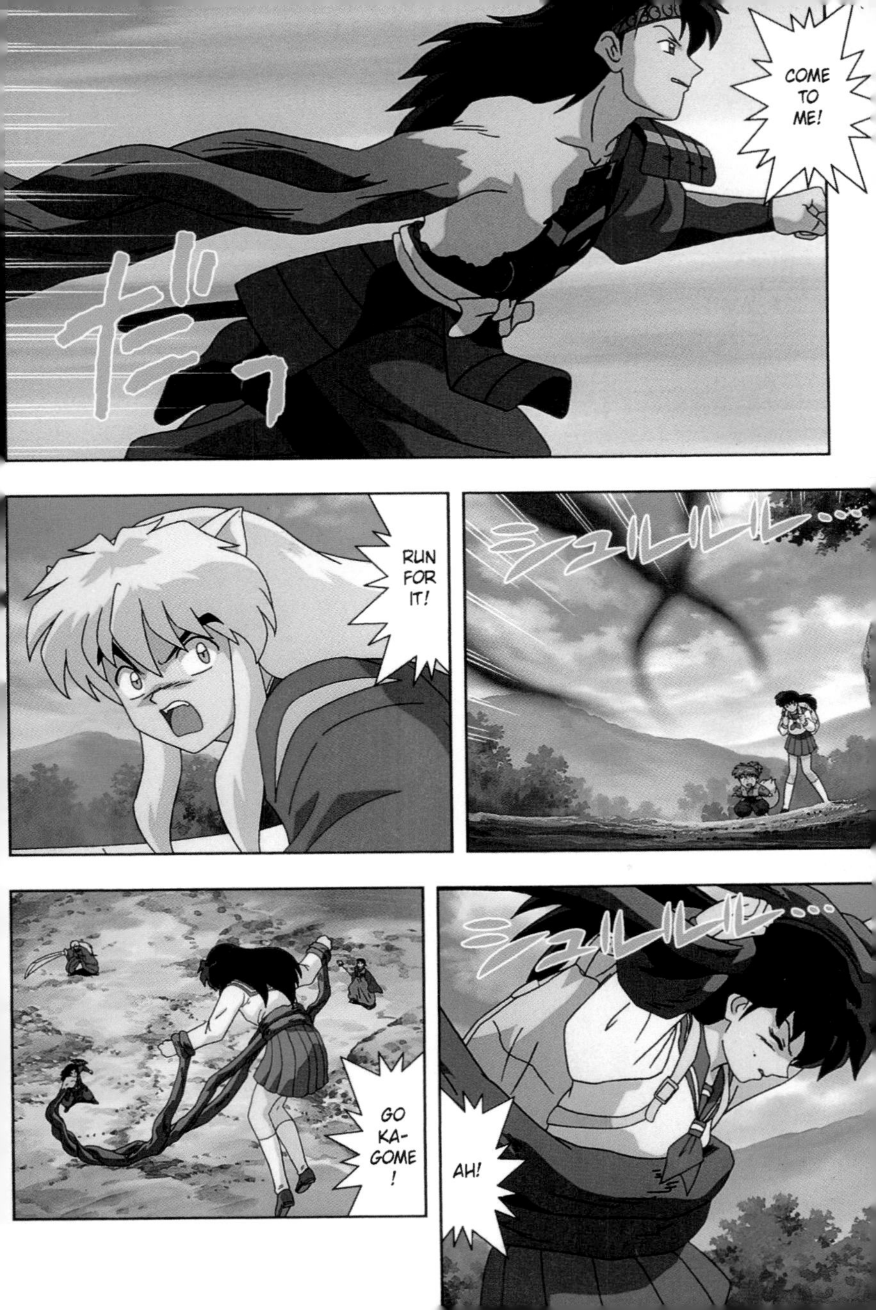
COME TO ME!
RUN FOR IT!
AH!
GO KA-GOME!

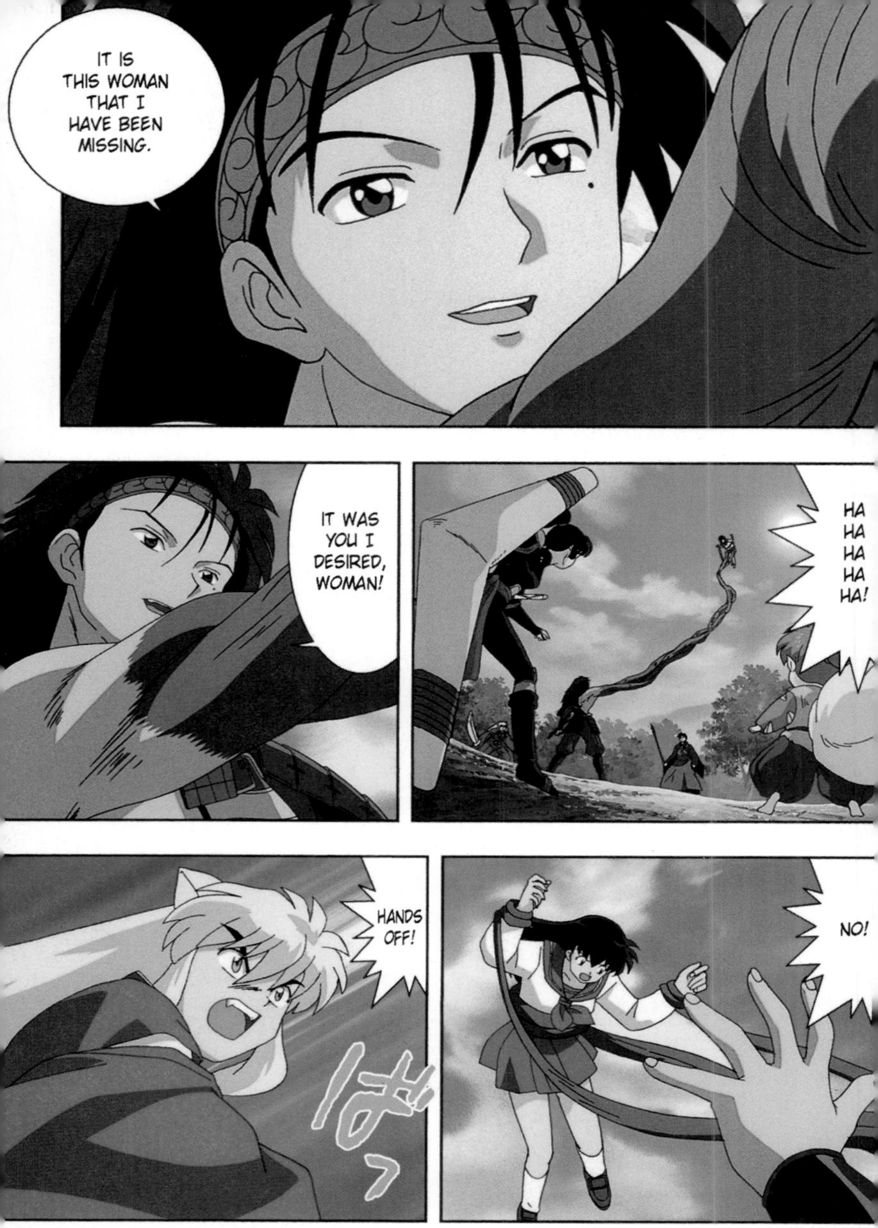
IT IS THIS WOMAN THAT I HAVE BEEN MISSING.
HA HA HA HA HA!
IT WAS YOU I DESIRED, WOMAN!
NO!
HANDS OFF!
ばっ

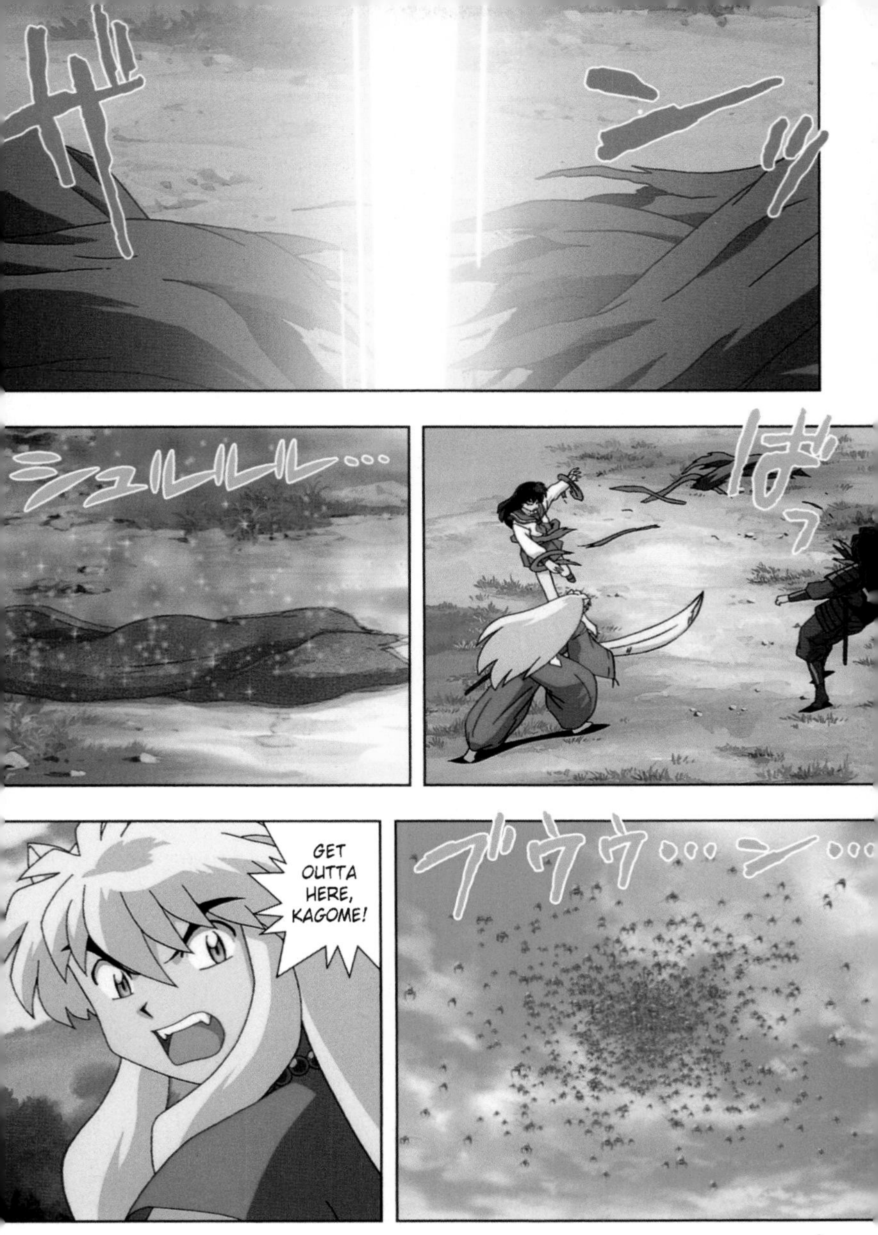
ザンッ
ぼっ
シュルルルル…
ブウウ…ン…
GET OUTTA HERE, KAGOME!

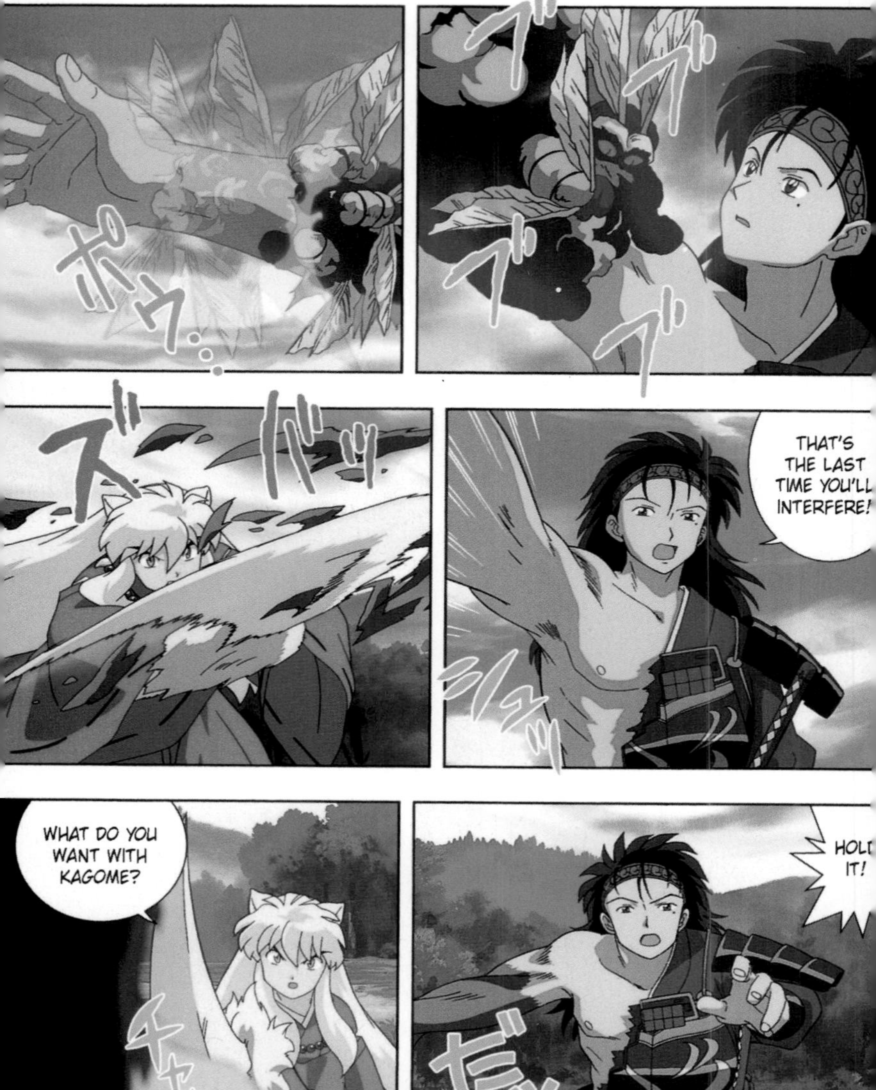
THAT'S THE LAST TIME YOU'LL INTERFERE!
HOLD IT!
WHAT DO YOU WANT WITH KAGOME?

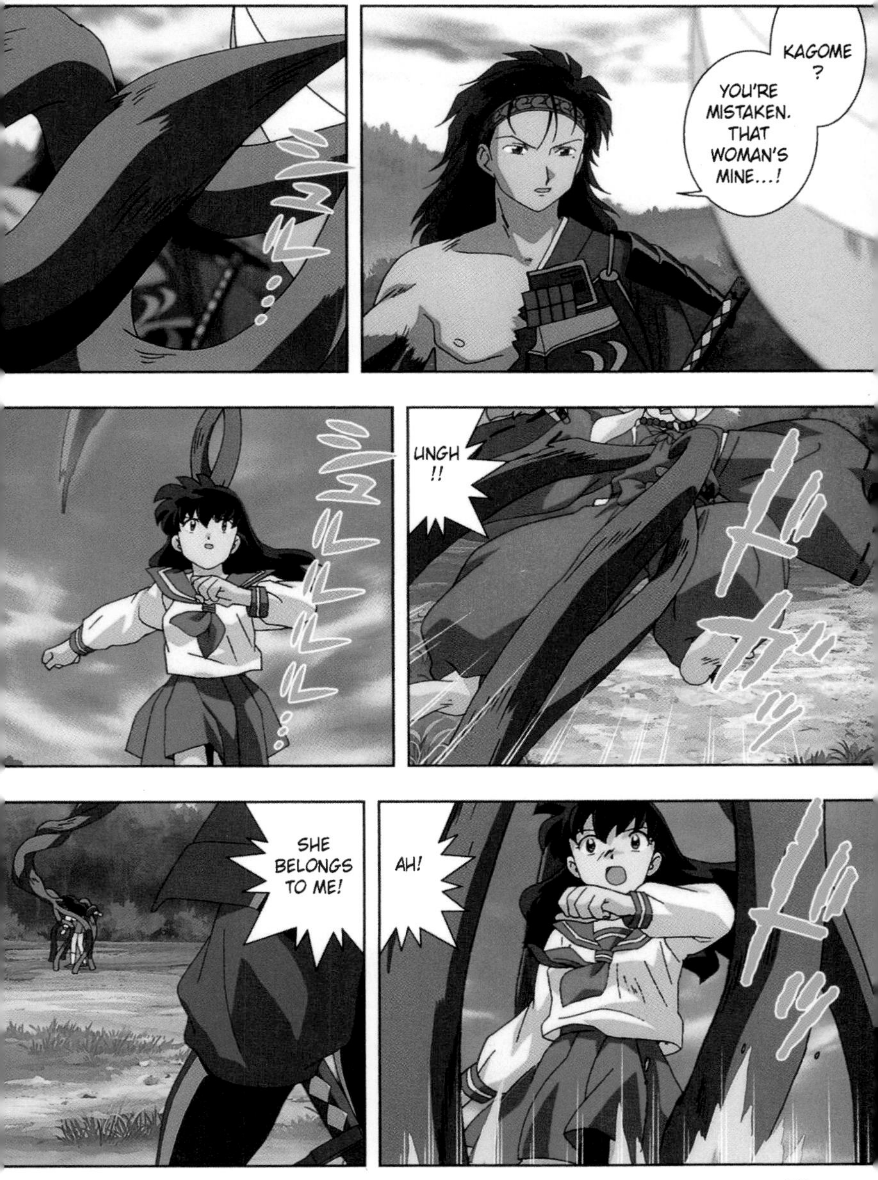
KAGOME ?
YOU'RE MISTAKEN. THAT WOMAN'S MINE...!
UNGH !!
AH!
SHE BELONGS TO ME!

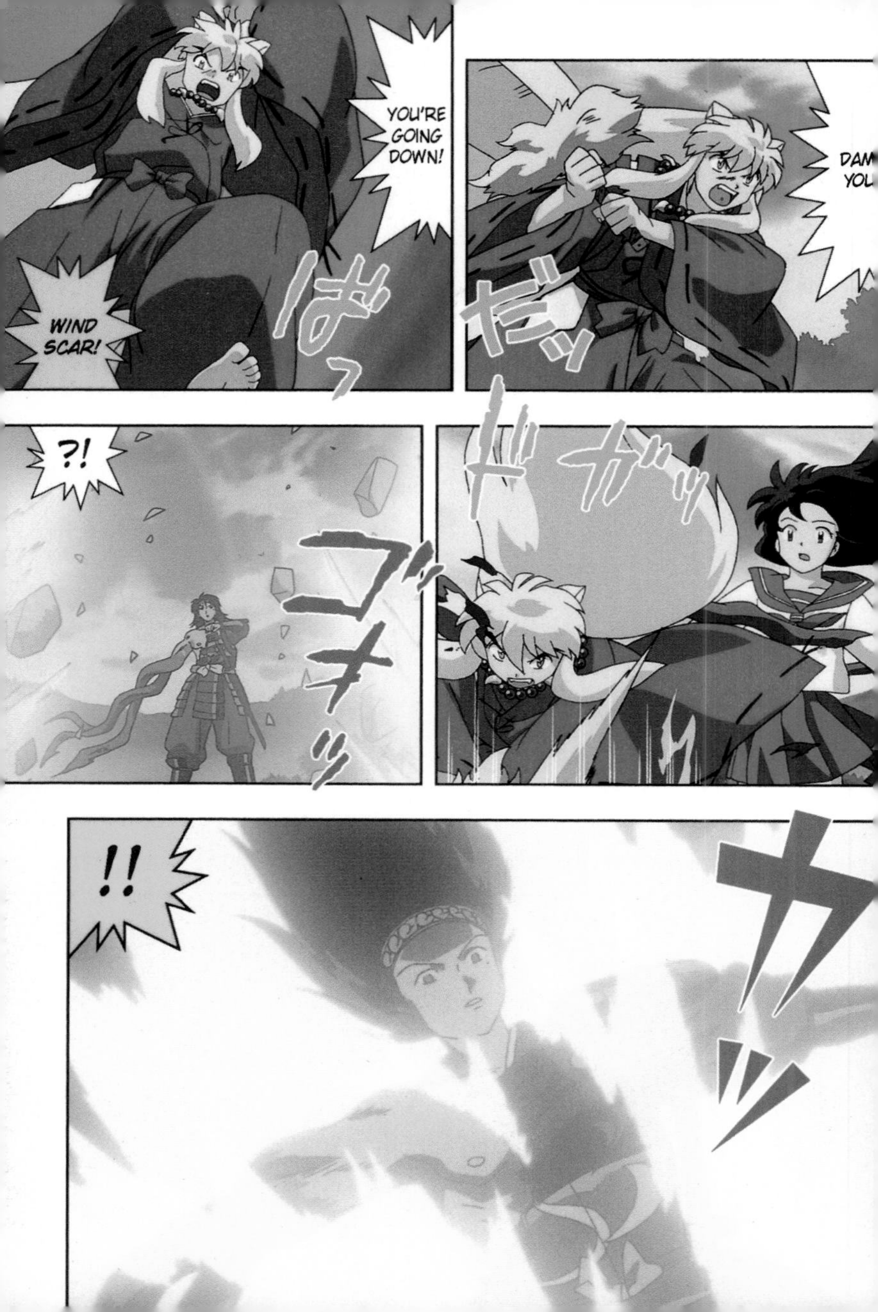

DAM YOU
YOU'RE GOING DOWN!
WIND SCAR!
?!
!!

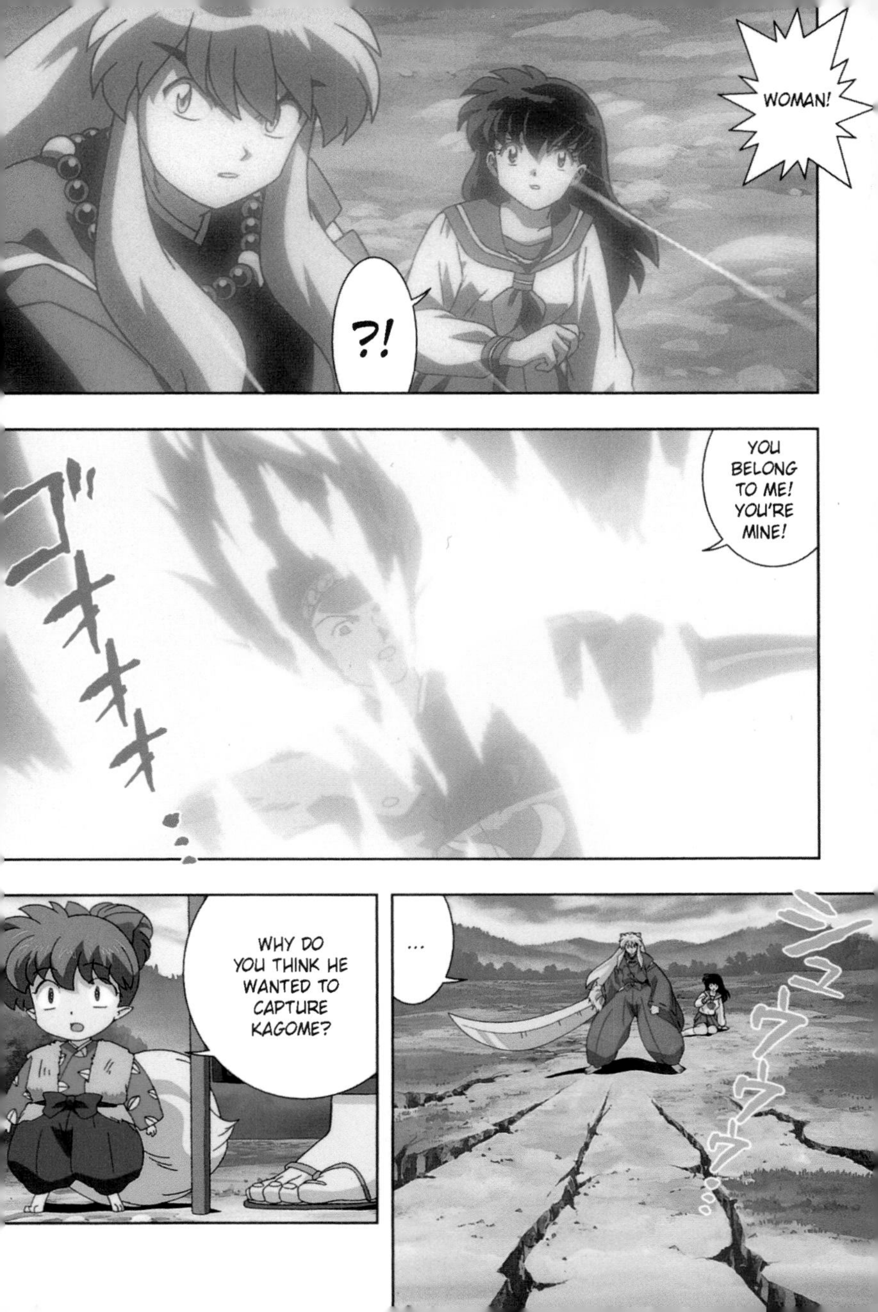
WOMAN!
?!
YOU BELONG TO ME! YOU'RE MINE!
ゴオオオ
...
シュウウウ
WHY DO YOU THINK HE WANTED TO CAPTURE KAGOME?

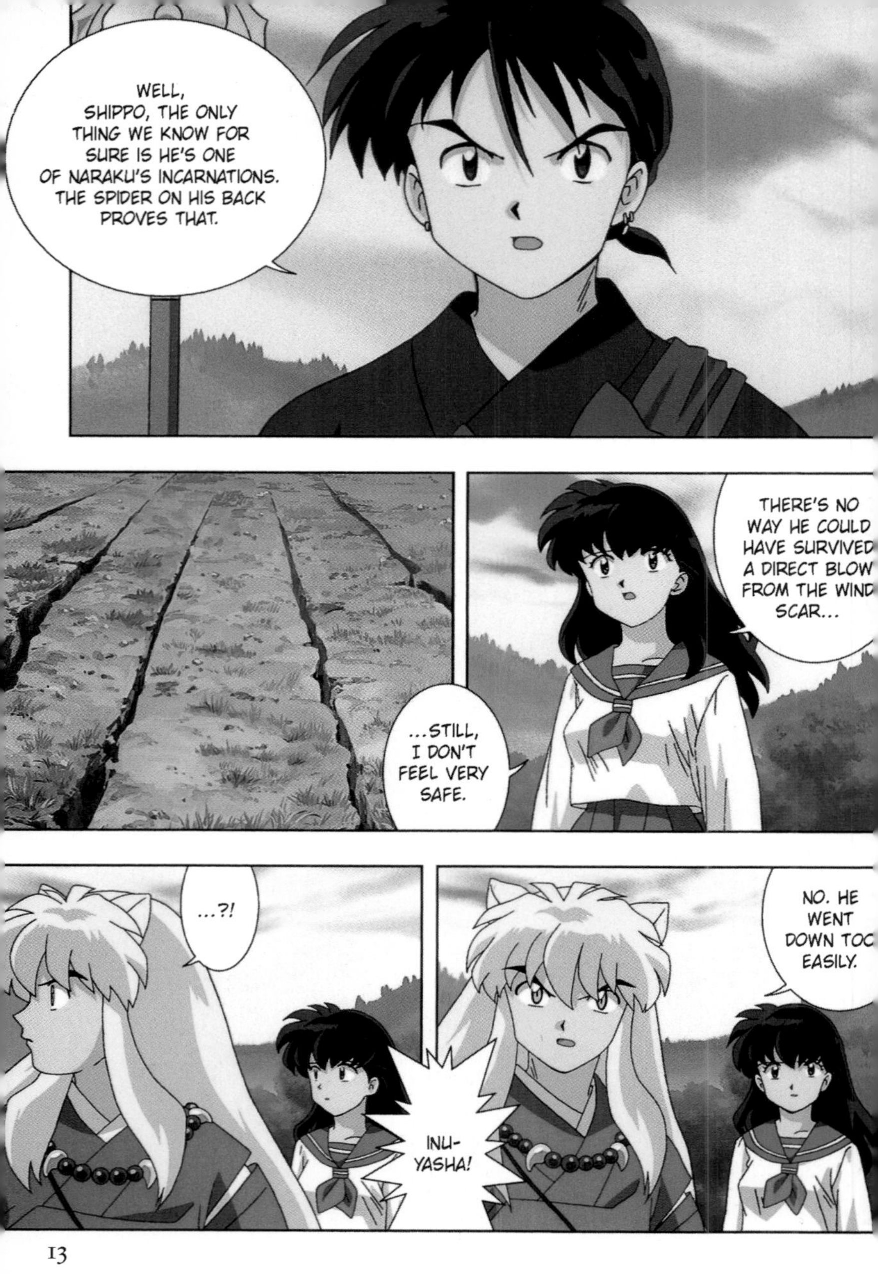
WELL, SHIPPO, THE ONLY THING WE KNOW FOR SURE IS HE'S ONE OF NARAKU'S INCARNATIONS. THE SPIDER ON HIS BACK PROVES THAT.
THERE'S NO WAY HE COULD HAVE SURVIVED A DIRECT BLOW FROM THE WIND SCAR...
...STILL, I DON'T FEEL VERY SAFE.
NO. HE WENT DOWN TOO EASILY.
INU-YASHA!
...?!

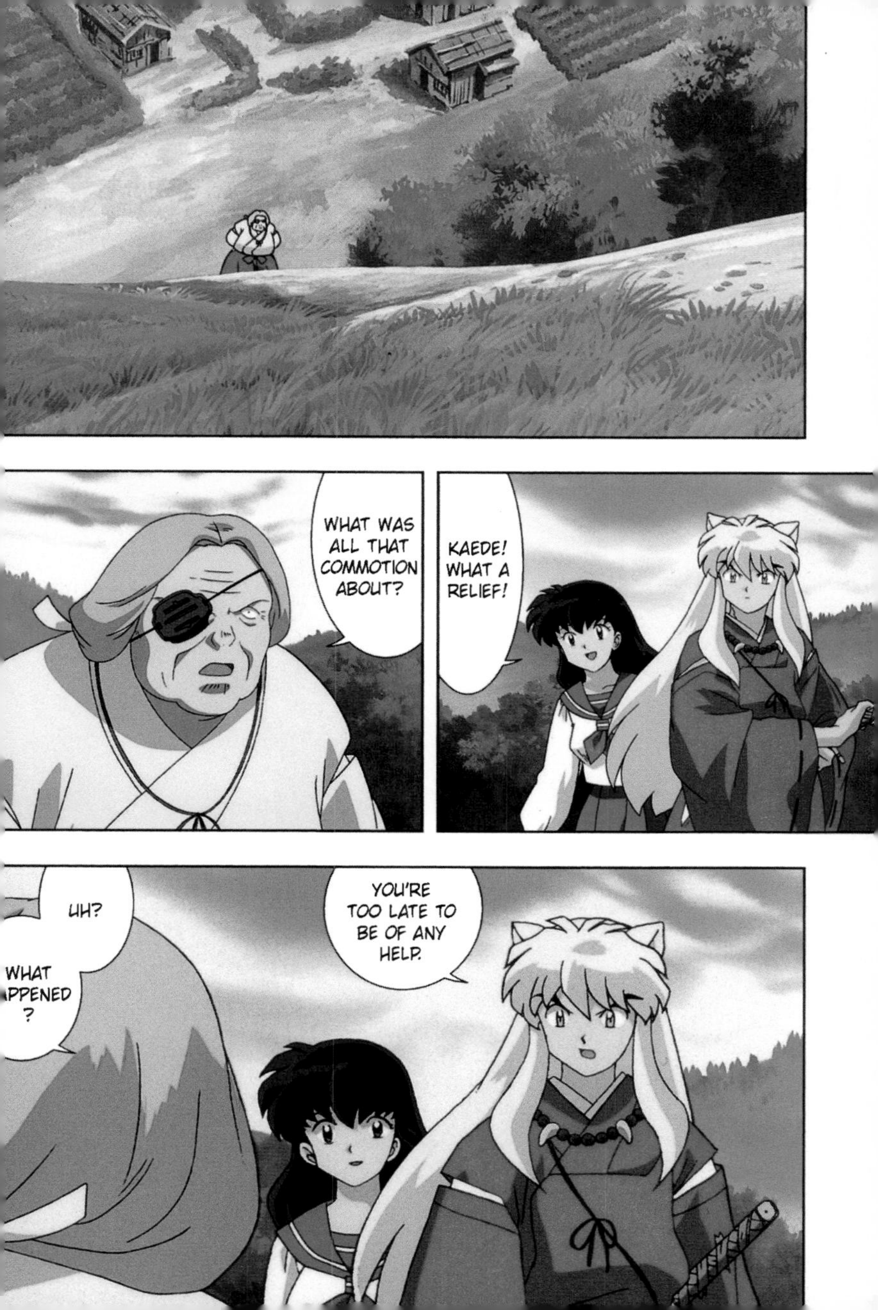
KAEDE! WHAT A RELIEF!
WHAT WAS ALL THAT COMMOTION ABOUT?
YOU'RE TOO LATE TO BE OF ANY HELP.
UH?
WHAT PPENED ?

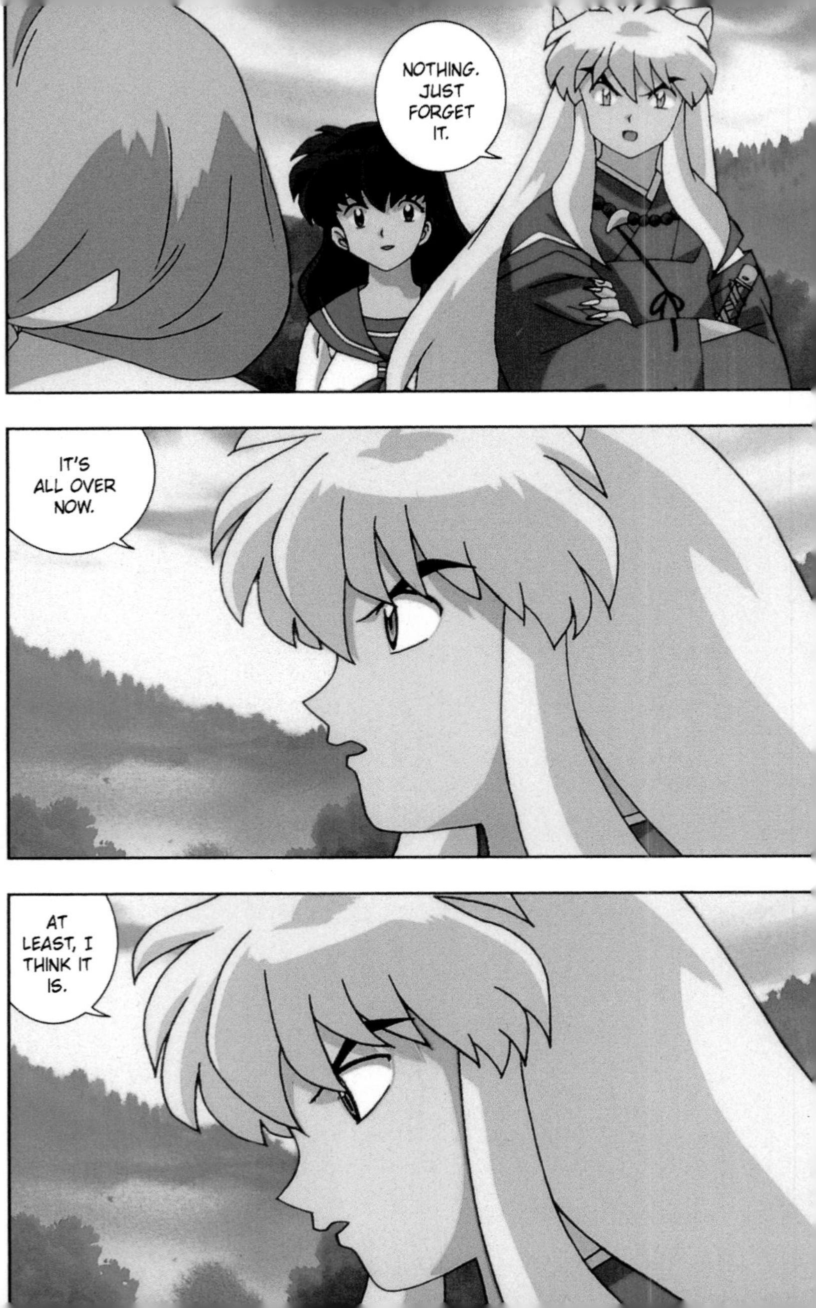
NOTHING. JUST FORGET IT.
IT'S ALL OVER NOW.
AT LEAST, I THINK IT IS.

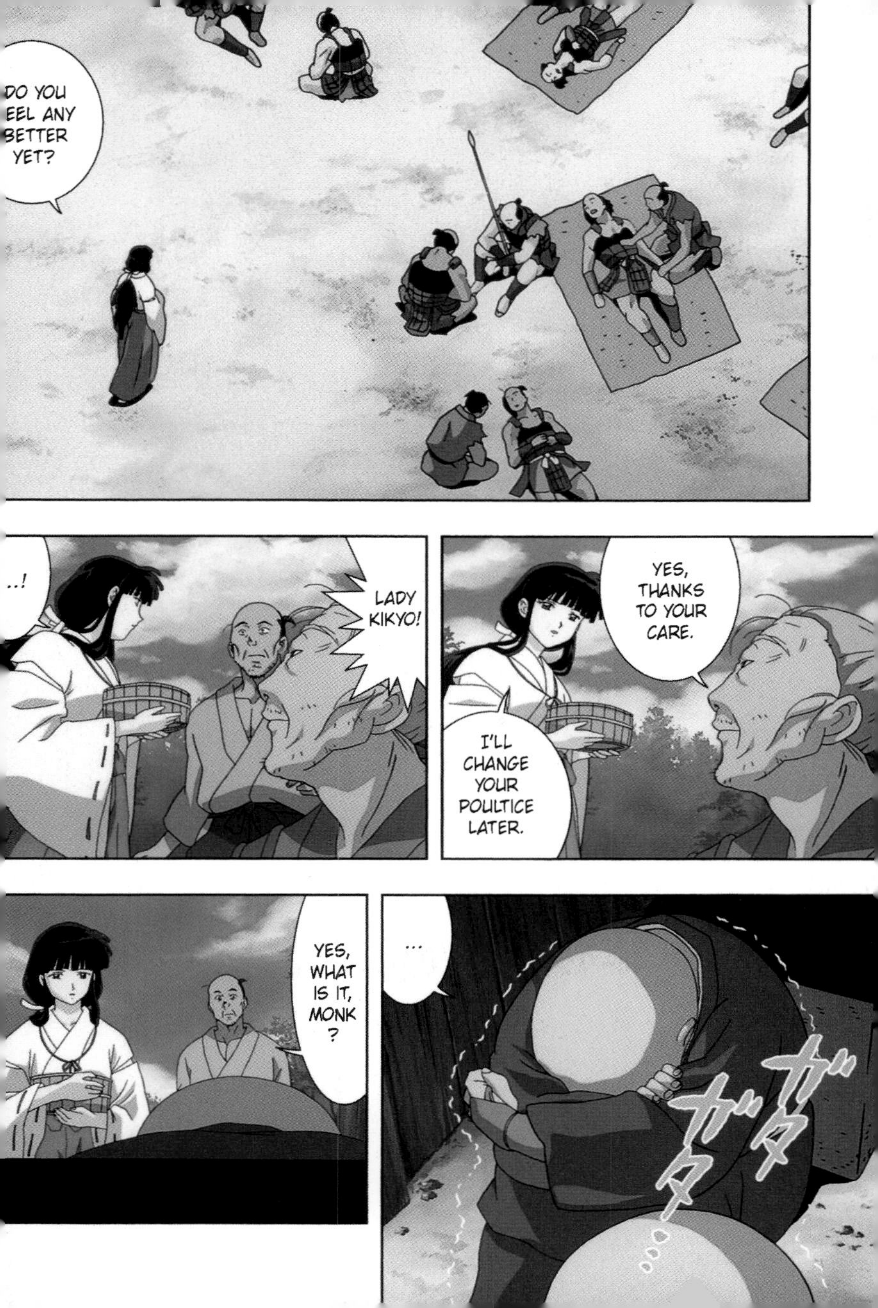
DO YOU EEL ANY BETTER YET?
YES, THANKS TO YOUR CARE.
I'LL CHANGE YOUR POULTICE LATER.
LADY KIKYO!
..!
...
ガタガタ
YES, WHAT IS IT, MONK?

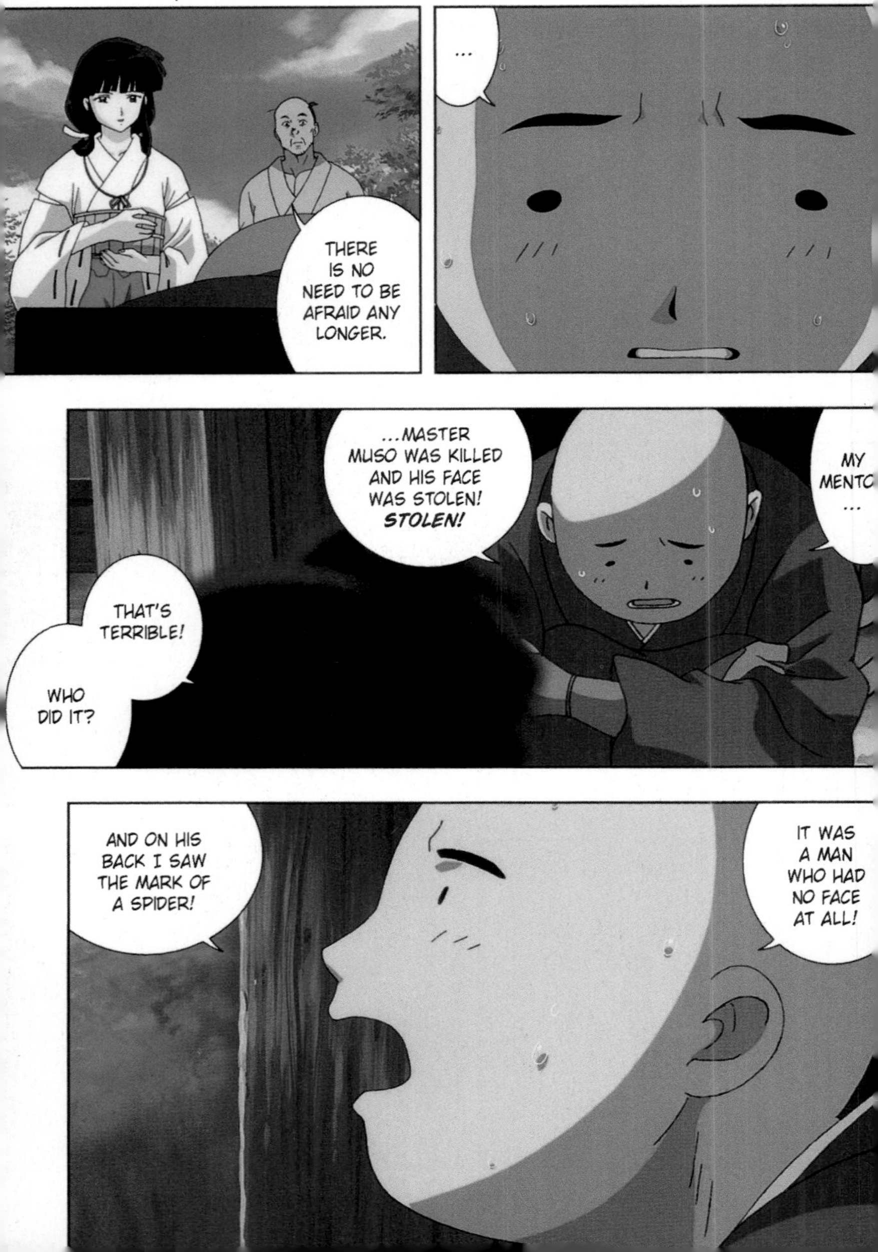
...
THERE IS NO NEED TO BE AFRAID ANY LONGER.
MY MENTO ...
...MASTER MUSO WAS KILLED AND HIS FACE WAS STOLEN! **STOLEN!**
THAT'S TERRIBLE!
WHO DID IT?
IT WAS A MAN WHO HAD NO FACE AT ALL!
AND ON HIS BACK I SAW THE MARK OF A SPIDER!

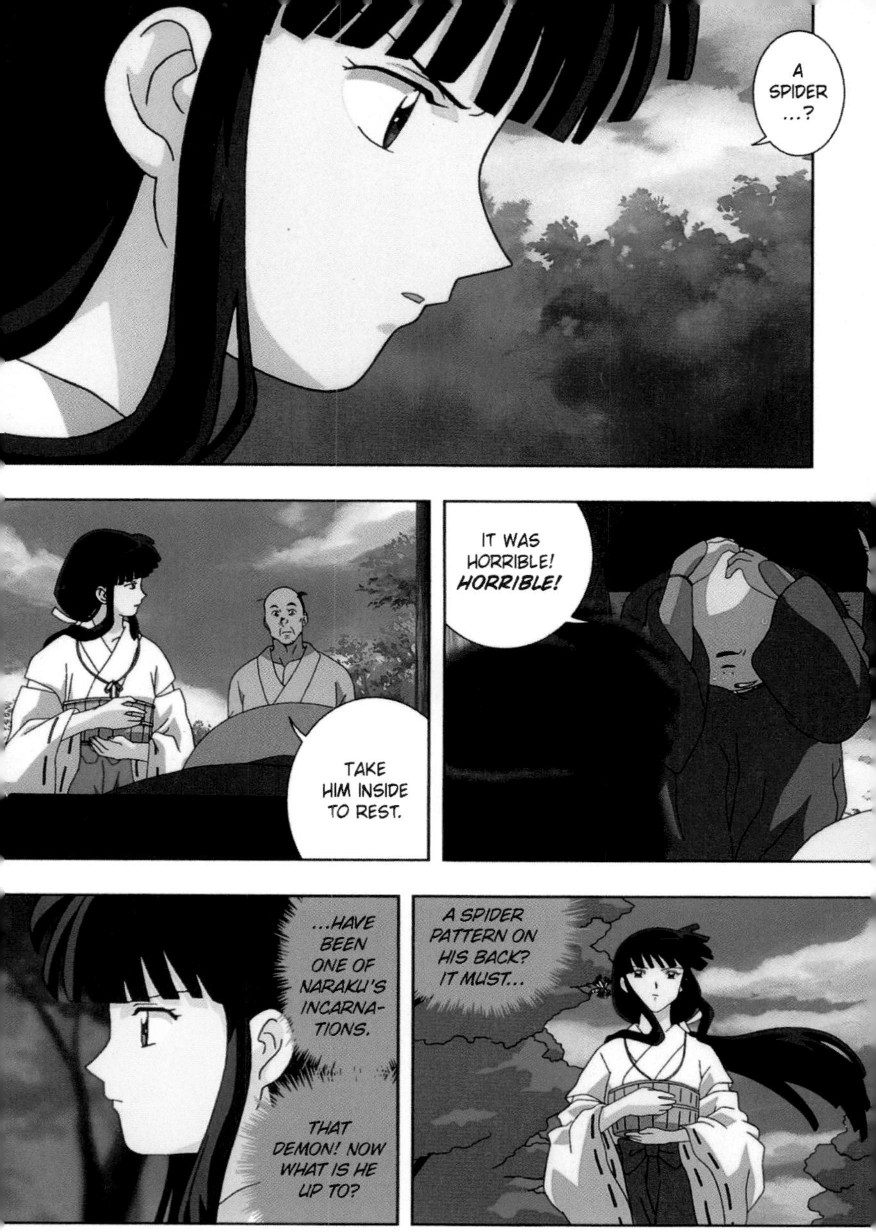
A SPIDER ...?
IT WAS HORRIBLE! ***HORRIBLE!***
TAKE HIM INSIDE TO REST.
A SPIDER PATTERN ON HIS BACK? IT MUST...
...HAVE BEEN ONE OF NARAKU'S INCARNATIONS.
THAT DEMON! NOW WHAT IS HE UP TO?

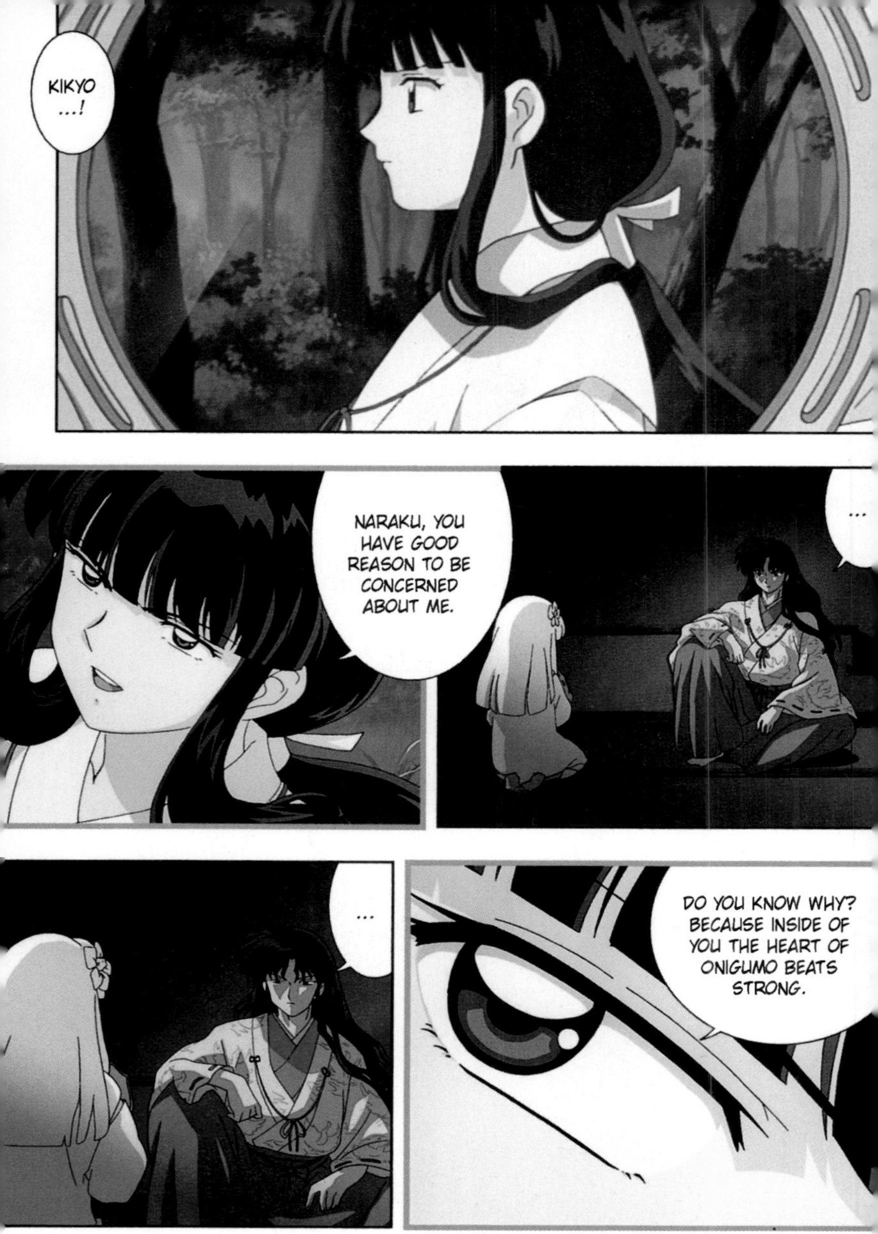
KIKYO ...!
...
NARAKU, YOU HAVE GOOD REASON TO BE CONCERNED ABOUT ME.
DO YOU KNOW WHY? BECAUSE INSIDE OF YOU THE HEART OF ONIGUMO BEATS STRONG.
...

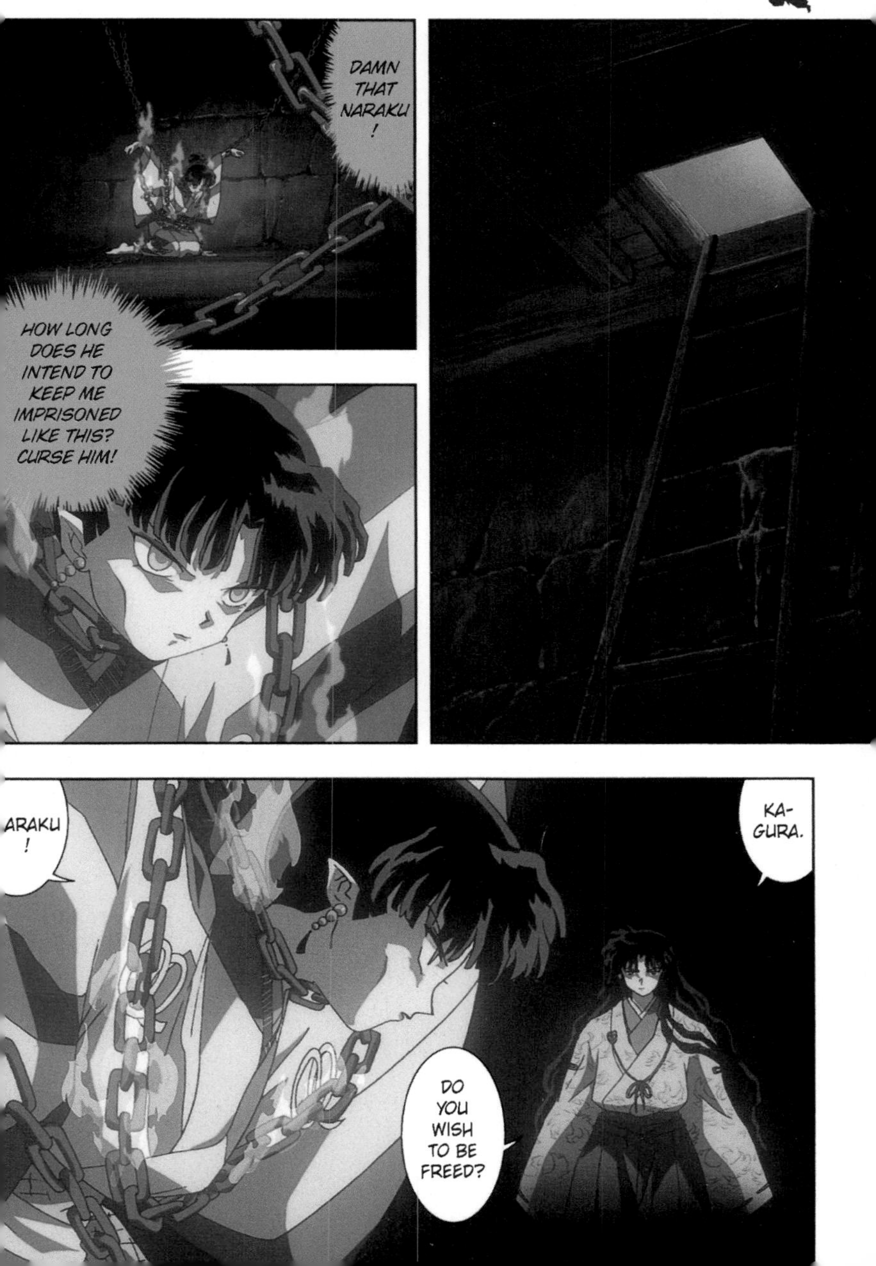
DAMN THAT NARAKU!
HOW LONG DOES HE INTEND TO KEEP ME IMPRISONED LIKE THIS? CURSE HIM!
KA-GURA.
ARAKU!
DO YOU WISH TO BE FREED?

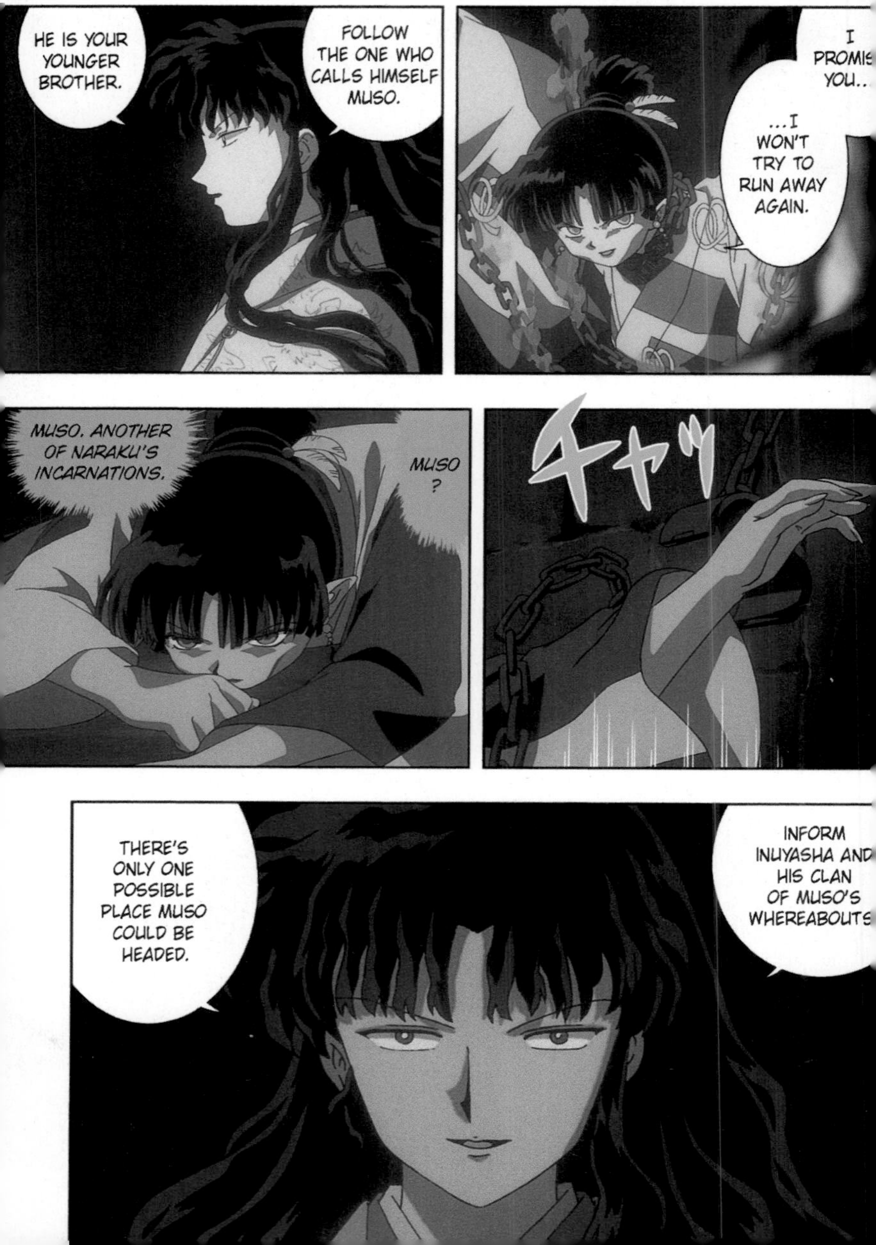
I PROMIS YOU...
...I WON'T TRY TO RUN AWAY AGAIN.
FOLLOW THE ONE WHO CALLS HIMSELF MUSO.
HE IS YOUR YOUNGER BROTHER.
チャッ
MUSO ?
MUSO. ANOTHER OF NARAKU'S INCARNATIONS.
INFORM INUYASHA AND HIS CLAN OF MUSO'S WHEREABOUTS
THERE'S ONLY ONE POSSIBLE PLACE MUSO COULD BE HEADED.

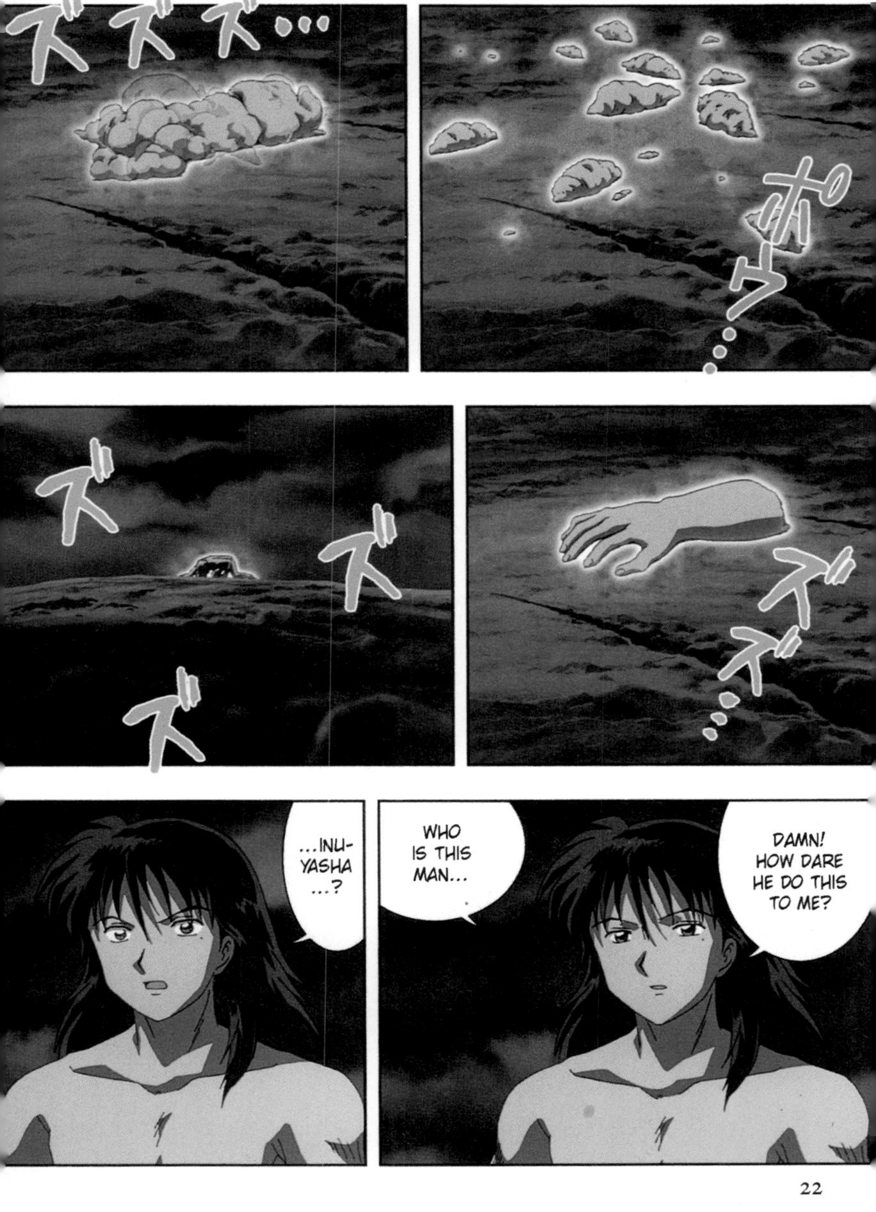
ポゥ…
ズズズ…
ズズ…
ズ
ズ
ズ
DAMN! HOW DARE HE DO THIS TO ME?
WHO IS THIS MAN…
…INU-YASHA …?

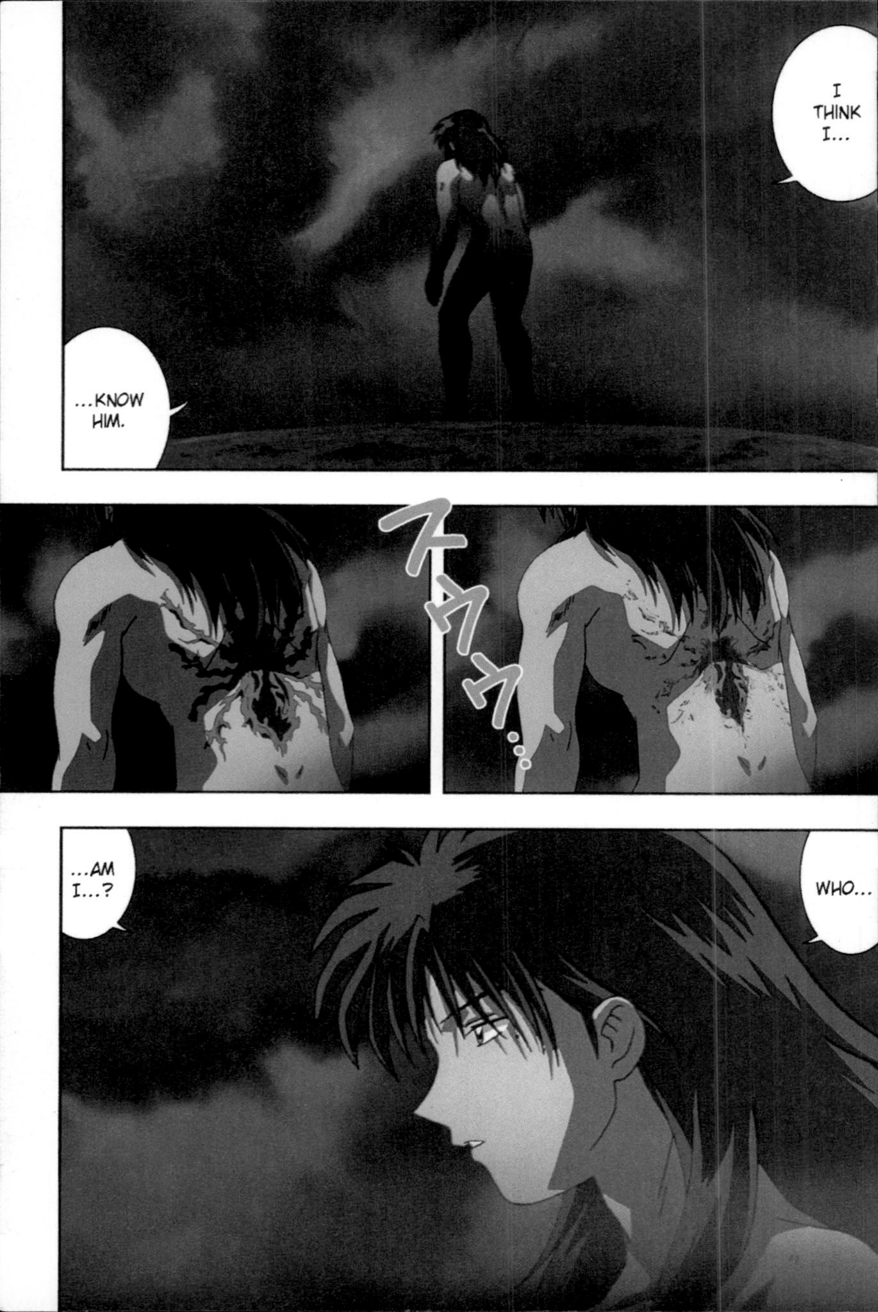
I THINK I...
...KNOW HIM.
スゥゥ...
WHO...
...AM I...?

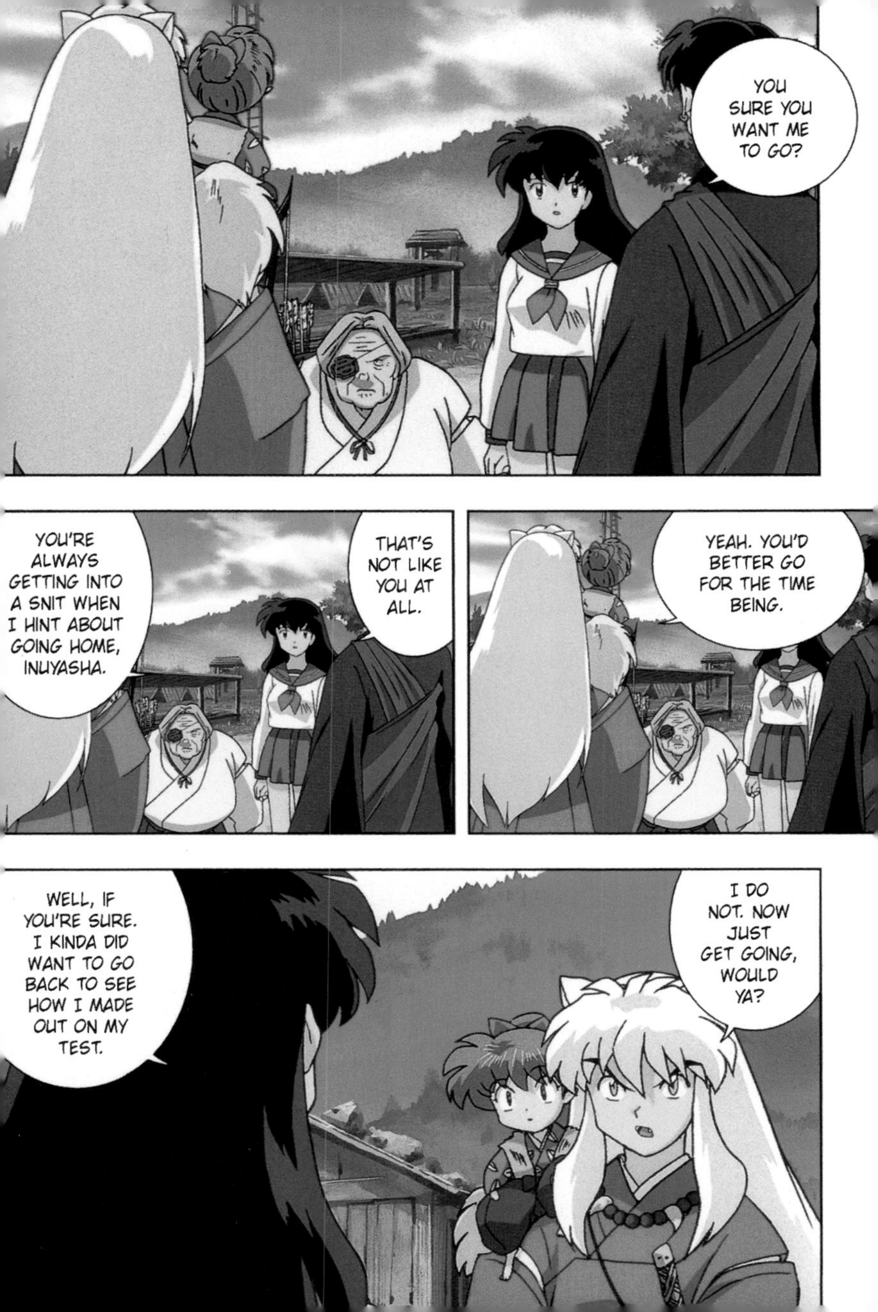
YOU SURE YOU WANT ME TO GO?
YEAH. YOU'D BETTER GO FOR THE TIME BEING.
THAT'S NOT LIKE YOU AT ALL.
YOU'RE ALWAYS GETTING INTO A SNIT WHEN I HINT ABOUT GOING HOME, INUYASHA.
I DO NOT. NOW JUST GET GOING, WOULD YA?
WELL, IF YOU'RE SURE. I KINDA DID WANT TO GO BACK TO SEE HOW I MADE OUT ON MY TEST.

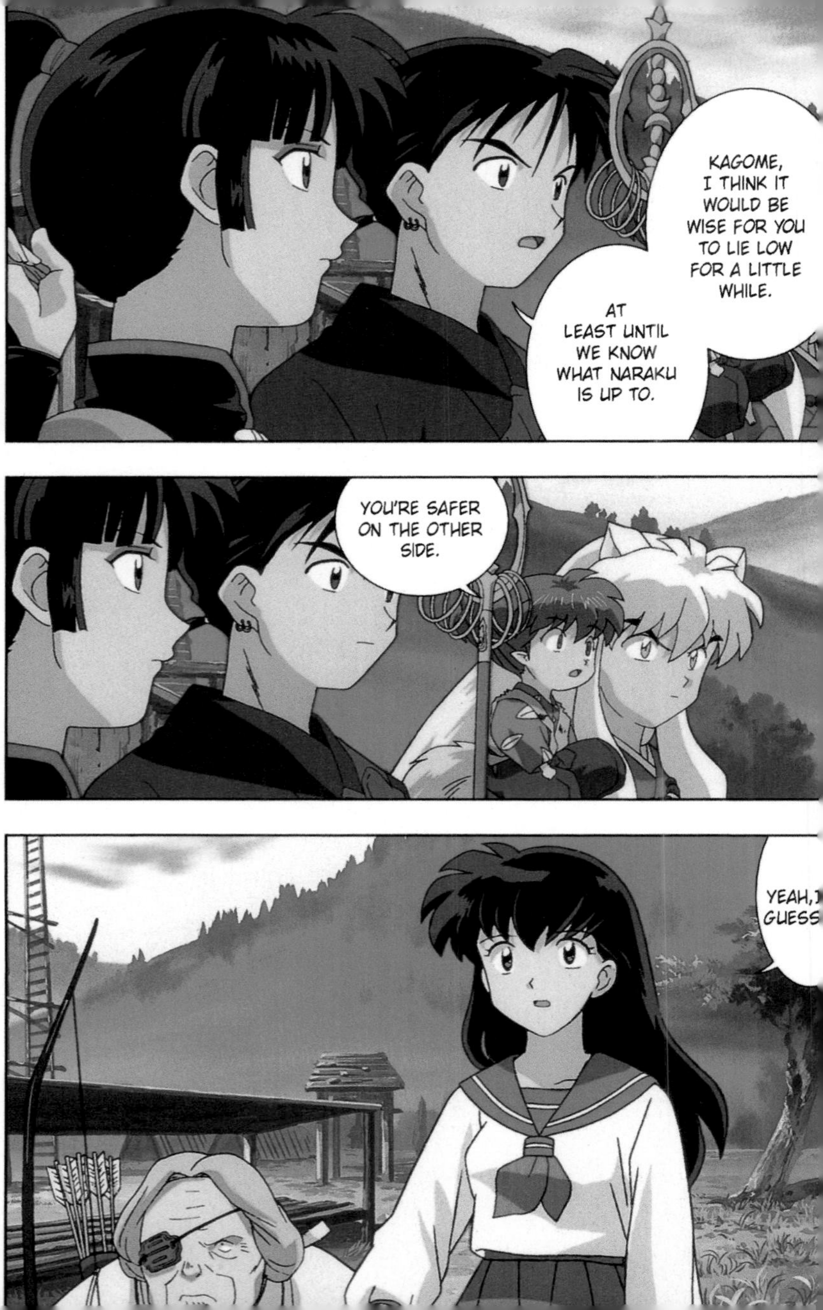
KAGOME, I THINK IT WOULD BE WISE FOR YOU TO LIE LOW FOR A LITTLE WHILE.
AT LEAST UNTIL WE KNOW WHAT NARAKU IS UP TO.
YOU'RE SAFER ON THE OTHER SIDE.
YEAH, I GUESS

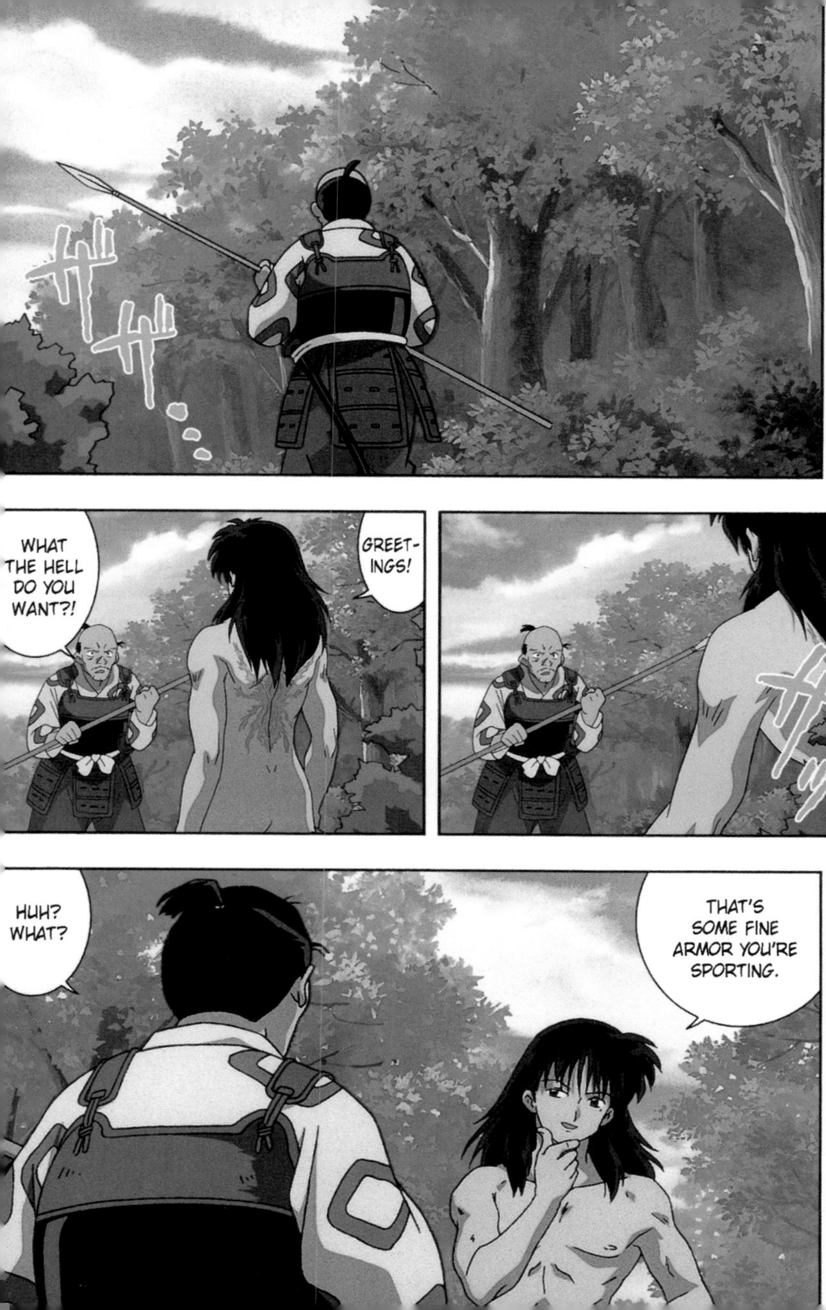
GREET-
INGS!
WHAT THE HELL DO YOU WANT?!
THAT'S SOME FINE ARMOR YOU'RE SPORTING.
HUH? WHAT?

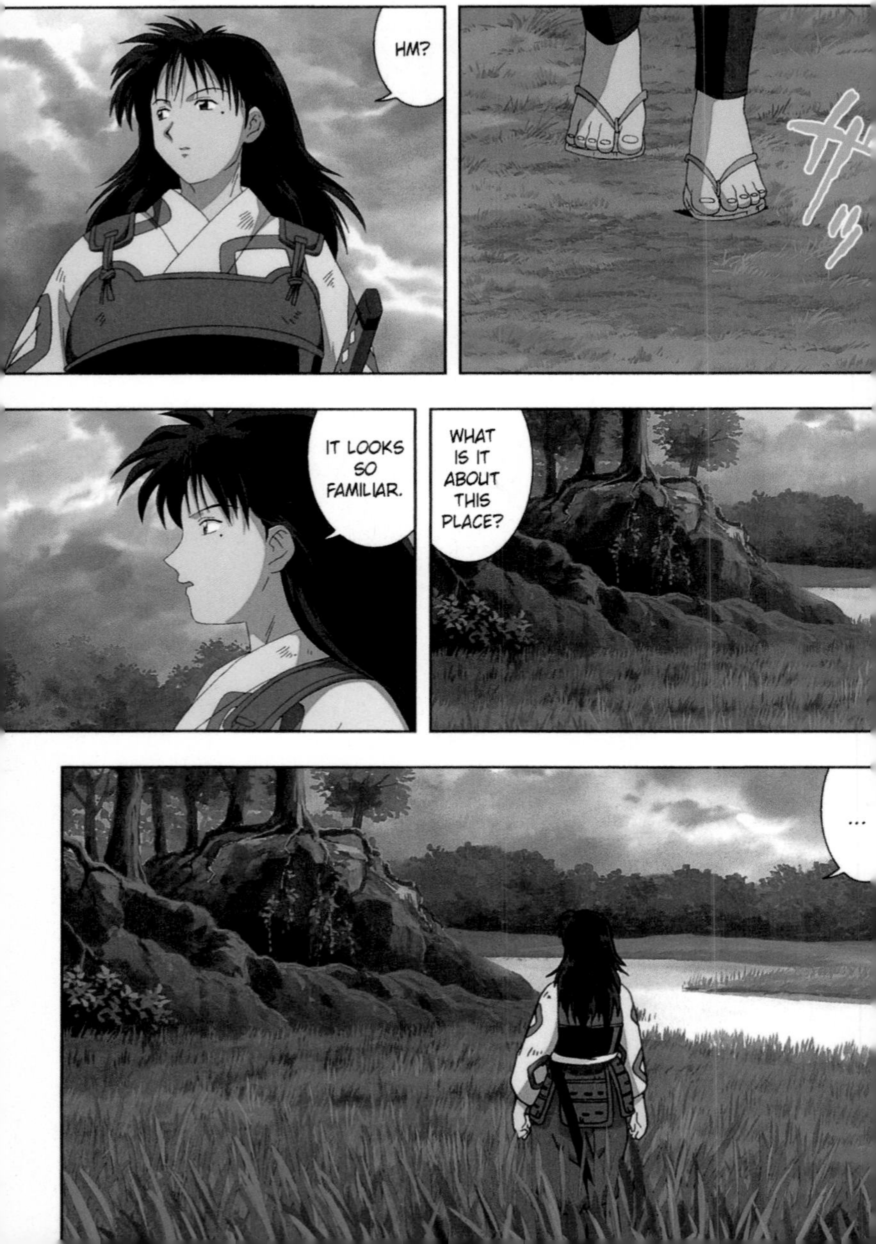
ザッ
HM?
WHAT IS IT ABOUT THIS PLACE?
IT LOOKS SO FAMILIAR.
...

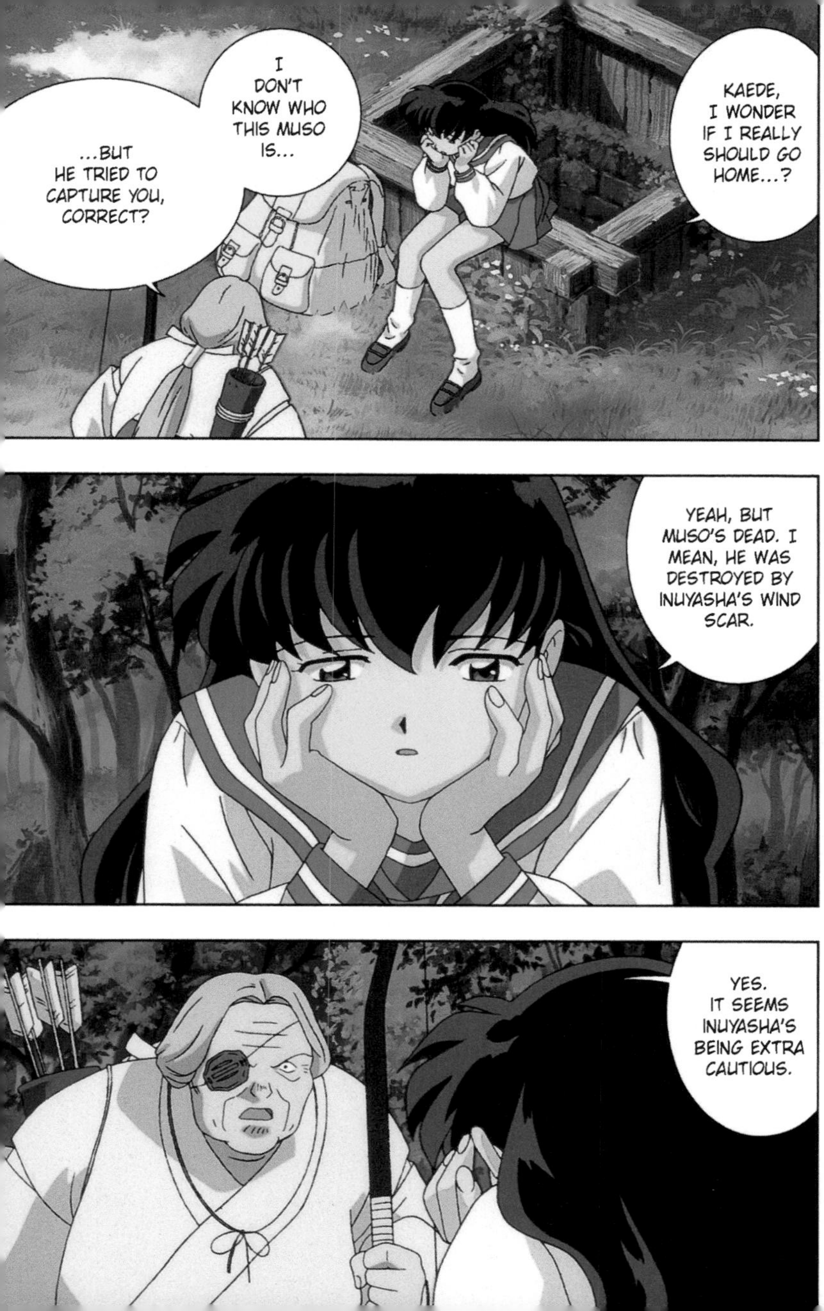
KAEDE, I WONDER IF I REALLY SHOULD GO HOME...?
I DON'T KNOW WHO THIS MUSO IS...
...BUT HE TRIED TO CAPTURE YOU, CORRECT?
YEAH, BUT MUSO'S DEAD. I MEAN, HE WAS DESTROYED BY INUYASHA'S WIND SCAR.
YES. IT SEEMS INUYASHA'S BEING EXTRA CAUTIOUS.

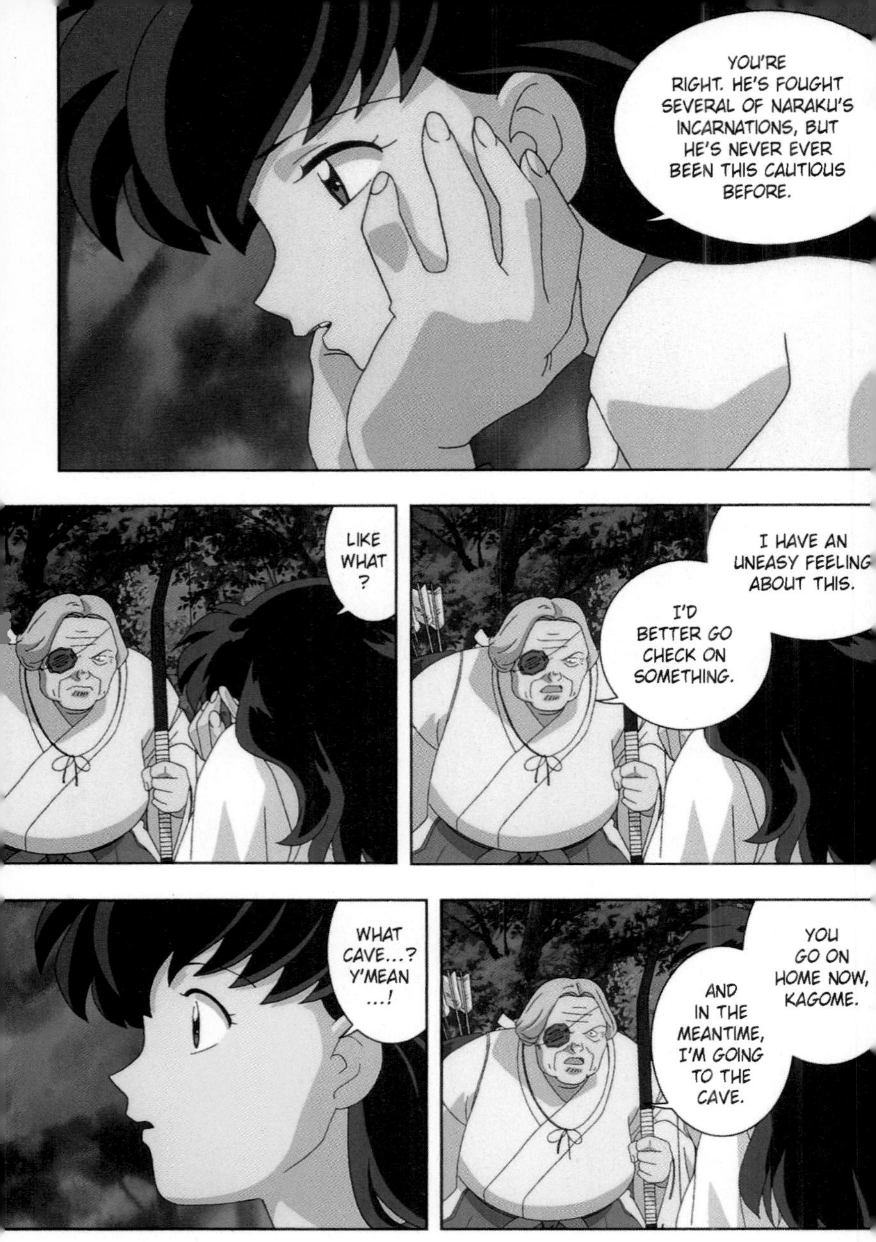
YOU'RE RIGHT. HE'S FOUGHT SEVERAL OF NARAKU'S INCARNATIONS, BUT HE'S NEVER EVER BEEN THIS CAUTIOUS BEFORE.
I HAVE AN UNEASY FEELING ABOUT THIS.
I'D BETTER GO CHECK ON SOMETHING.
LIKE WHAT?
YOU GO ON HOME NOW, KAGOME.
AND IN THE MEANTIME, I'M GOING TO THE CAVE.
WHAT CAVE...? Y'MEAN...!

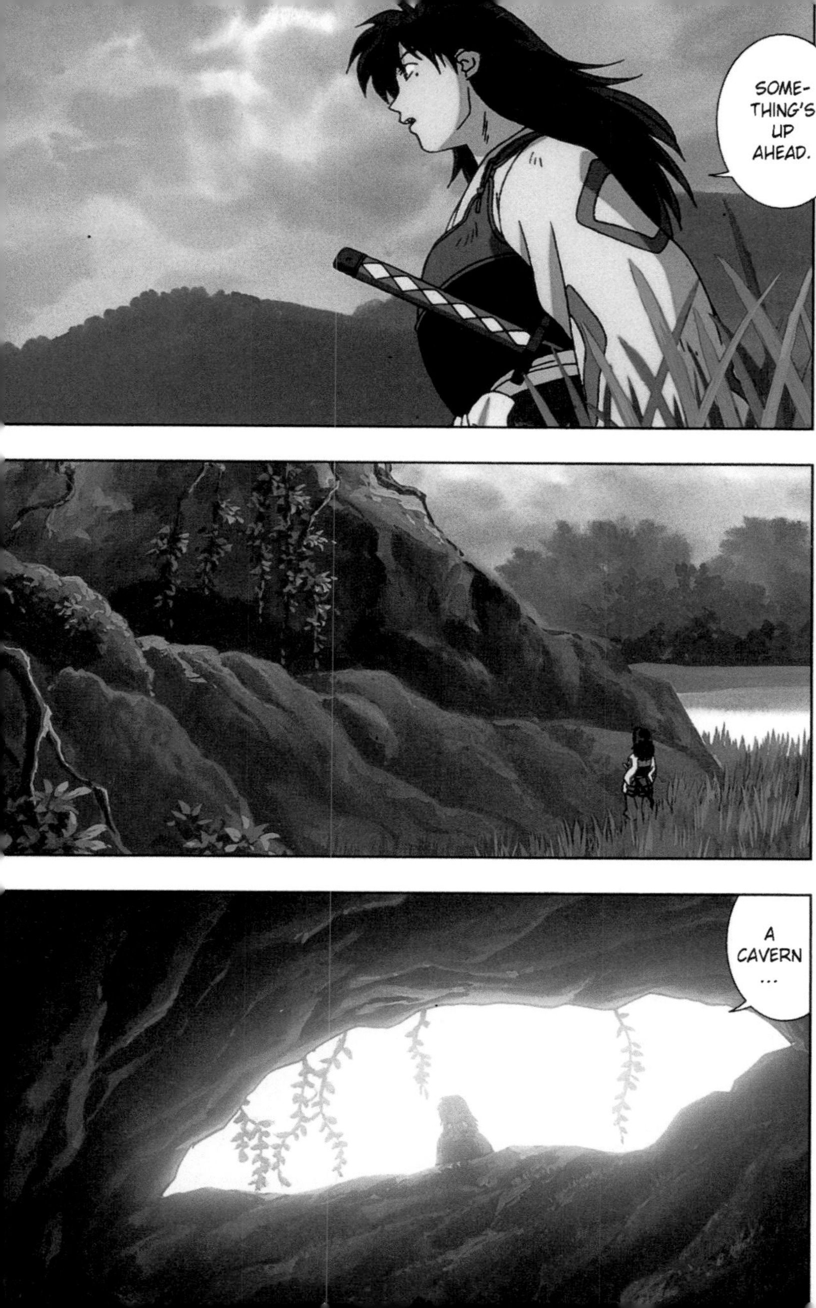
SOME-THING'S UP AHEAD.
A CAVERN ...

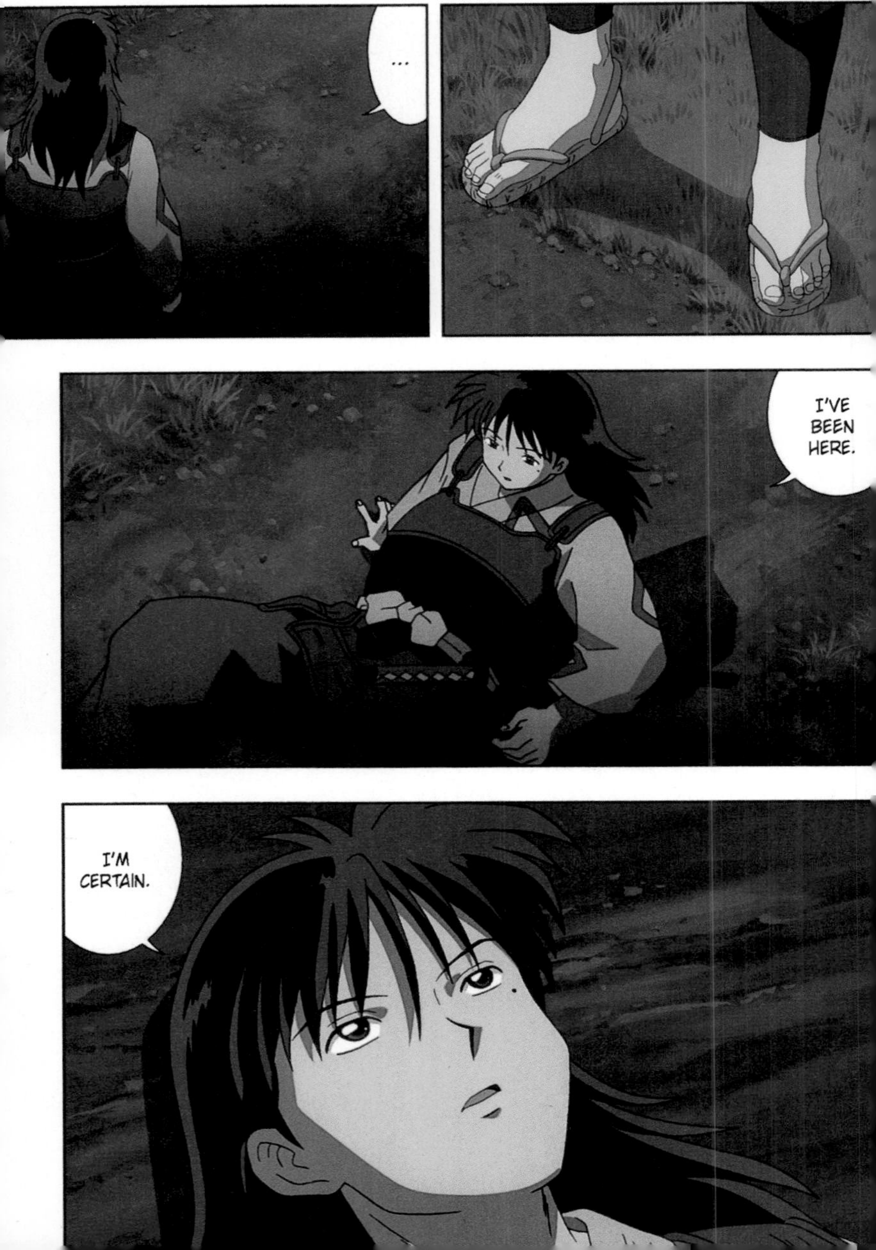
...
I'VE BEEN HERE.
I'M CERTAIN.

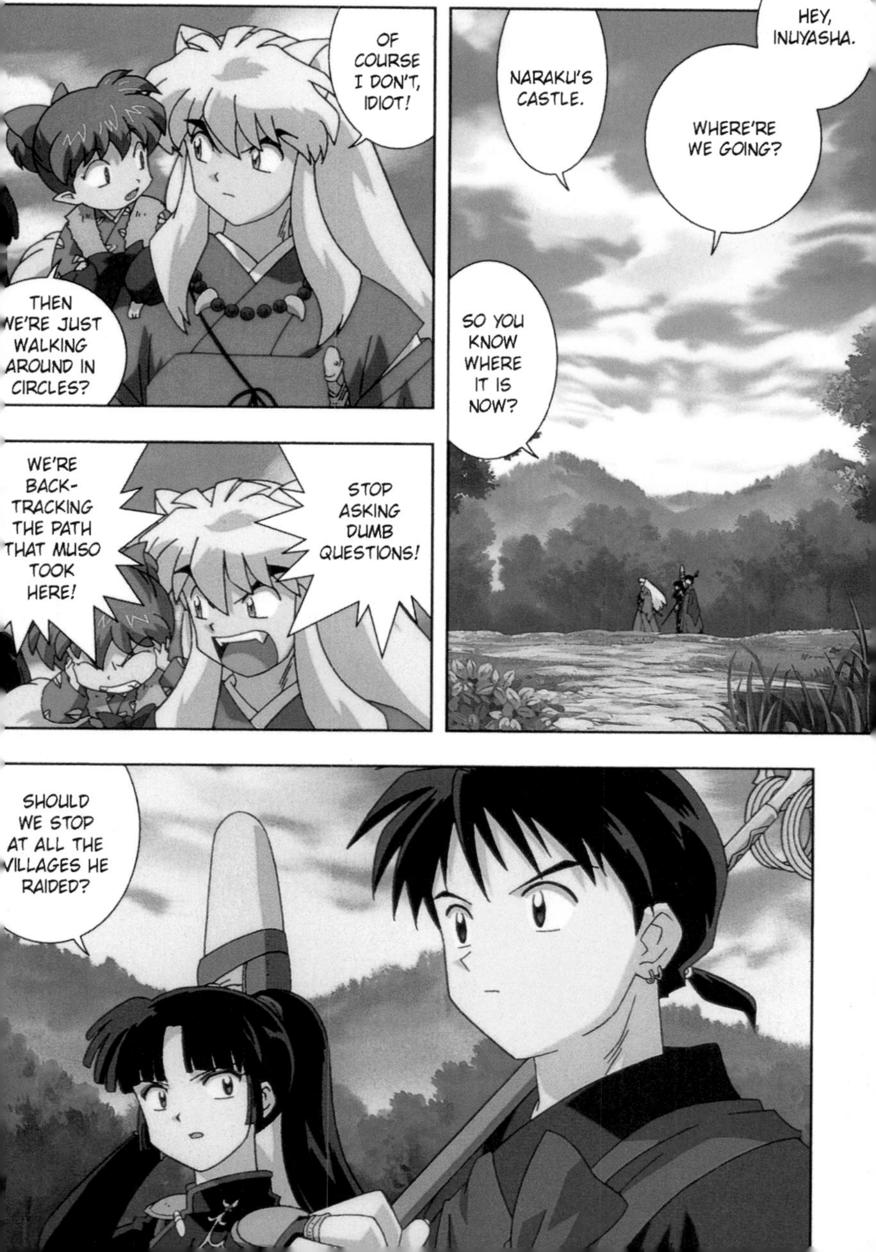
HEY, INUYASHA.
WHERE'RE WE GOING?
NARAKU'S CASTLE.
SO YOU KNOW WHERE IT IS NOW?
OF COURSE I DON'T, IDIOT!
THEN WE'RE JUST WALKING AROUND IN CIRCLES?
STOP ASKING DUMB QUESTIONS!
WE'RE BACK-TRACKING THE PATH THAT MUSO TOOK HERE!
SHOULD WE STOP AT ALL THE VILLAGES HE RAIDED?

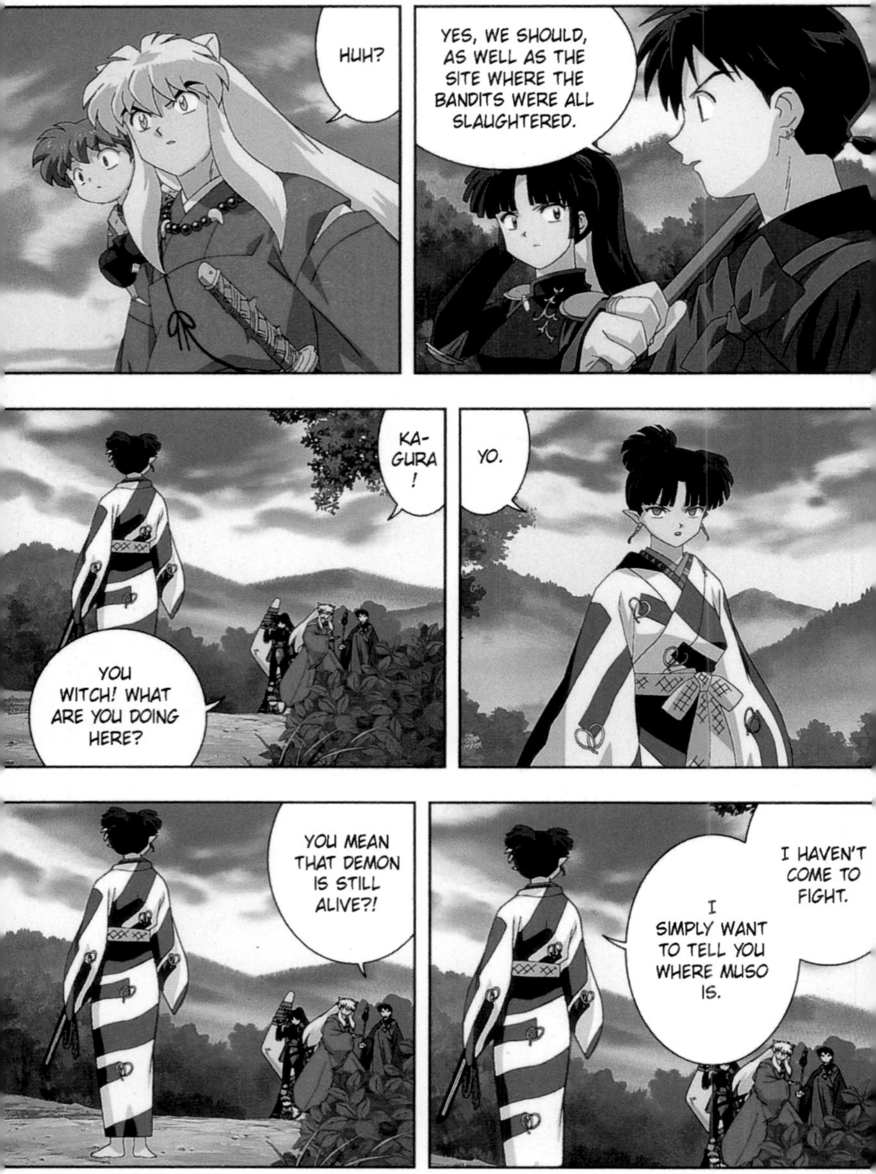
YES, WE SHOULD, AS WELL AS THE SITE WHERE THE BANDITS WERE ALL SLAUGHTERED.
HUH?
YO.
KA-GURA!
YOU WITCH! WHAT ARE YOU DOING HERE?
I HAVEN'T COME TO FIGHT.
I SIMPLY WANT TO TELL YOU WHERE MUSO IS.
YOU MEAN THAT DEMON IS STILL ALIVE?!

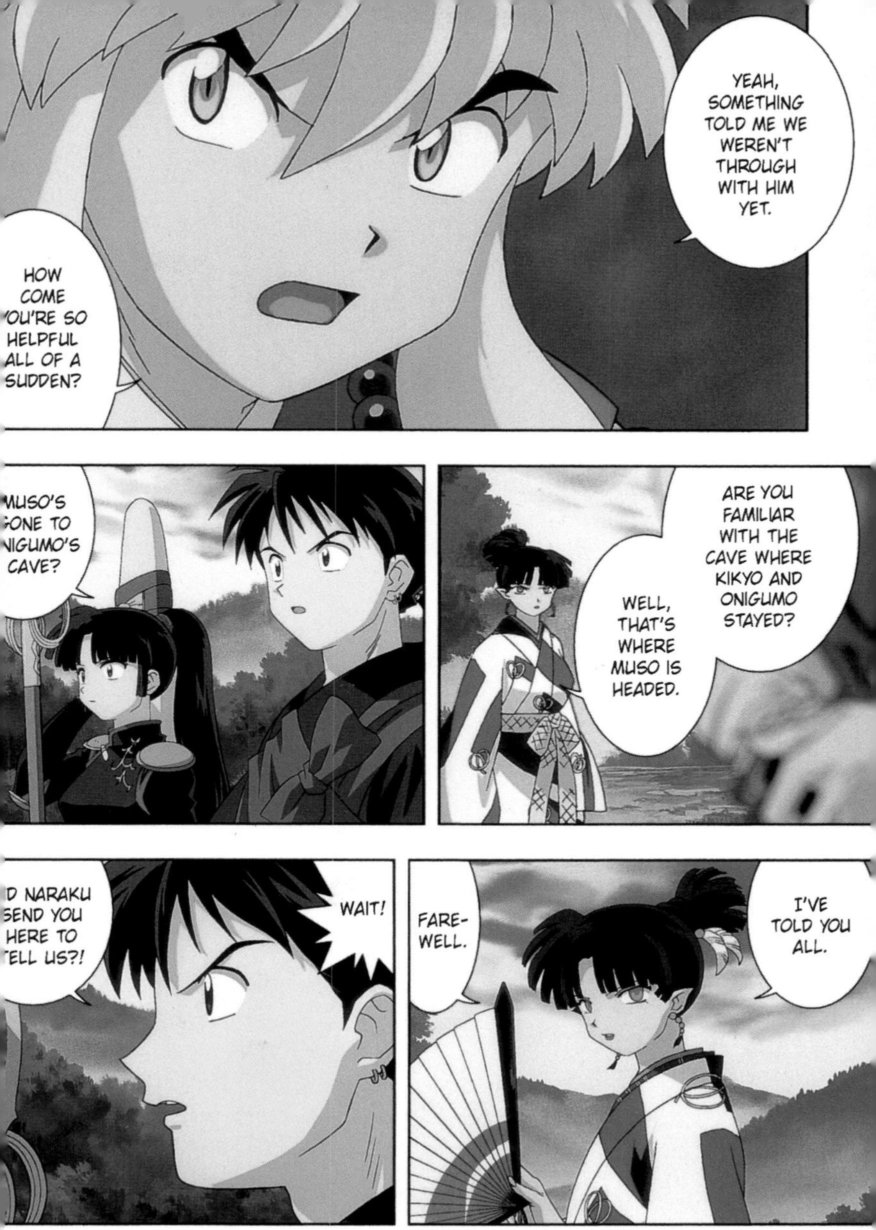
YEAH, SOMETHING TOLD ME WE WEREN'T THROUGH WITH HIM YET.
HOW COME OU'RE SO HELPFUL ALL OF A SUDDEN?
ARE YOU FAMILIAR WITH THE CAVE WHERE KIKYO AND ONIGUMO STAYED?
WELL, THAT'S WHERE MUSO IS HEADED.
IUSO'S ONE TO NIGUMO'S CAVE?
I'VE TOLD YOU ALL.
FARE-WELL.
WAIT!
D NARAKU SEND YOU HERE TO ELL US?!

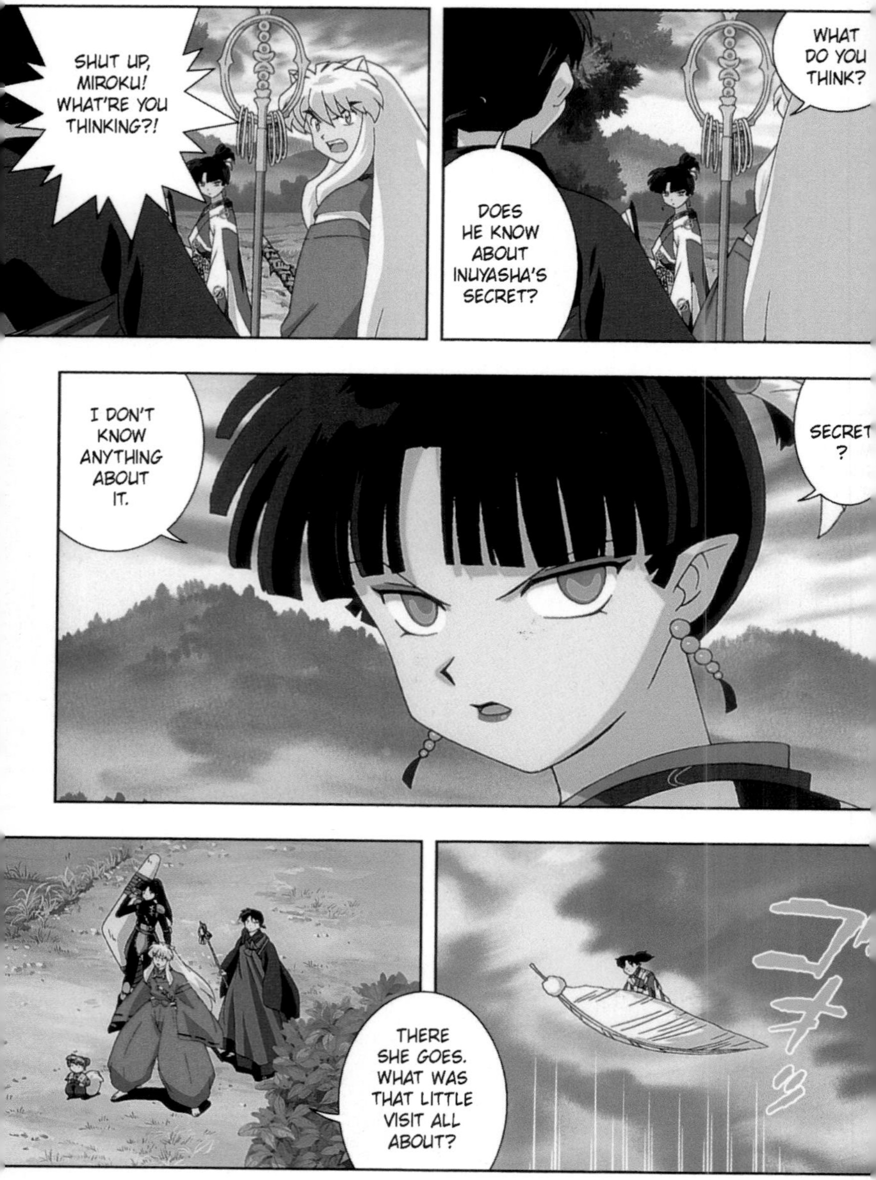
WHAT DO YOU THINK?
DOES HE KNOW ABOUT INUYASHA'S SECRET?
SHUT UP, MIROKU! WHAT'RE YOU THINKING?!
SECRET ?
I DON'T KNOW ANYTHING ABOUT IT.
THERE SHE GOES. WHAT WAS THAT LITTLE VISIT ALL ABOUT?

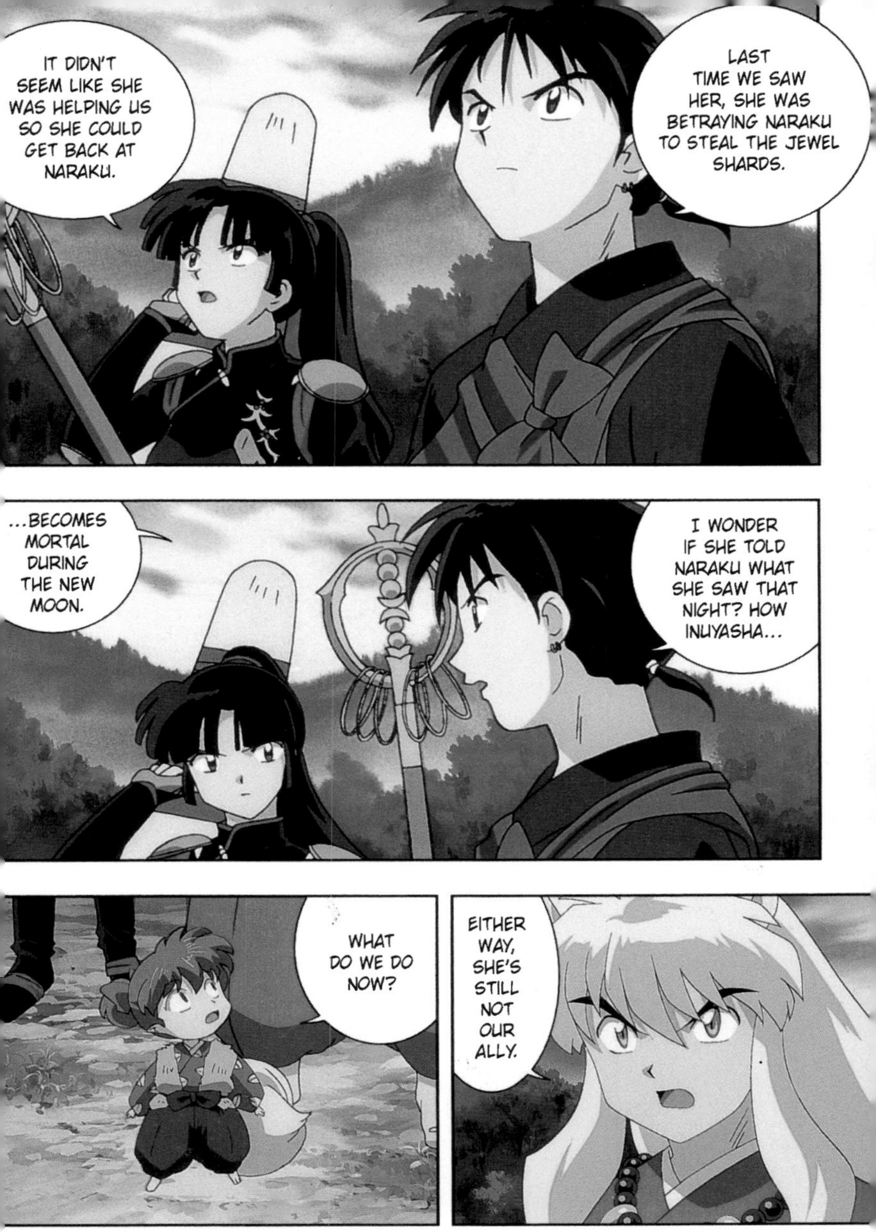
LAST TIME WE SAW HER, SHE WAS BETRAYING NARAKU TO STEAL THE JEWEL SHARDS.
IT DIDN'T SEEM LIKE SHE WAS HELPING US SO SHE COULD GET BACK AT NARAKU.
I WONDER IF SHE TOLD NARAKU WHAT SHE SAW THAT NIGHT? HOW INUYASHA...
...BECOMES MORTAL DURING THE NEW MOON.
EITHER WAY, SHE'S STILL NOT OUR ALLY.
WHAT DO WE DO NOW?

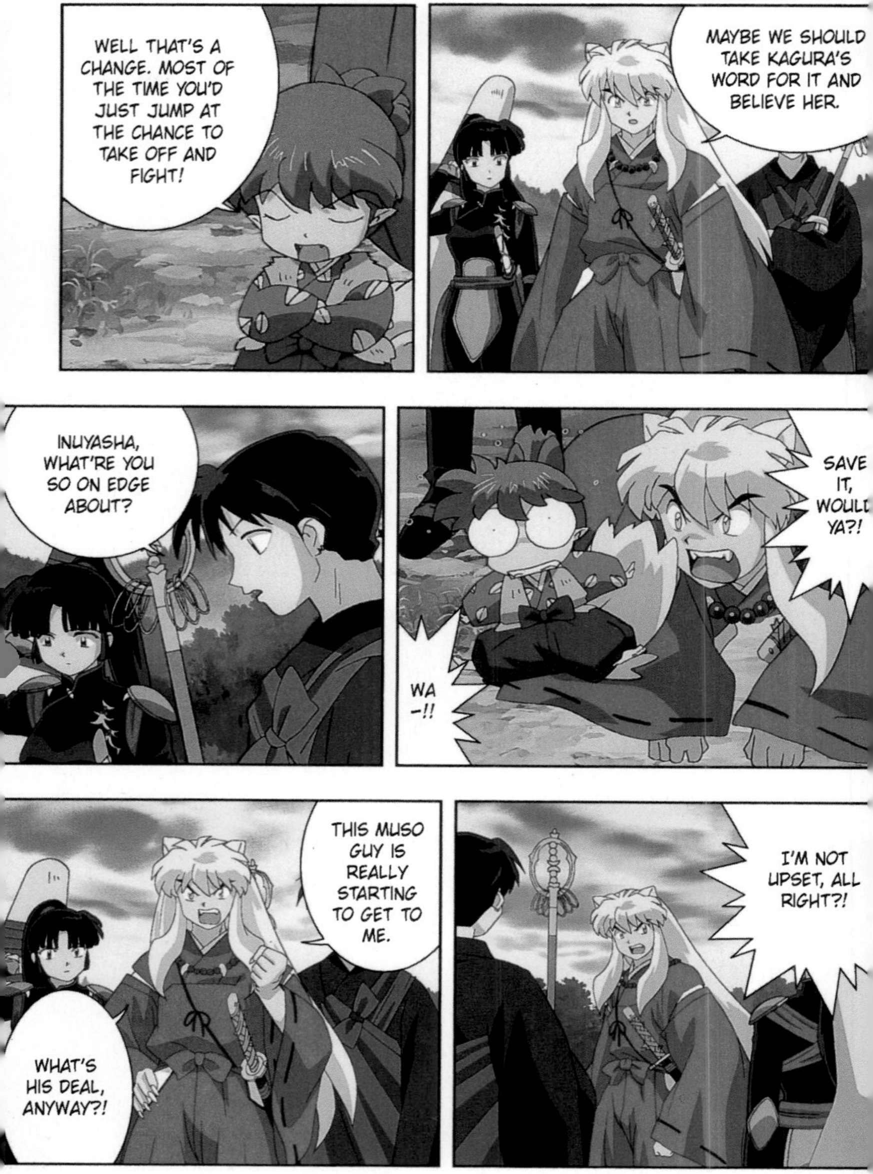
MAYBE WE SHOULD TAKE KAGURA'S WORD FOR IT AND BELIEVE HER.
WELL THAT'S A CHANGE. MOST OF THE TIME YOU'D JUST JUMP AT THE CHANCE TO TAKE OFF AND FIGHT!
SAVE IT, WOULD YA?!
WA-!!
INUYASHA, WHAT'RE YOU SO ON EDGE ABOUT?
I'M NOT UPSET, ALL RIGHT?!
THIS MUSO GUY IS REALLY STARTING TO GET TO ME.
WHAT'S HIS DEAL, ANYWAY?!

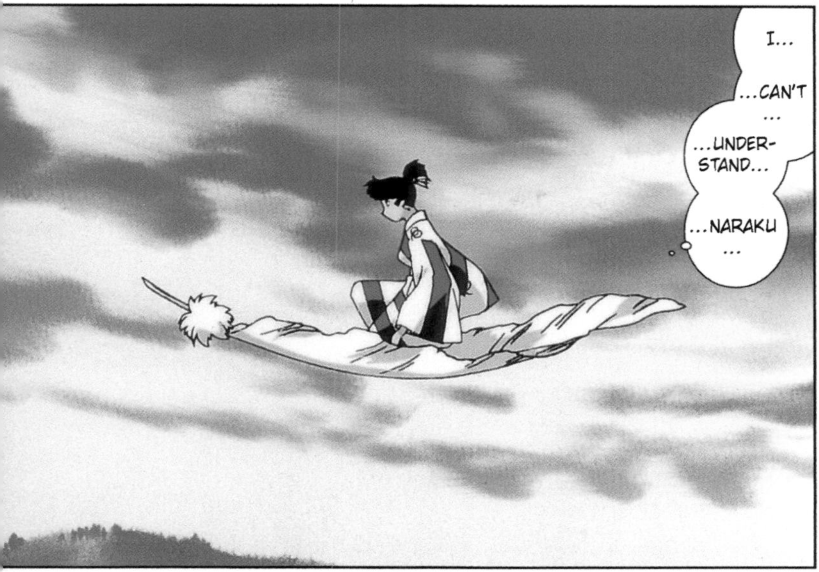
I...
...CAN'T ...
...UNDER-STAND...
...NARAKU ...

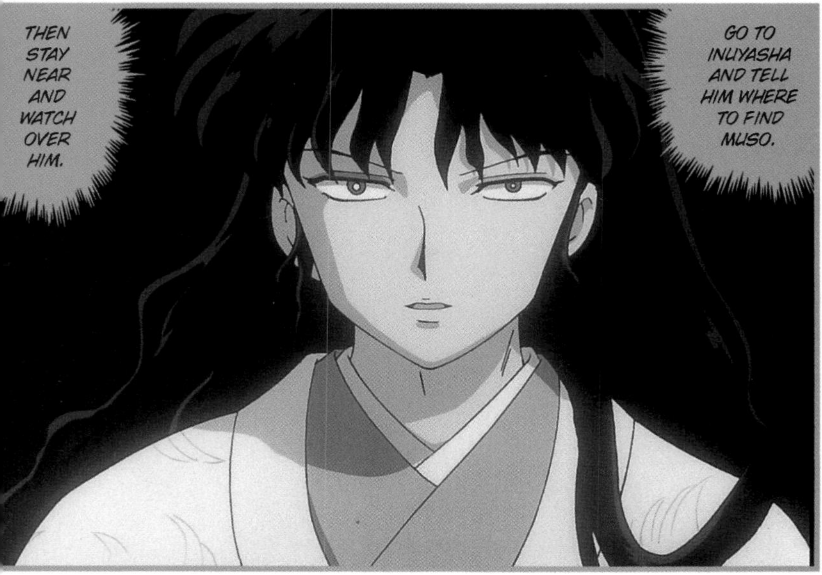
GO TO INUYASHA AND TELL HIM WHERE TO FIND MUSO.
THEN STAY NEAR AND WATCH OVER HIM.

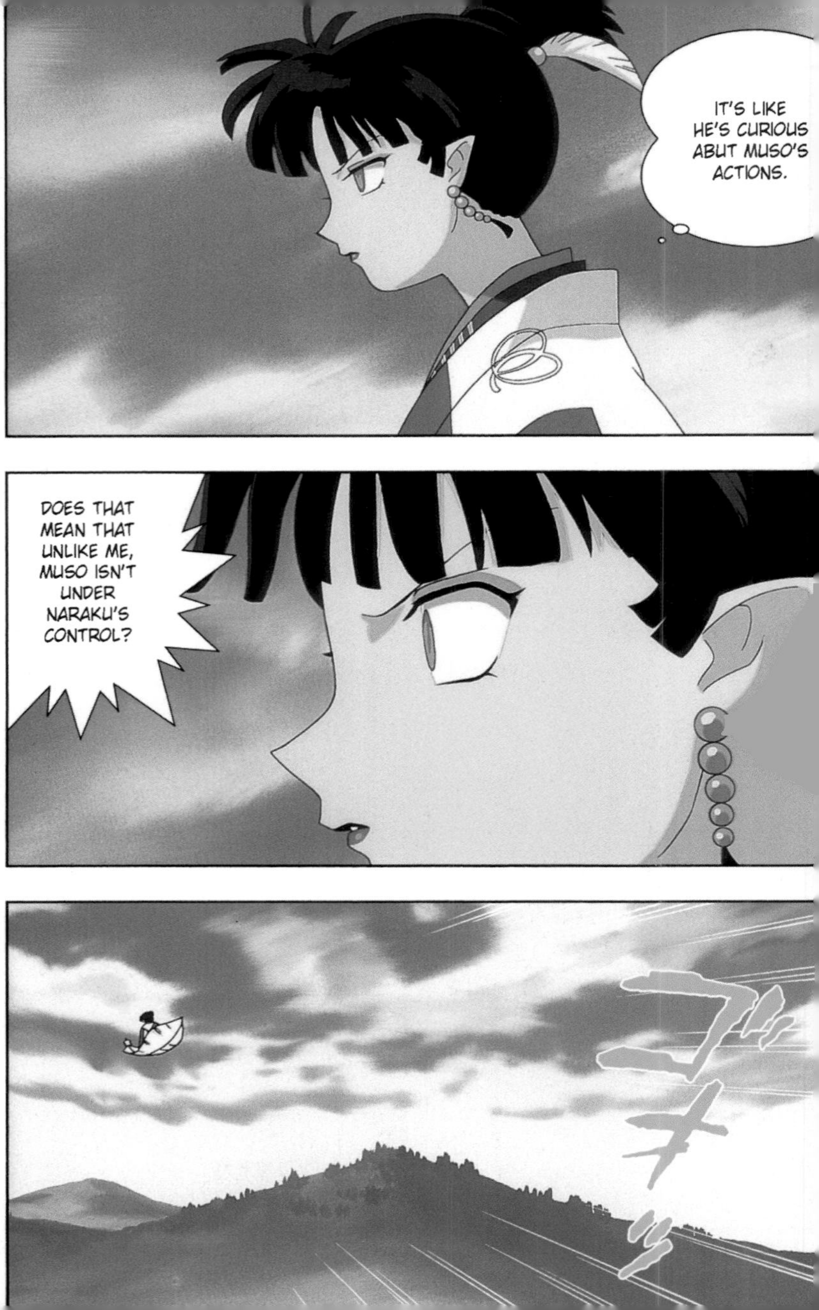
IT'S LIKE HE'S CURIOUS ABUT MUSO'S ACTIONS.
DOES THAT MEAN THAT UNLIKE ME, MUSO ISN'T UNDER NARAKU'S CONTROL?

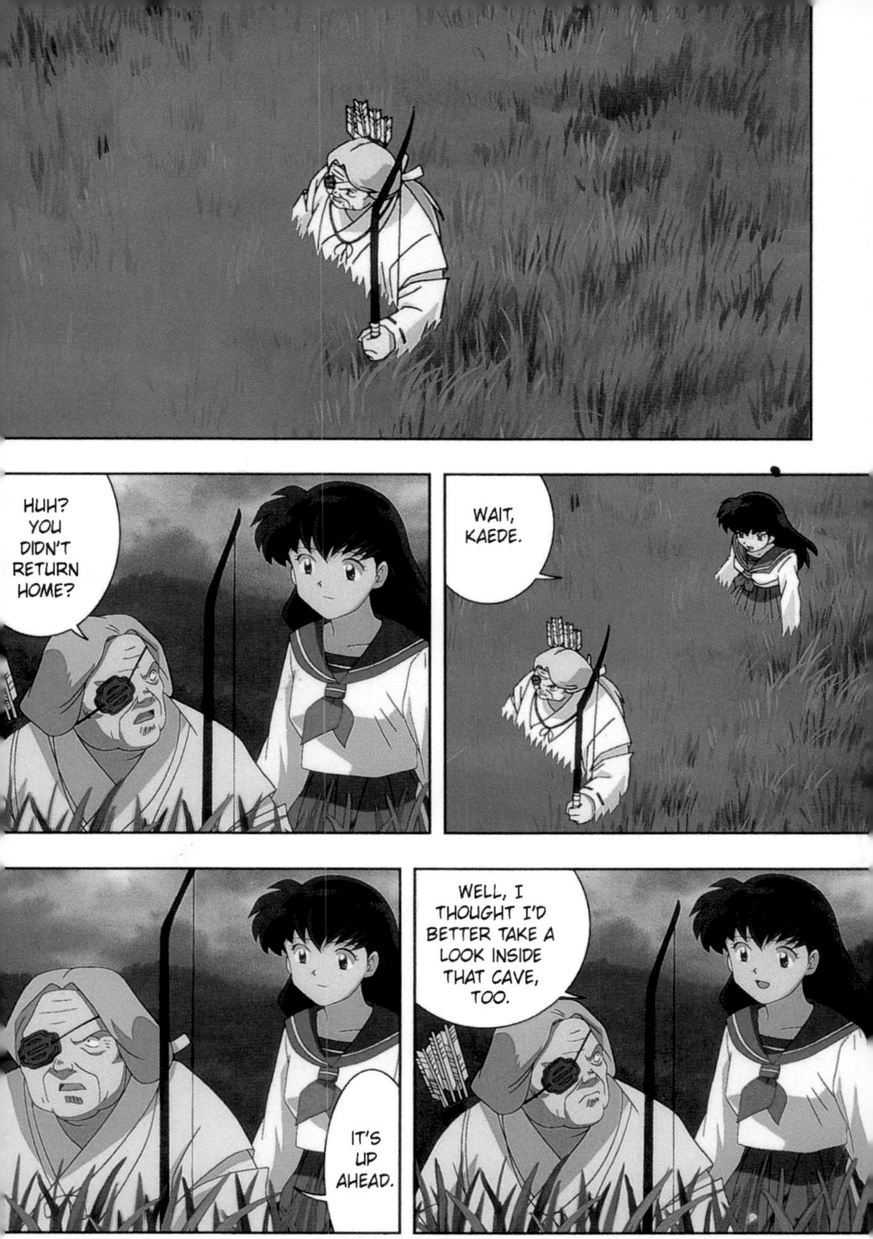
WAIT, KAEDE.
HUH? YOU DIDN'T RETURN HOME?
WELL, I THOUGHT I'D BETTER TAKE A LOOK INSIDE THAT CAVE, TOO.
IT'S UP AHEAD.

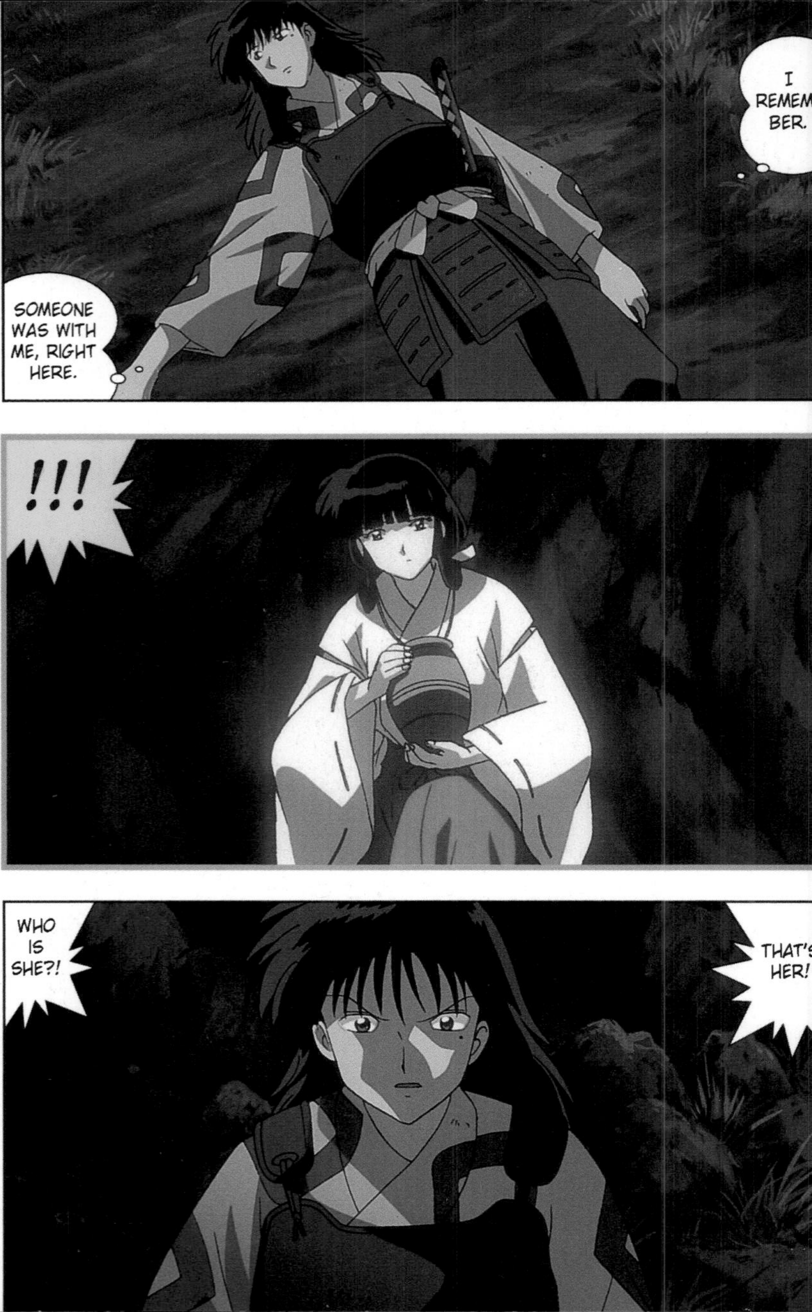
I REMEMBER.
SOMEONE WAS WITH ME, RIGHT HERE.
!!!
THAT'S HER!
WHO IS SHE?!

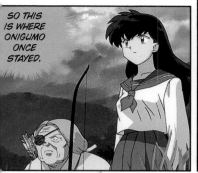

SO THIS IS WHERE ONIGUMO ONCE STAYED.

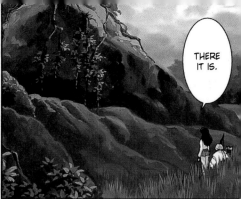

THERE IT IS.

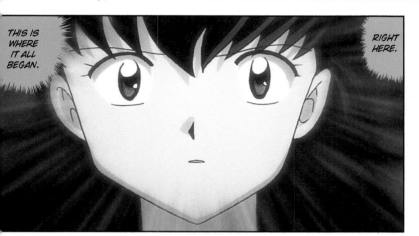

THIS IS WHERE IT ALL BEGAN.

RIGHT HERE.

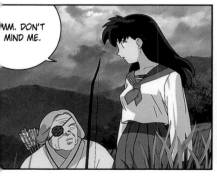

MM. DON'T MIND ME.

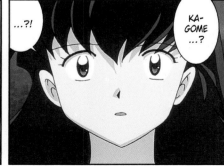

...?!

KA-GOME...?

42

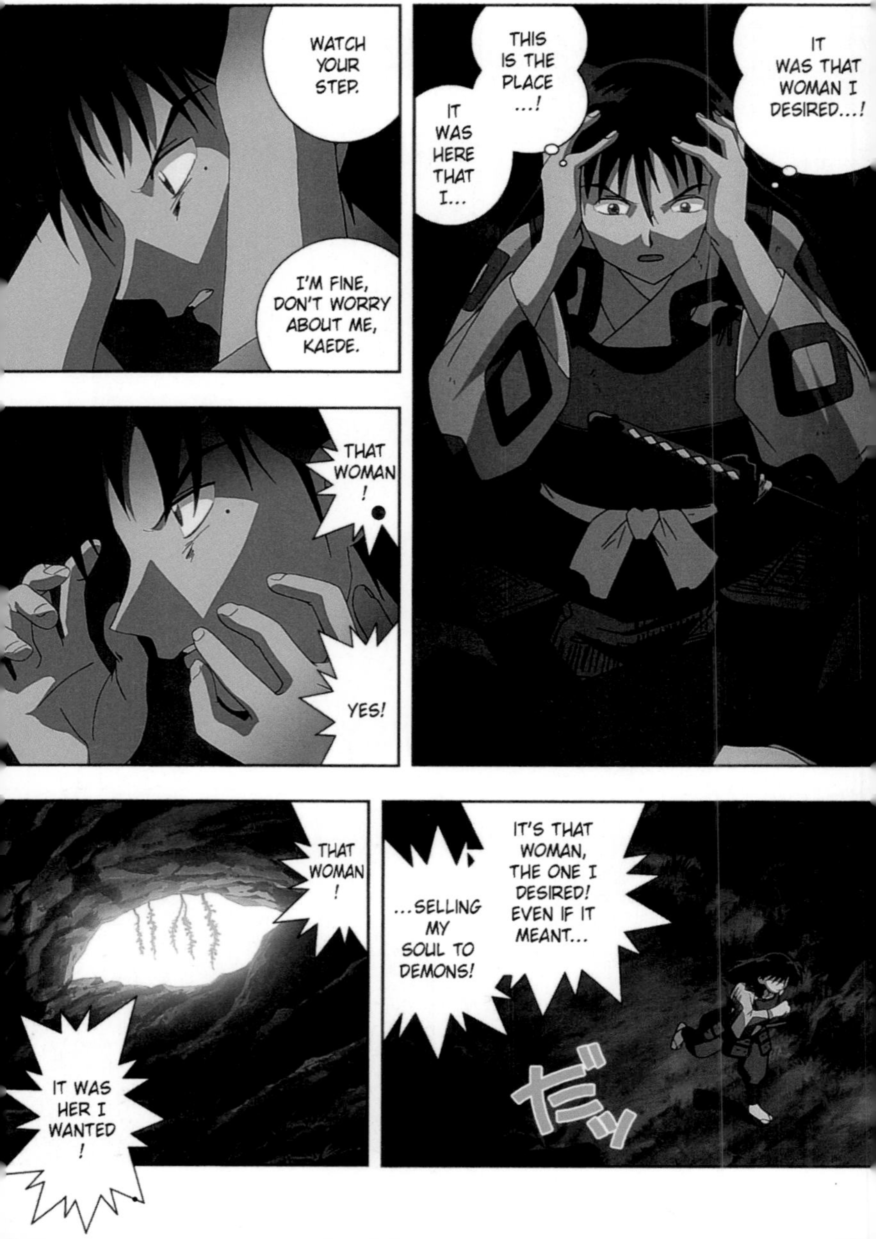
IT WAS THAT WOMAN I DESIRED...!
THIS IS THE PLACE...!
IT WAS HERE THAT I...
WATCH YOUR STEP.
I'M FINE, DON'T WORRY ABOUT ME, KAEDE.
THAT WOMAN!
YES!
IT'S THAT WOMAN, THE ONE I DESIRED! EVEN IF IT MEANT...
...SELLING MY SOUL TO DEMONS!
ダッ
THAT WOMAN!
IT WAS HER I WANTED!

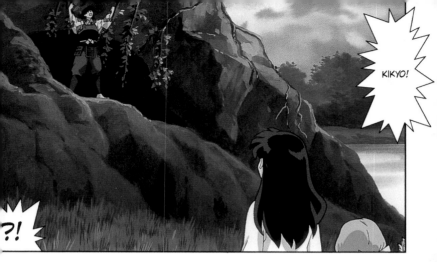

KIKYO!

?!

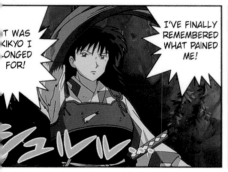

IT WAS KIKYO I LONGED FOR!

I'VE FINALLY REMEMBERED WHAT PAINED ME!

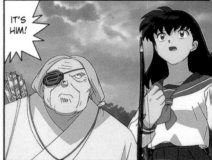

IT'S HIM!

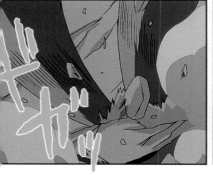

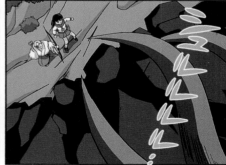

44

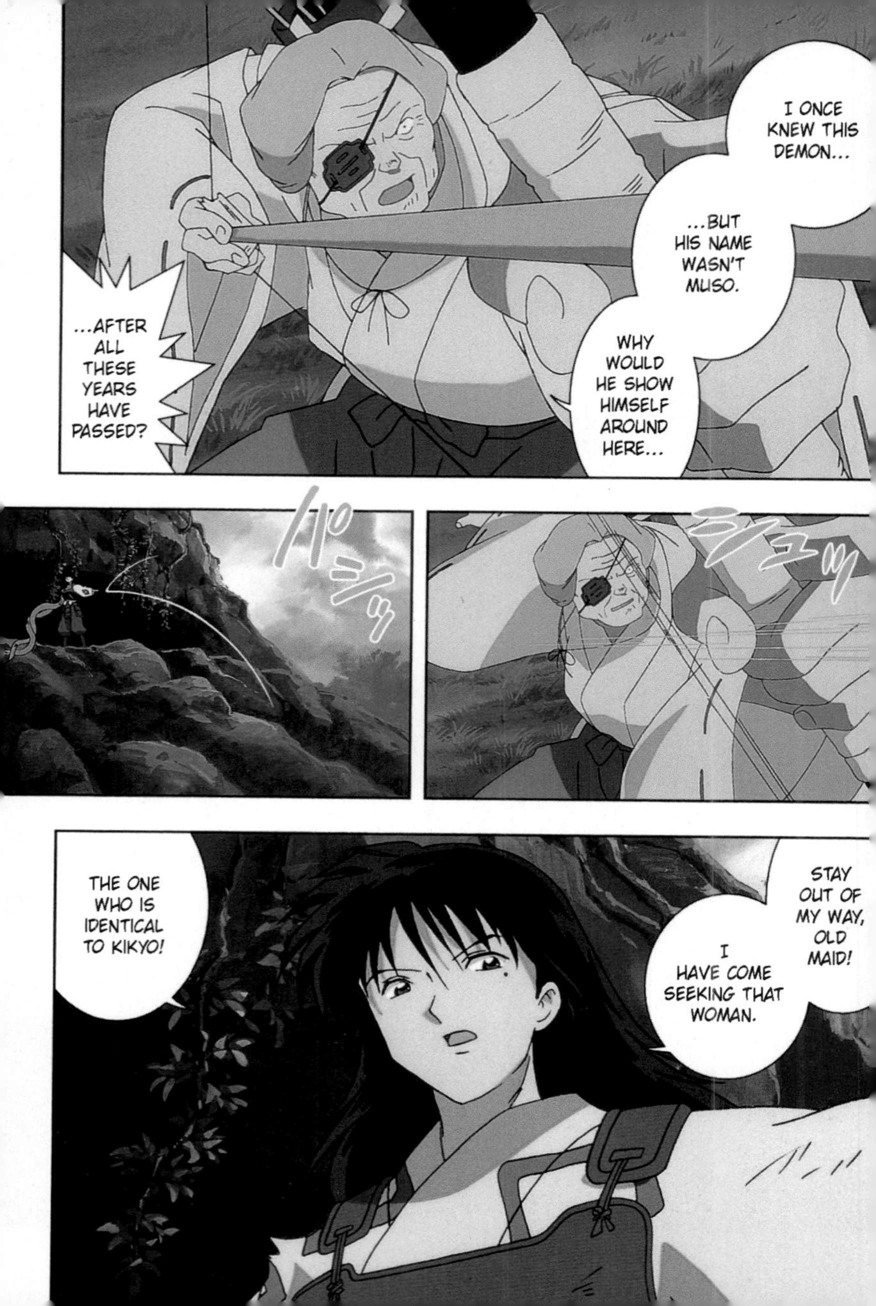
I ONCE KNEW THIS DEMON...
...BUT HIS NAME WASN'T MUSO.
WHY WOULD HE SHOW HIMSELF AROUND HERE...
...AFTER ALL THESE YEARS HAVE PASSED?
シュッ
パシッ
STAY OUT OF MY WAY, OLD MAID!
I HAVE COME SEEKING THAT WOMAN.
THE ONE WHO IS IDENTICAL TO KIKYO!

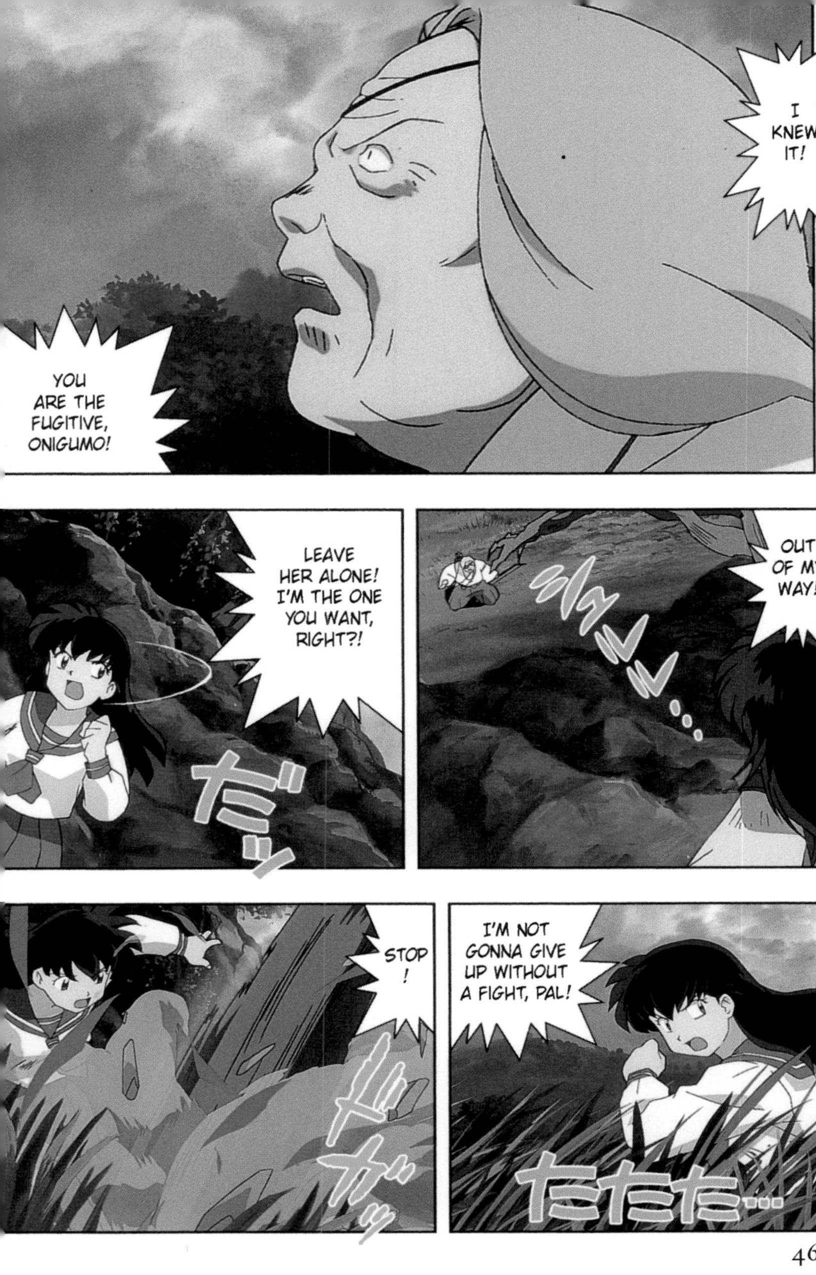
I KNEW IT!
YOU ARE THE FUGITIVE, ONIGUMO!
OUT OF MY WAY!
LEAVE HER ALONE! I'M THE ONE YOU WANT, RIGHT?!
だッ
I'M NOT GONNA GIVE UP WITHOUT A FIGHT, PAL!
たたたた…
STOP!
ドガッ

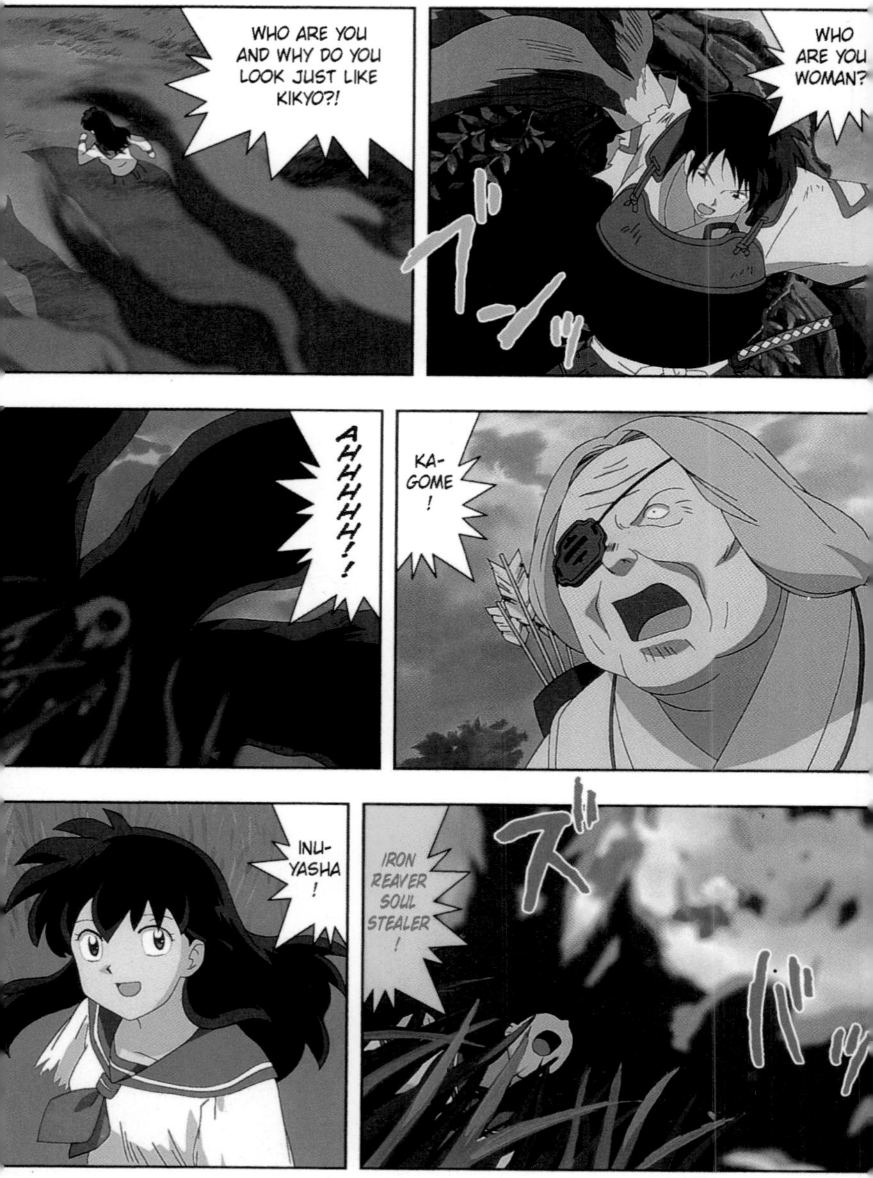
WHO ARE YOU WOMAN?
WHO ARE YOU AND WHY DO YOU LOOK JUST LIKE KIKYO?!
KA-GOME!
AHHHHHH!!
IRON REAVER SOUL STEALER!
INU-YASHA!

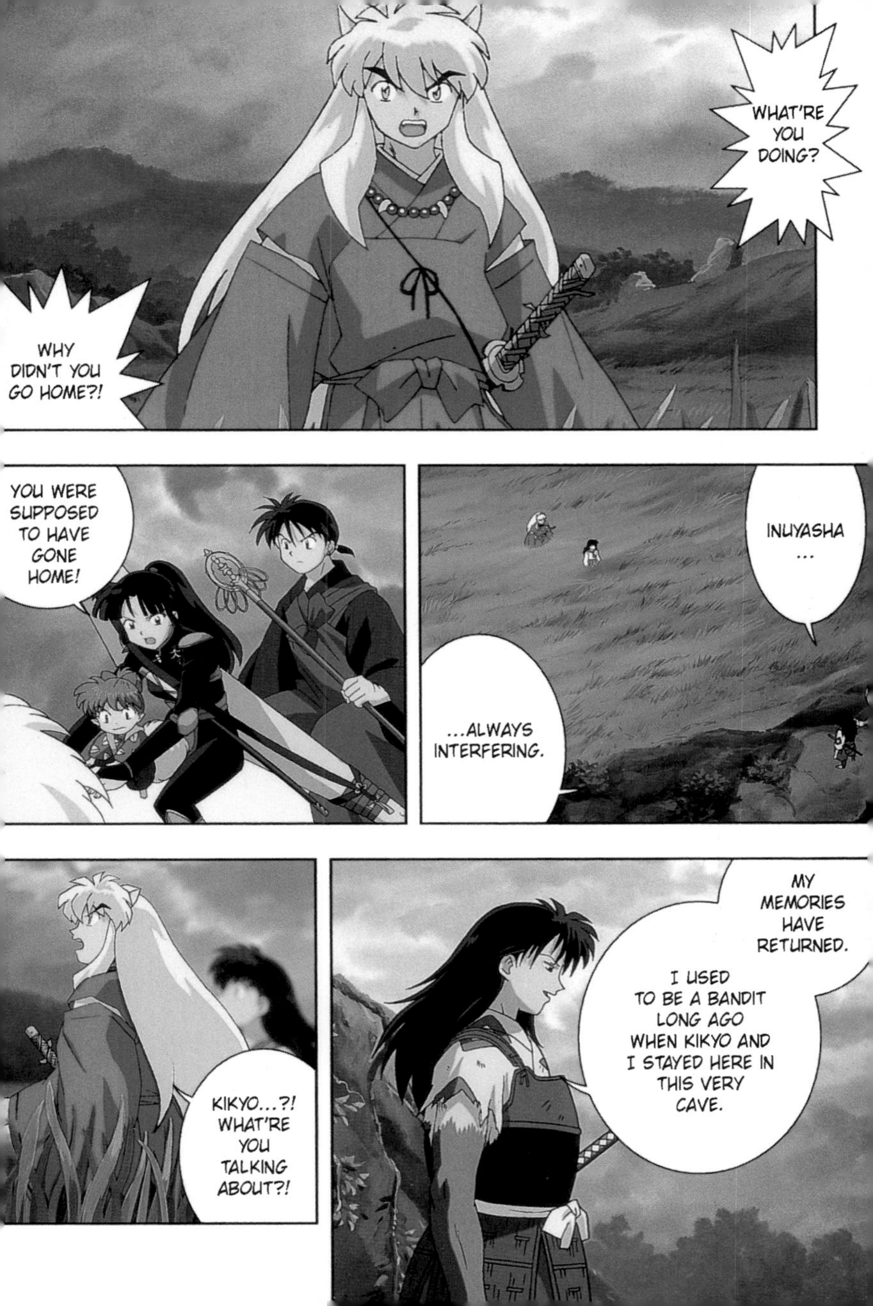
WHAT'RE YOU DOING?
WHY DIDN'T YOU GO HOME?!
INUYASHA ...
...ALWAYS INTERFERING.
YOU WERE SUPPOSED TO HAVE GONE HOME!
MY MEMORIES HAVE RETURNED.
I USED TO BE A BANDIT LONG AGO WHEN KIKYO AND I STAYED HERE IN THIS VERY CAVE.
KIKYO...?! WHAT'RE YOU TALKING ABOUT?!

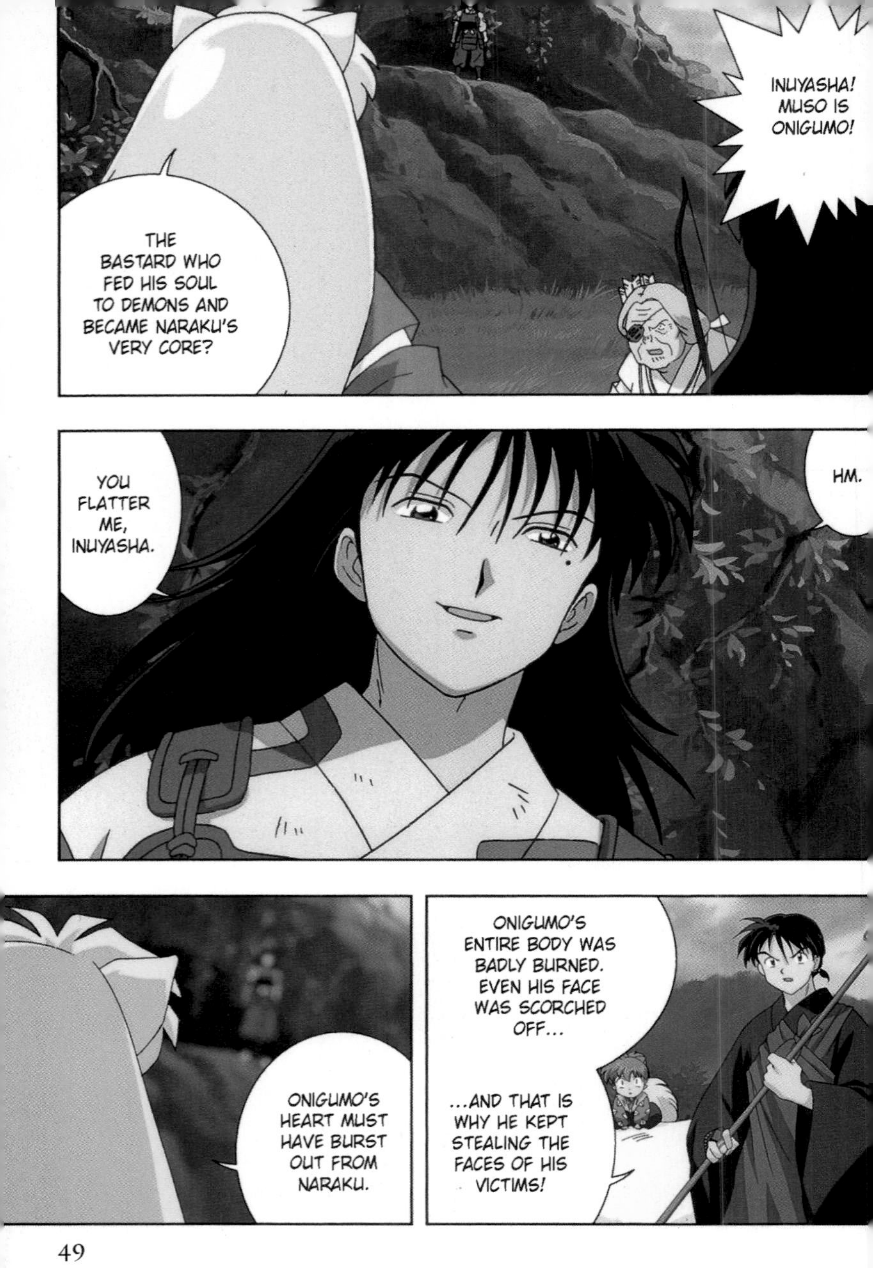
INUYASHA! MUSO IS ONIGUMO!
THE BASTARD WHO FED HIS SOUL TO DEMONS AND BECAME NARAKU'S VERY CORE?
HM.
YOU FLATTER ME, INUYASHA.
ONIGUMO'S ENTIRE BODY WAS BADLY BURNED. EVEN HIS FACE WAS SCORCHED OFF...
...AND THAT IS WHY HE KEPT STEALING THE FACES OF HIS VICTIMS!
ONIGUMO'S HEART MUST HAVE BURST OUT FROM NARAKU.

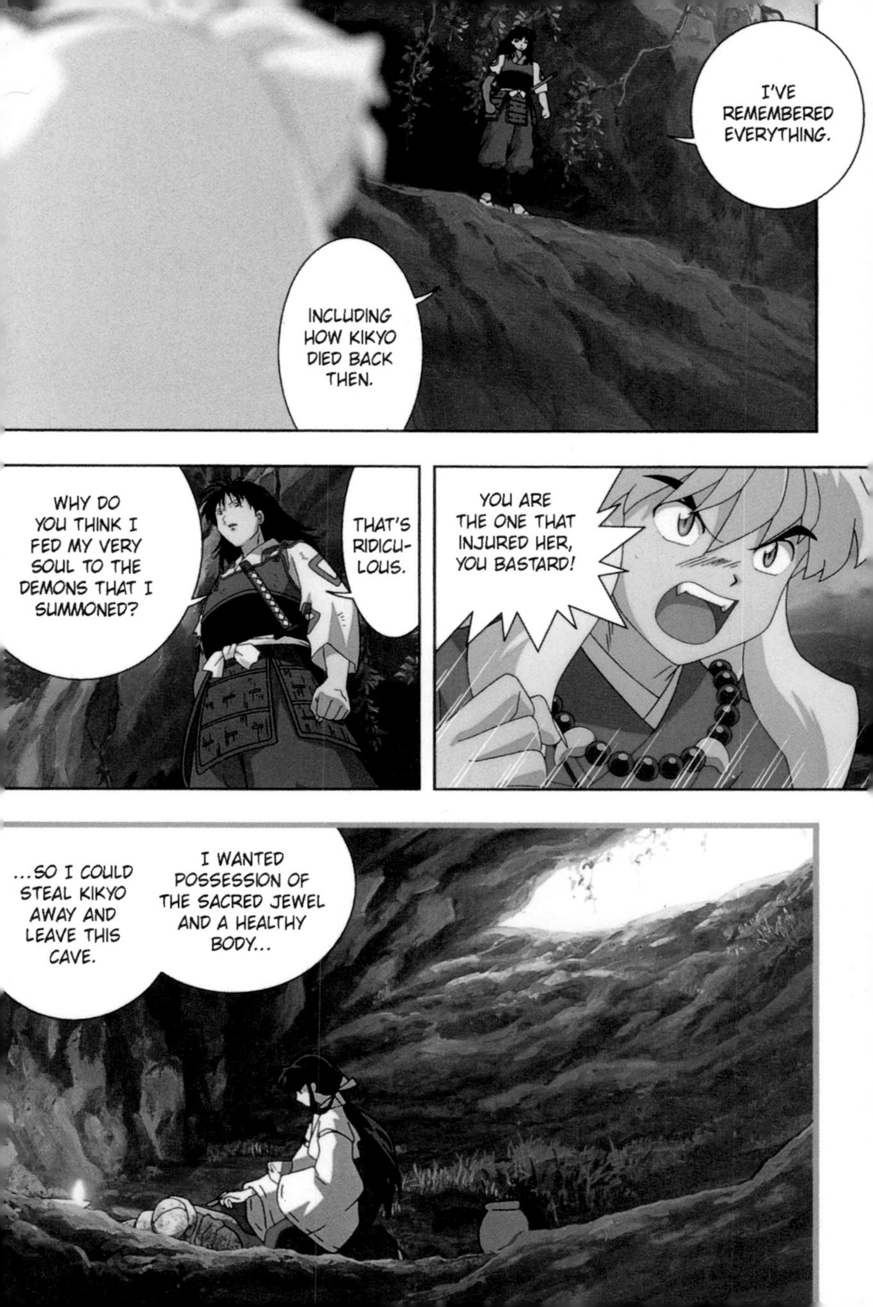
I'VE REMEMBERED EVERYTHING.
INCLUDING HOW KIKYO DIED BACK THEN.
YOU ARE THE ONE THAT INJURED HER, YOU BASTARD!
THAT'S RIDICU-LOUS.
WHY DO YOU THINK I FED MY VERY SOUL TO THE DEMONS THAT I SUMMONED?
I WANTED POSSESSION OF THE SACRED JEWEL AND A HEALTHY BODY...
...SO I COULD STEAL KIKYO AWAY AND LEAVE THIS CAVE.

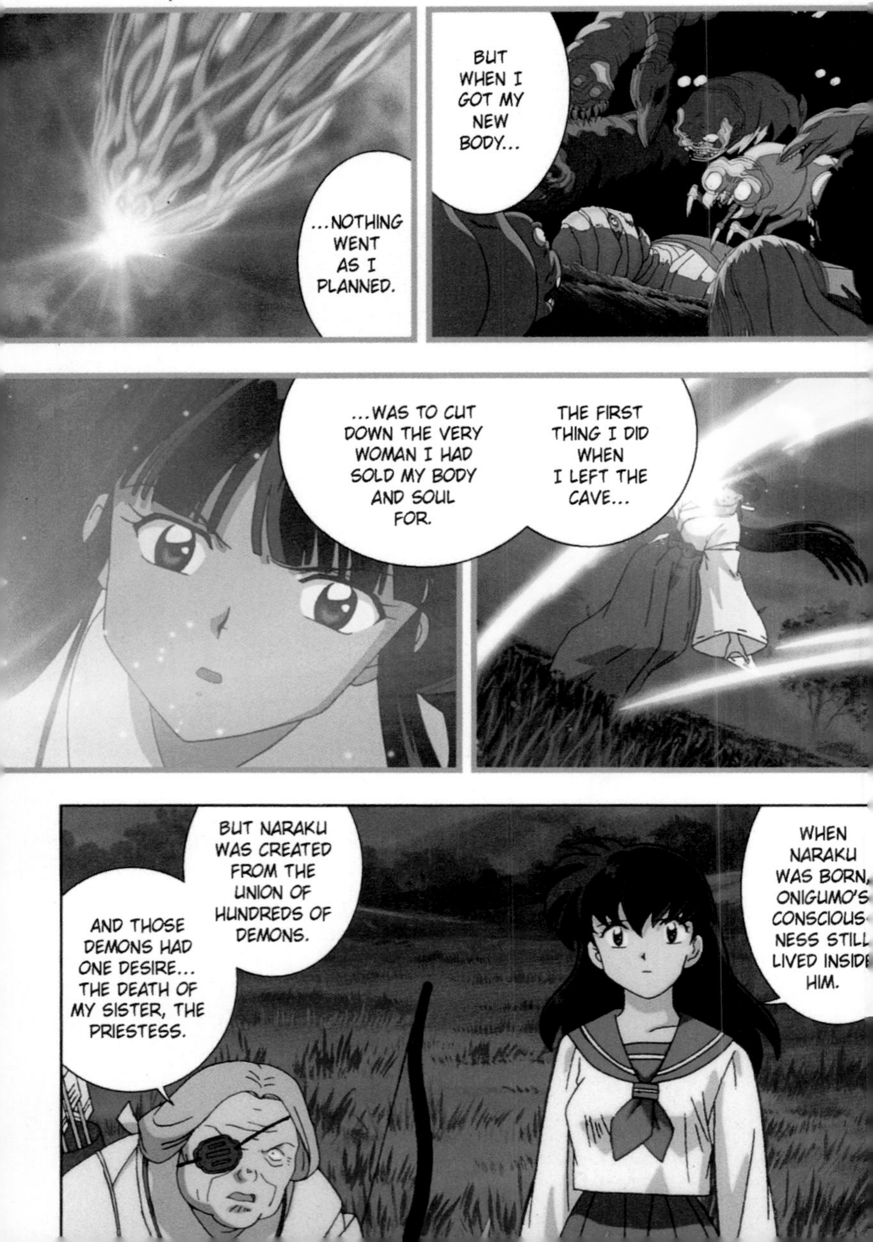
BUT WHEN I GOT MY NEW BODY...
...NOTHING WENT AS I PLANNED.
THE FIRST THING I DID WHEN I LEFT THE CAVE...
...WAS TO CUT DOWN THE VERY WOMAN I HAD SOLD MY BODY AND SOUL FOR.
WHEN NARAKU WAS BORN, ONIGUMO'S CONSCIOUS-NESS STILL LIVED INSIDE HIM.
BUT NARAKU WAS CREATED FROM THE UNION OF HUNDREDS OF DEMONS.
AND THOSE DEMONS HAD ONE DESIRE... THE DEATH OF MY SISTER, THE PRIESTESS.

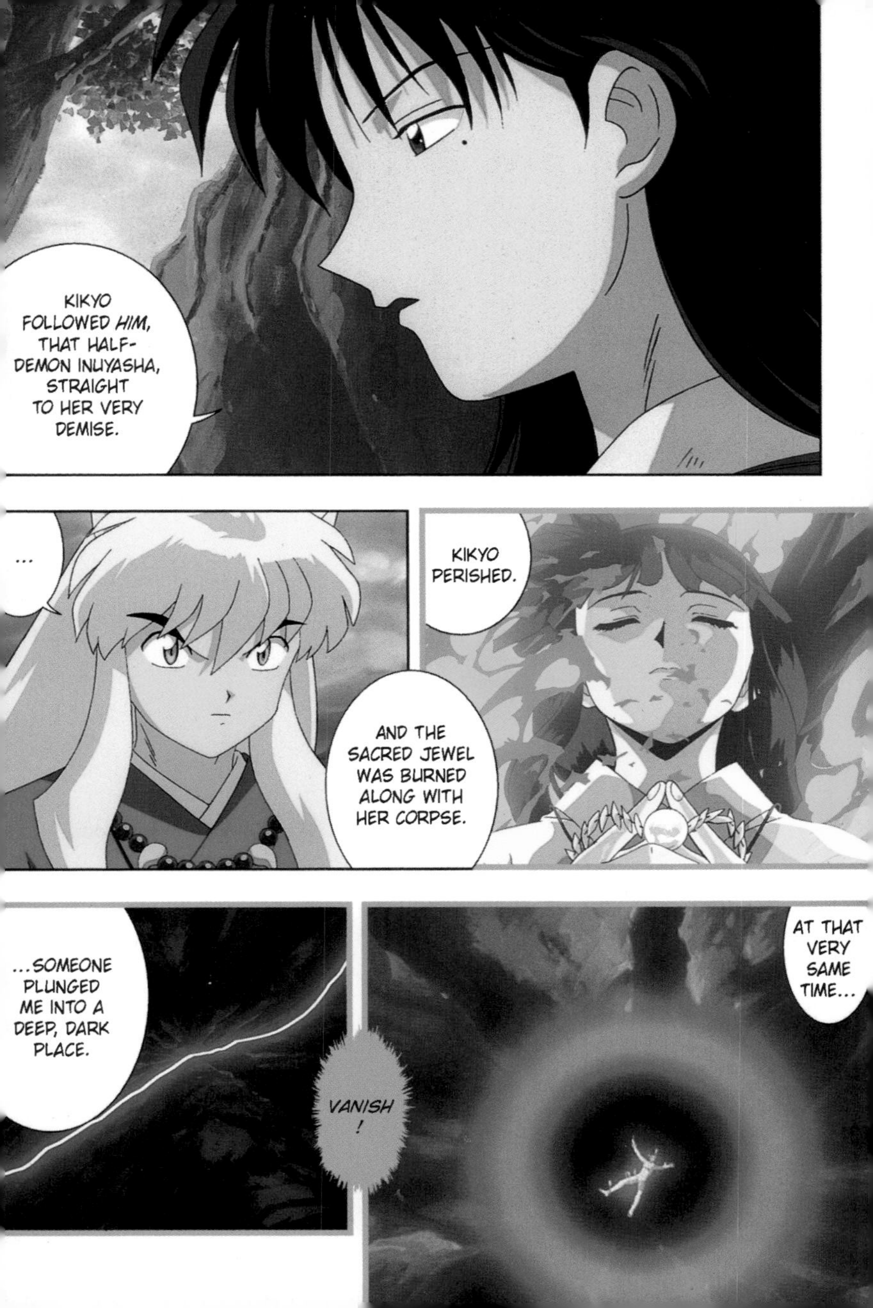
KIKYO FOLLOWED *HIM*, THAT HALF-DEMON INUYASHA, STRAIGHT TO HER VERY DEMISE.
KIKYO PERISHED.
AND THE SACRED JEWEL WAS BURNED ALONG WITH HER CORPSE.
...
AT THAT VERY SAME TIME...
VANISH!
...SOMEONE PLUNGED ME INTO A DEEP, DARK PLACE.

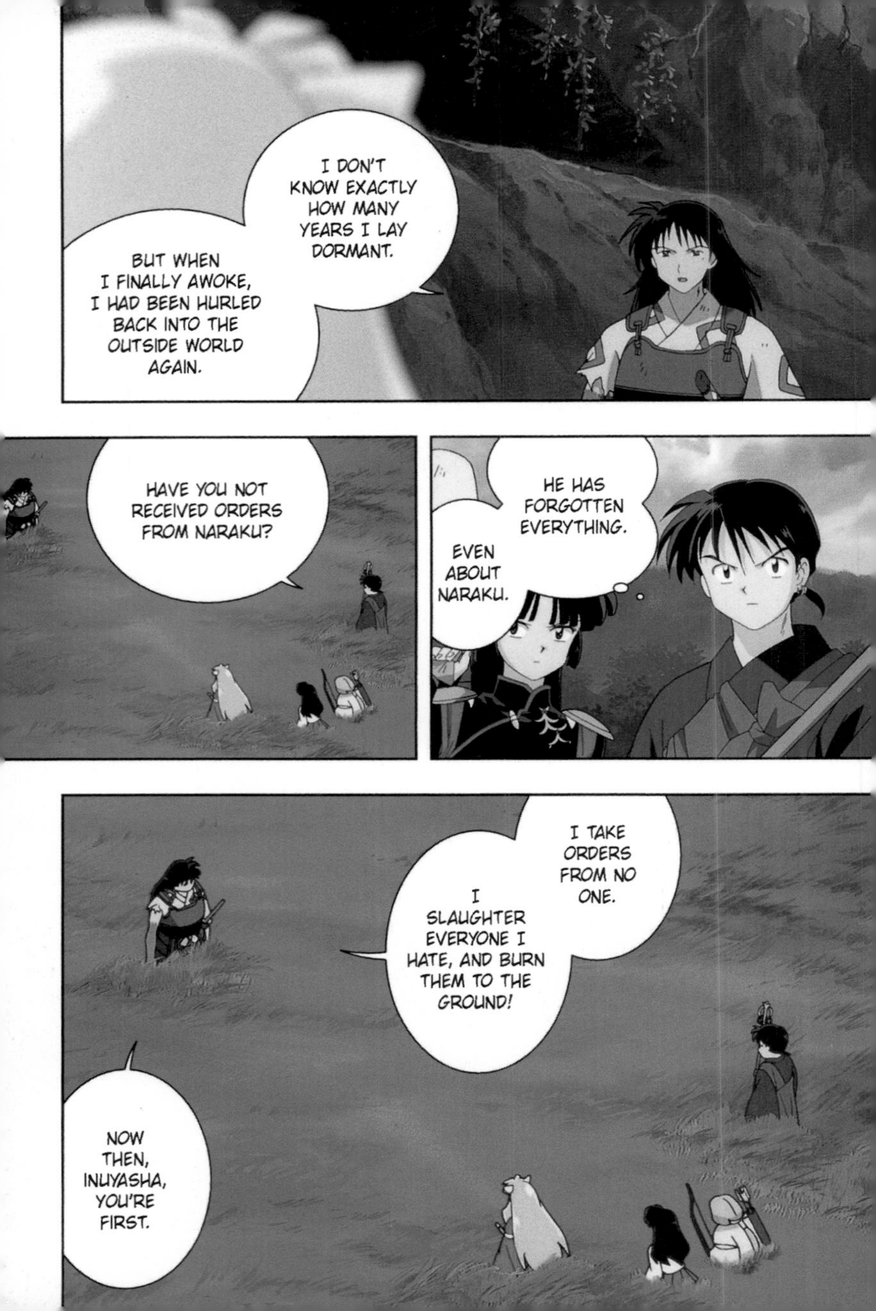
I DON'T KNOW EXACTLY HOW MANY YEARS I LAY DORMANT.
BUT WHEN I FINALLY AWOKE, I HAD BEEN HURLED BACK INTO THE OUTSIDE WORLD AGAIN.
HE HAS FORGOTTEN EVERYTHING.
EVEN ABOUT NARAKU.
HAVE YOU NOT RECEIVED ORDERS FROM NARAKU?
I TAKE ORDERS FROM NO ONE.
I SLAUGHTER EVERYONE I HATE, AND BURN THEM TO THE GROUND!
NOW THEN, INUYASHA, YOU'RE FIRST.

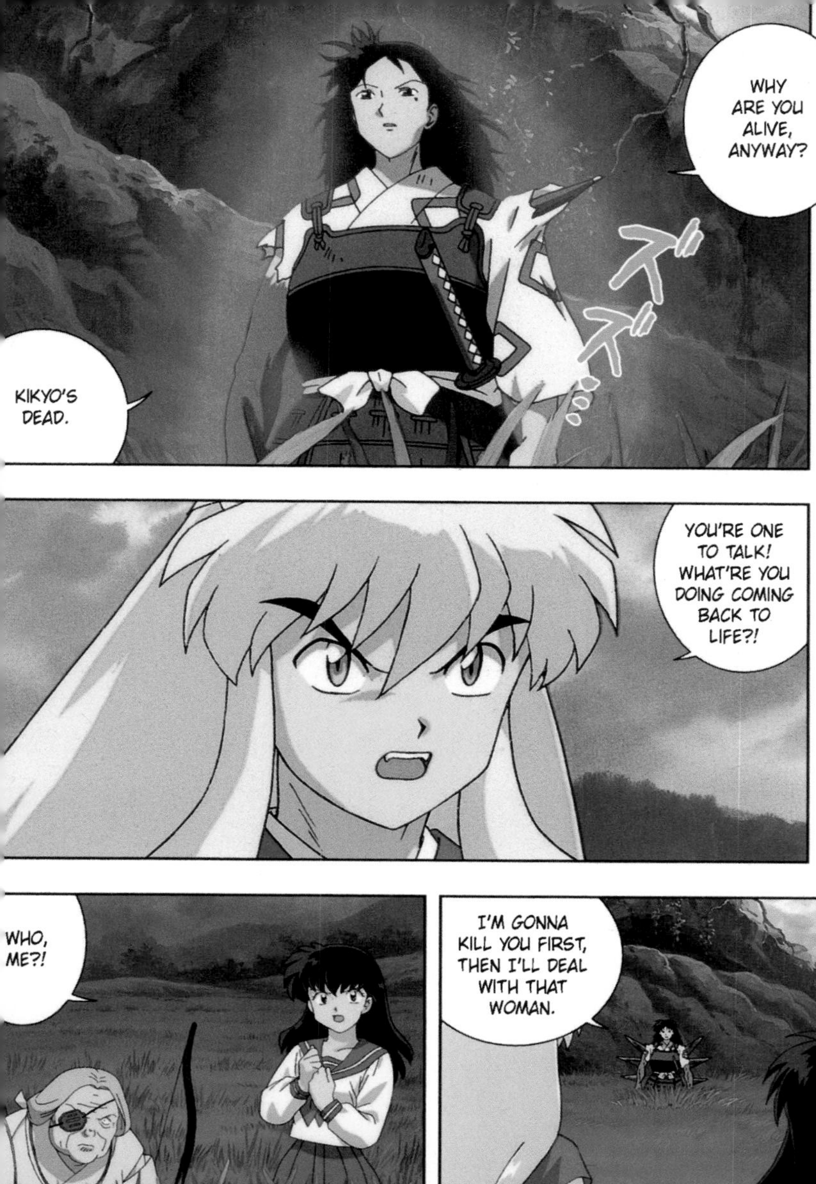
WHY ARE YOU ALIVE, ANYWAY?
ズズ
KIKYO'S DEAD.
YOU'RE ONE TO TALK! WHAT'RE YOU DOING COMING BACK TO LIFE?!
I'M GONNA KILL YOU FIRST, THEN I'LL DEAL WITH THAT WOMAN.
WHO, ME?!

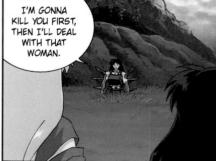

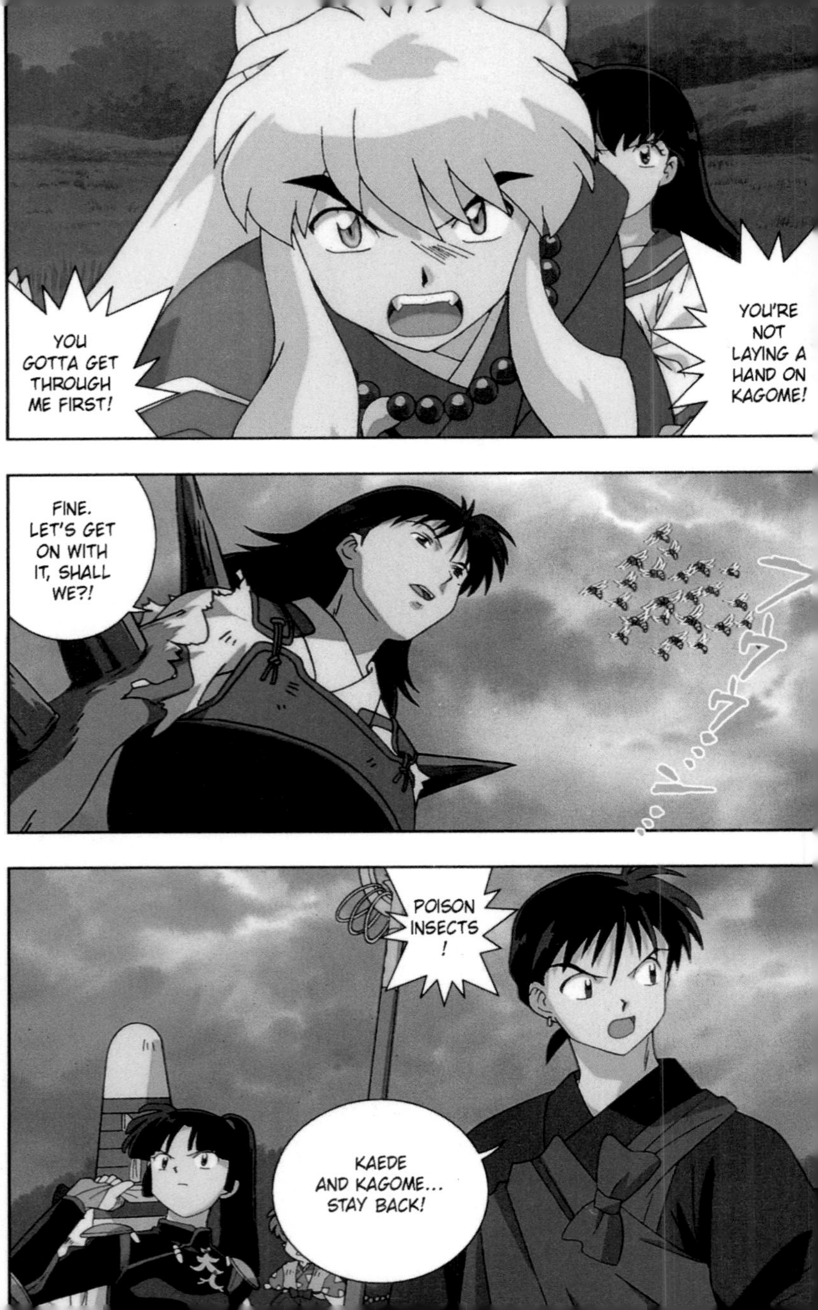
YOU'RE NOT LAYING A HAND ON KAGOME!
YOU GOTTA GET THROUGH ME FIRST!
FINE. LET'S GET ON WITH IT, SHALL WE?!
POISON INSECTS!
KAEDE AND KAGOME... STAY BACK!

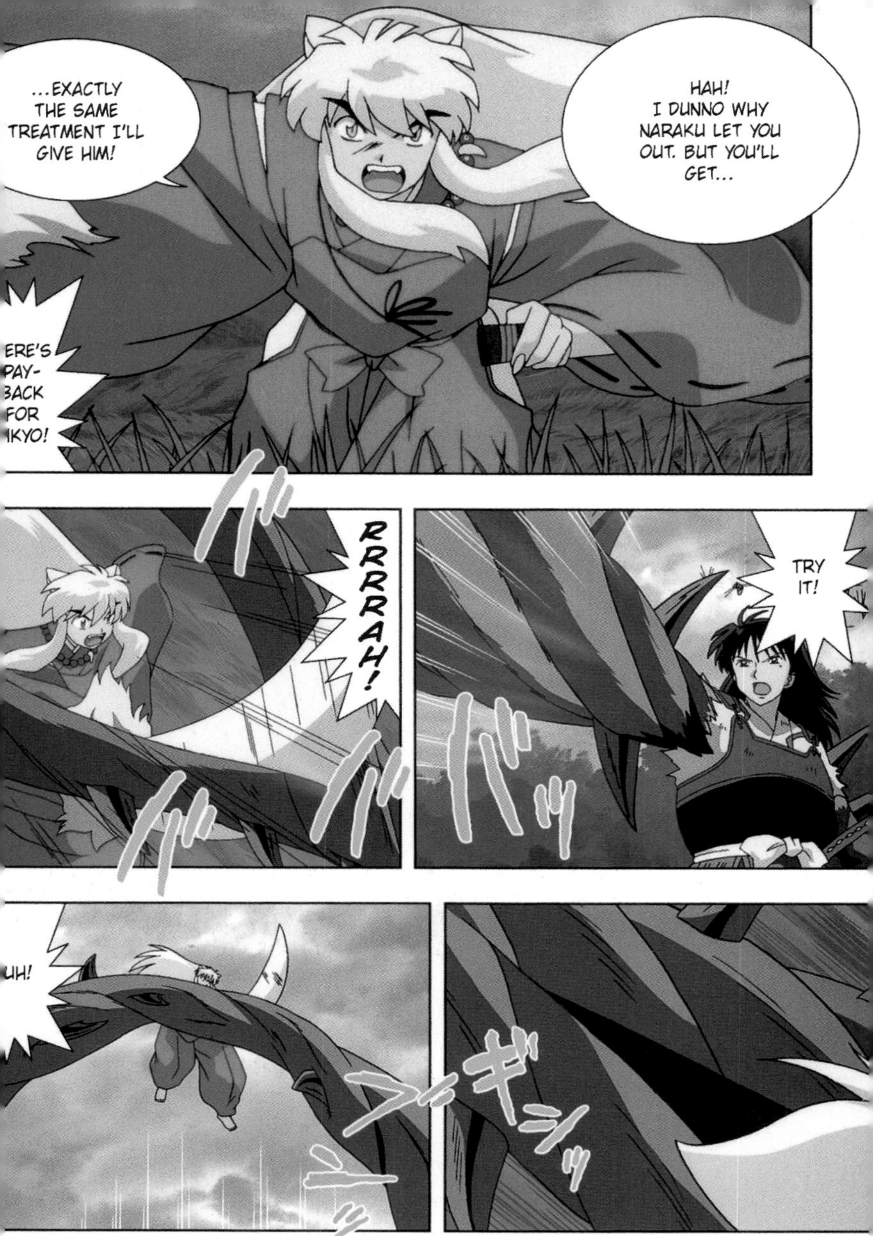
HAH! I DUNNO WHY NARAKU LET YOU OUT. BUT YOU'LL GET...
...EXACTLY THE SAME TREATMENT I'LL GIVE HIM!
ERE'S PAY-BACK FOR KYO!
TRY IT!
RRRRAH!
UH!

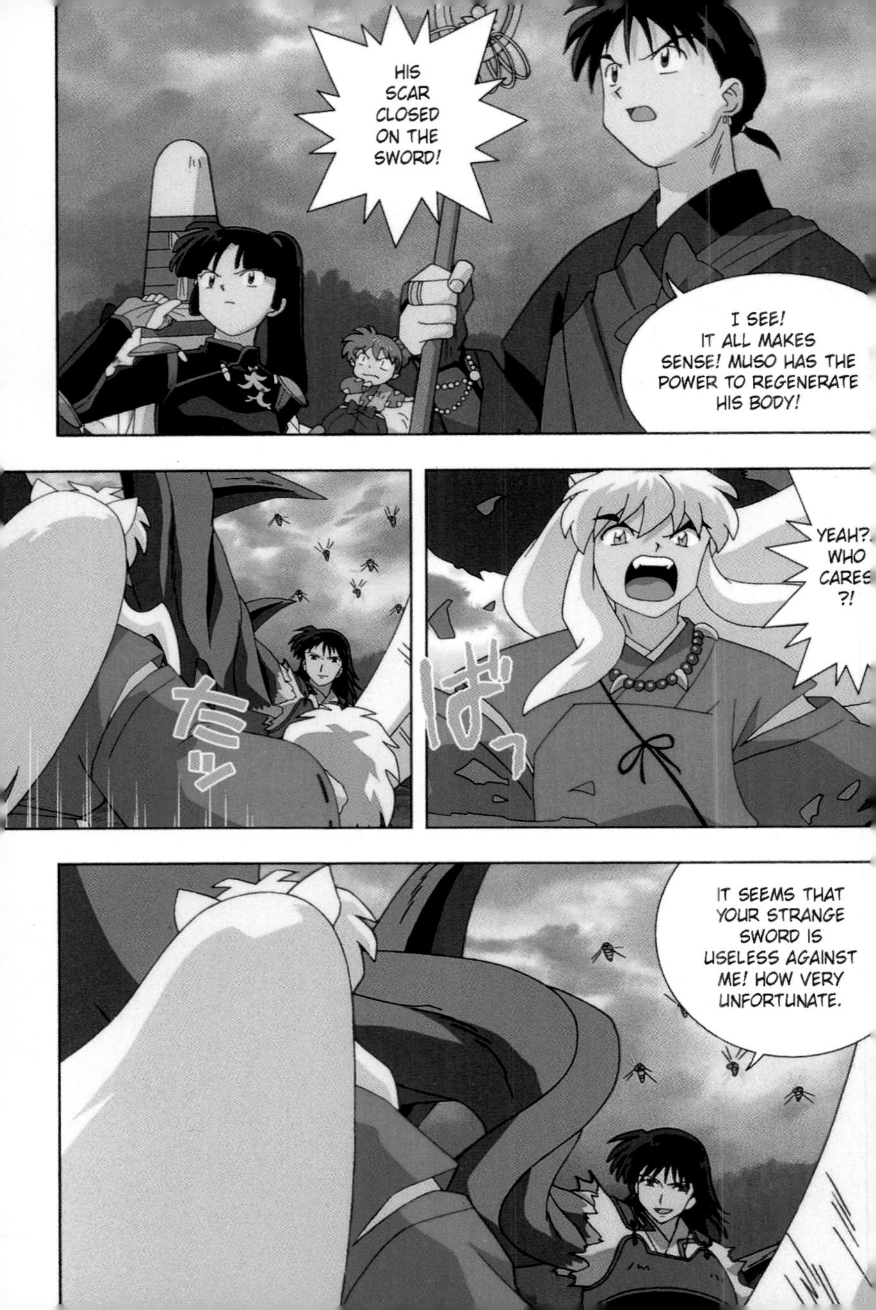
I SEE! IT ALL MAKES SENSE! MUSO HAS THE POWER TO REGENERATE HIS BODY!
HIS SCAR CLOSED ON THE SWORD!
YEAH?! WHO CARES?!
ばっ
たッ
IT SEEMS THAT YOUR STRANGE SWORD IS USELESS AGAINST ME! HOW VERY UNFORTUNATE.

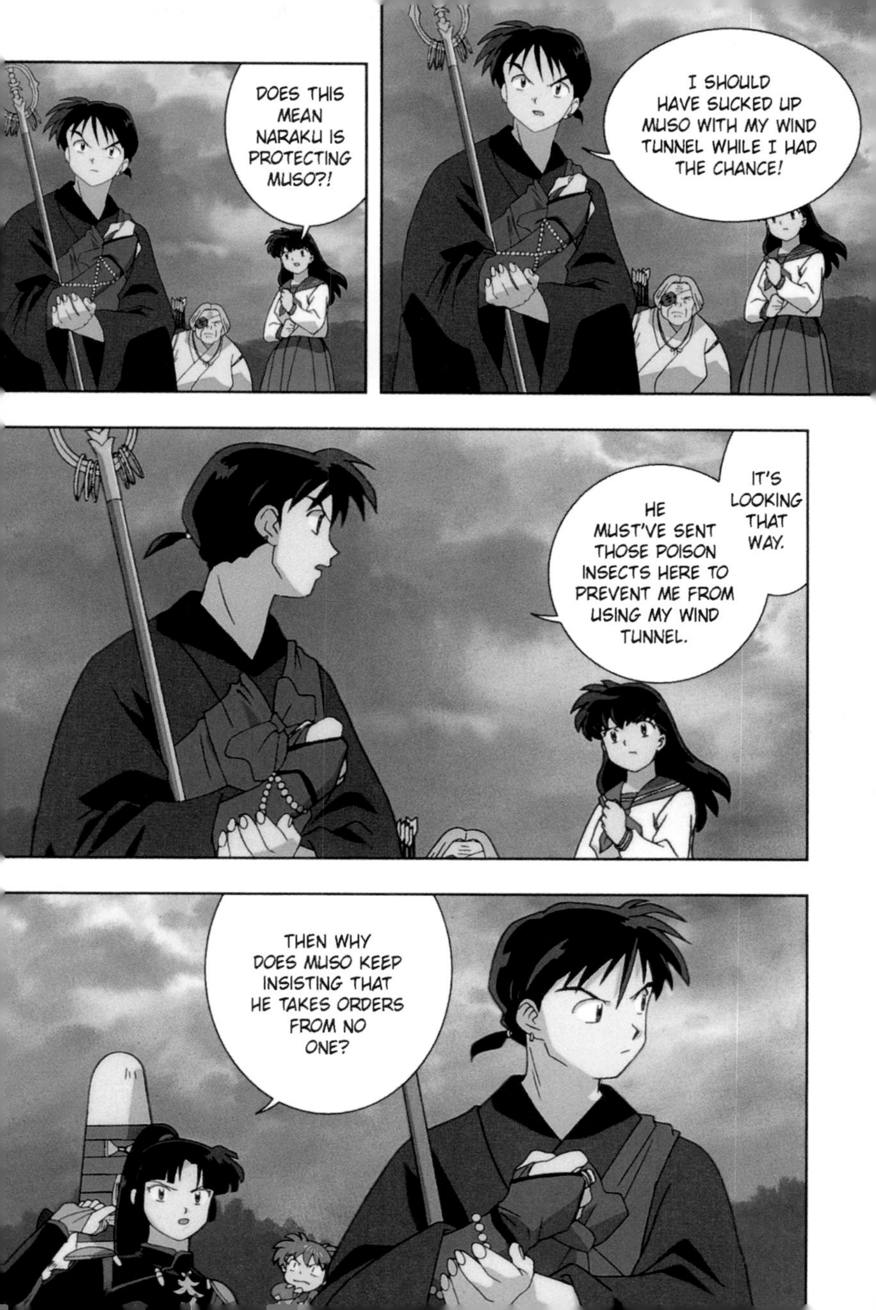
I SHOULD HAVE SUCKED UP MUSO WITH MY WIND TUNNEL WHILE I HAD THE CHANCE!
DOES THIS MEAN NARAKU IS PROTECTING MUSO?!
IT'S LOOKING THAT WAY.
HE MUST'VE SENT THOSE POISON INSECTS HERE TO PREVENT ME FROM USING MY WIND TUNNEL.
THEN WHY DOES MUSO KEEP INSISTING THAT HE TAKES ORDERS FROM NO ONE?

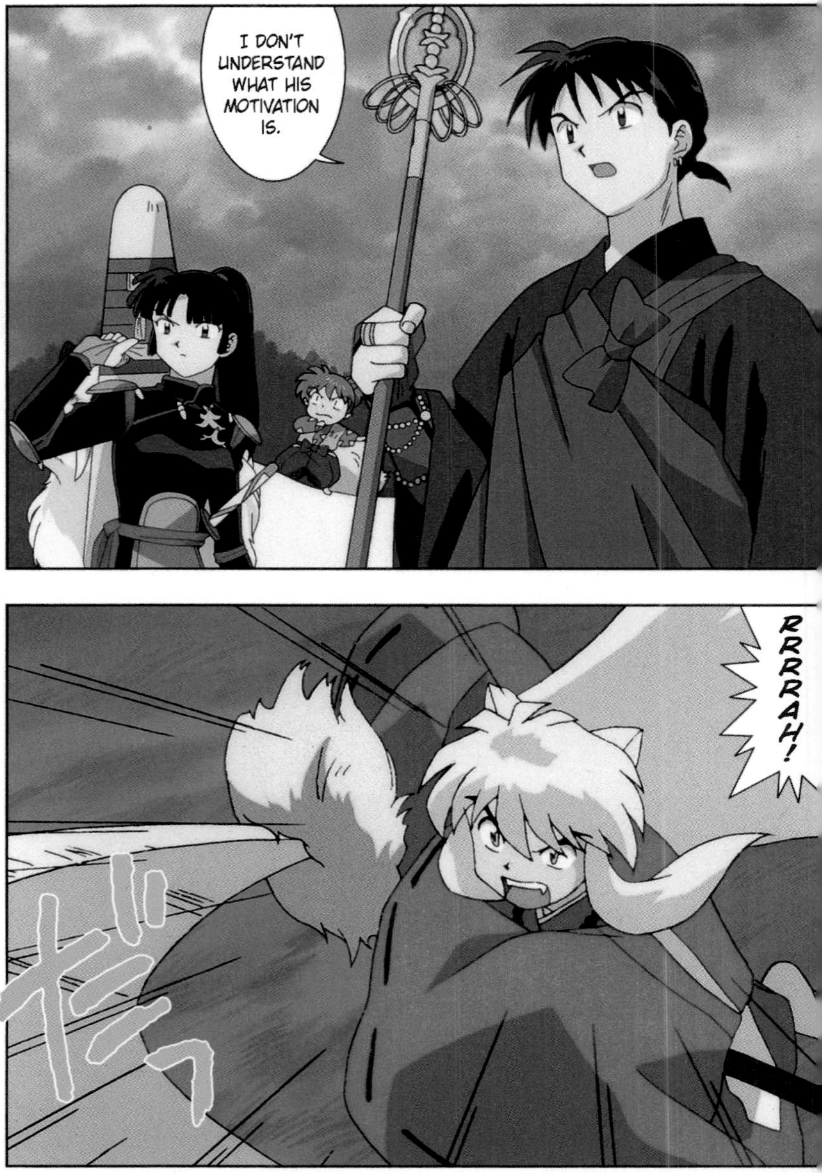
I DON'T UNDERSTAND WHAT HIS MOTIVATION IS.
RRRRAH!

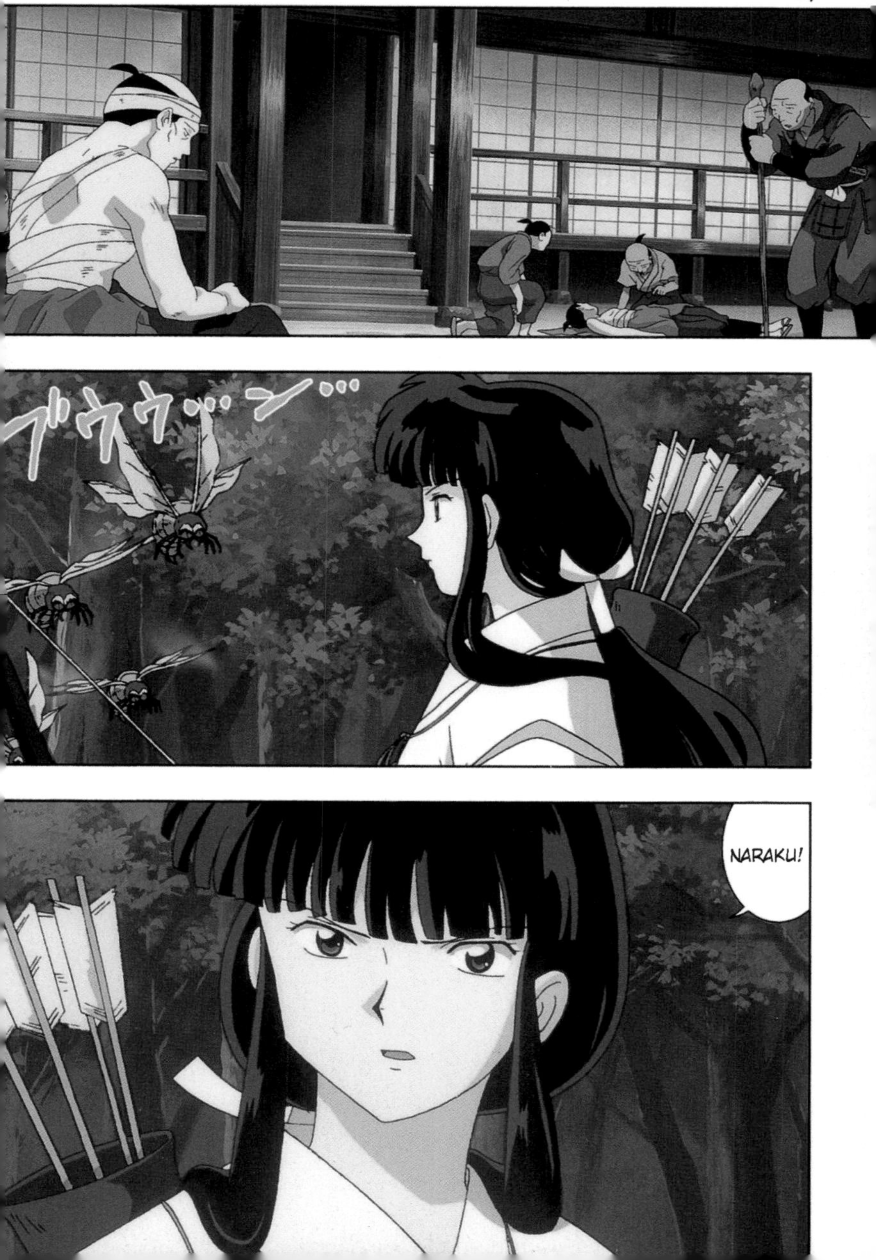
ブウウ…ン…
NARAKU!

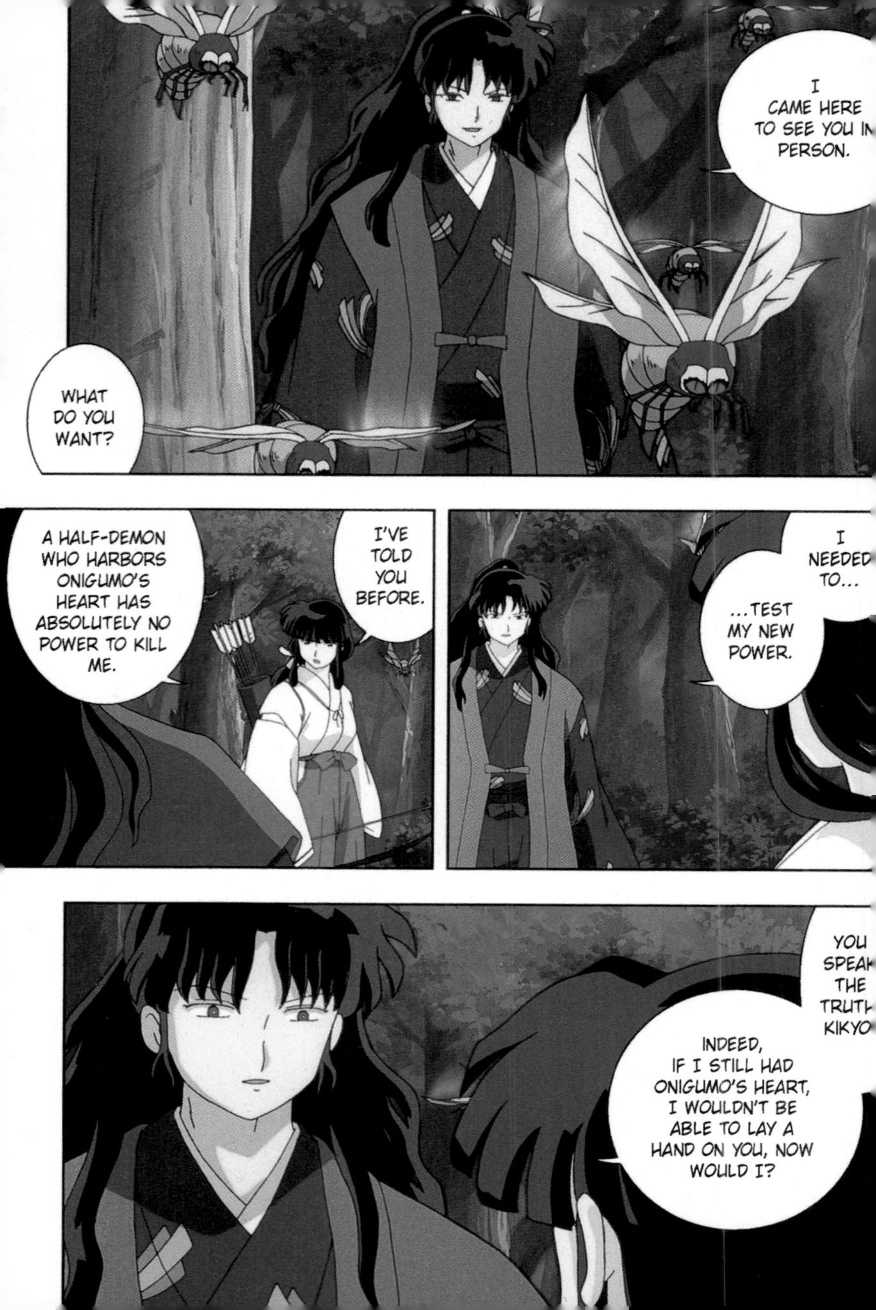
I CAME HERE TO SEE YOU IN PERSON.
WHAT DO YOU WANT?
I NEEDED TO...
...TEST MY NEW POWER.
I'VE TOLD YOU BEFORE.
A HALF-DEMON WHO HARBORS ONIGUMO'S HEART HAS ABSOLUTELY NO POWER TO KILL ME.
YOU SPEAK THE TRUTH KIKYO
INDEED, IF I STILL HAD ONIGUMO'S HEART, I WOULDN'T BE ABLE TO LAY A HAND ON YOU, NOW WOULD I?

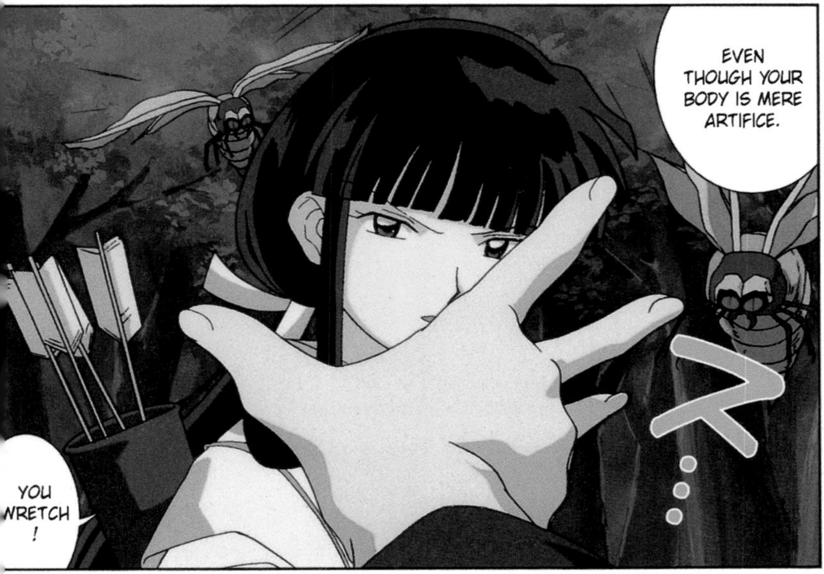
EVEN THOUGH YOUR BODY IS MERE ARTIFICE.
YOU WRETCH!
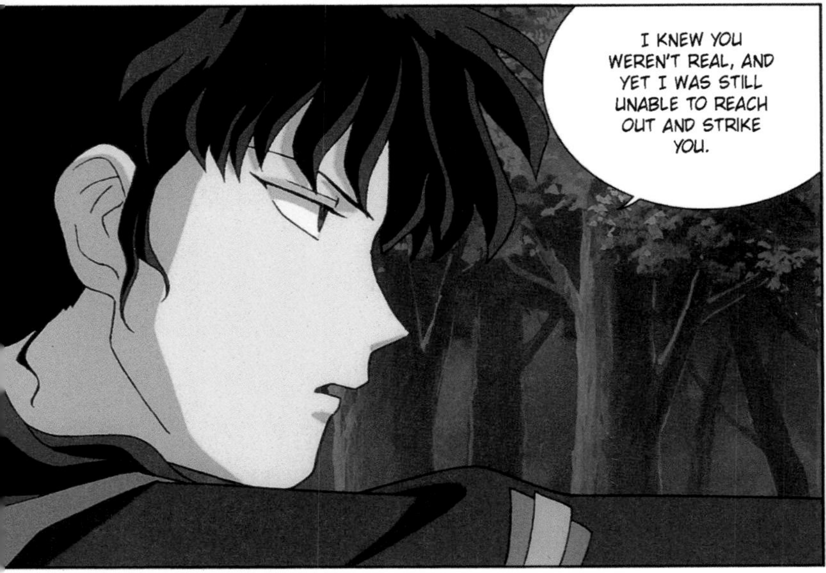
I KNEW YOU WEREN'T REAL, AND YET I WAS STILL UNABLE TO REACH OUT AND STRIKE YOU.

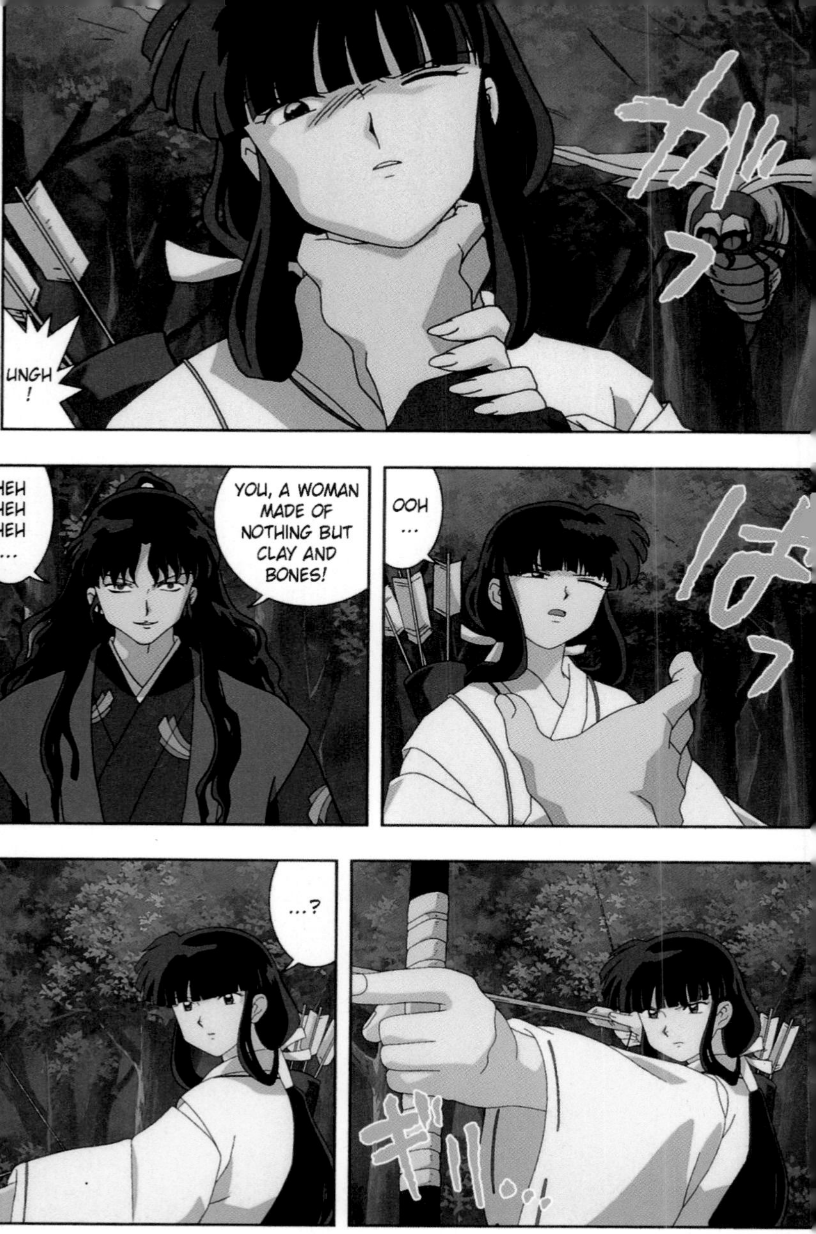
UNGH !
OOH ...
YOU, A WOMAN MADE OF NOTHING BUT CLAY AND BONES!
HEH HEH HEH ...
...?

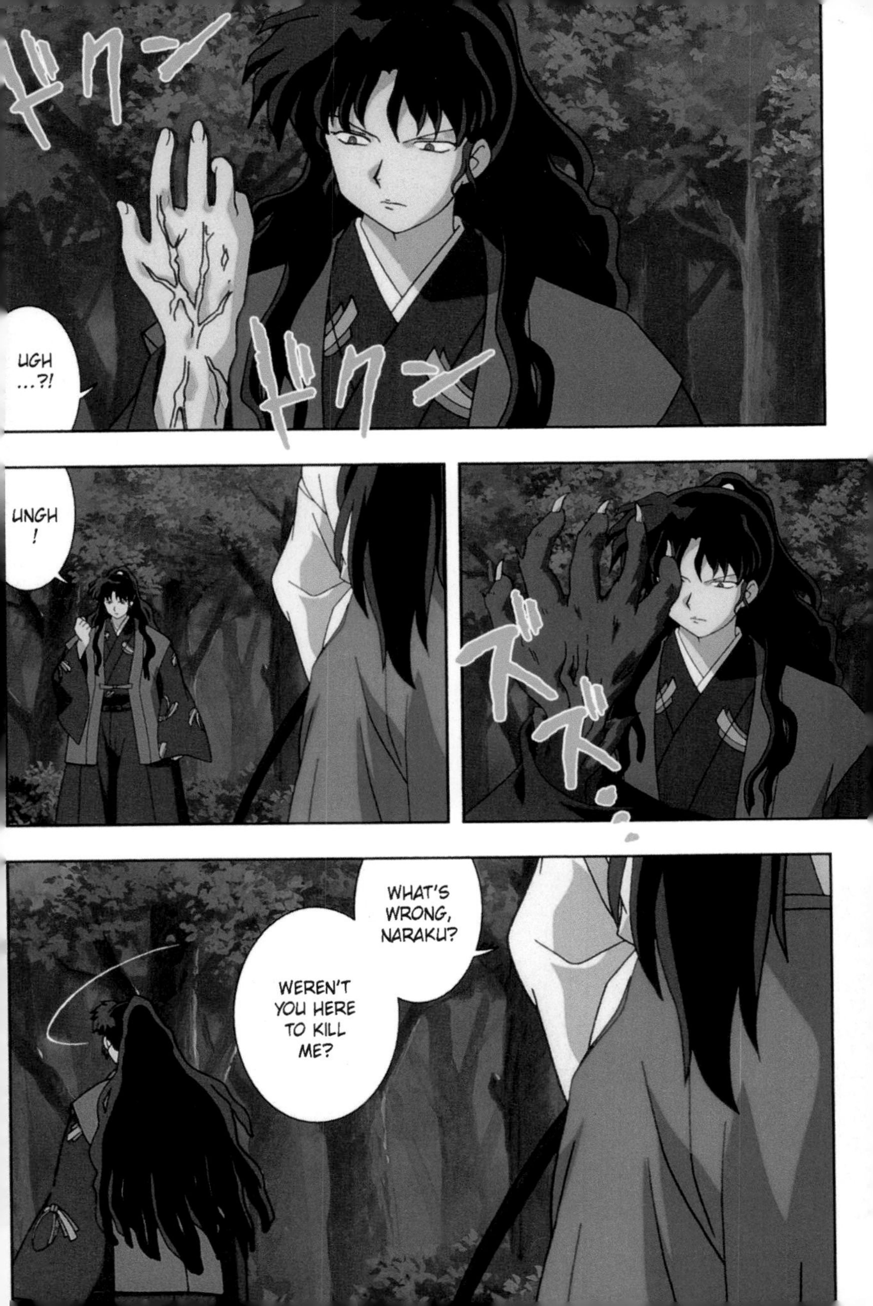
ドクン
ドクン
UGH ...?!
ズズ…
UNGH !
WHAT'S WRONG, NARAKU?
WEREN'T YOU HERE TO KILL ME?

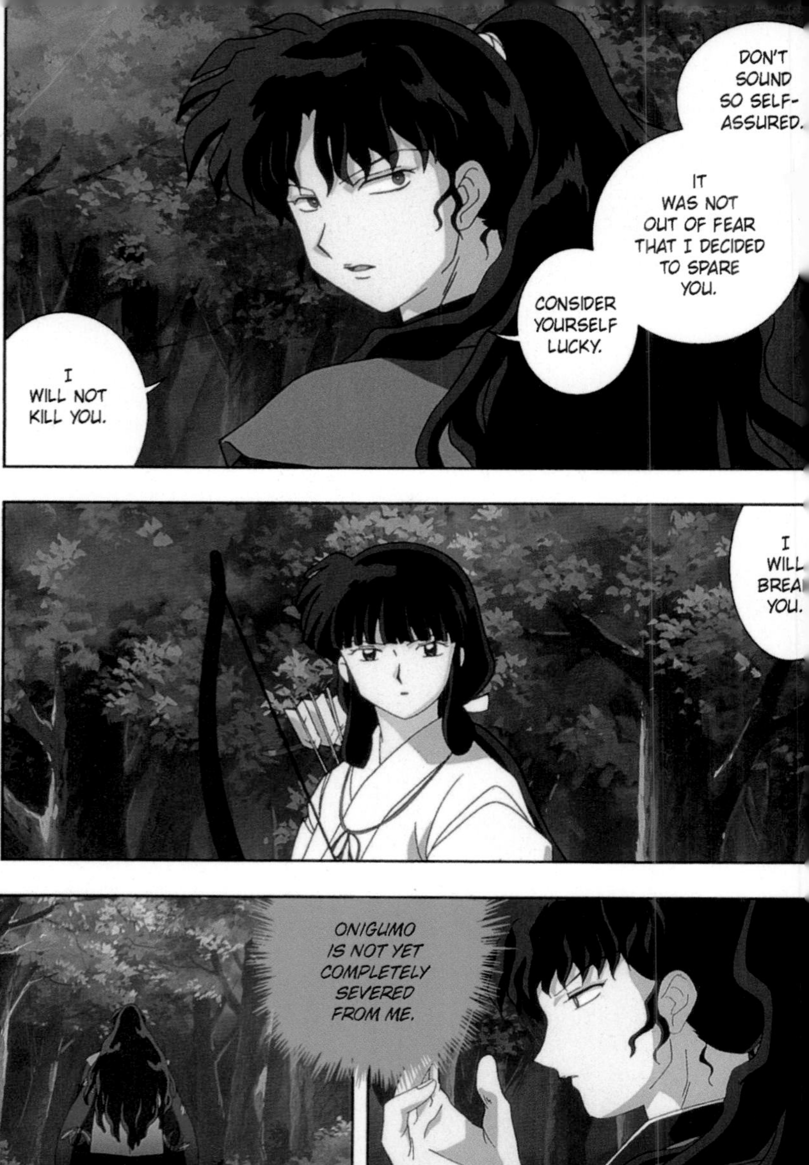
DON'T SOUND SO SELF-ASSURED.
IT WAS NOT OUT OF FEAR THAT I DECIDED TO SPARE YOU.
CONSIDER YOURSELF LUCKY.
I WILL NOT KILL YOU.
I WILL BREA YOU.
ONIGUMO IS NOT YET COMPLETELY SEVERED FROM ME.

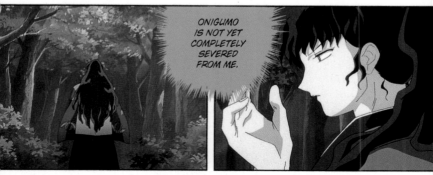

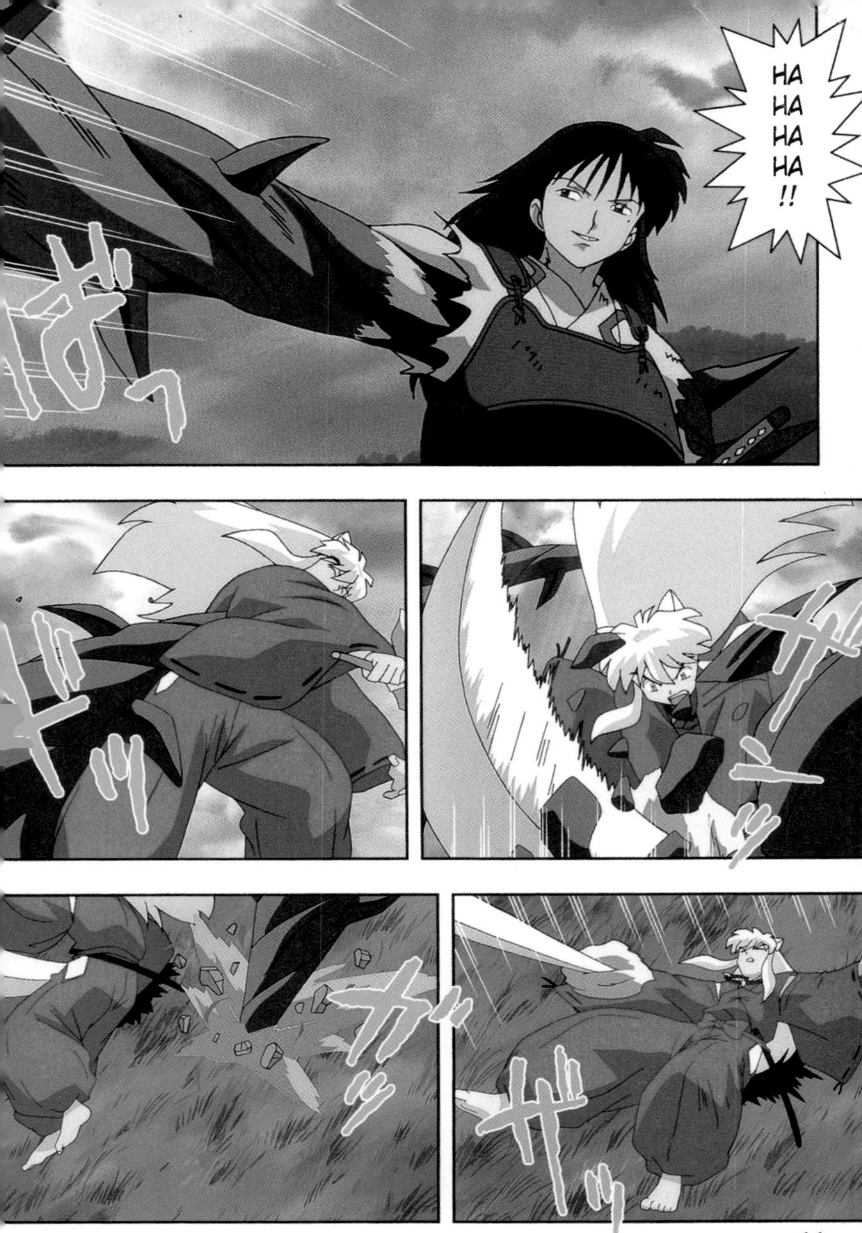
HA HA HA HA !!
ばっ
ドッ
ガッ

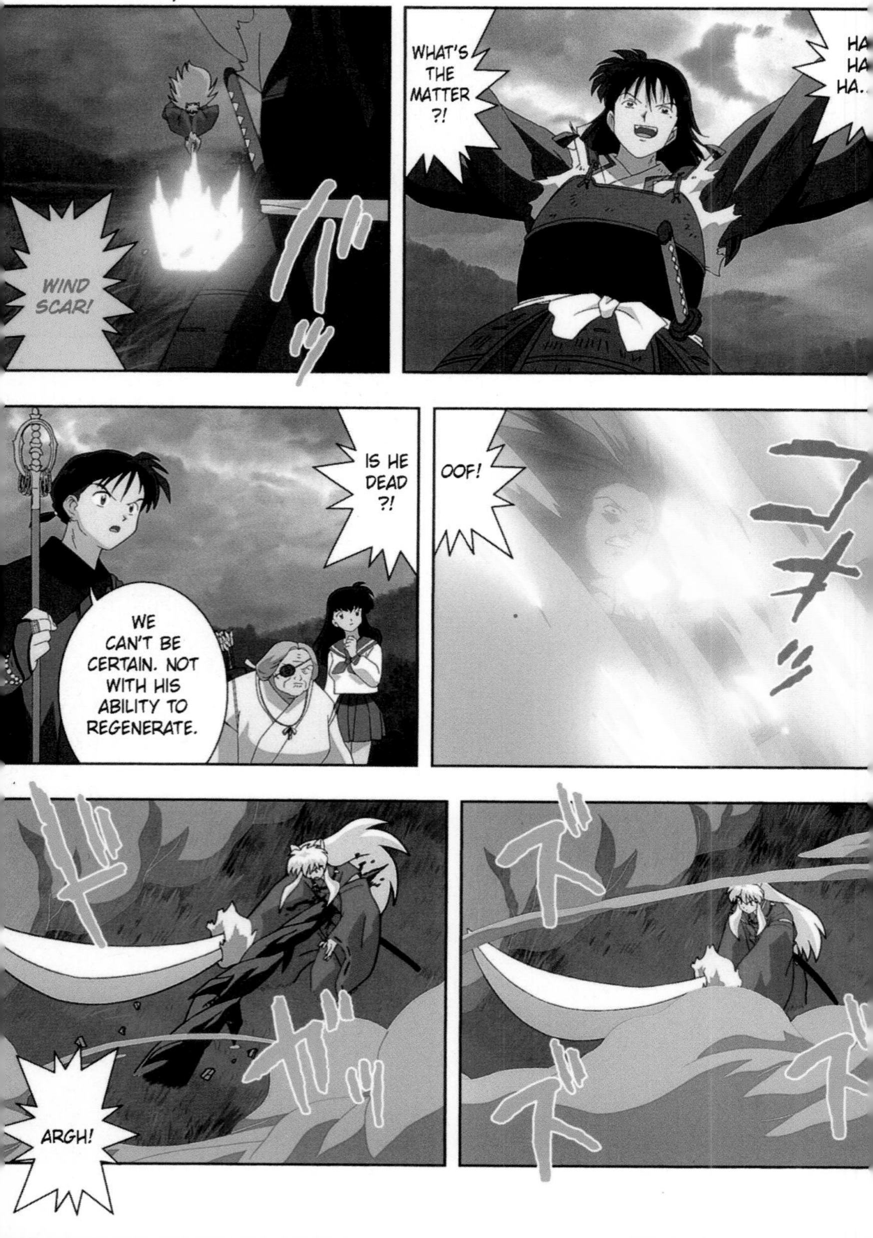
WHAT'S THE MATTER ?!
HA HA HA...
WIND SCAR!
OOF!
IS HE DEAD ?!
WE CAN'T BE CERTAIN. NOT WITH HIS ABILITY TO REGENERATE.
ARGH!

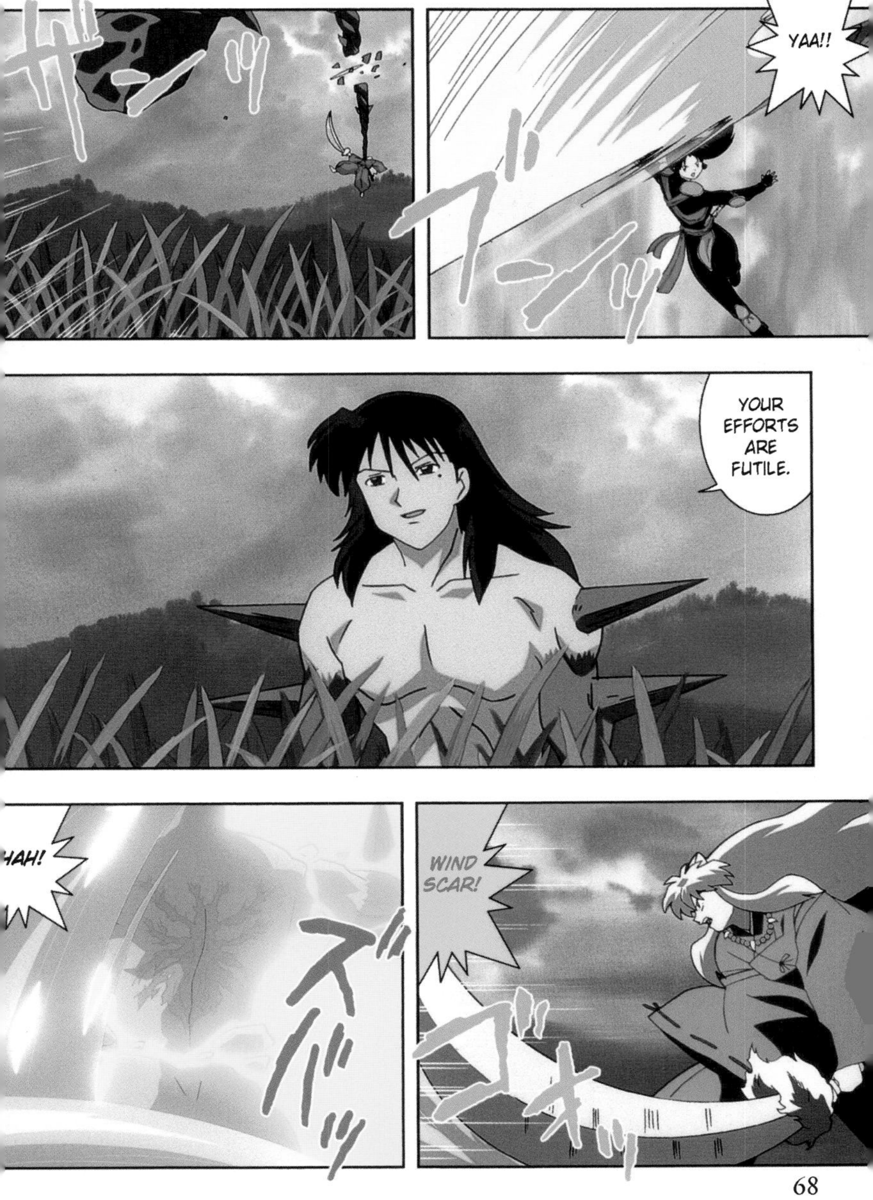
YAA!!
YOUR EFFORTS ARE FUTILE.
WIND SCAR!
HAH!

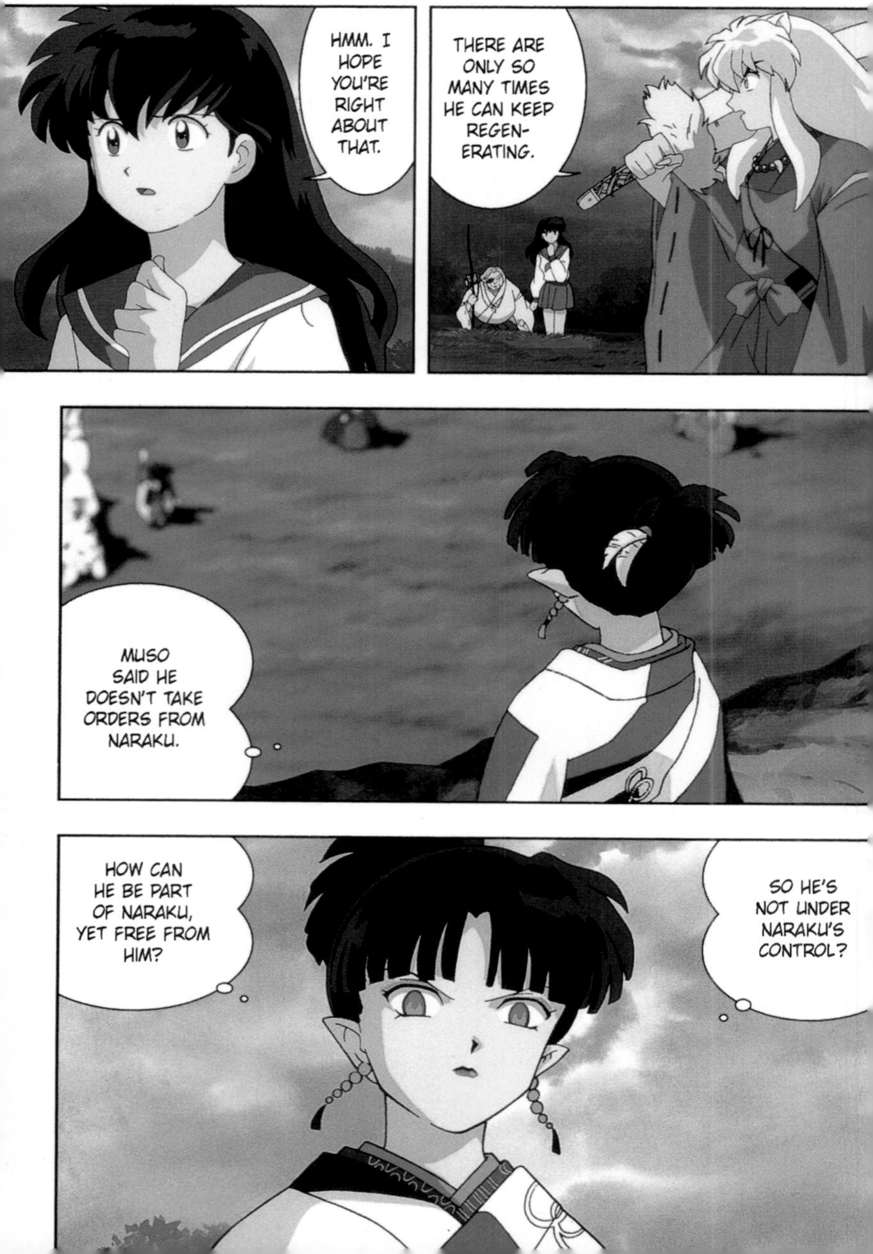
THERE ARE ONLY SO MANY TIMES HE CAN KEEP REGEN-ERATING.
HMM. I HOPE YOU'RE RIGHT ABOUT THAT.
MUSO SAID HE DOESN'T TAKE ORDERS FROM NARAKU.
SO HE'S NOT UNDER NARAKU'S CONTROL?
HOW CAN HE BE PART OF NARAKU, YET FREE FROM HIM?

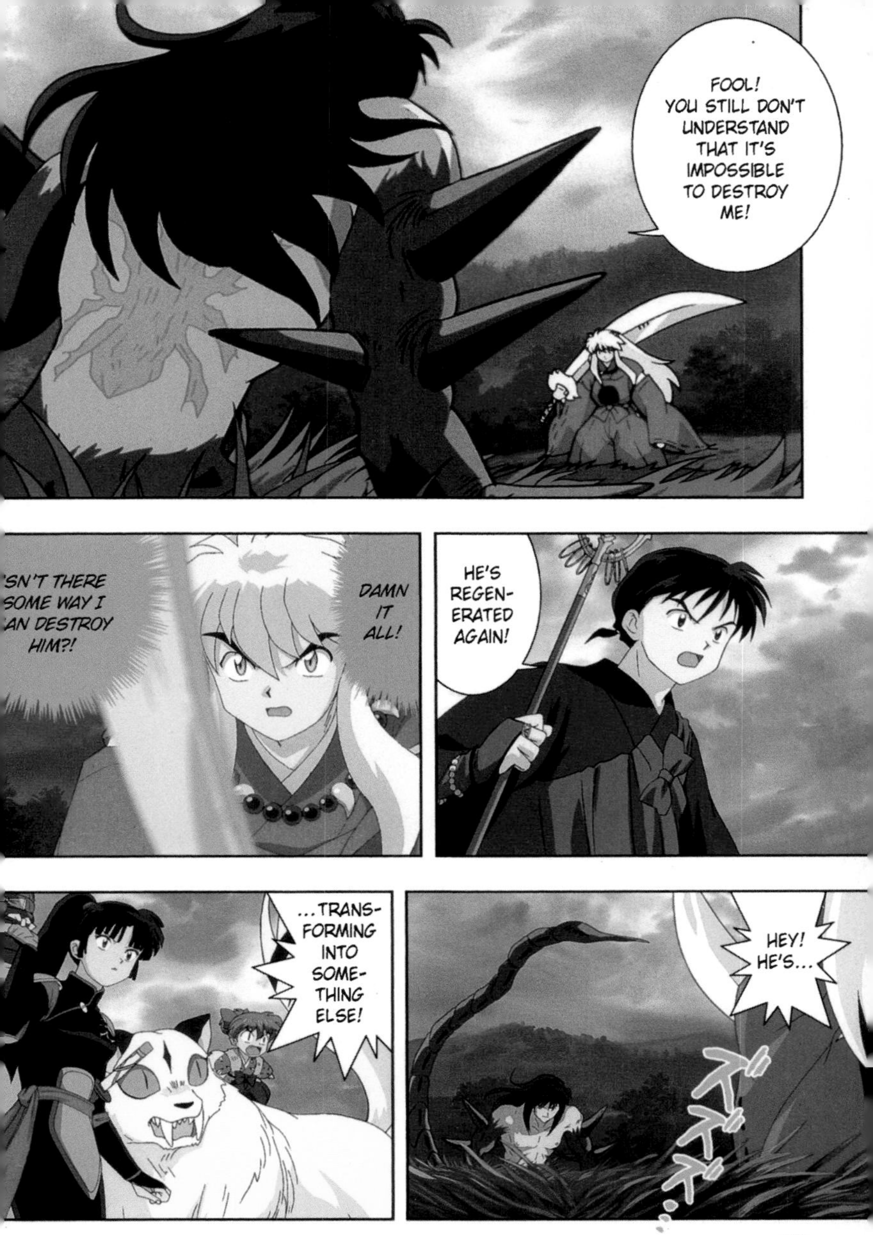
FOOL! YOU STILL DON'T UNDERSTAND THAT IT'S IMPOSSIBLE TO DESTROY ME!
HE'S REGEN-ERATED AGAIN!
DAMN IT ALL!
SN'T THERE SOME WAY I AN DESTROY HIM?!
HEY! HE'S...
...TRANS-FORMING INTO SOME-THING ELSE!

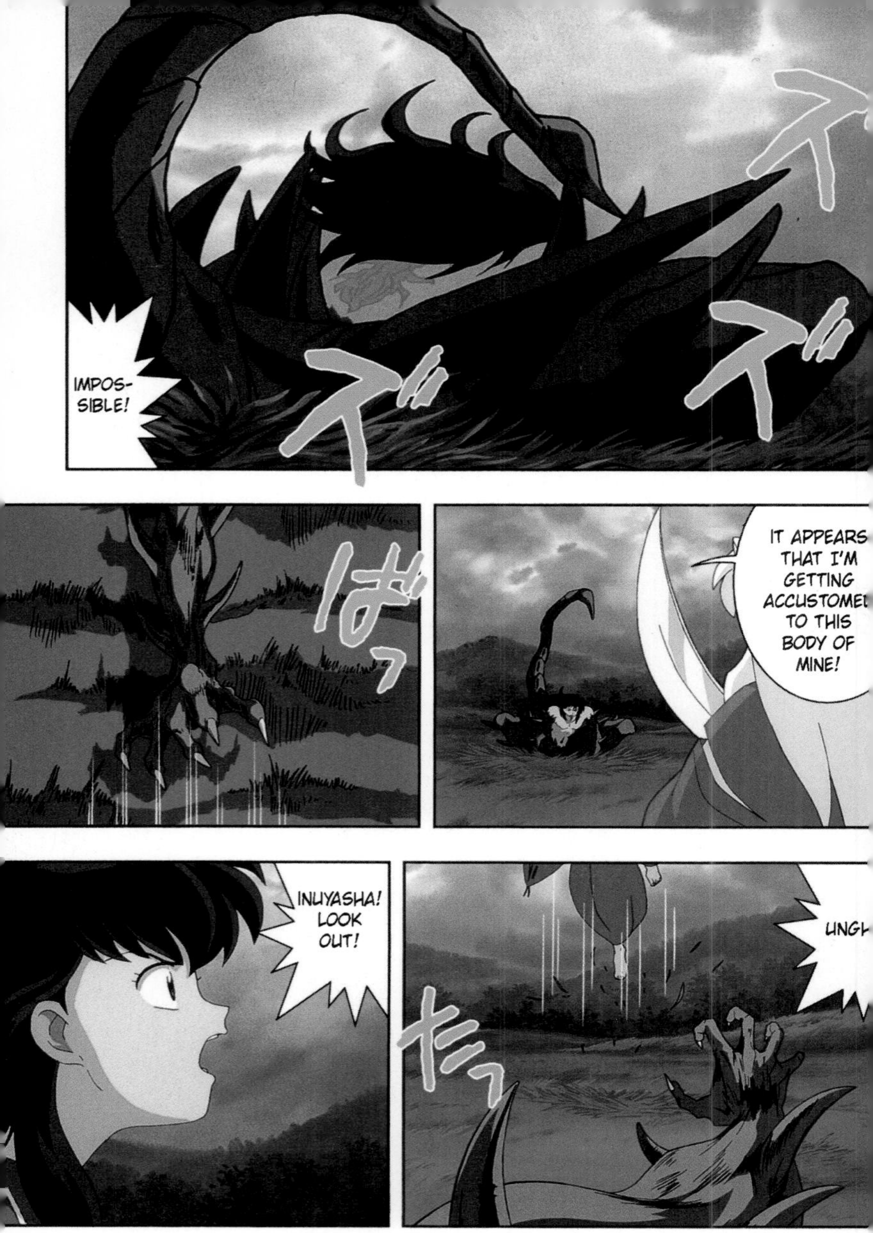
ズ
ズ
ズ
IMPOS-SIBLE!
IT APPEARS THAT I'M GETTING ACCUSTOME TO THIS BODY OF MINE!
ぱっ
UNG
たっ
INUYASHA! LOOK OUT!

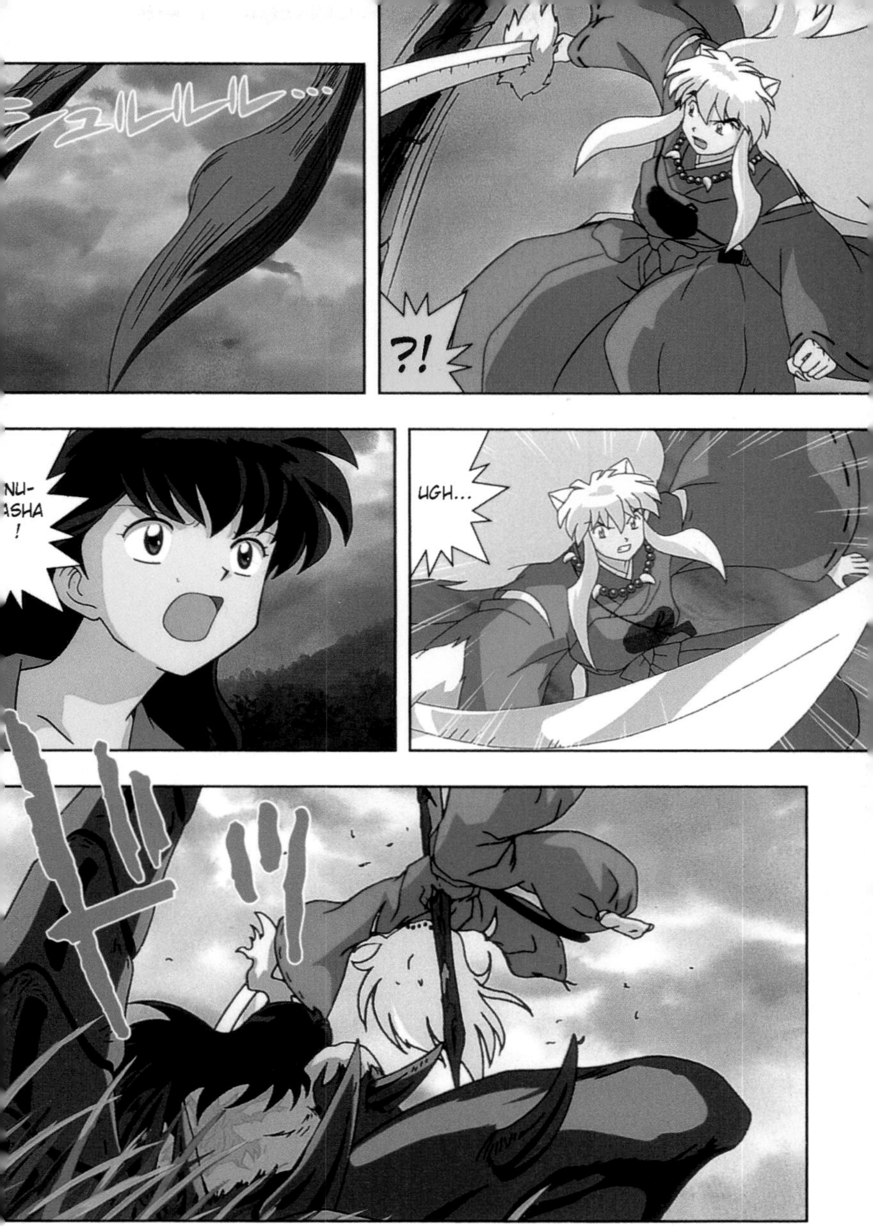
?!
シュルルル…
UGH…
NU-ASHA!

71
Three-sided Battle to the Death

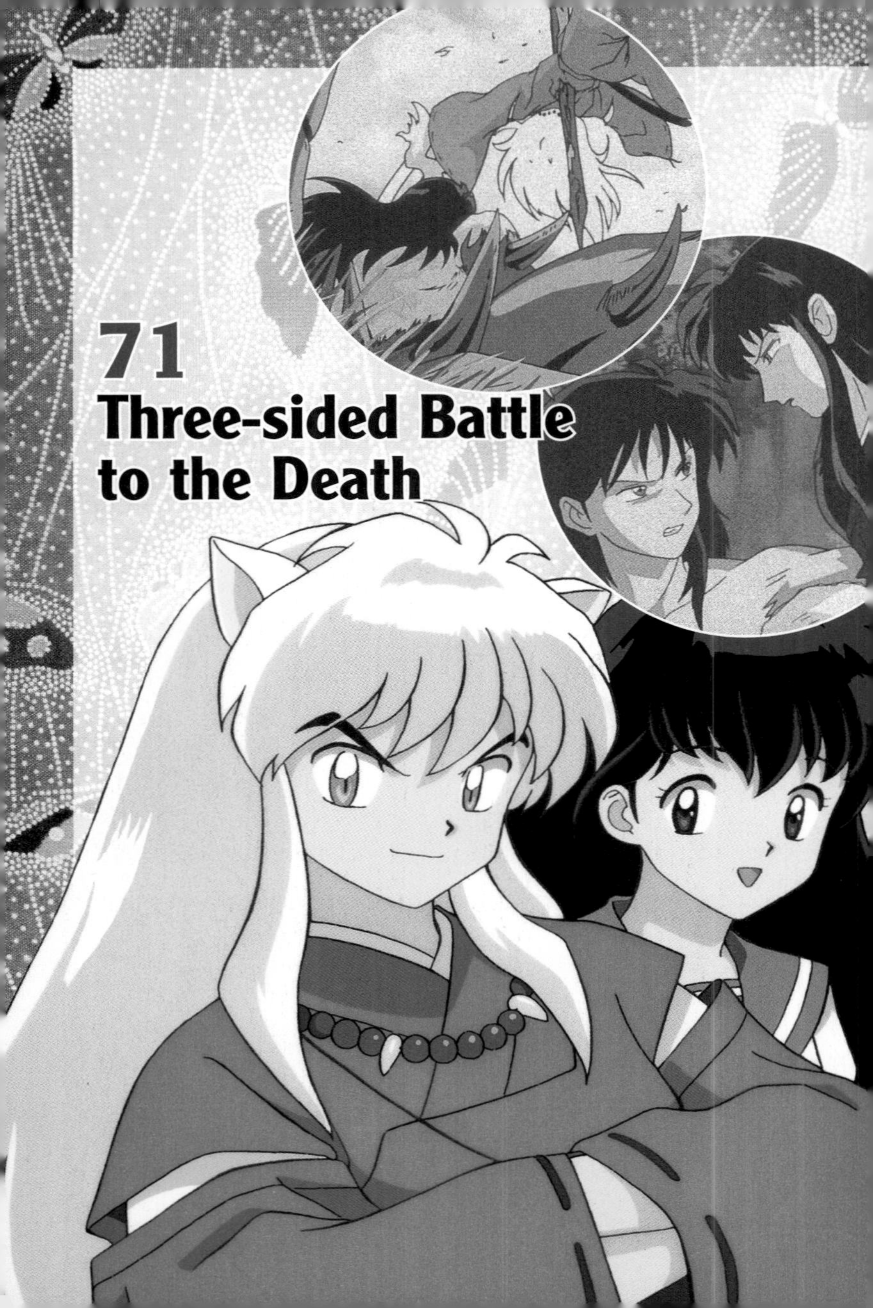

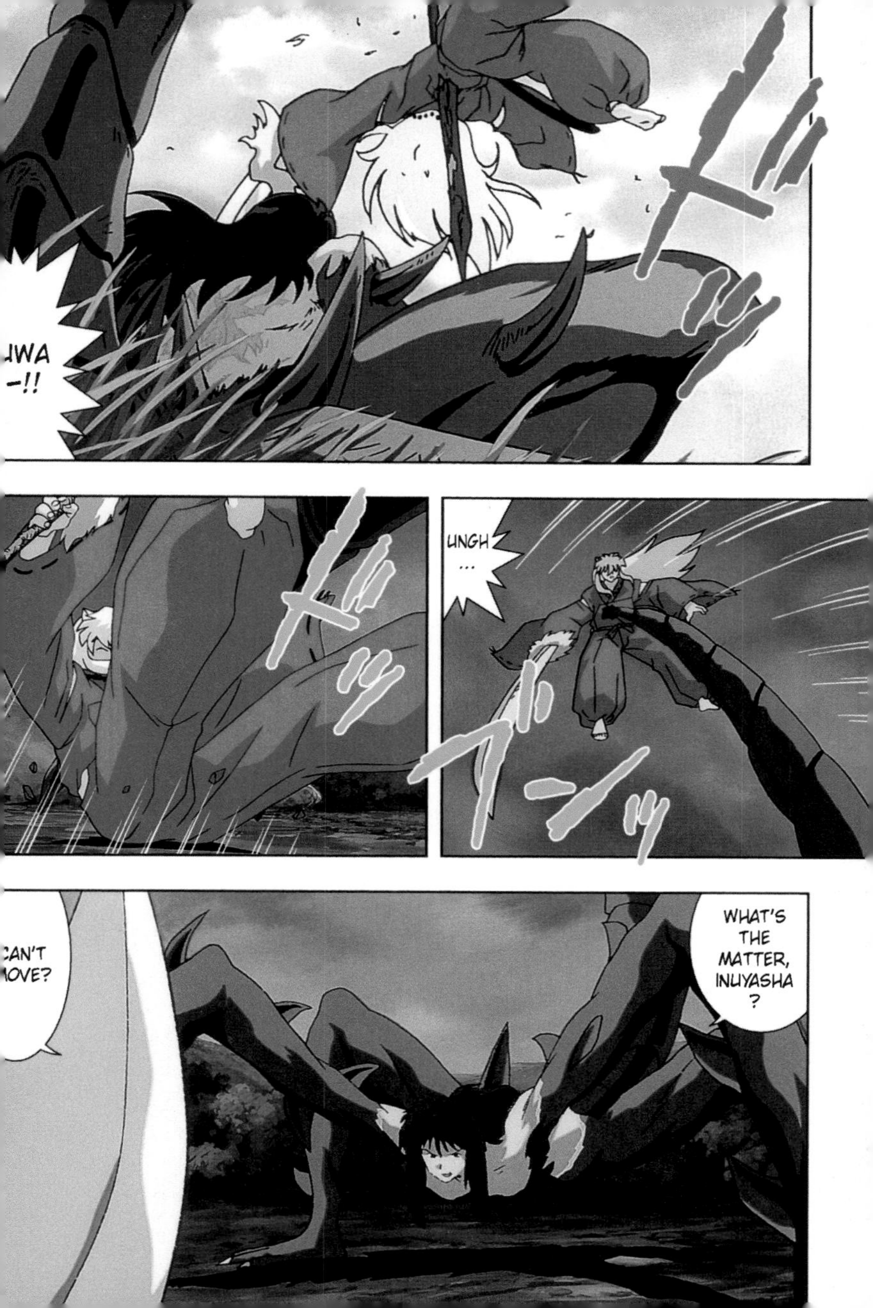
WA —!!
UNGH ...
WHAT'S THE MATTER, INUYASHA?
CAN'T MOVE?

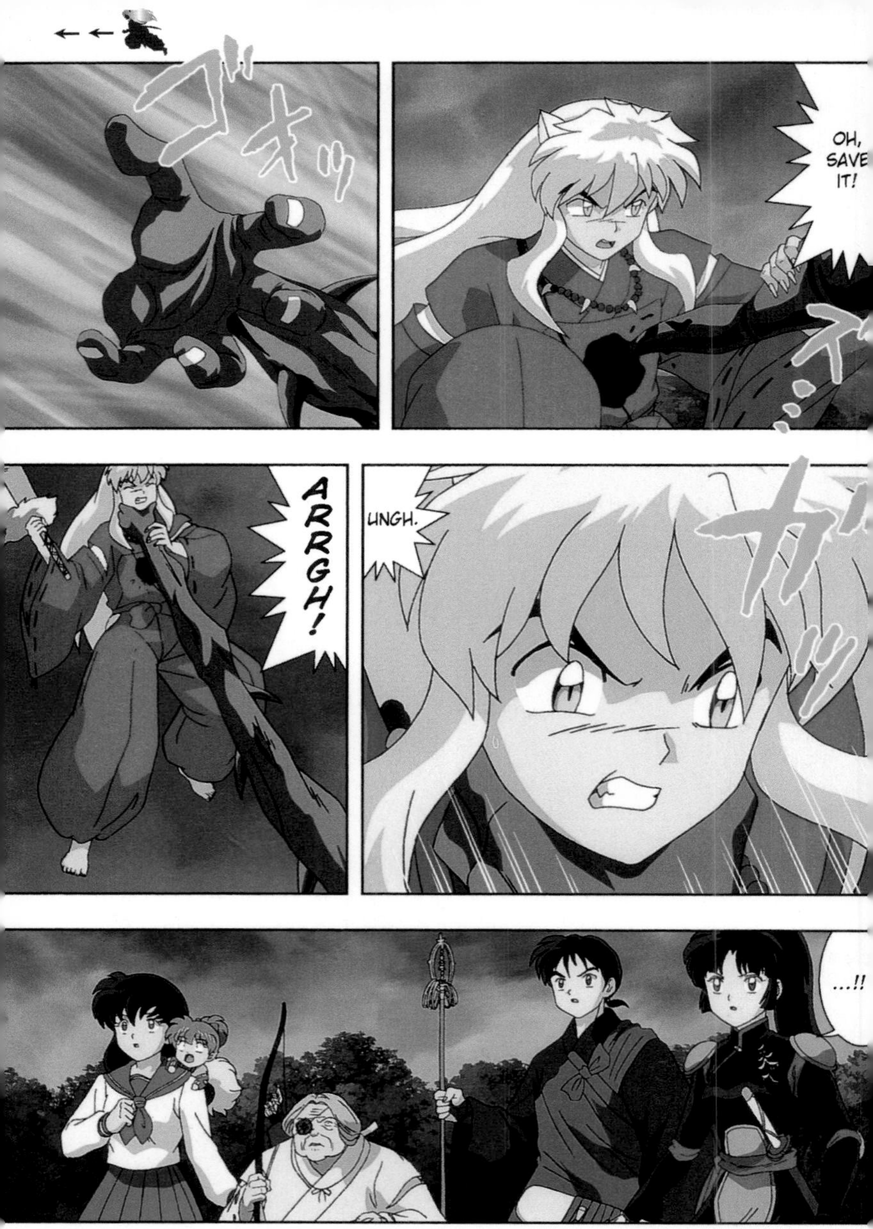
OH, SAVE IT!
ゴォッ
UNGH.
ARRGH!
...!!

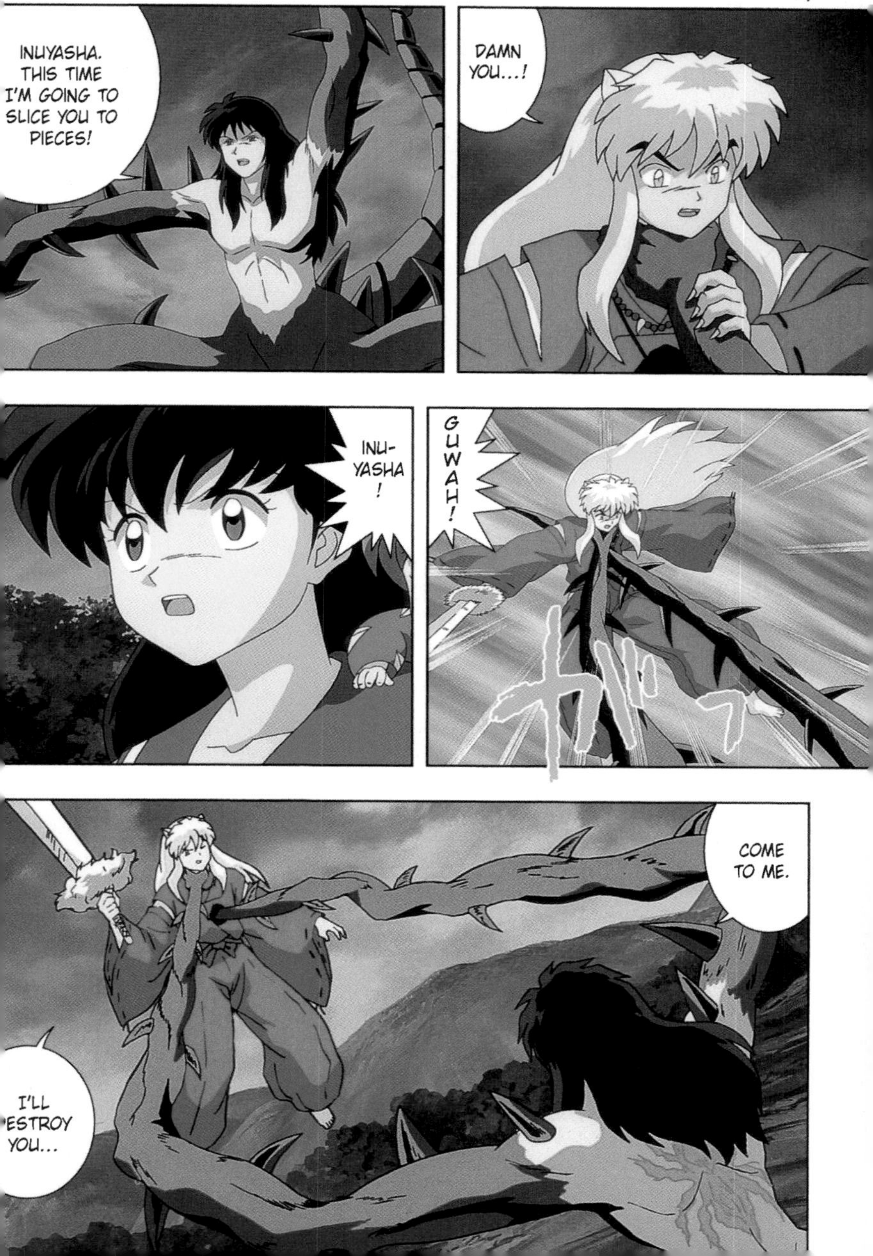
DAMN YOU...!
INUYASHA. THIS TIME I'M GOING TO SLICE YOU TO PIECES!
GUWAH!
ガッ
INU-YASHA!
COME TO ME.
I'LL 'ESTROY YOU...

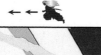

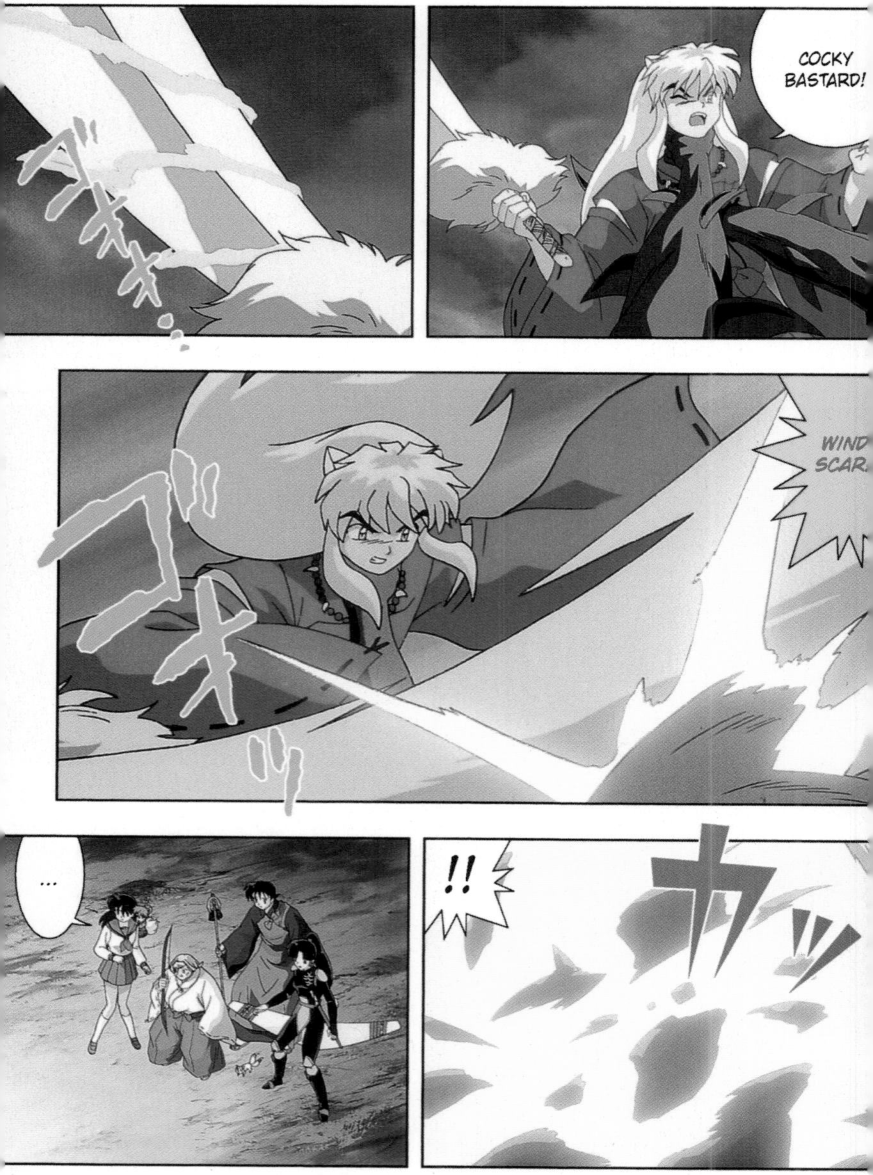
COCKY BASTARD!
WIND SCAR
!!
...

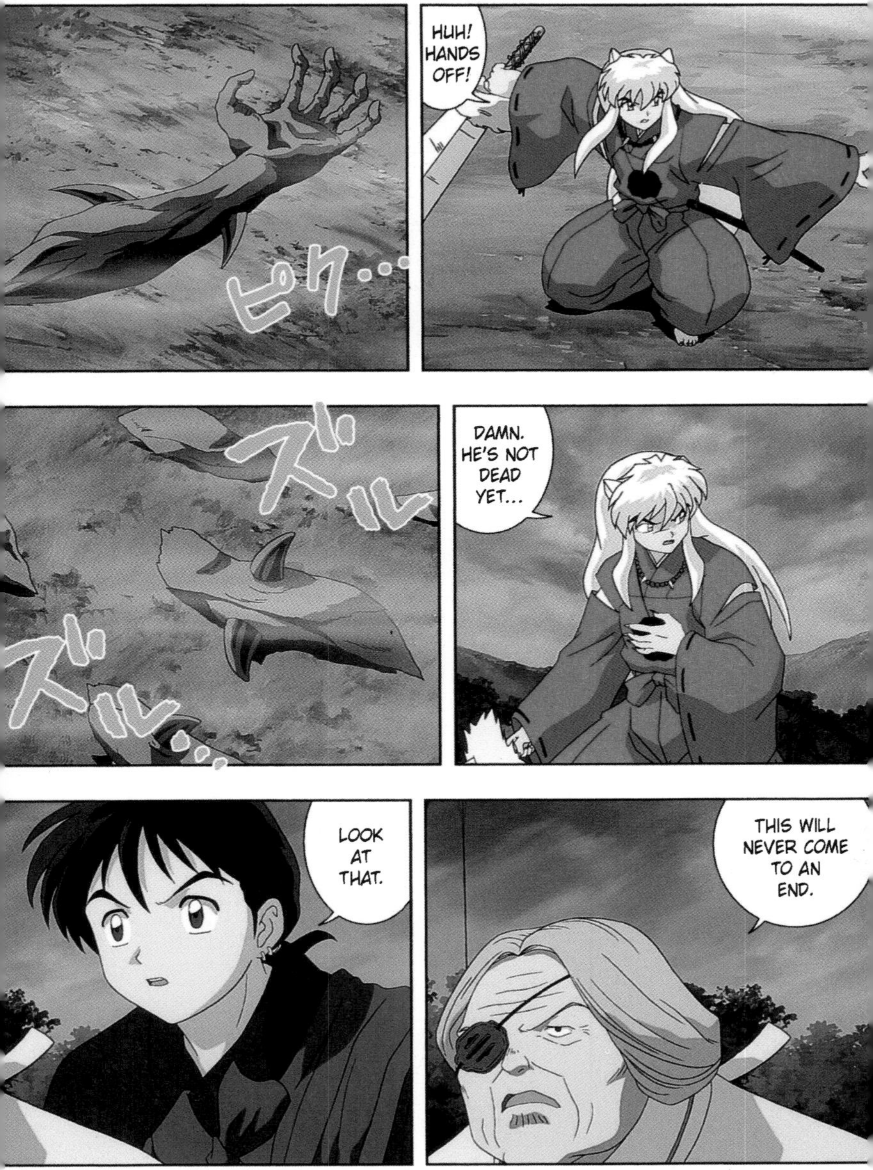
HUH! HANDS OFF!
DAMN. HE'S NOT DEAD YET...
ズル
ズル...
THIS WILL NEVER COME TO AN END.
LOOK AT THAT.

ドクン…
ドクン
ドクン…
A SPIDER!
ズズ…
メキッ…

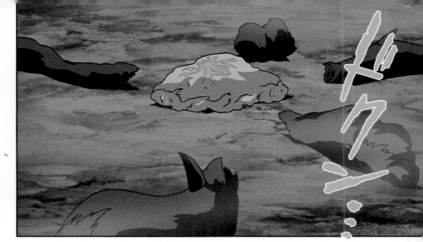

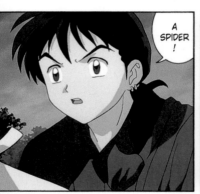

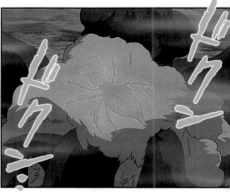

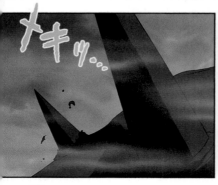

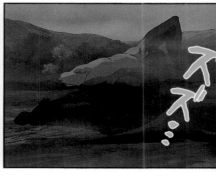

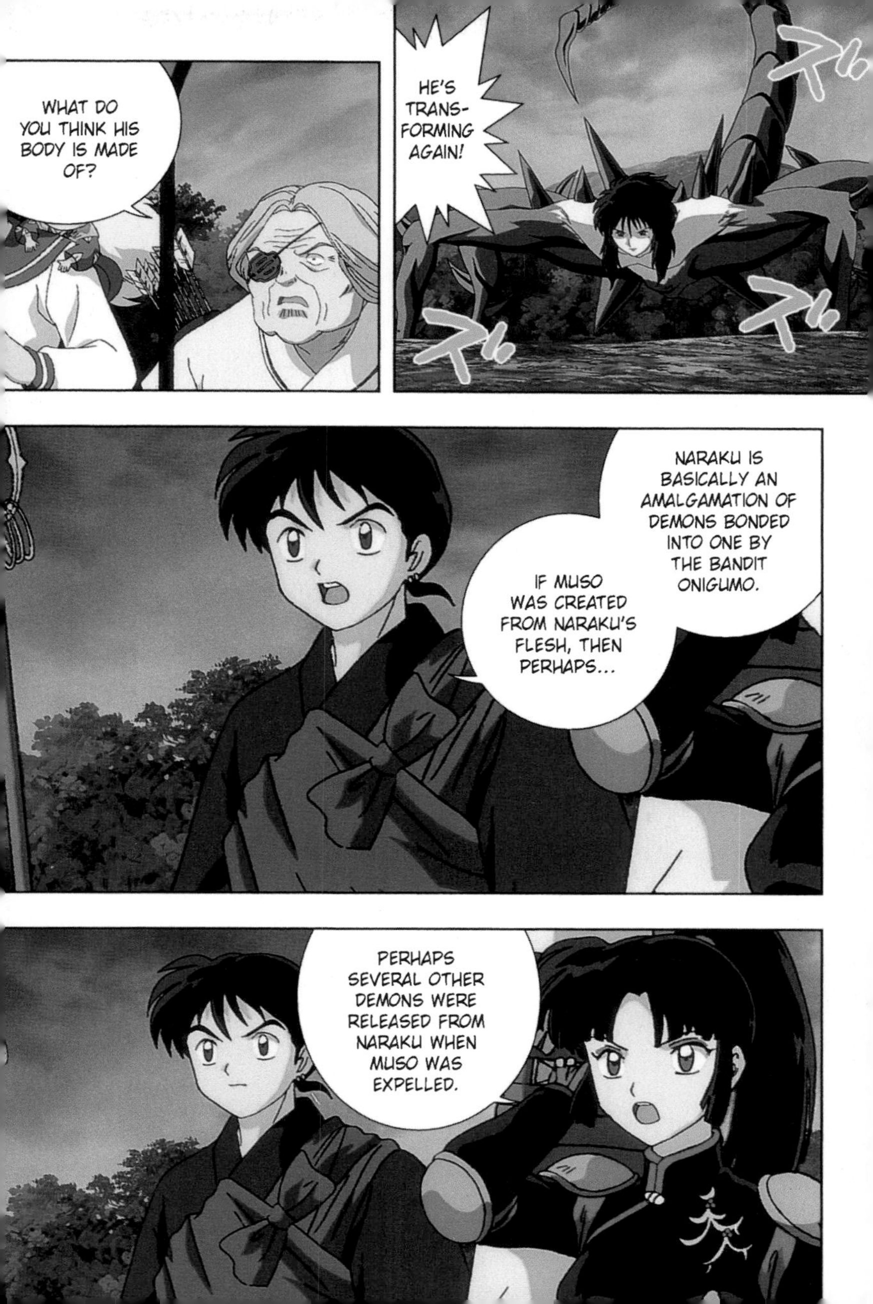
HE'S TRANS-FORMING AGAIN!
WHAT DO YOU THINK HIS BODY IS MADE OF?
NARAKU IS BASICALLY AN AMALGAMATION OF DEMONS BONDED INTO ONE BY THE BANDIT ONIGUMO.
IF MUSO WAS CREATED FROM NARAKU'S FLESH, THEN PERHAPS...
PERHAPS SEVERAL OTHER DEMONS WERE RELEASED FROM NARAKU WHEN MUSO WAS EXPELLED.

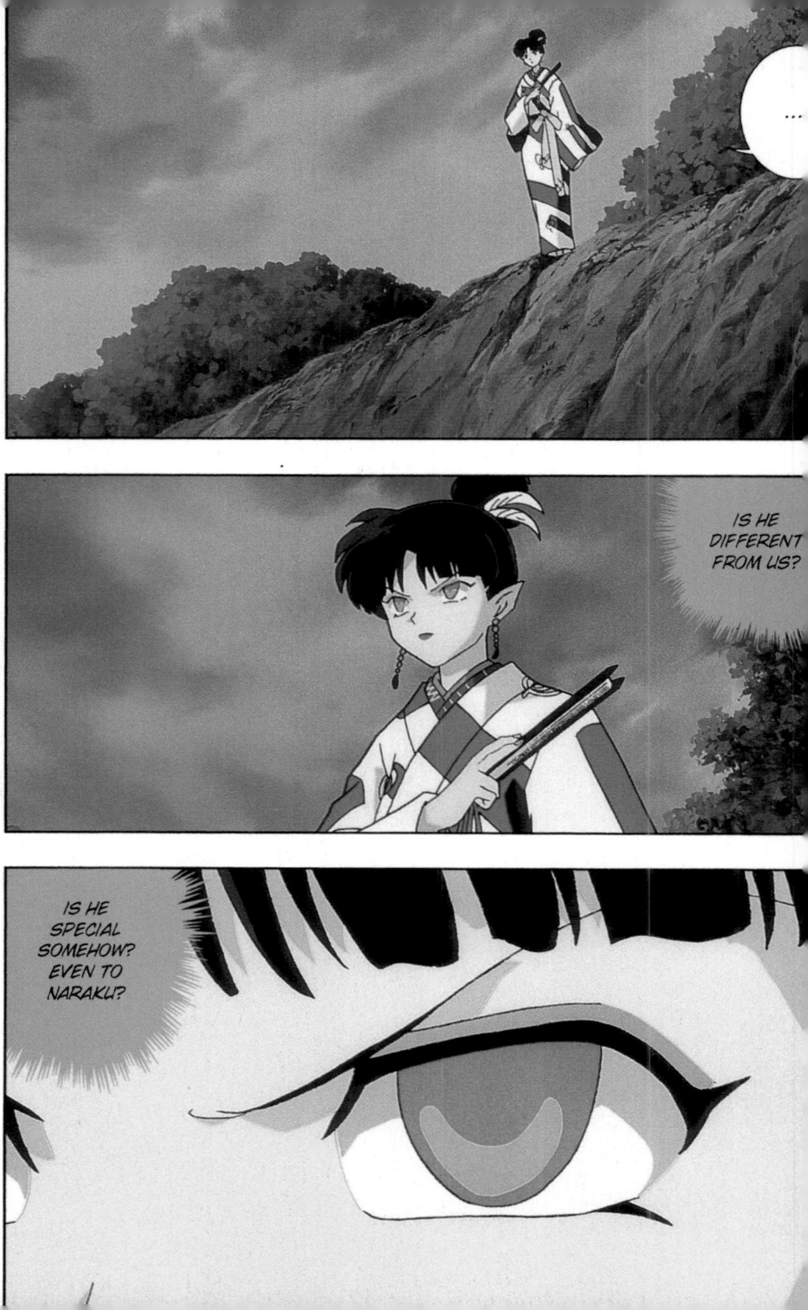
...
IS HE DIFFERENT FROM US?
IS HE SPECIAL SOMEHOW? EVEN TO NARAKU?

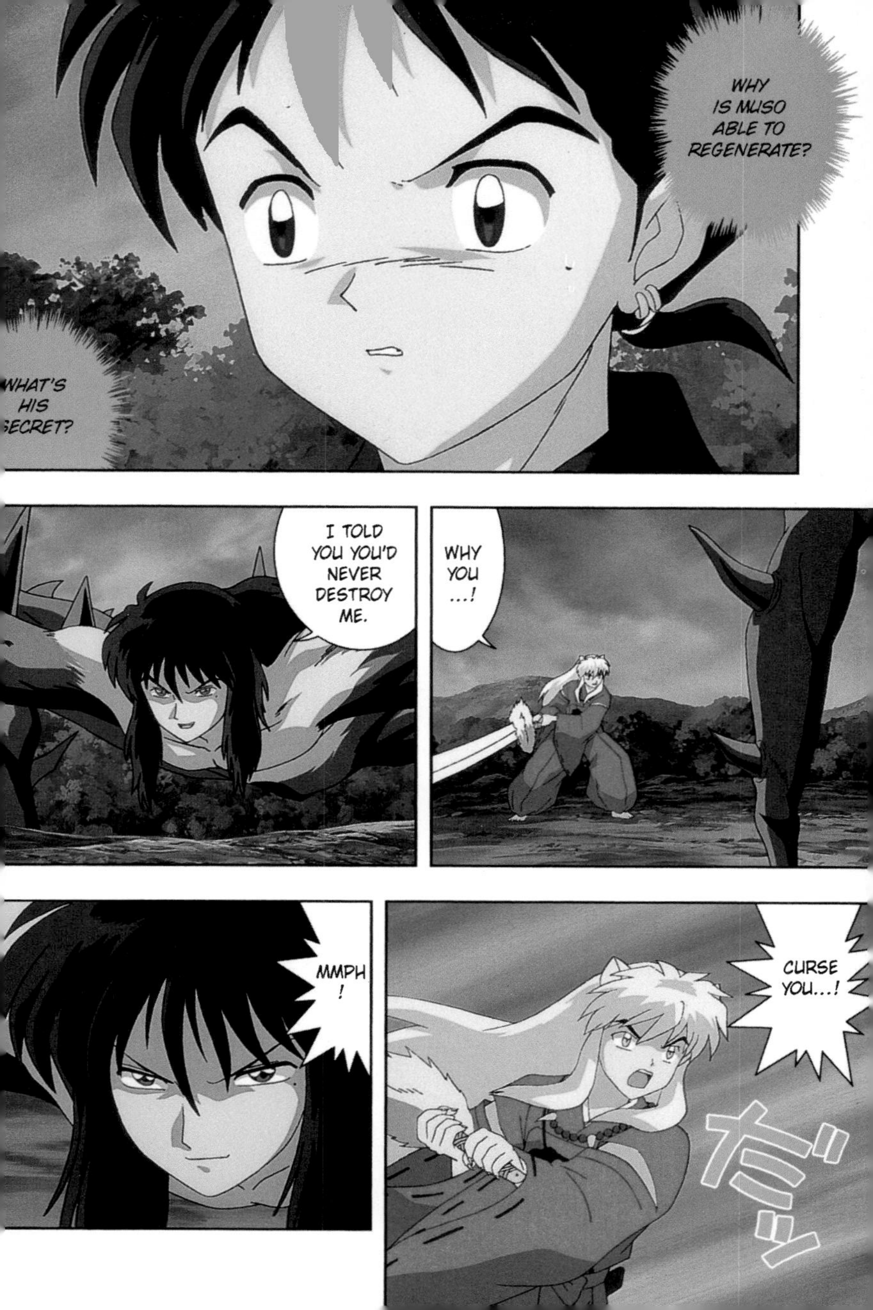
WHY IS MUSO ABLE TO REGENERATE?
WHAT'S HIS SECRET?
WHY YOU ...!
I TOLD YOU YOU'D NEVER DESTROY ME.
CURSE YOU...!
ダッ
MMPH !

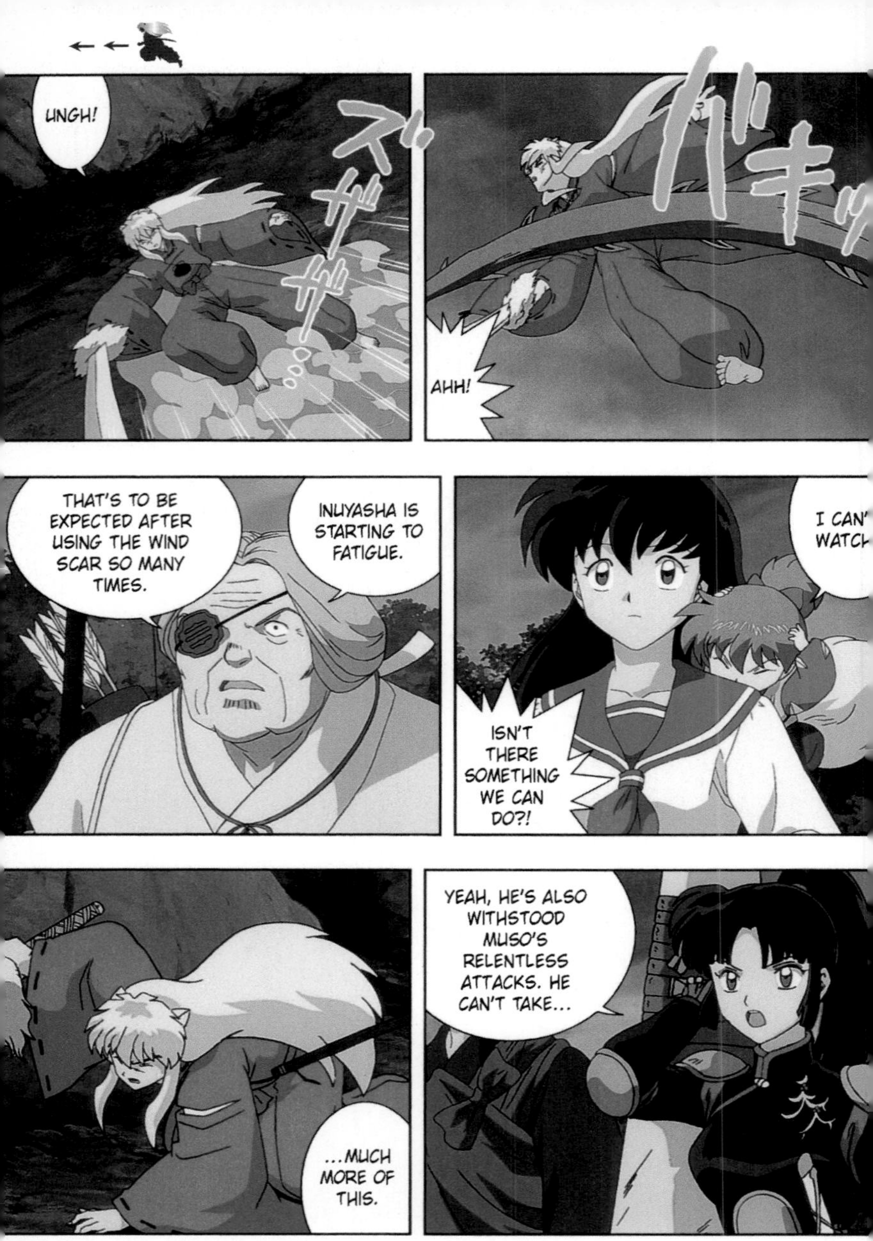
バキッ
AHH!
UNGH!
ズザザ
I CAN'
WATCH
ISN'T THERE SOMETHING WE CAN DO?!
INUYASHA IS STARTING TO FATIGUE.
THAT'S TO BE EXPECTED AFTER USING THE WIND SCAR SO MANY TIMES.
YEAH, HE'S ALSO WITHSTOOD MUSO'S RELENTLESS ATTACKS. HE CAN'T TAKE...
...MUCH MORE OF THIS.

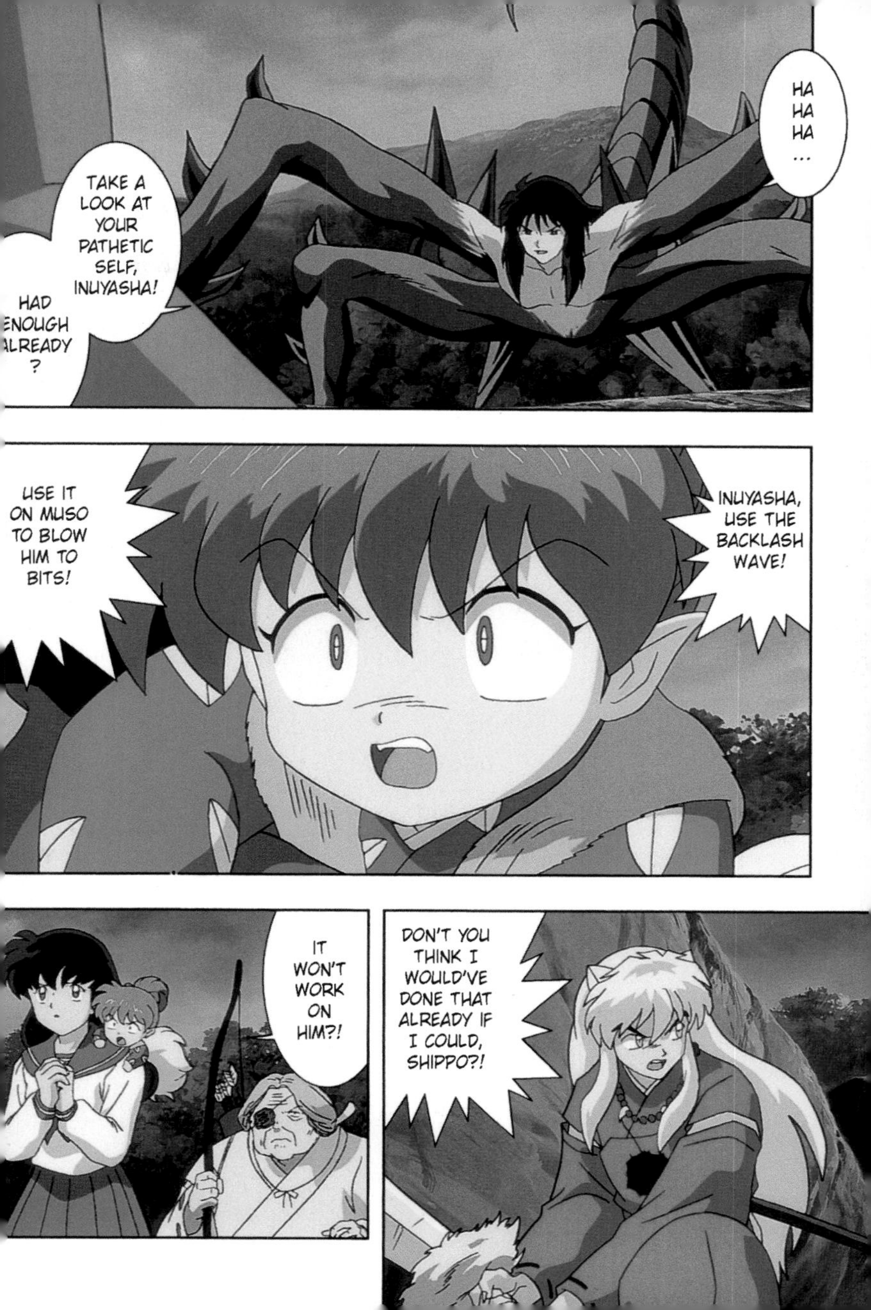
HA HA HA ...
TAKE A LOOK AT YOUR PATHETIC SELF, INUYASHA!
HAD ENOUGH ALREADY?
INUYASHA, USE THE BACKLASH WAVE!
USE IT ON MUSO TO BLOW HIM TO BITS!
DON'T YOU THINK I WOULD'VE DONE THAT ALREADY IF I COULD, SHIPPO?!
IT WON'T WORK ON HIM?!

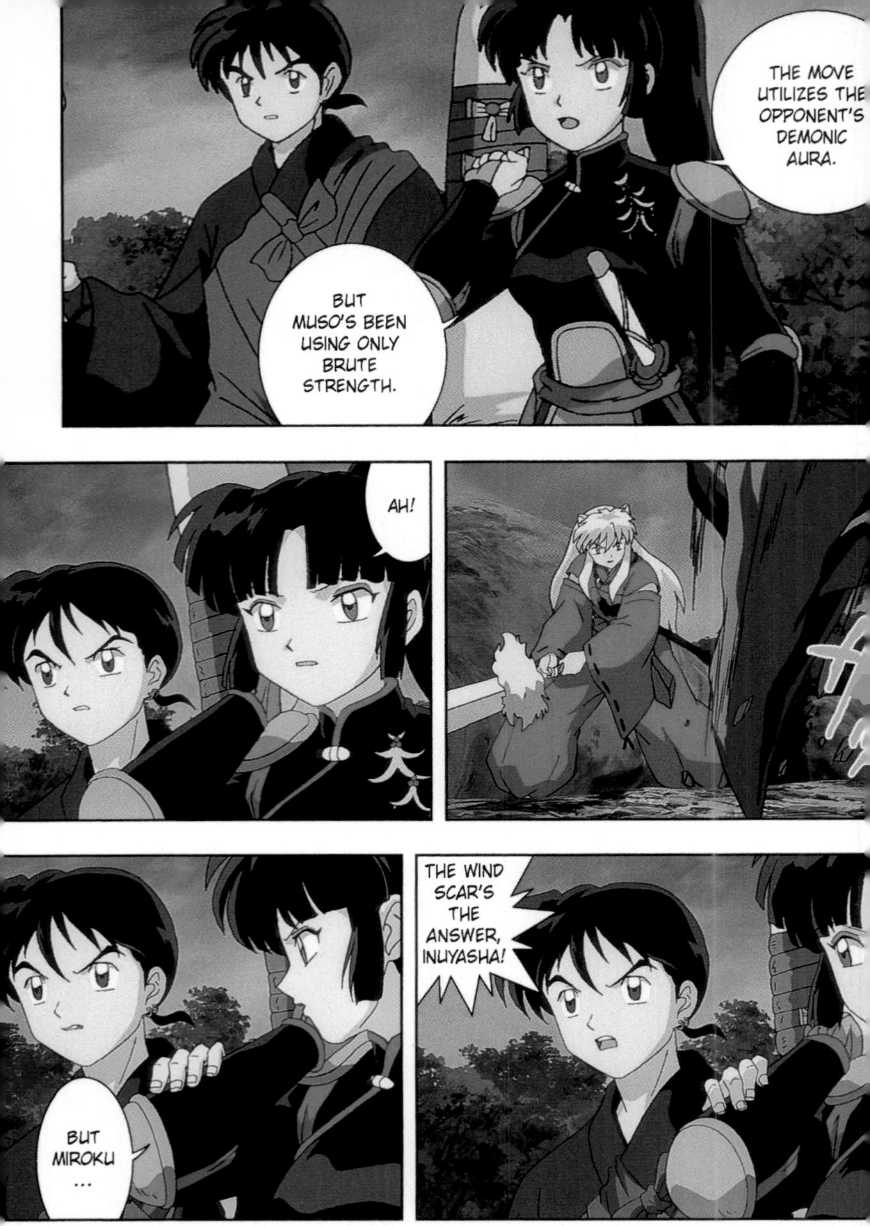
THE MOVE UTILIZES THE OPPONENT'S DEMONIC AURA.
BUT MUSO'S BEEN USING ONLY BRUTE STRENGTH.
AH!
THE WIND SCAR'S THE ANSWER, INUYASHA!
BUT MIROKU ...

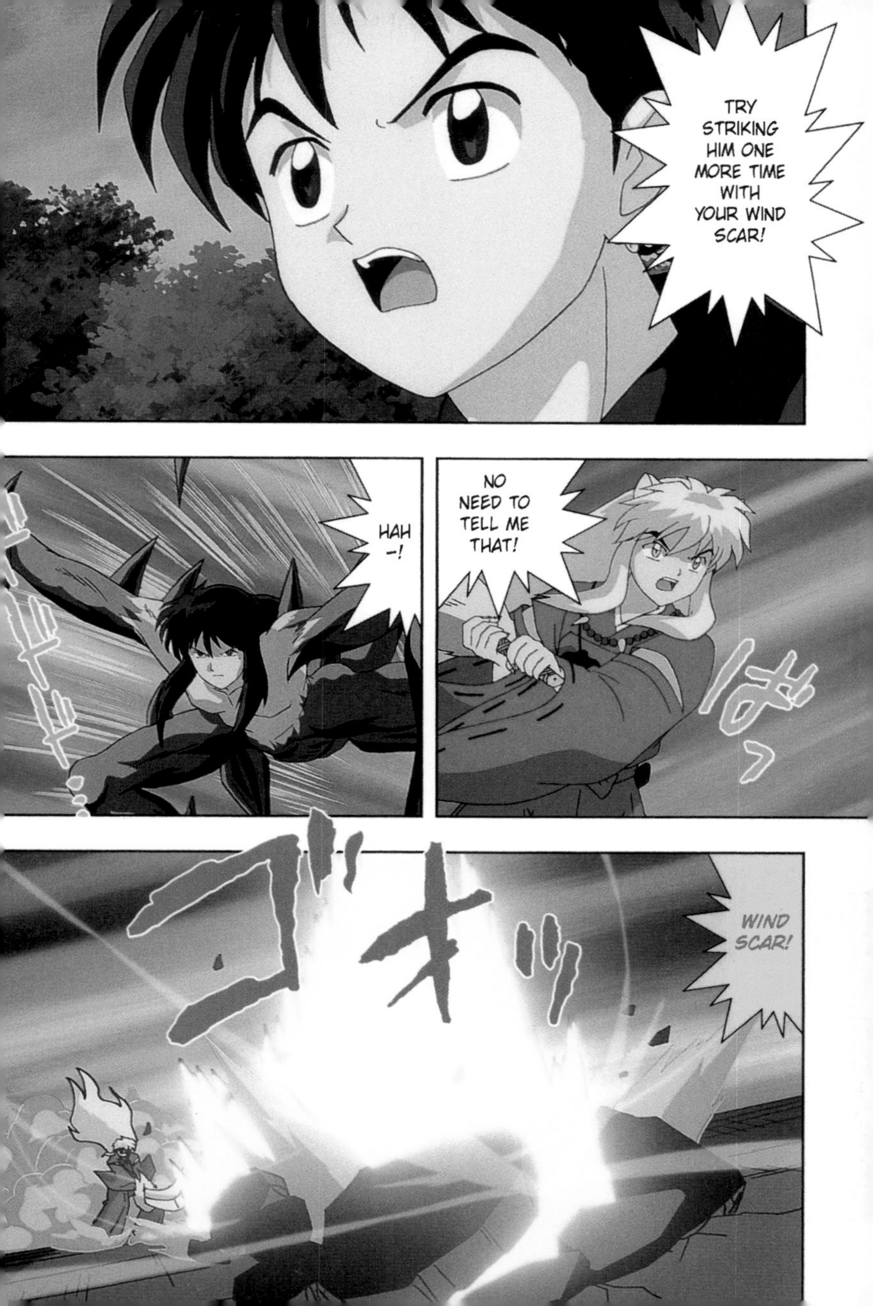
TRY STRIKING HIM ONE MORE TIME WITH YOUR WIND SCAR!
NO NEED TO TELL ME THAT!
ぱっ
HAH —!
ゴオッ
WIND SCAR!

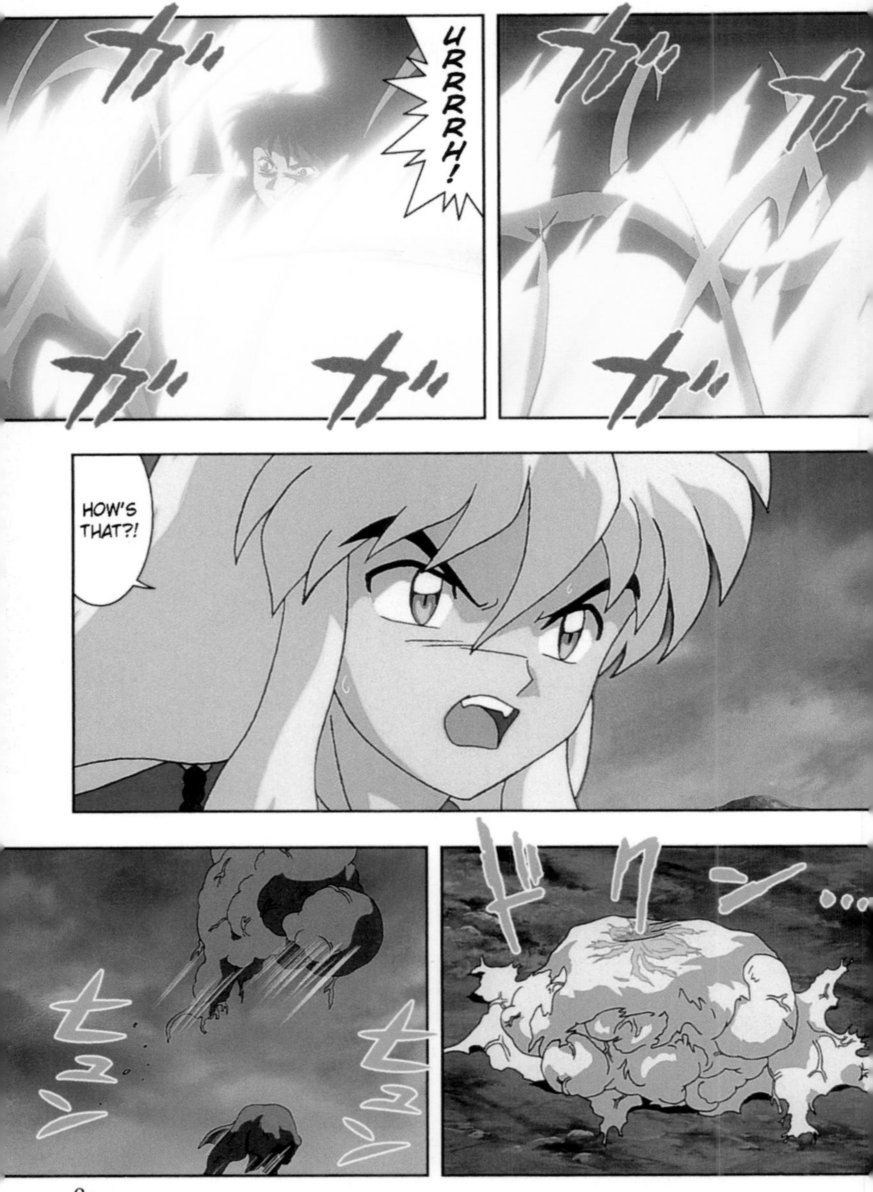
URRRRH!
HOW'S THAT?!
ドクン…
ヒュン
ヒュン

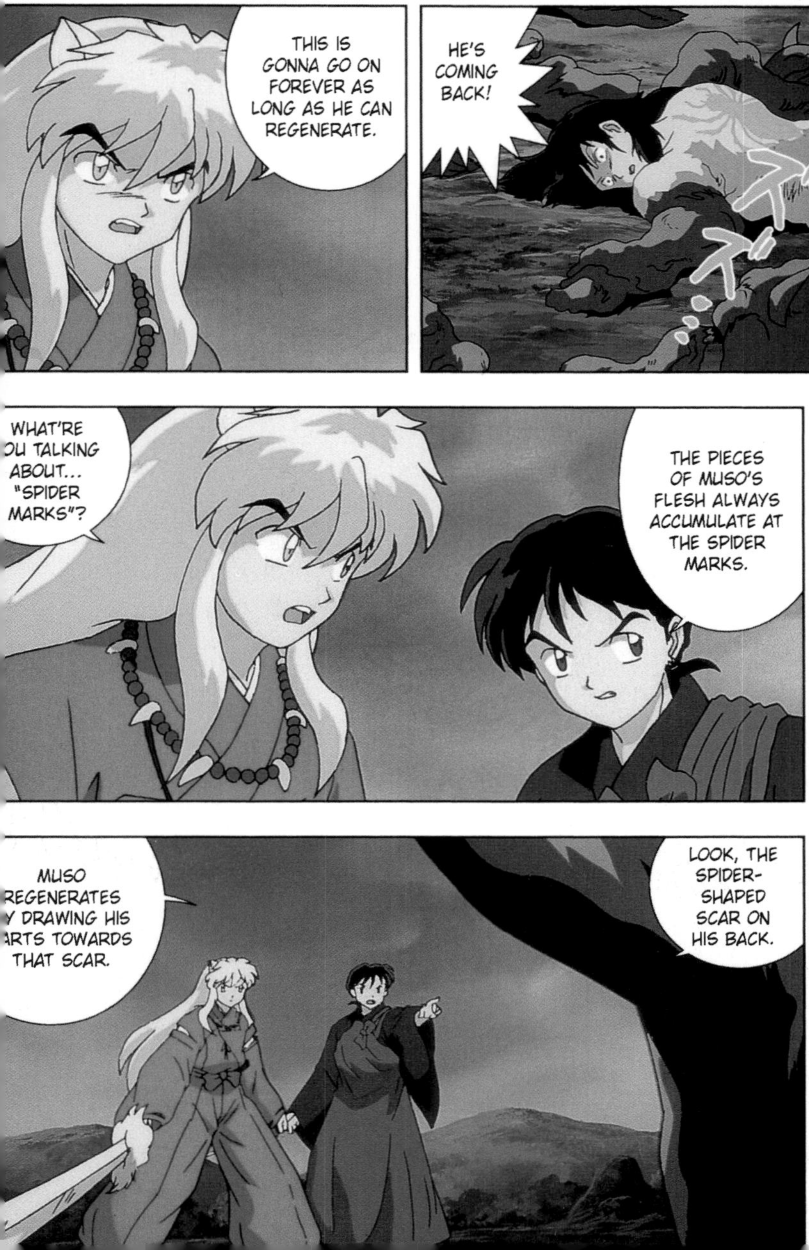
HE'S COMING BACK!
ズズ…
THIS IS GONNA GO ON FOREVER AS LONG AS HE CAN REGENERATE.
THE PIECES OF MUSO'S FLESH ALWAYS ACCUMULATE AT THE SPIDER MARKS.
WHAT'RE OU TALKING ABOUT... "SPIDER MARKS"?
LOOK, THE SPIDER-SHAPED SCAR ON HIS BACK.
MUSO EGENERATES Y DRAWING HIS ARTS TOWARDS THAT SCAR.

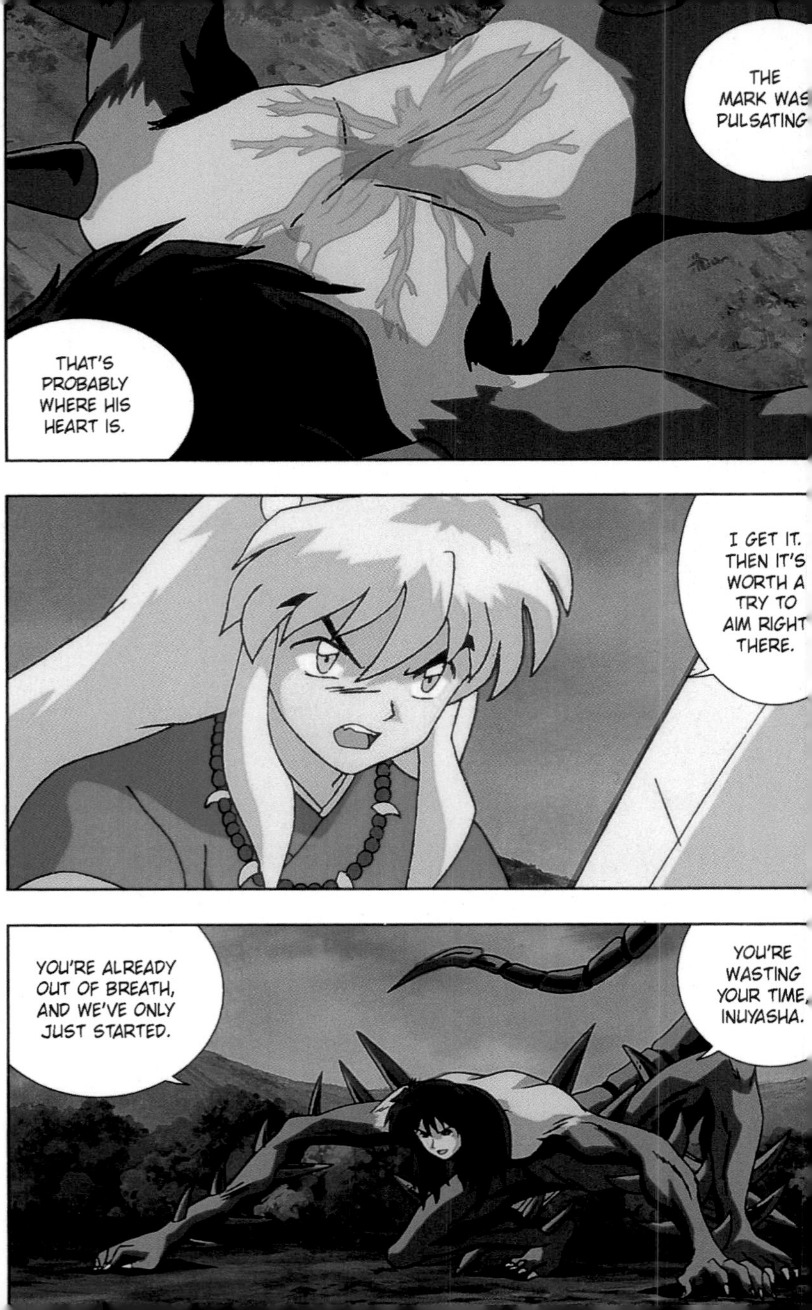
THE MARK WAS PULSATING
THAT'S PROBABLY WHERE HIS HEART IS.
I GET IT. THEN IT'S WORTH A TRY TO AIM RIGHT THERE.
YOU'RE WASTING YOUR TIME, INUYASHA.
YOU'RE ALREADY OUT OF BREATH, AND WE'VE ONLY JUST STARTED.

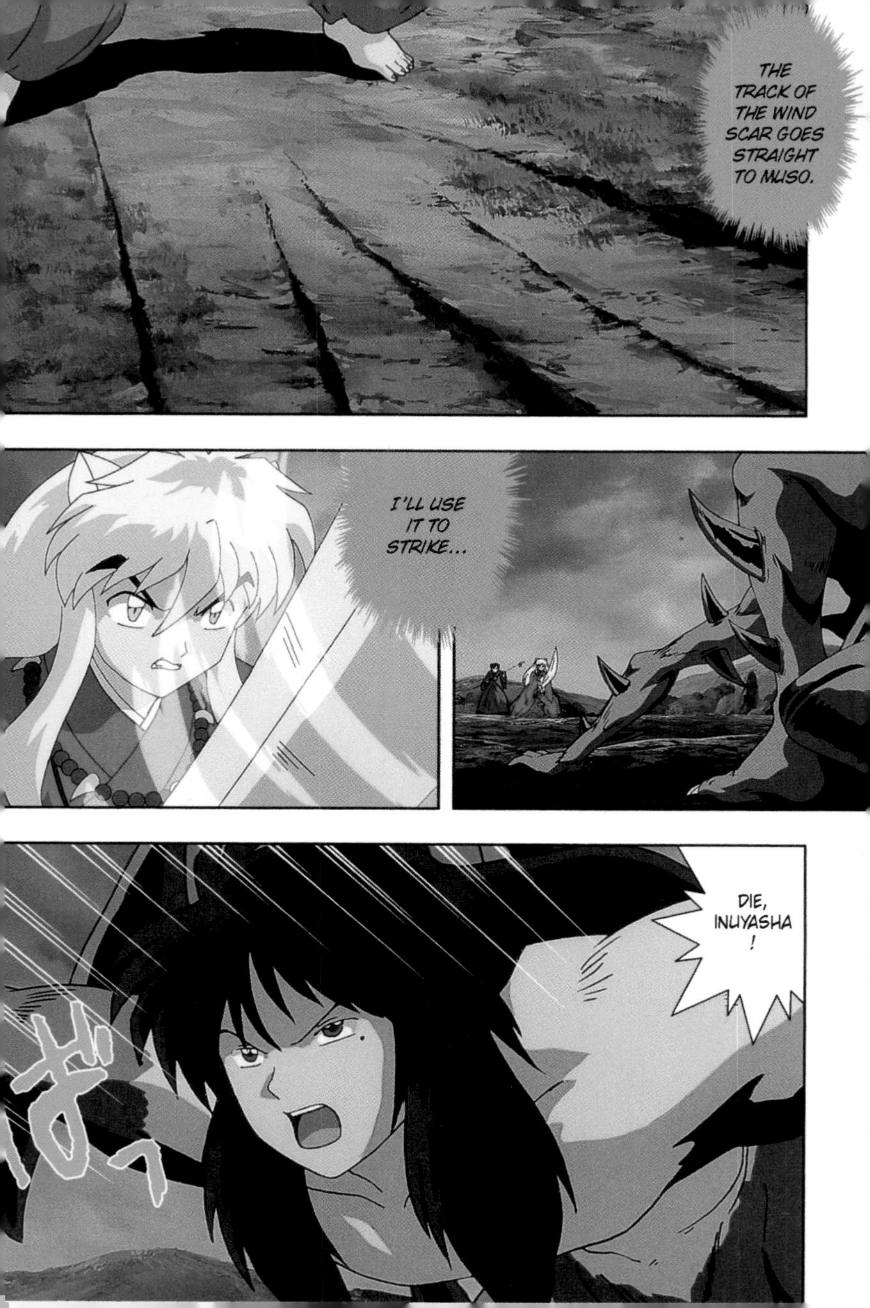
THE TRACK OF THE WIND SCAR GOES STRAIGHT TO MUSO.
I'LL USE IT TO STRIKE...
DIE, INUYASHA!

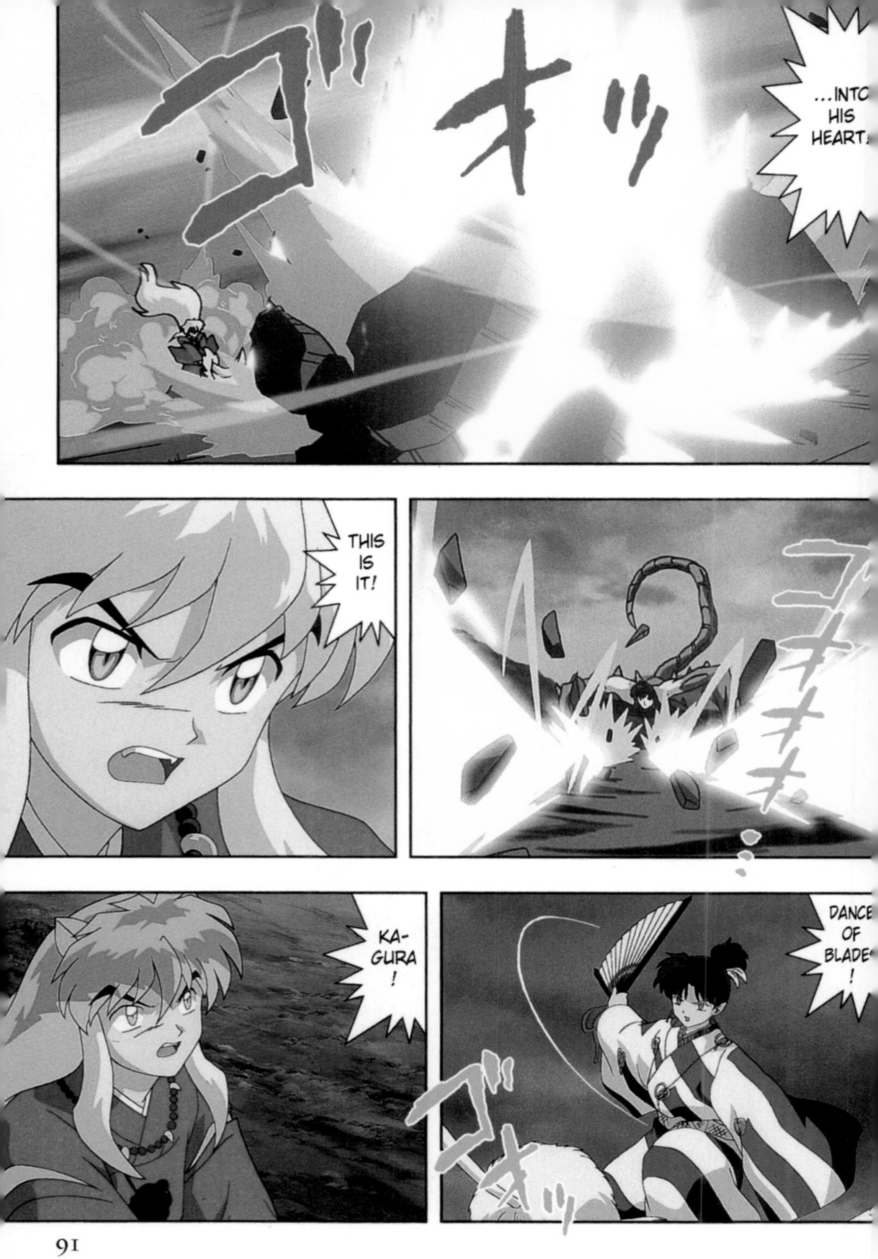
ゴオッ
...INTO HIS HEART!
ゴオオオオ...
THIS IS IT!
DANCE OF BLADES!
ゴオッ
KA-GURA!

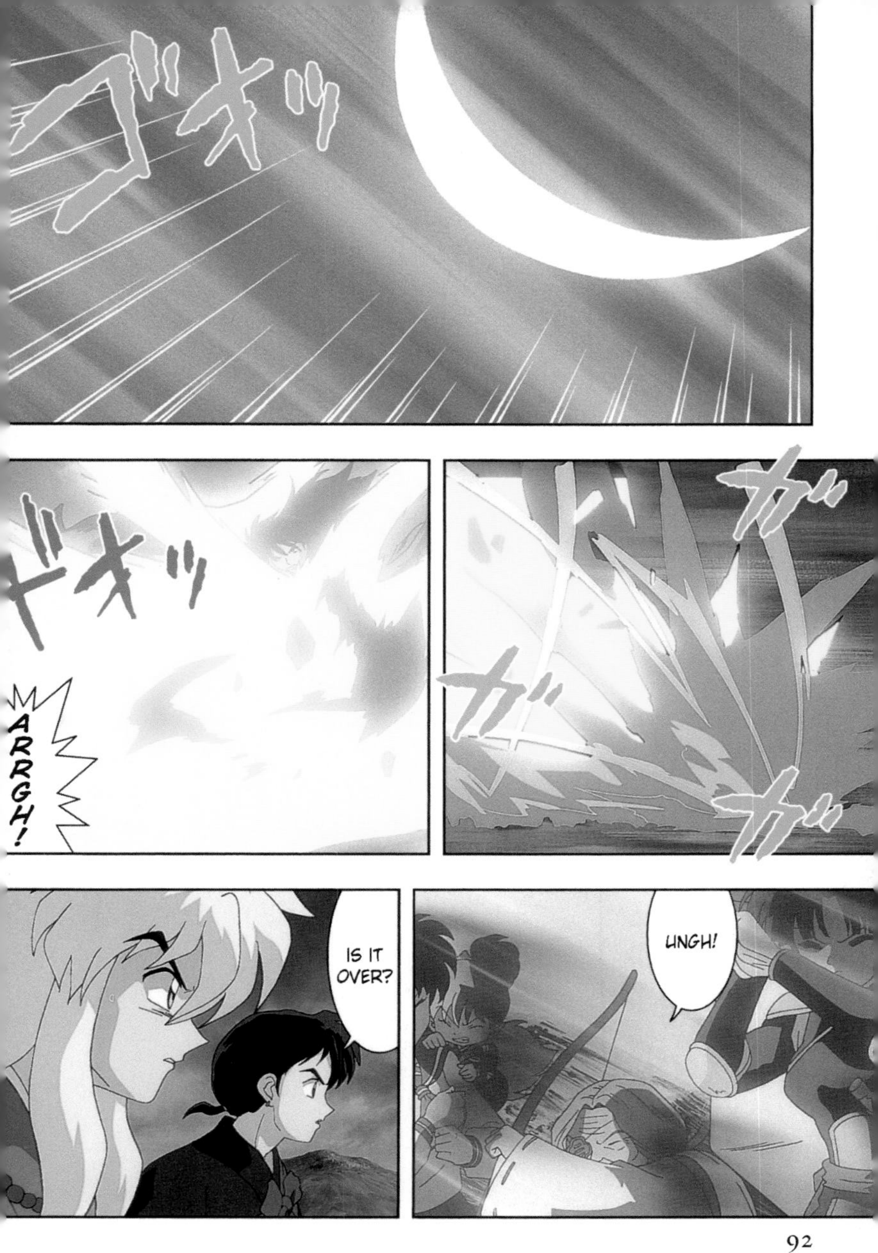
ゴオッ
ガ
ガ
ガ
ドオッ
ARRGH!
UNGH!
IS IT OVER?

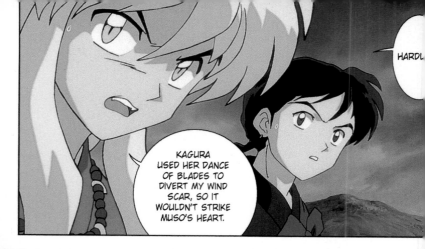

HARDL

KAGURA USED HER DANCE OF BLADES TO DIVERT MY WIND SCAR, SO IT WOULDN'T STRIKE MUSO'S HEART.

AT LEAST WE'VE DISCOVERED ONE THING.

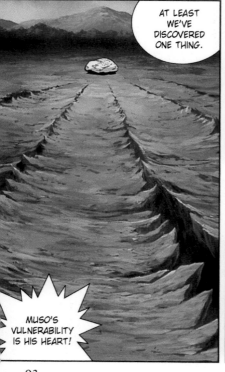

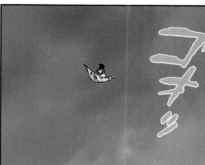

...

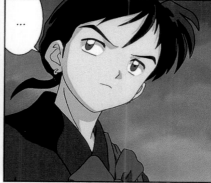

MUSO'S VULNERABILITY IS HIS HEART!

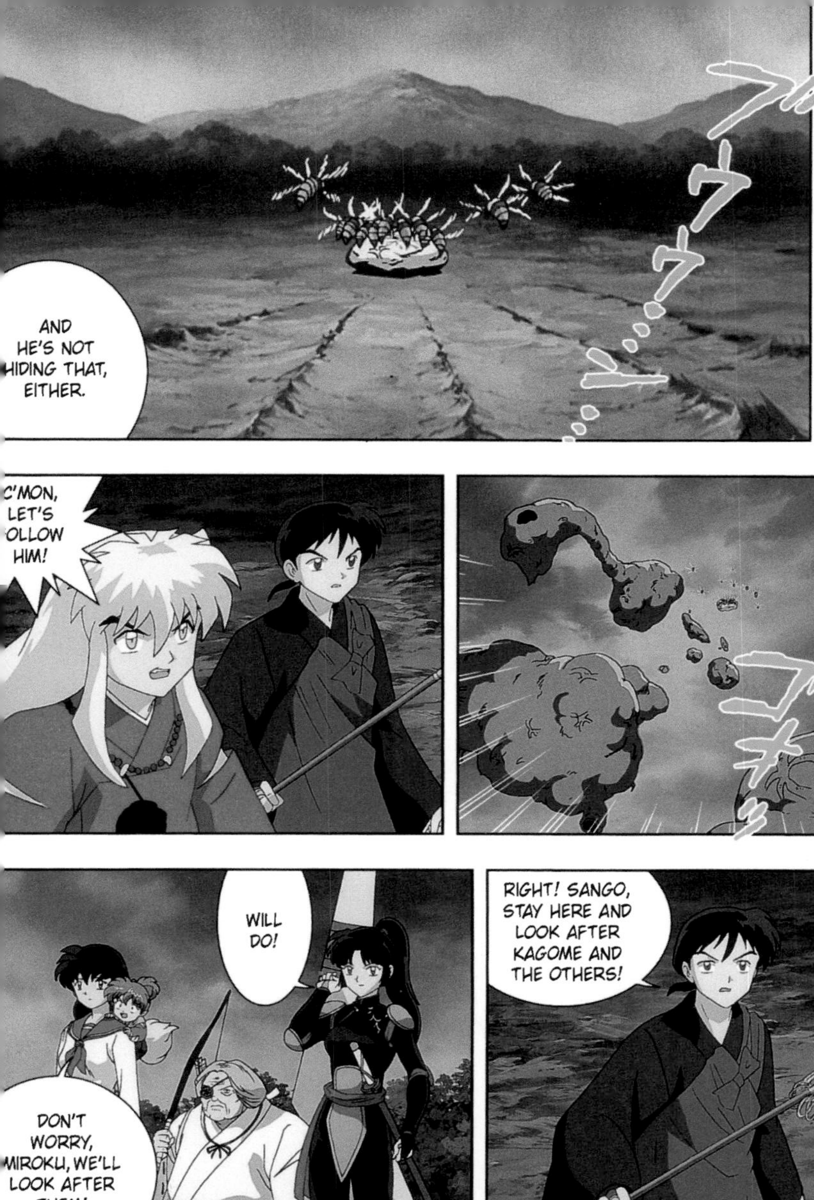
AND HE'S NOT HIDING THAT, EITHER.
C'MON, LET'S OLLOW HIM!
RIGHT! SANGO, STAY HERE AND LOOK AFTER KAGOME AND THE OTHERS!
WILL DO!
DON'T WORRY, MIROKU, WE'LL LOOK AFTER THEM!

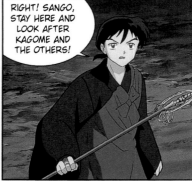

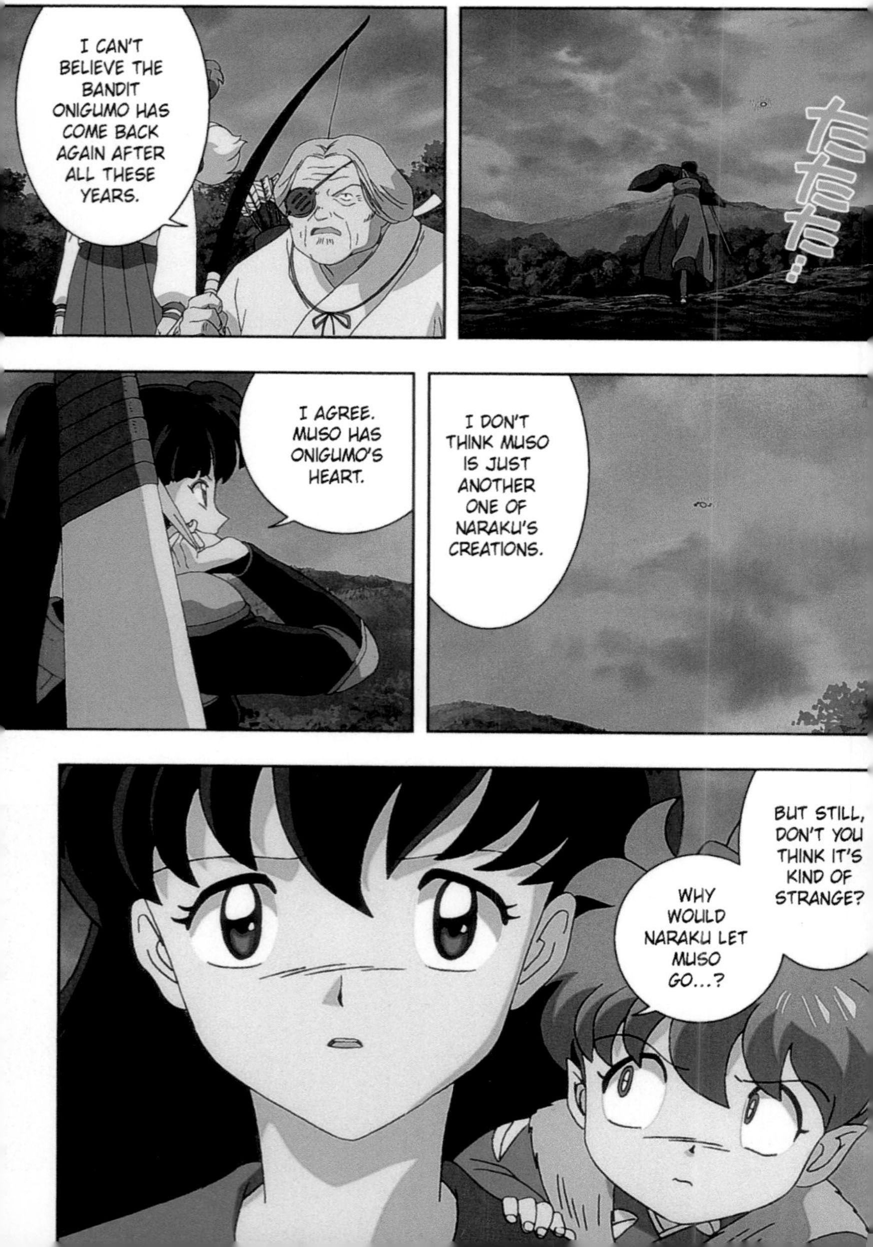
たたた…
I CAN'T BELIEVE THE BANDIT ONIGUMO HAS COME BACK AGAIN AFTER ALL THESE YEARS.
I DON'T THINK MUSO IS JUST ANOTHER ONE OF NARAKU'S CREATIONS.
I AGREE. MUSO HAS ONIGUMO'S HEART.
BUT STILL, DON'T YOU THINK IT'S KIND OF STRANGE?
WHY WOULD NARAKU LET MUSO GO...?

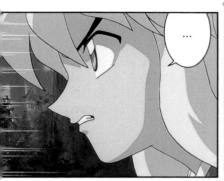

...

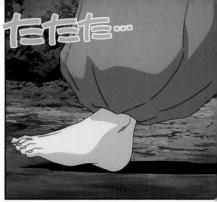

たたた...

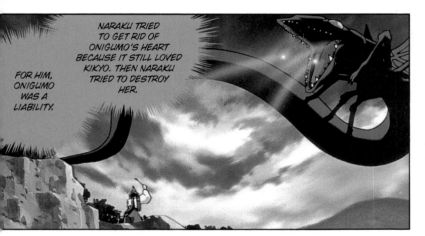

NARAKU TRIED TO GET RID OF ONIGUMO'S HEART BECAUSE IT STILL LOVED KIKYO. THEN NARAKU TRIED TO DESTROY HER.

FOR HIM, ONIGUMO WAS A LIABILITY.

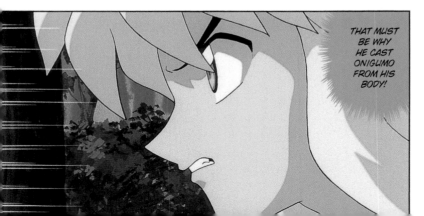

THAT MUST BE WHY HE CAST ONIGUMO FROM HIS BODY!

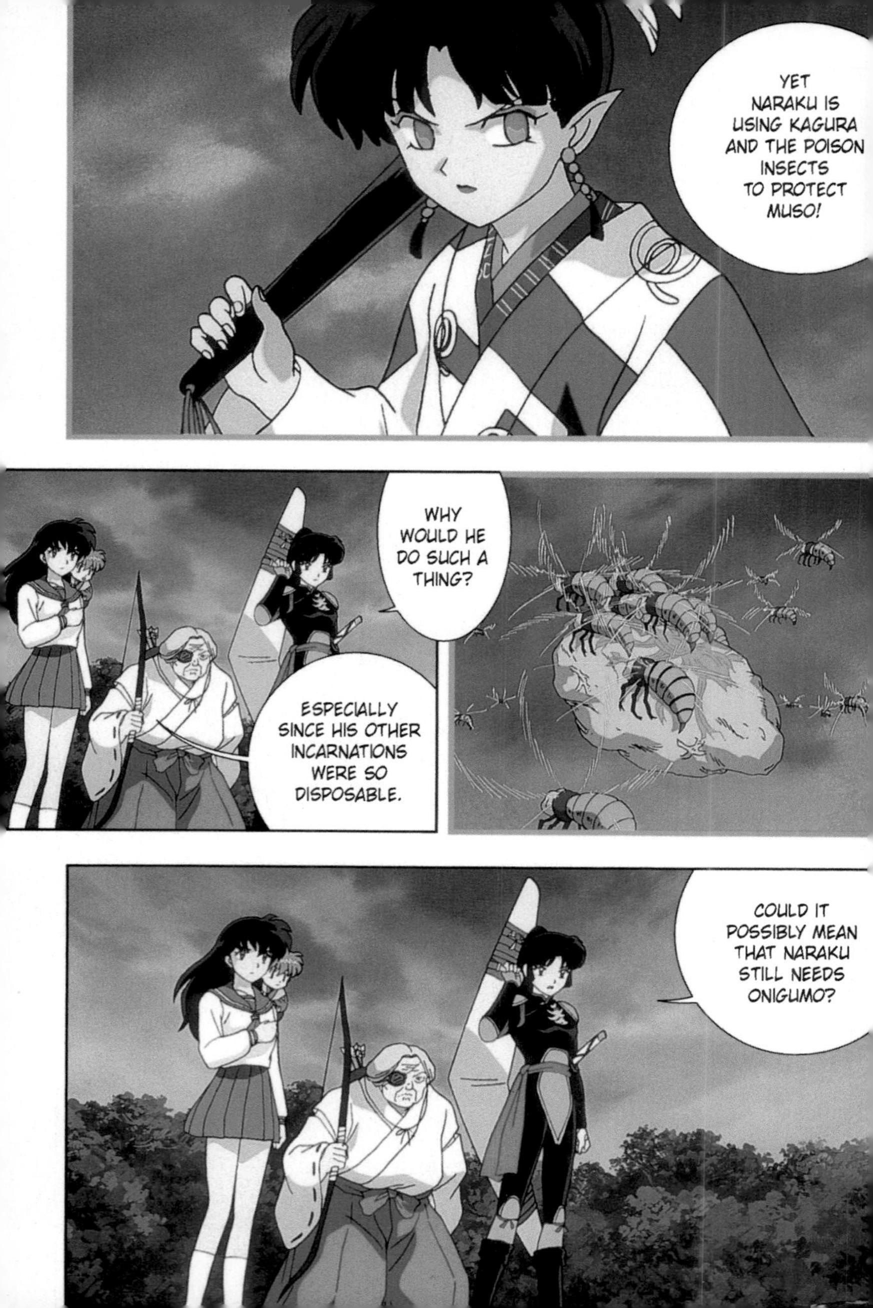
YET NARAKU IS USING KAGURA AND THE POISON INSECTS TO PROTECT MUSO!
WHY WOULD HE DO SUCH A THING?
ESPECIALLY SINCE HIS OTHER INCARNATIONS WERE SO DISPOSABLE.
COULD IT POSSIBLY MEAN THAT NARAKU STILL NEEDS ONIGUMO?

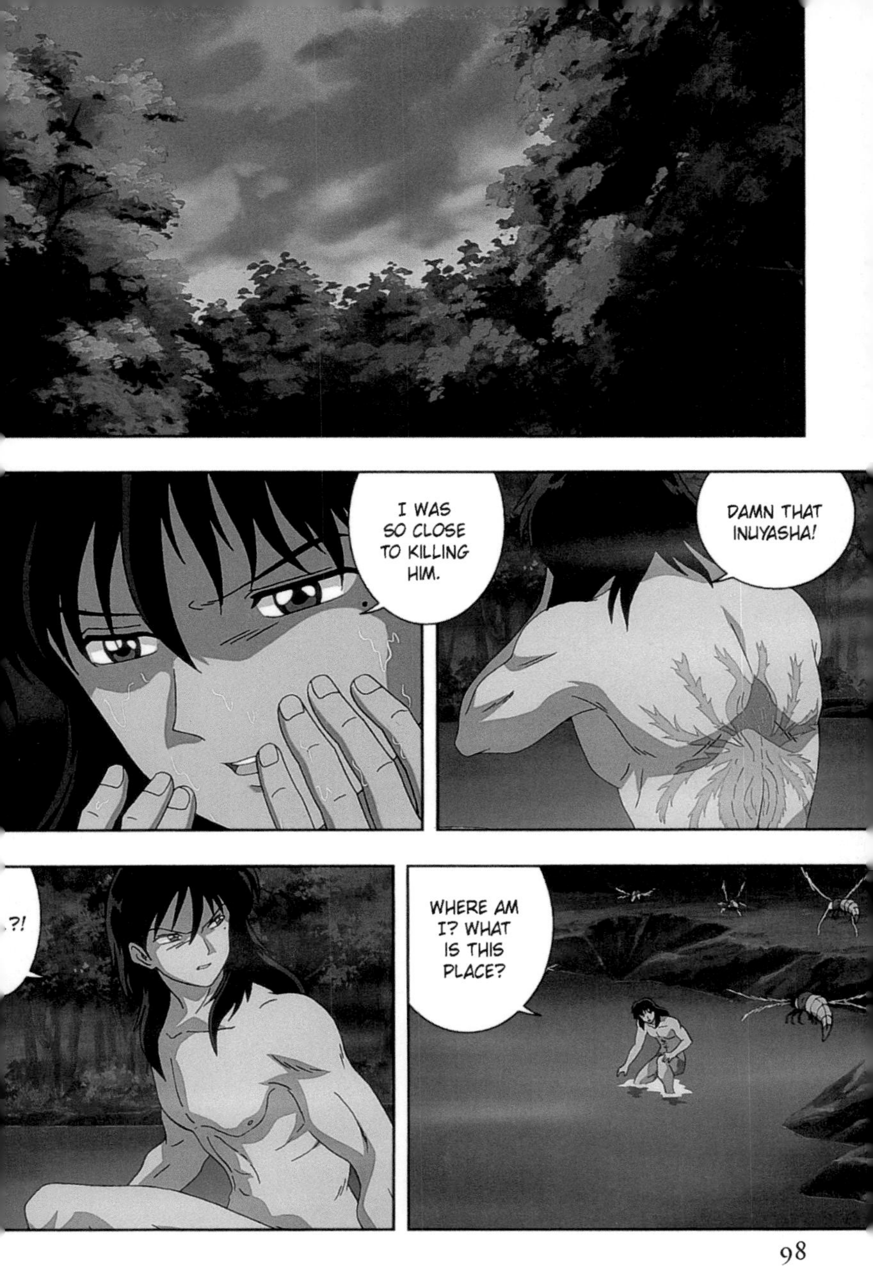
DAMN THAT INUYASHA!
I WAS SO CLOSE TO KILLING HIM.
WHERE AM I? WHAT IS THIS PLACE?
?!

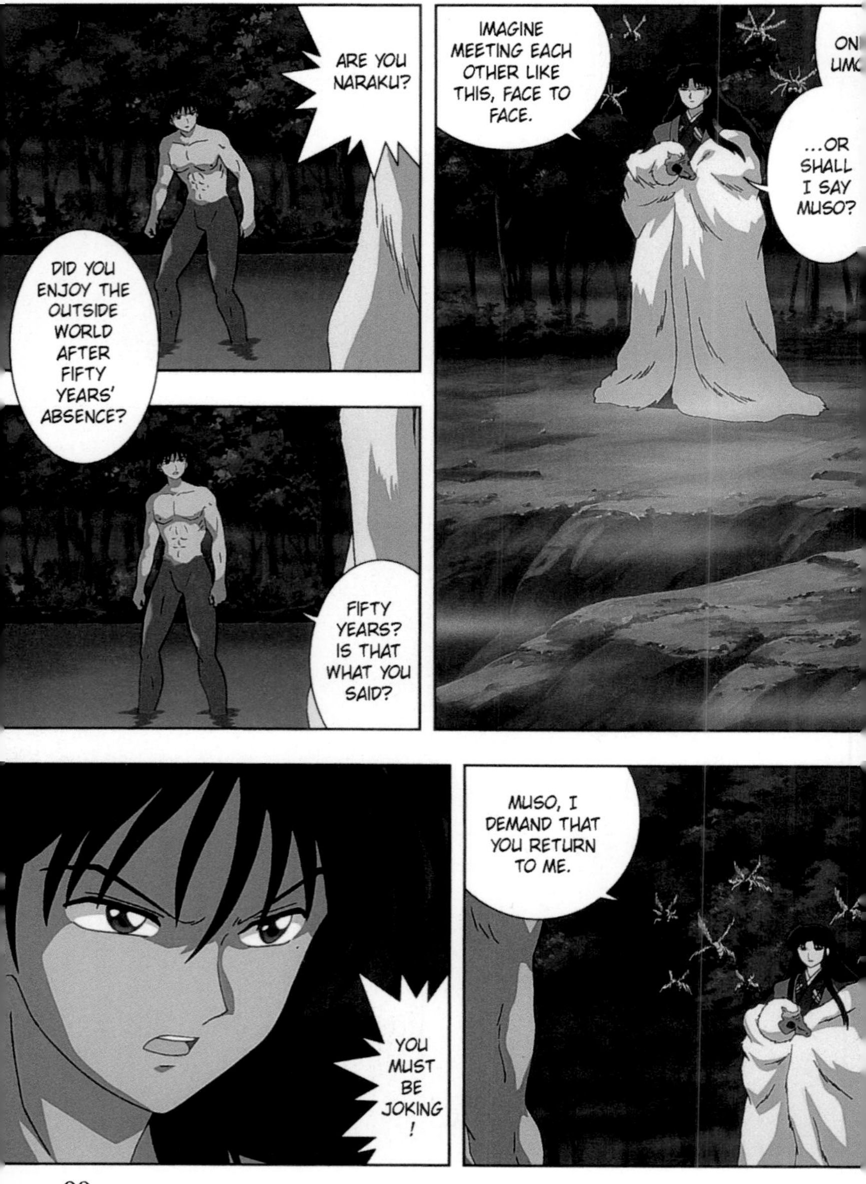
IMAGINE MEETING EACH OTHER LIKE THIS, FACE TO FACE.
...OR SHALL I SAY MUSO?
ARE YOU NARAKU?
DID YOU ENJOY THE OUTSIDE WORLD AFTER FIFTY YEARS' ABSENCE?
FIFTY YEARS? IS THAT WHAT YOU SAID?
MUSO, I DEMAND THAT YOU RETURN TO ME.
YOU MUST BE JOKING!

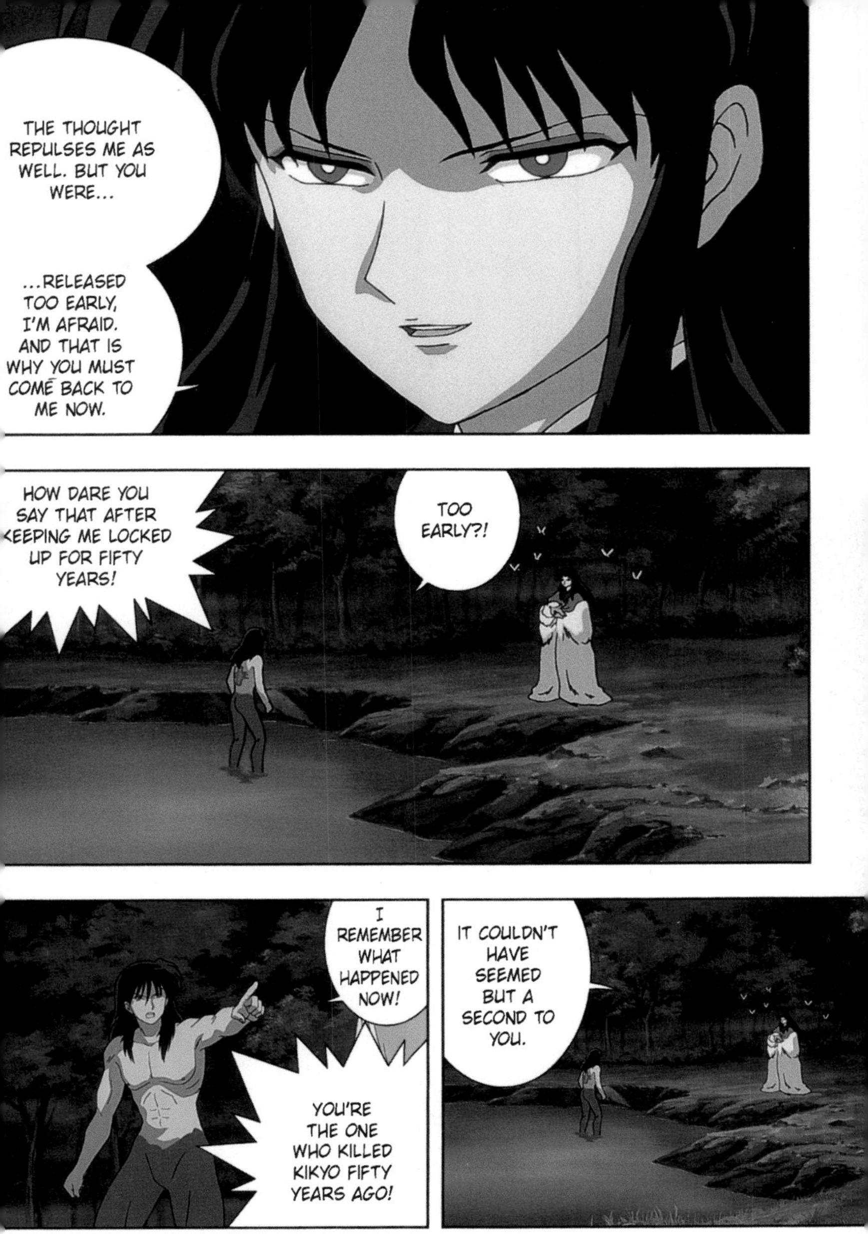
THE THOUGHT REPULSES ME AS WELL. BUT YOU WERE...
...RELEASED TOO EARLY, I'M AFRAID. AND THAT IS WHY YOU MUST COME BACK TO ME NOW.
TOO EARLY?!
HOW DARE YOU SAY THAT AFTER KEEPING ME LOCKED UP FOR FIFTY YEARS!
IT COULDN'T HAVE SEEMED BUT A SECOND TO YOU.
I REMEMBER WHAT HAPPENED NOW!
YOU'RE THE ONE WHO KILLED KIKYO FIFTY YEARS AGO!

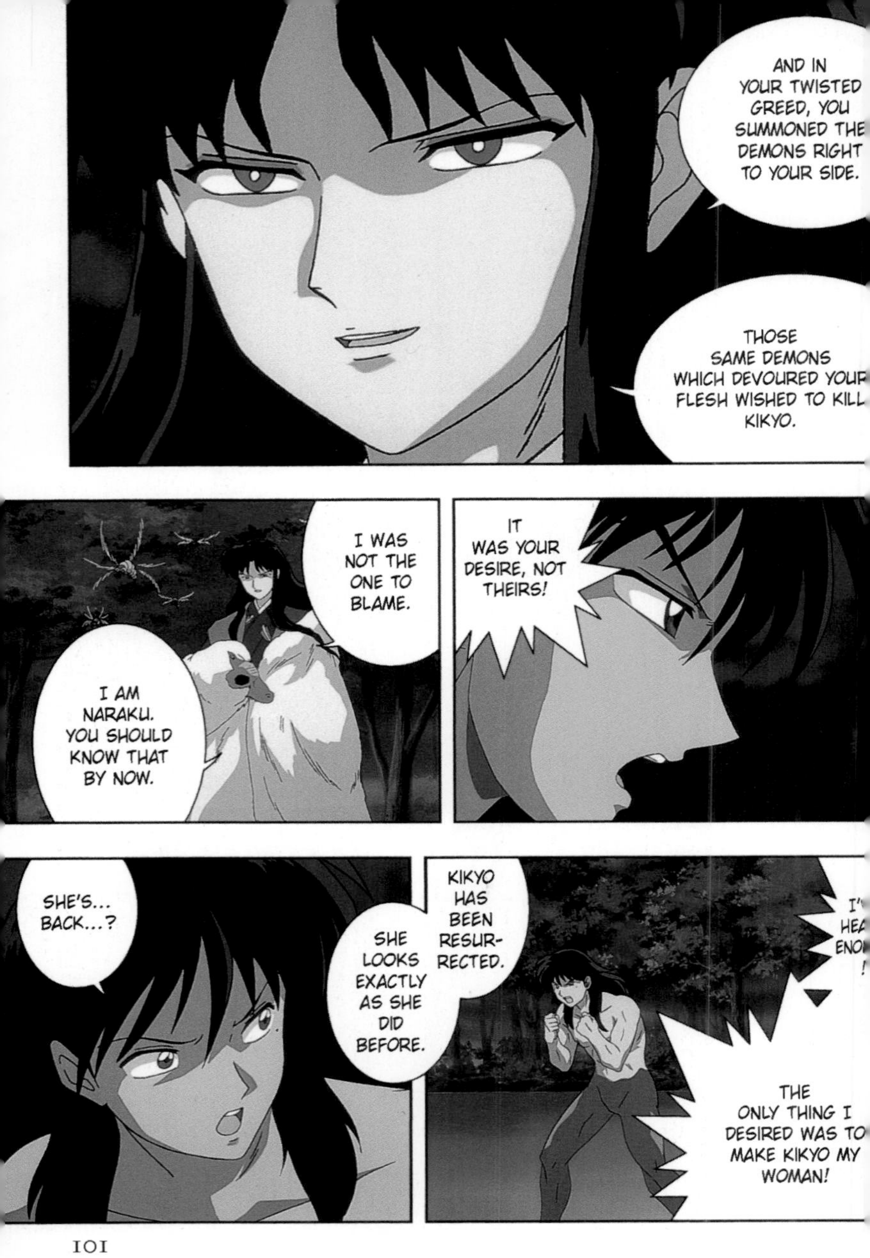

AND IN YOUR TWISTED GREED, YOU SUMMONED THE DEMONS RIGHT TO YOUR SIDE.
THOSE SAME DEMONS WHICH DEVOURED YOUR FLESH WISHED TO KILL KIKYO.
IT WAS YOUR DESIRE, NOT THEIRS!
I WAS NOT THE ONE TO BLAME.
I AM NARAKU. YOU SHOULD KNOW THAT BY NOW.
THE ONLY THING I DESIRED WAS TO MAKE KIKYO MY WOMAN!
KIKYO HAS BEEN RESURRECTED.
SHE LOOKS EXACTLY AS SHE DID BEFORE.
SHE'S... BACK...?

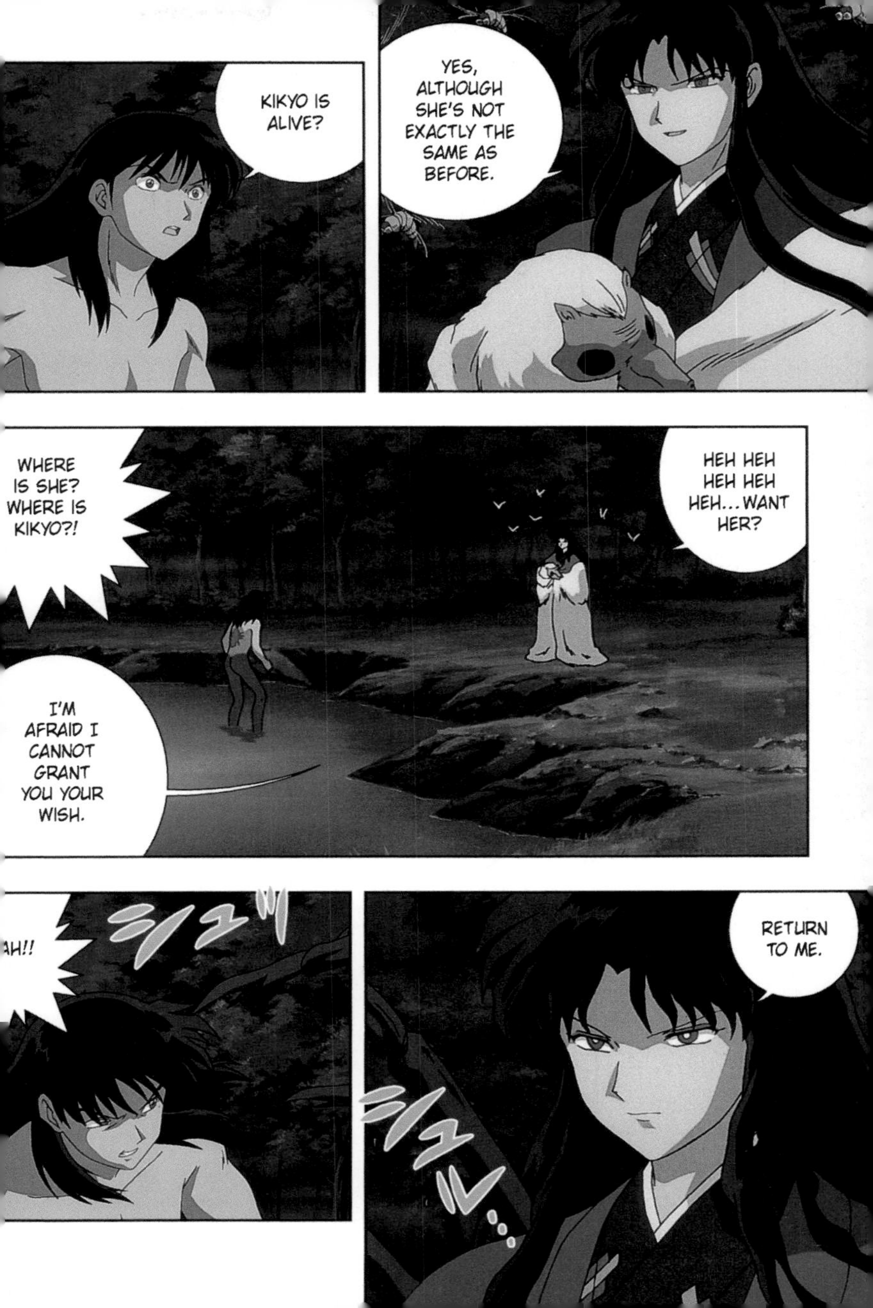
YES, ALTHOUGH SHE'S NOT EXACTLY THE SAME AS BEFORE.
KIKYO IS ALIVE?
HEH HEH HEH HEH HEH...WANT HER?
WHERE IS SHE? WHERE IS KIKYO?!
I'M AFRAID I CANNOT GRANT YOU YOUR WISH.
RETURN TO ME.
シュル…
AH!!
シュル

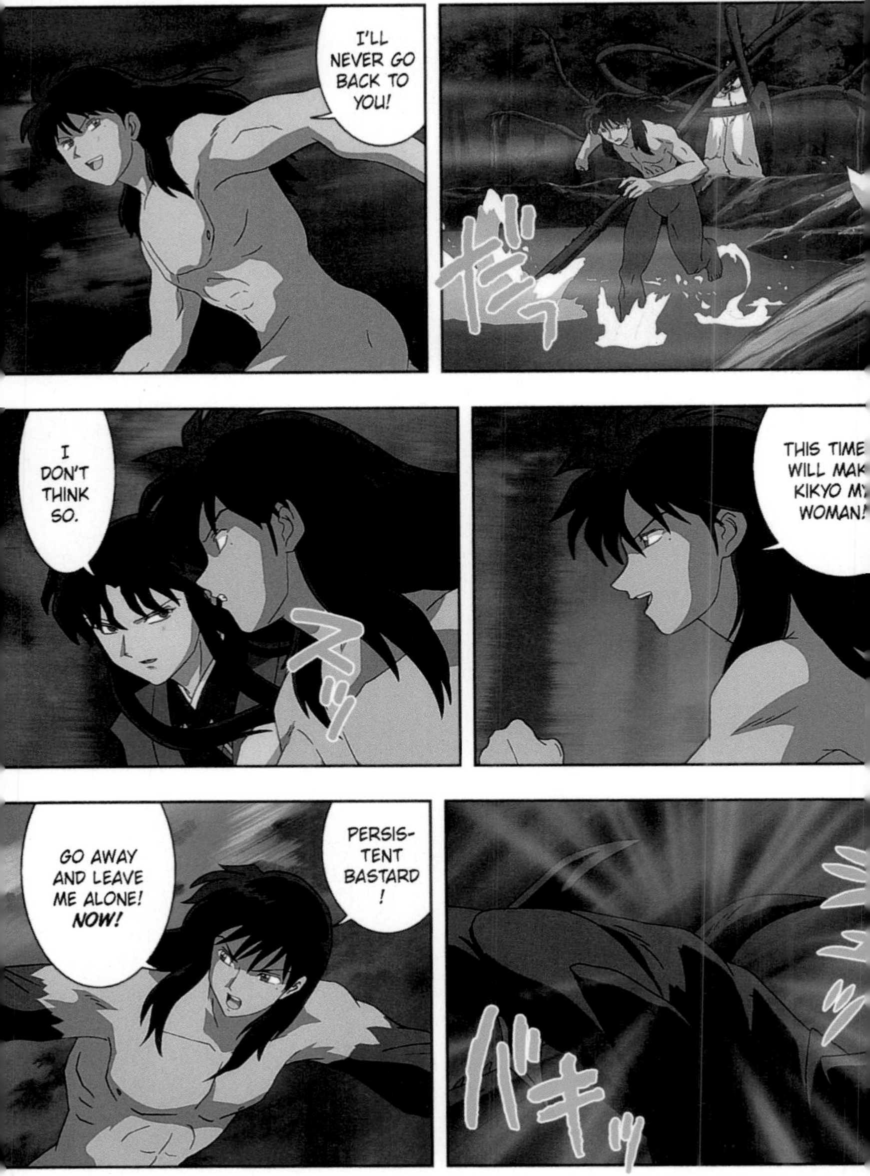
I'LL NEVER GO BACK TO YOU!
THIS TIME WILL MAK KIKYO MY WOMAN!
I DON'T THINK SO.
スッ
バキッ
PERSIS-TENT BASTARD!
GO AWAY AND LEAVE ME ALONE! NOW!

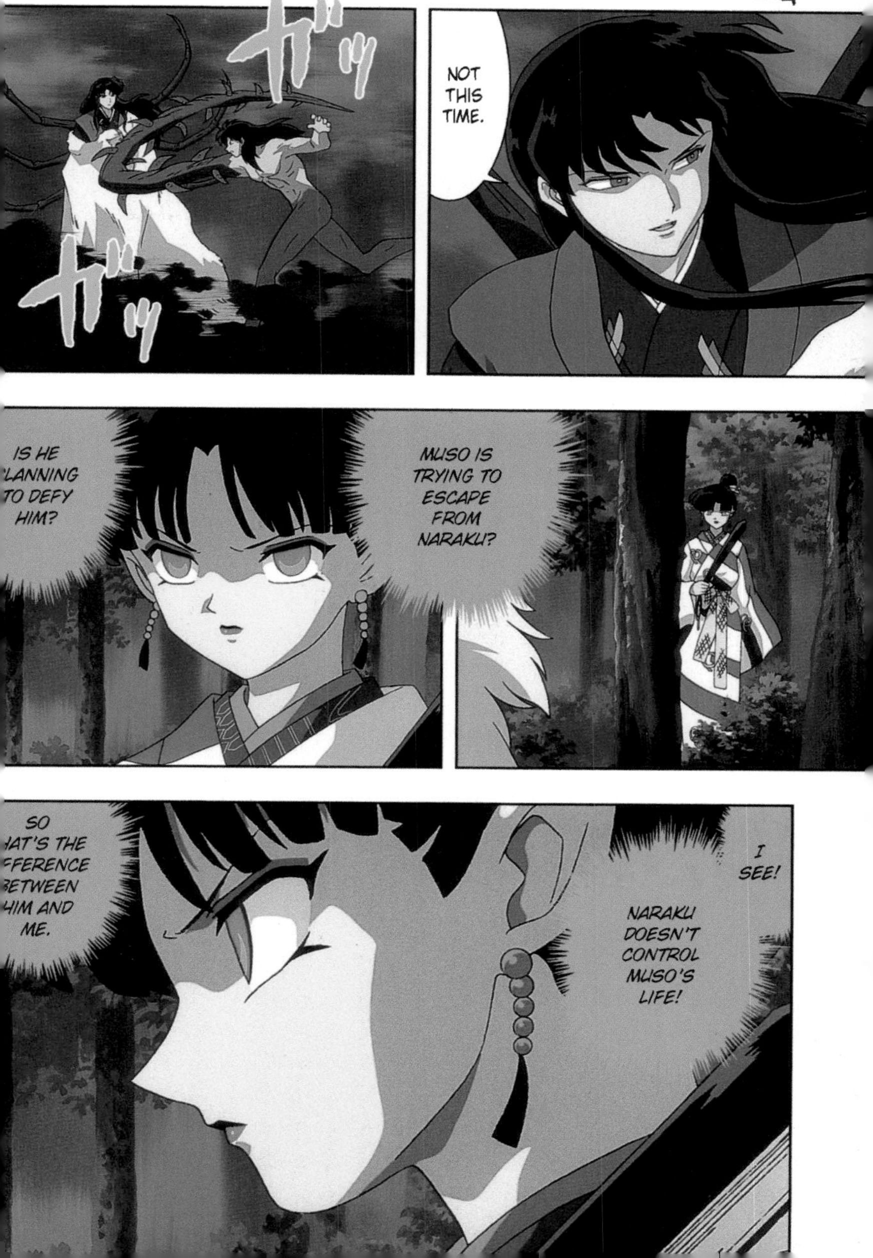
NOT THIS TIME.
ガッ
ガッ
MUSO IS TRYING TO ESCAPE FROM NARAKU?
IS HE LANNING TO DEFY HIM?
I SEE!
NARAKU DOESN'T CONTROL MUSO'S LIFE!
SO HAT'S THE FFERENCE BETWEEN HIM AND ME.

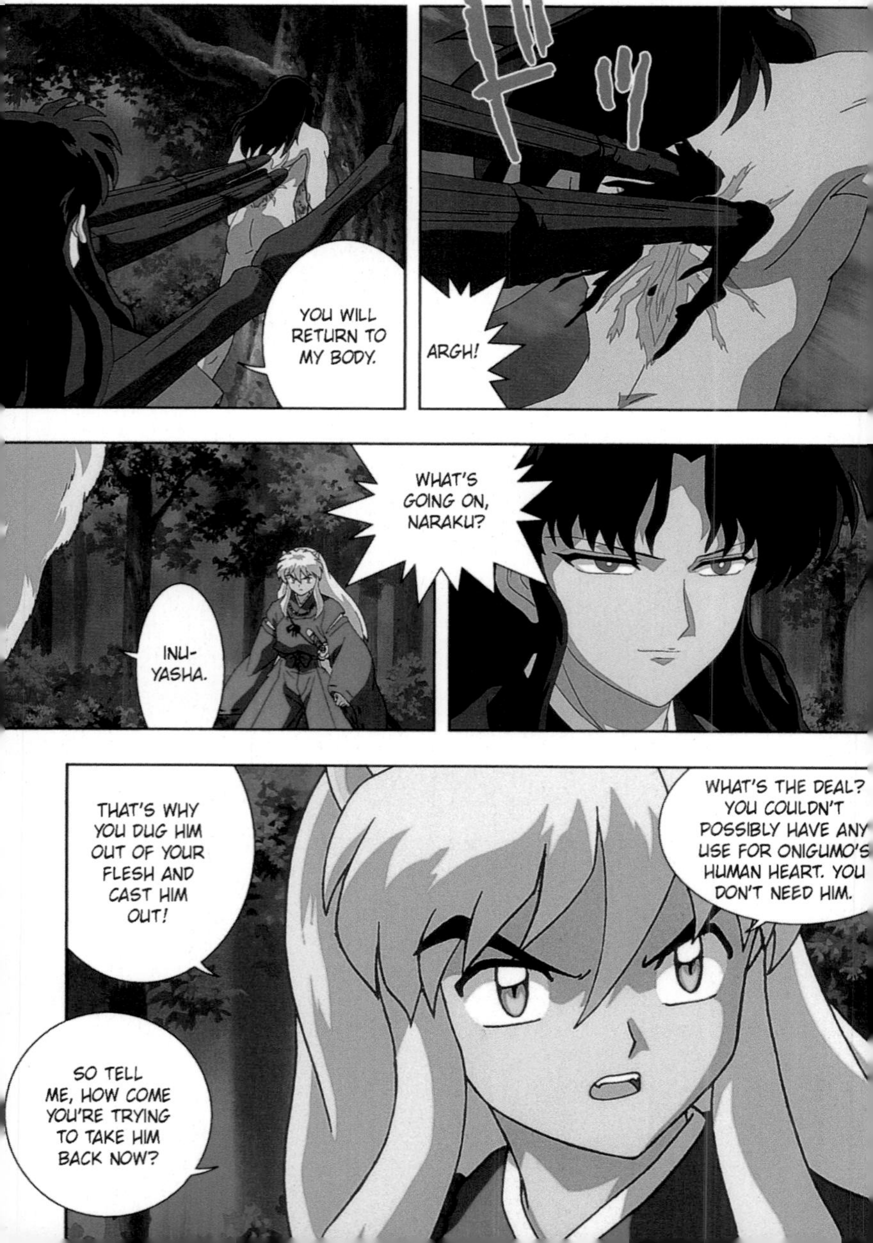
ドッ
ARGH!
YOU WILL RETURN TO MY BODY.
WHAT'S GOING ON, NARAKU?
INU-YASHA.
WHAT'S THE DEAL? YOU COULDN'T POSSIBLY HAVE ANY USE FOR ONIGUMO'S HUMAN HEART. YOU DON'T NEED HIM.
THAT'S WHY YOU DUG HIM OUT OF YOUR FLESH AND CAST HIM OUT!
SO TELL ME, HOW COME YOU'RE TRYING TO TAKE HIM BACK NOW?

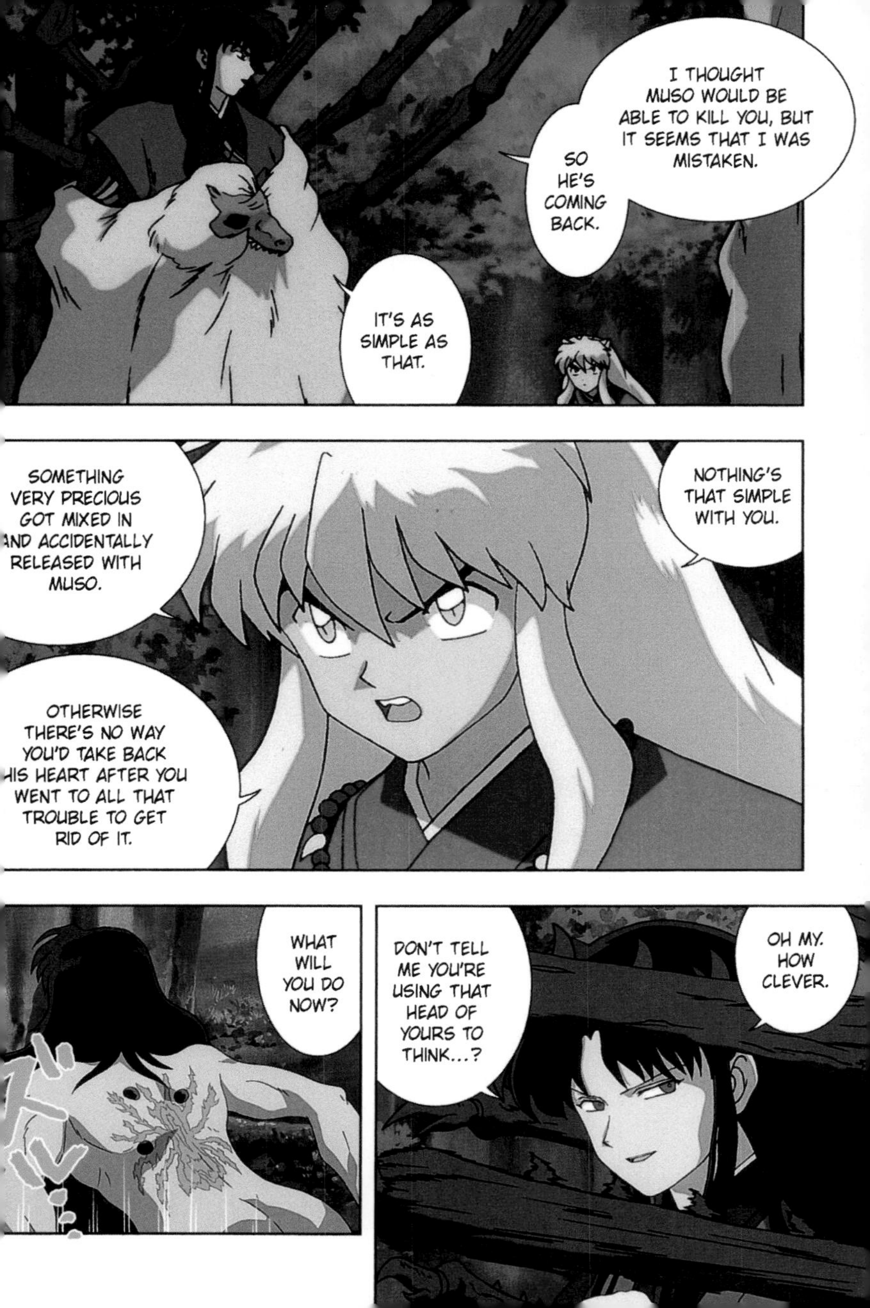
I THOUGHT MUSO WOULD BE ABLE TO KILL YOU, BUT IT SEEMS THAT I WAS MISTAKEN.
SO HE'S COMING BACK.
IT'S AS SIMPLE AS THAT.
NOTHING'S THAT SIMPLE WITH YOU.
SOMETHING VERY PRECIOUS GOT MIXED IN AND ACCIDENTALLY RELEASED WITH MUSO.
OTHERWISE THERE'S NO WAY YOU'D TAKE BACK HIS HEART AFTER YOU WENT TO ALL THAT TROUBLE TO GET RID OF IT.
OH MY. HOW CLEVER.
DON'T TELL ME YOU'RE USING THAT HEAD OF YOURS TO THINK...?
WHAT WILL YOU DO NOW?

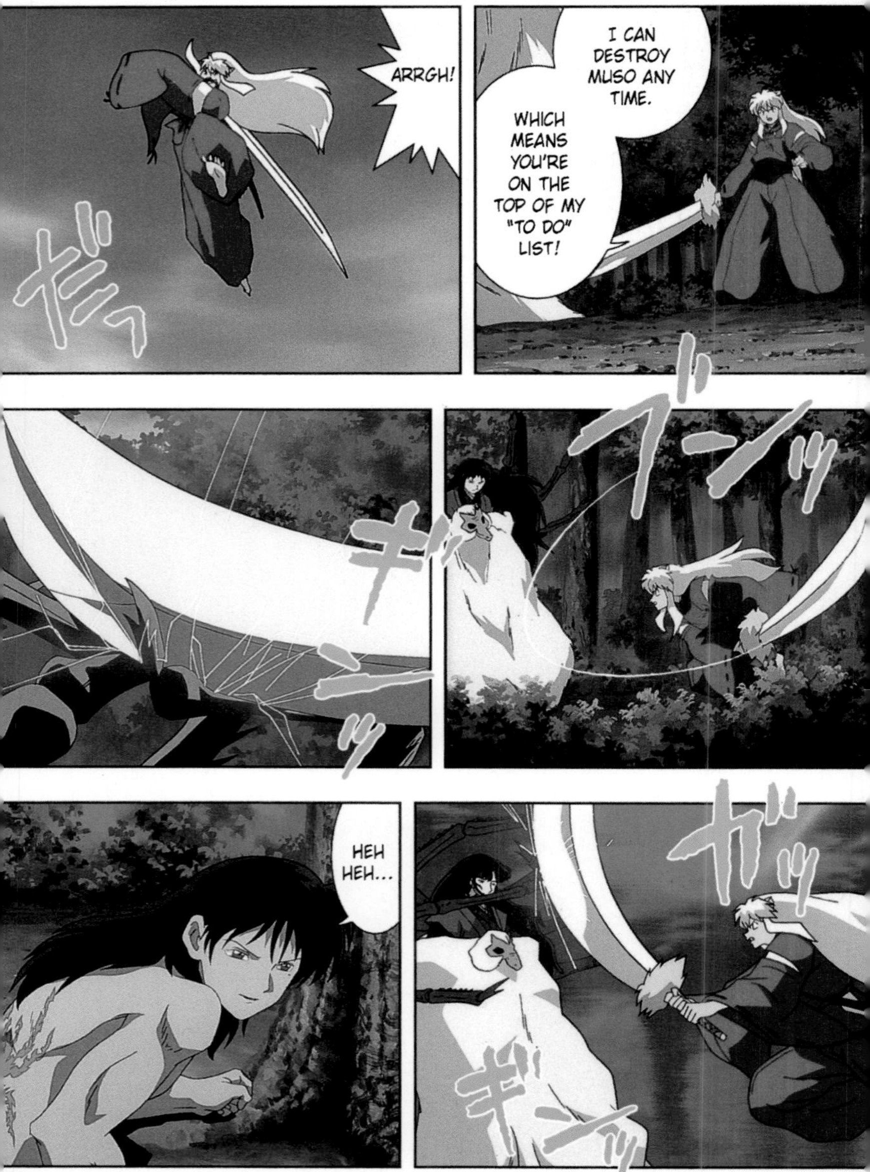
I CAN DESTROY MUSO ANY TIME.
WHICH MEANS YOU'RE ON THE TOP OF MY "TO DO" LIST!
ARRGH!
HEH HEH...

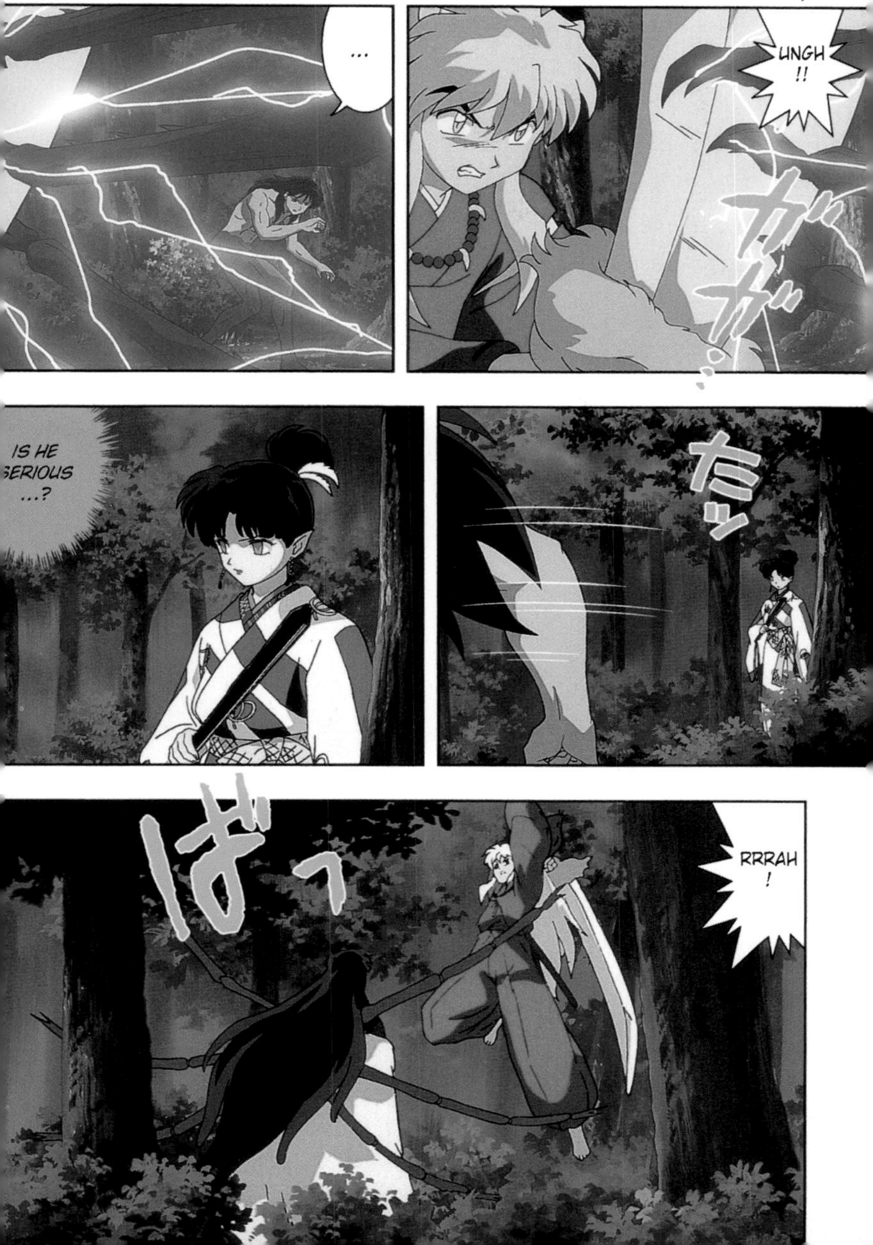
UNGH !!
ガガ…
...
タッ
IS HE SERIOUS ...?
ぱっ
RRRAH !

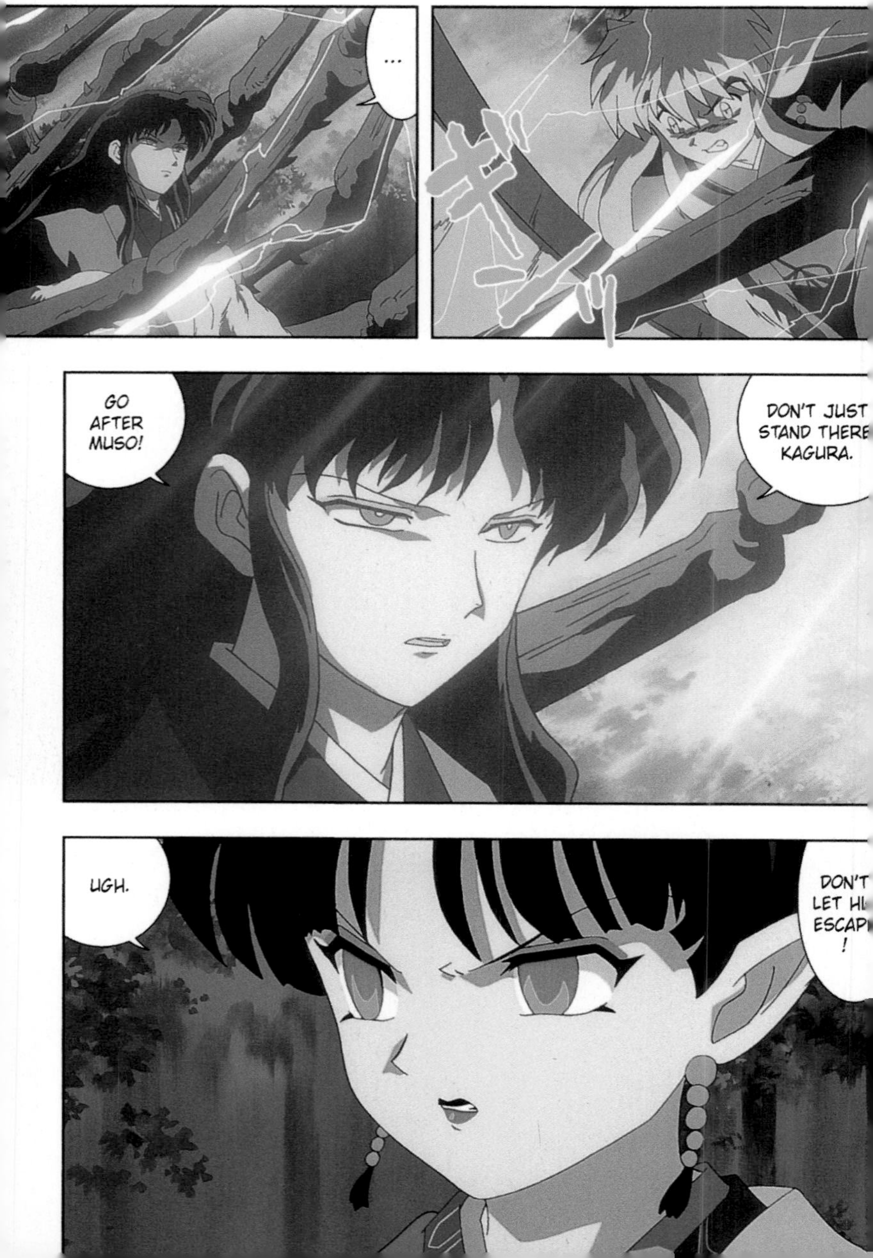
ギーッ
...
DON'T JUST STAND THERE KAGURA.
GO AFTER MUSO!
DON'T LET HI ESCAP !
UGH.

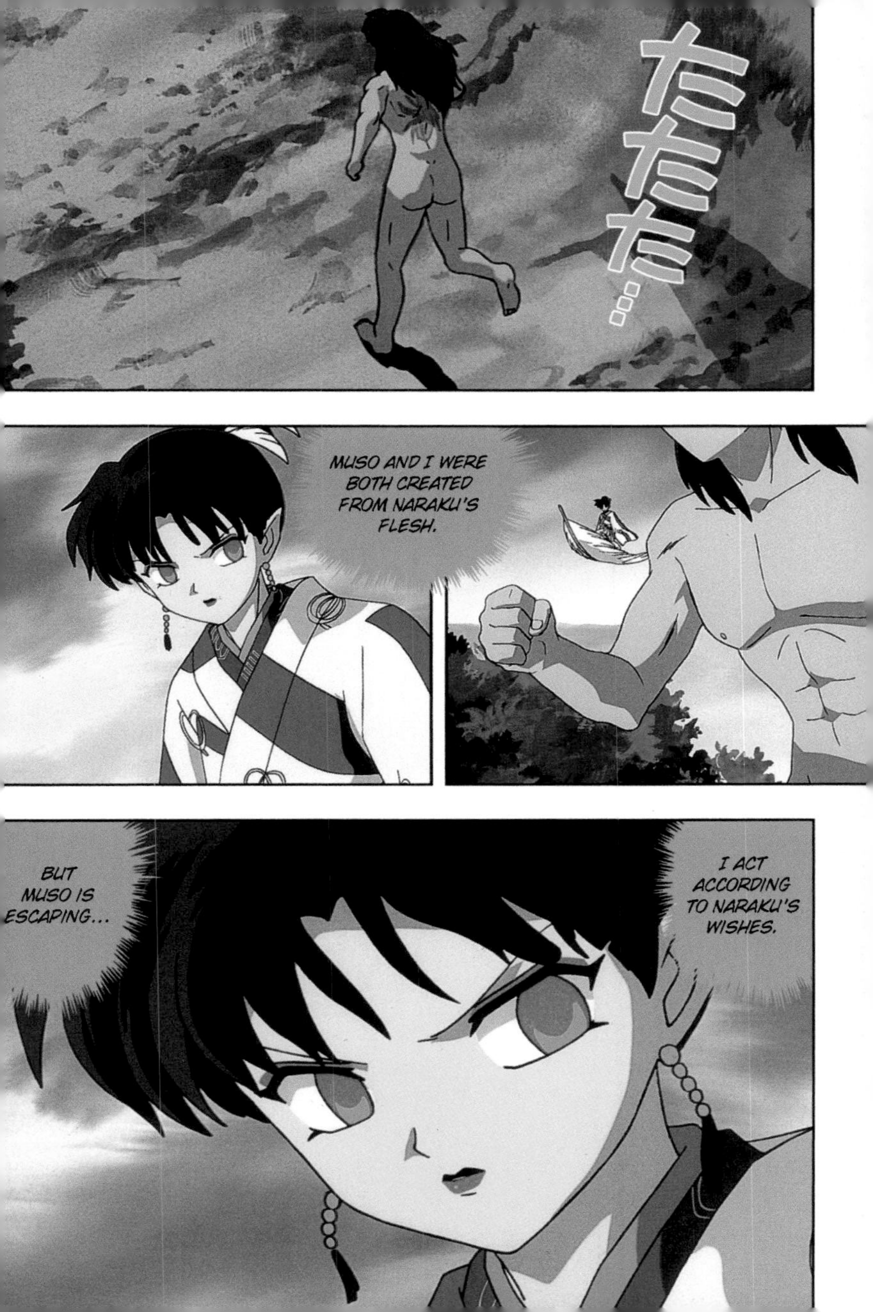
たたた…
MUSO AND I WERE BOTH CREATED FROM NARAKU'S FLESH.
I ACT ACCORDING TO NARAKU'S WISHES.
BUT MUSO IS ESCAPING...

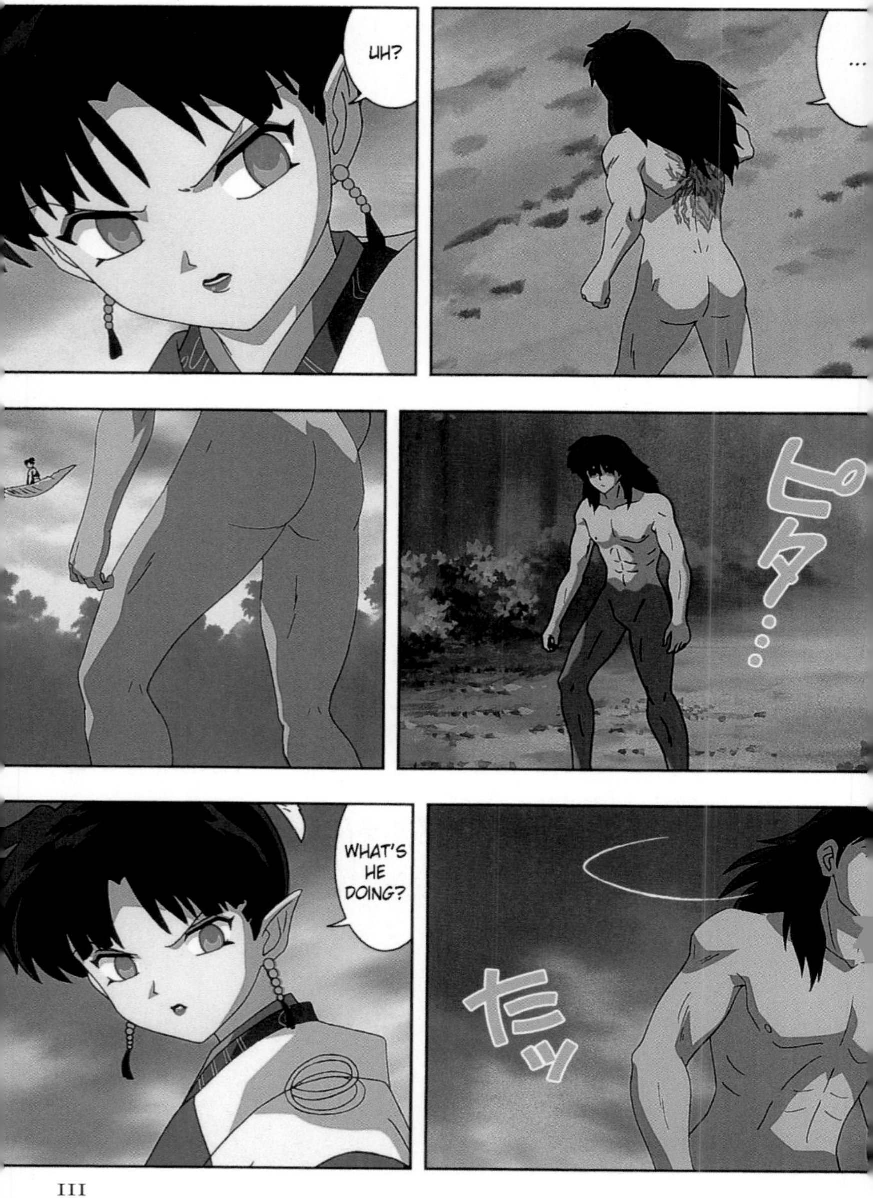
...
UH?
ピタ・・・
タッ
WHAT'S HE DOING?

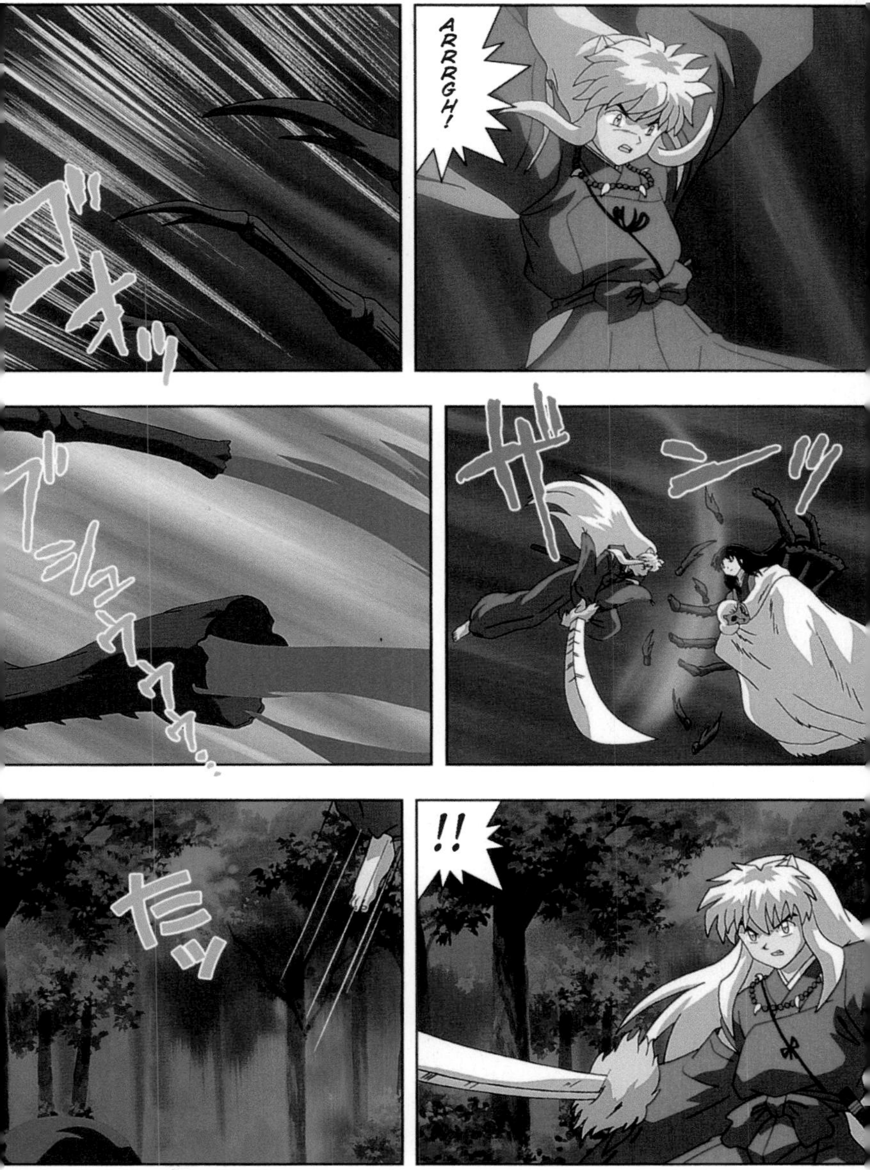
ARRRGH!
!!

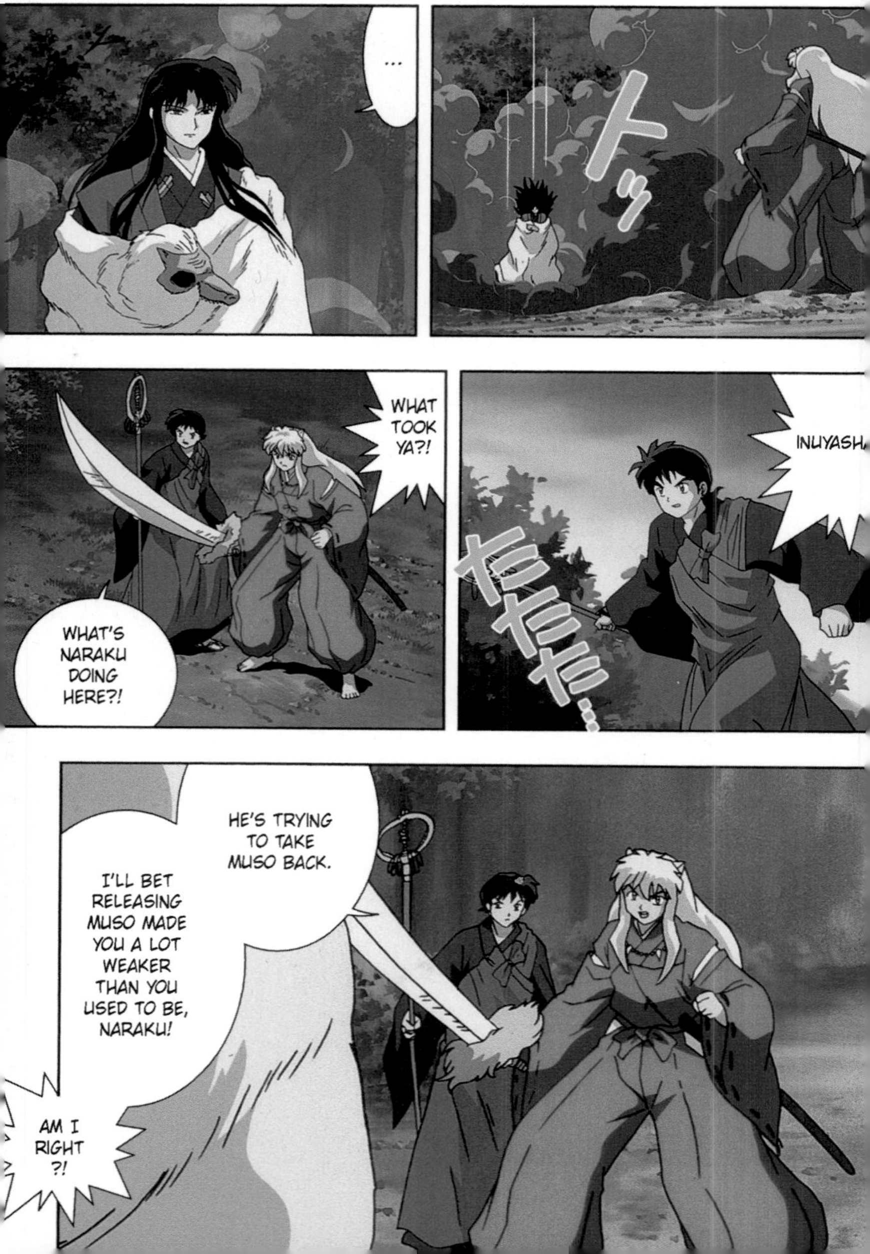
トッ
...
INUYASH
WHAT TOOK YA?!
WHAT'S NARAKU DOING HERE?!
HE'S TRYING TO TAKE MUSO BACK.
I'LL BET RELEASING MUSO MADE YOU A LOT WEAKER THAN YOU USED TO BE, NARAKU!
AM I RIGHT ?!

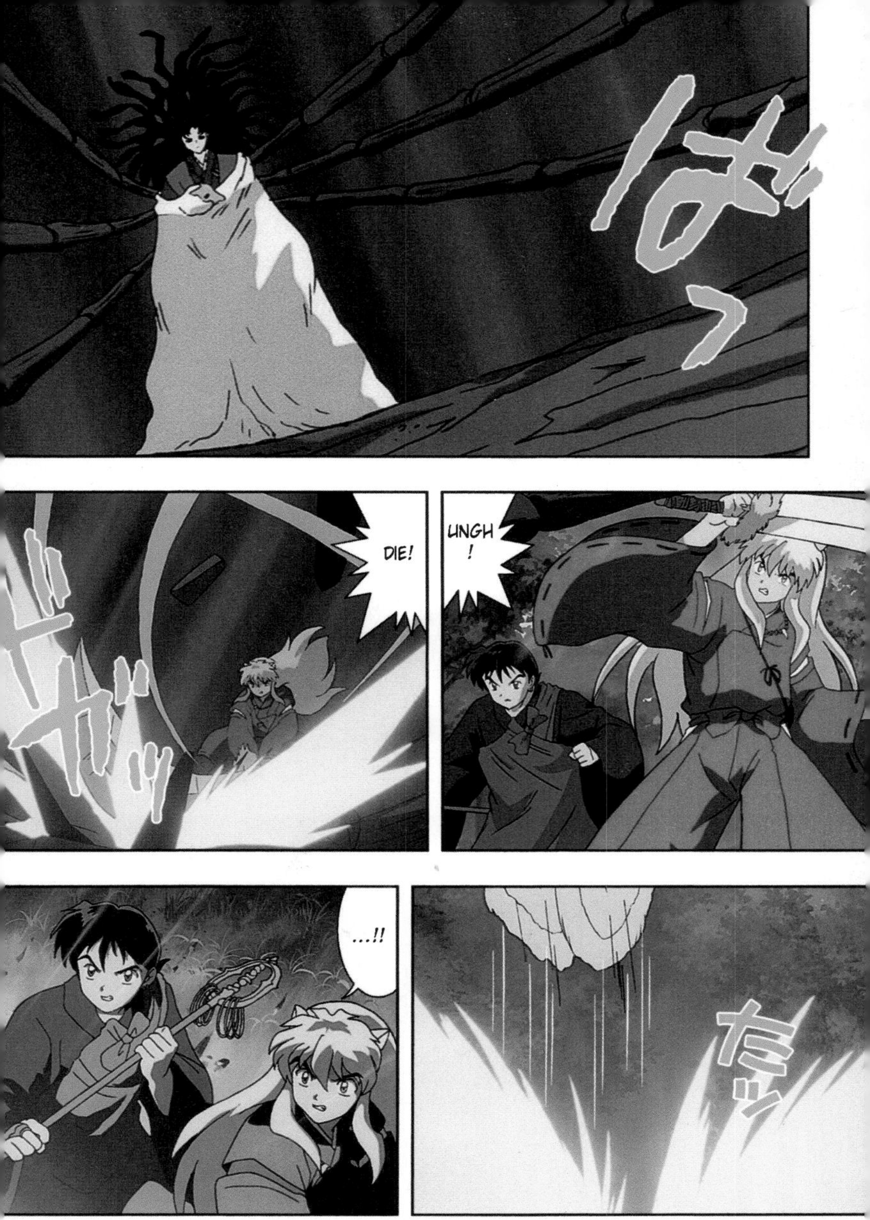
ばっ
UNGH!
DIE!
たッ
...!!

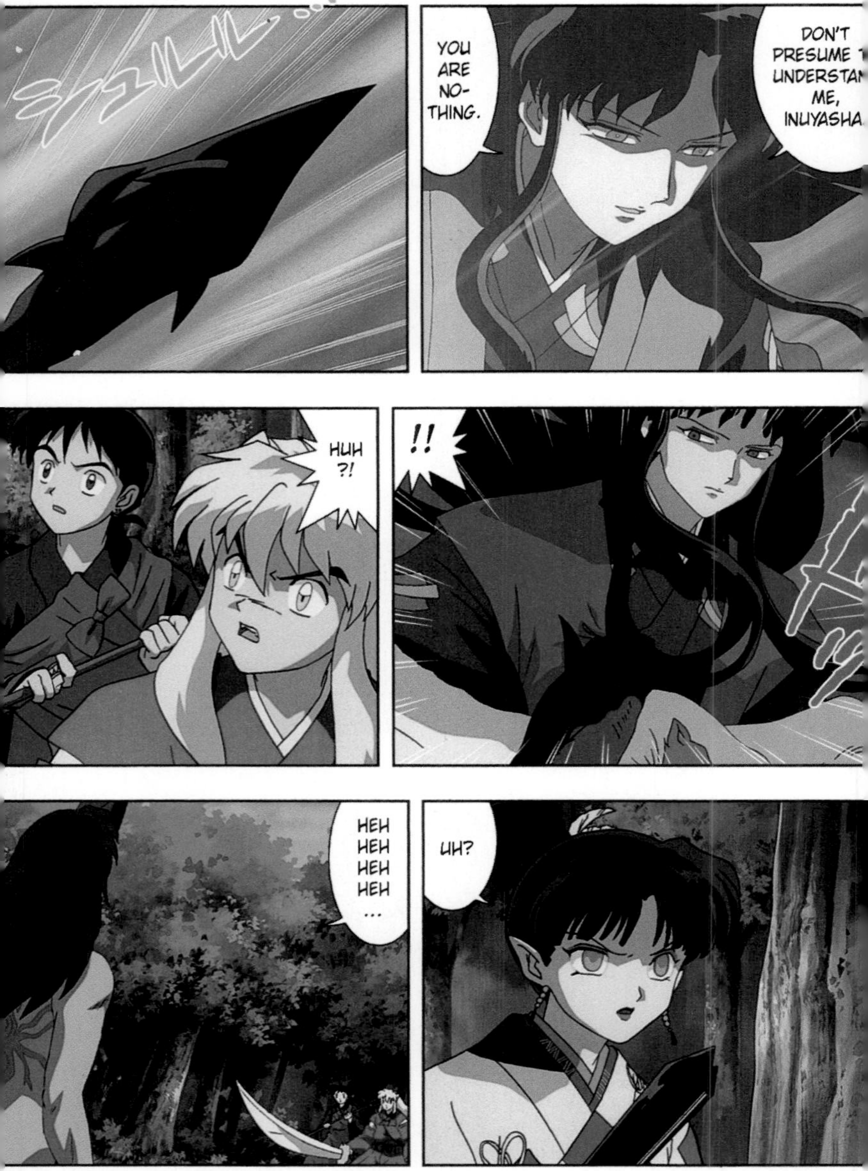
DON'T PRESUME T UNDERSTAN ME, INUYASHA.
YOU ARE NO-THING.
シュルルル...
!!
HUH ?!
UH?
HEH HEH HEH HEH ...

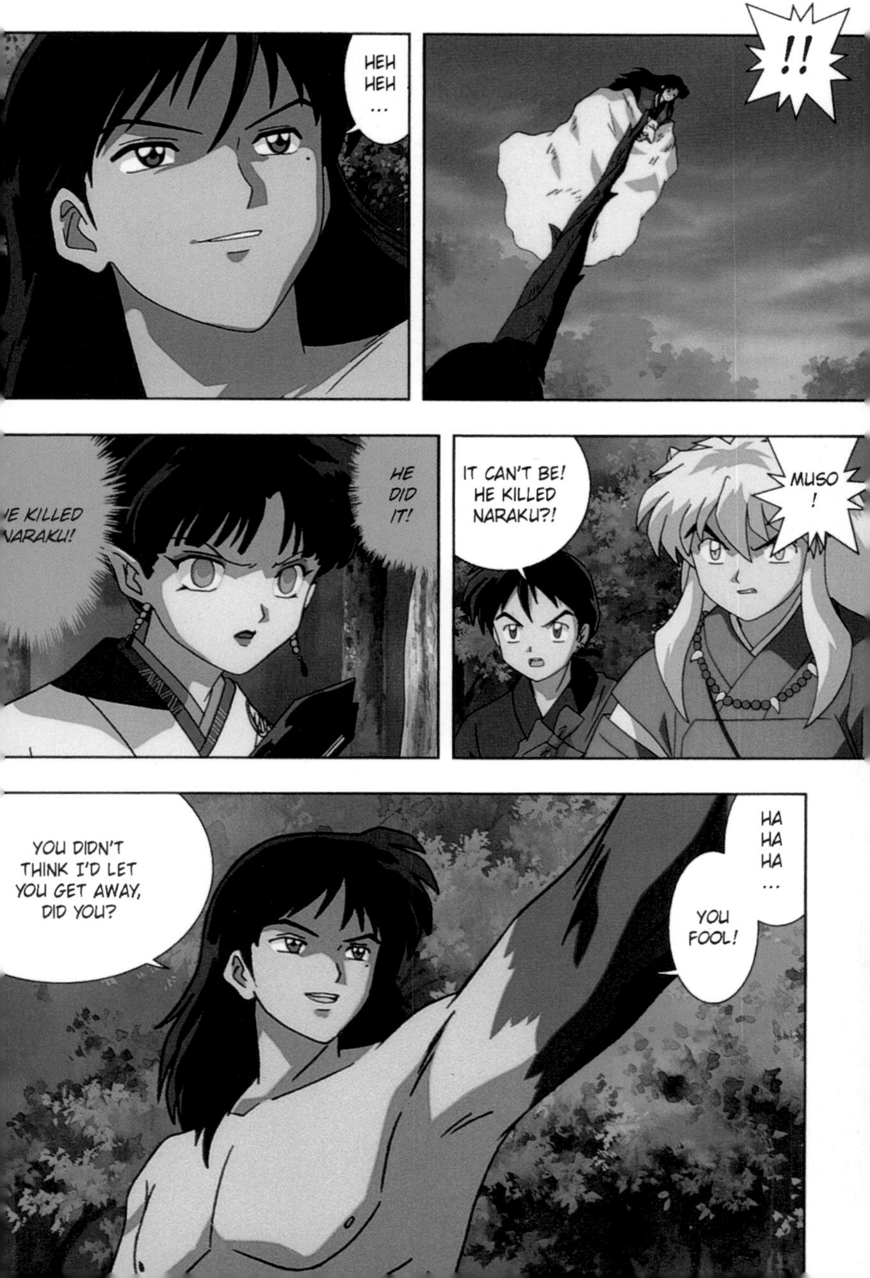
!!
HEH HEH ...
MUSO!
IT CAN'T BE! HE KILLED NARAKU?!
HE DID IT!
E KILLED NARAKU!
HA HA HA ...
YOU FOOL!
YOU DIDN'T THINK I'D LET YOU GET AWAY, DID YOU?

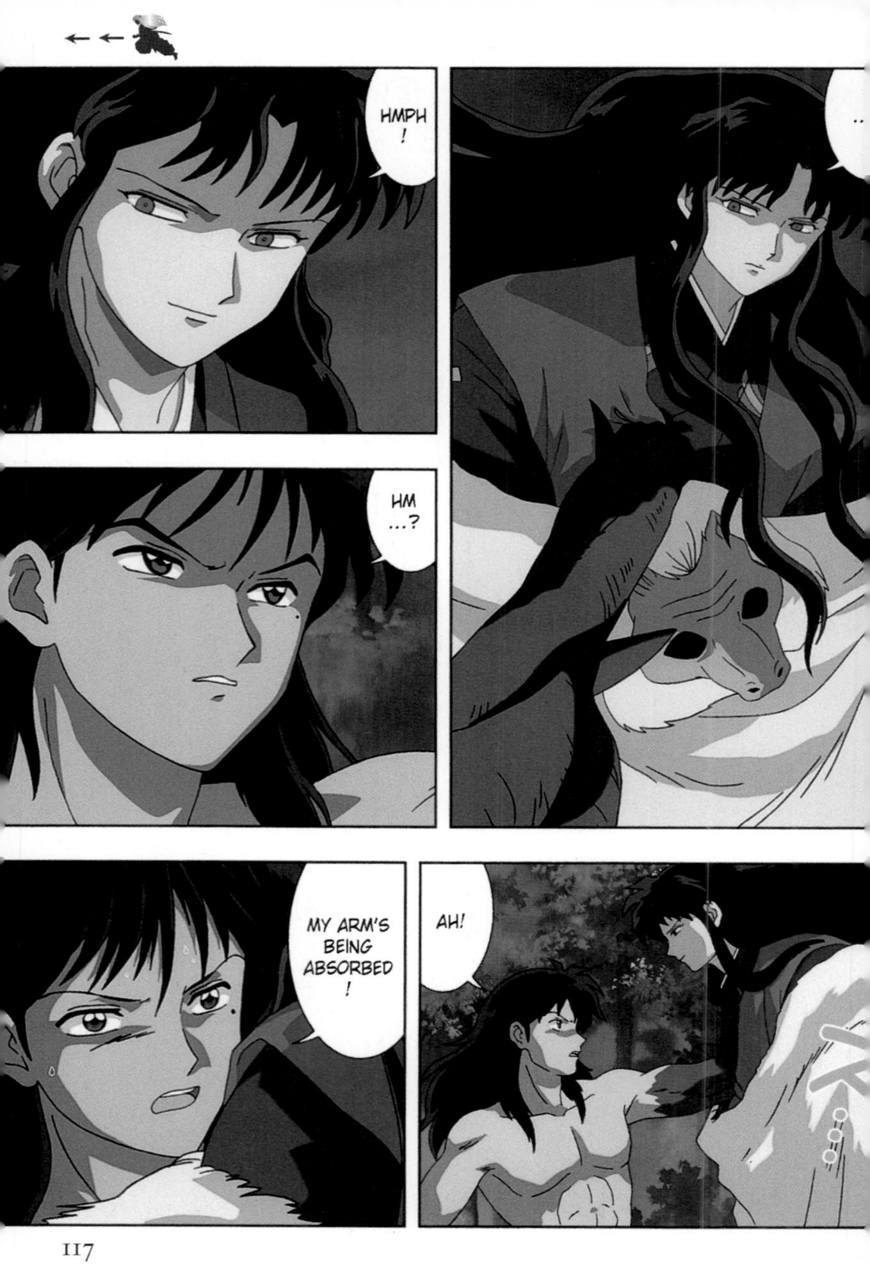
..
HMPH!
HM...?
AH!
MY ARM'S BEING ABSORBED!

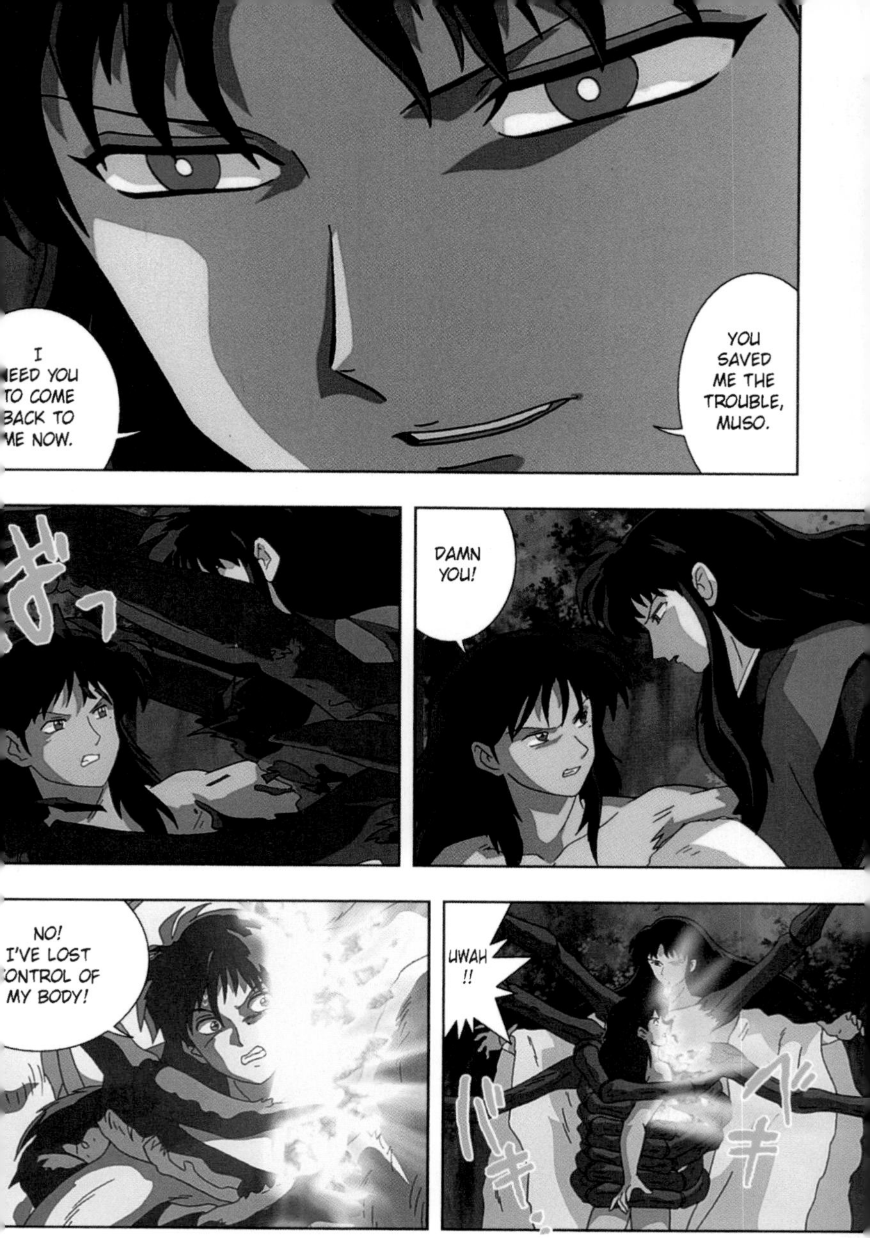

YOU SAVED ME THE TROUBLE, MUSO.
I NEED YOU TO COME BACK TO ME NOW.
DAMN YOU!
UWAH !!
NO! I'VE LOST CONTROL OF MY BODY!

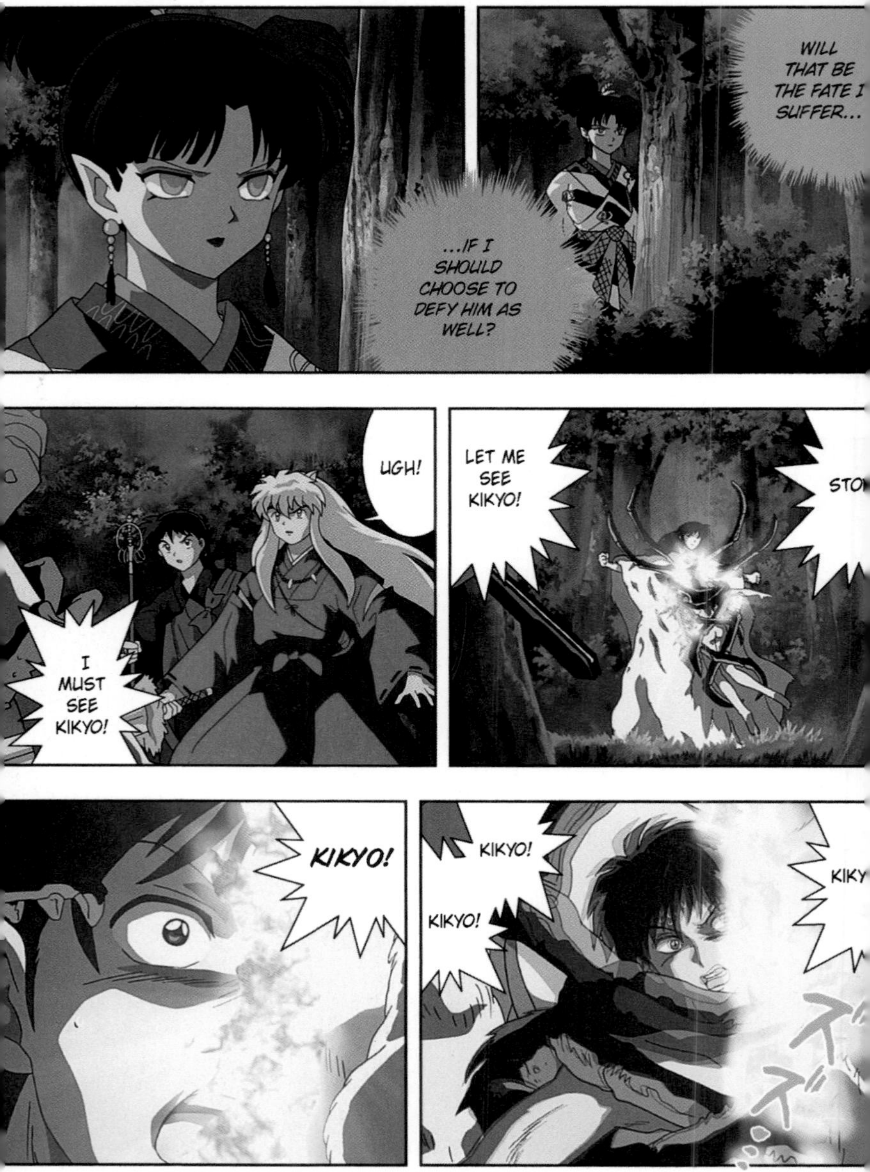

WILL THAT BE THE FATE I SUFFER...
...IF I SHOULD CHOOSE TO DEFY HIM AS WELL?
STO
LET ME SEE KIKYO!
UGH!
I MUST SEE KIKYO!
KIKY
KIKYO!
KIKYO!
ズ
ズ
KIKYO!

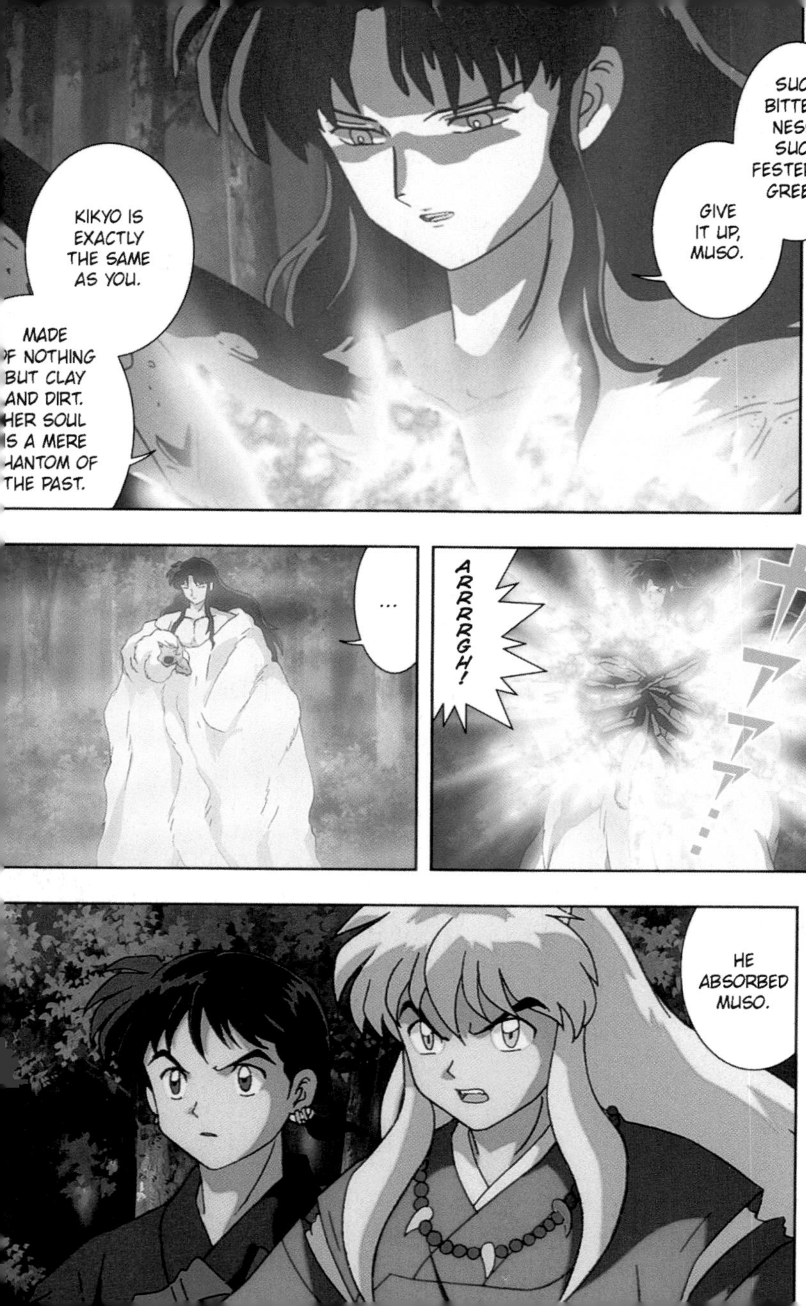
SUCH BITTERNESS. SUCH FESTERING GREED.
GIVE IT UP, MUSO.
KIKYO IS EXACTLY THE SAME AS YOU.
MADE OF NOTHING BUT CLAY AND DIRT. HER SOUL IS A MERE HANTOM OF THE PAST.
ARRRRGH!
カァァァ…
...
HE ABSORBED MUSO.

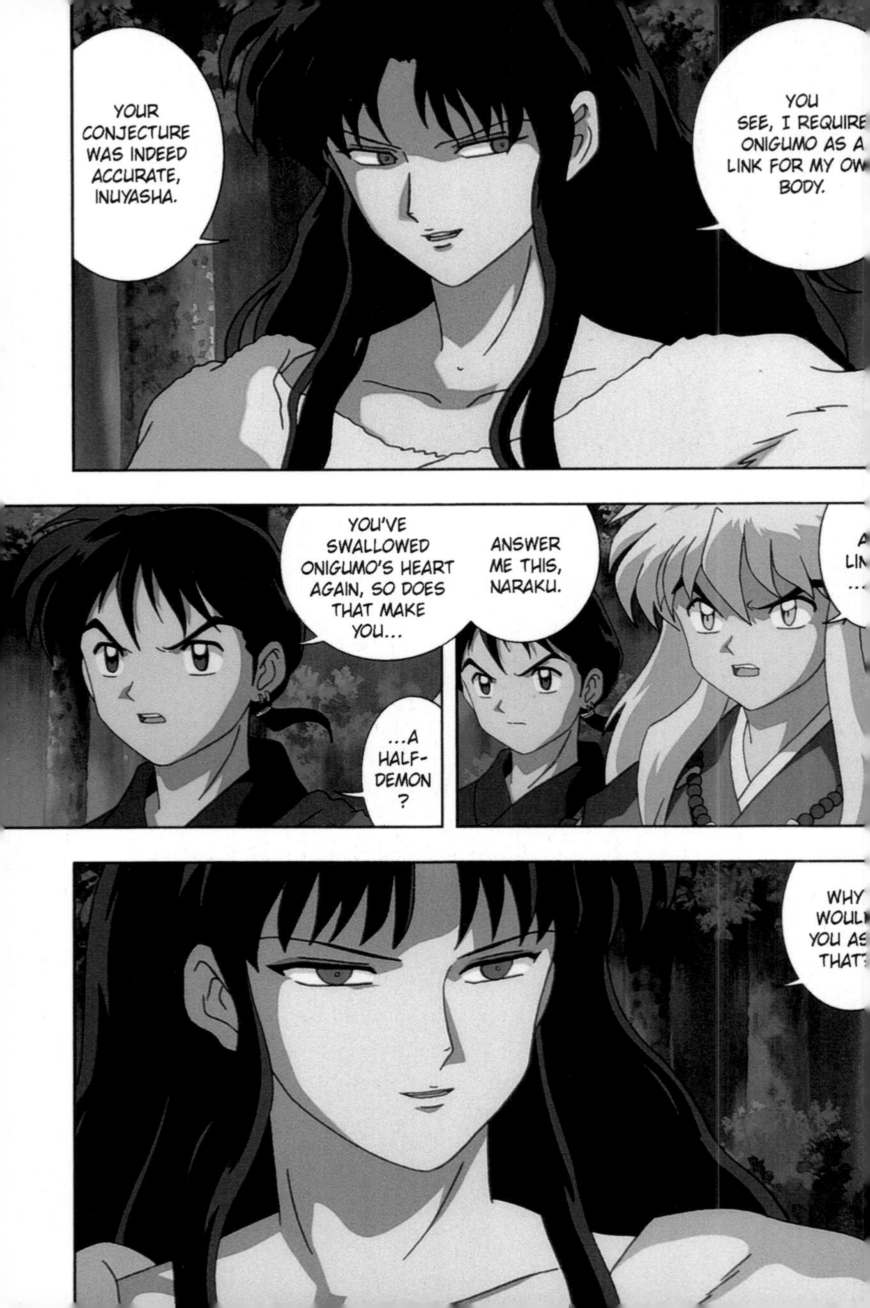
YOU SEE, I REQUIRE ONIGUMO AS A LINK FOR MY OW BODY.
YOUR CONJECTURE WAS INDEED ACCURATE, INUYASHA.
A LIN …
ANSWER ME THIS, NARAKU.
YOU'VE SWALLOWED ONIGUMO'S HEART AGAIN, SO DOES THAT MAKE YOU...
...A HALF-DEMON?
WHY WOUL YOU AS THAT

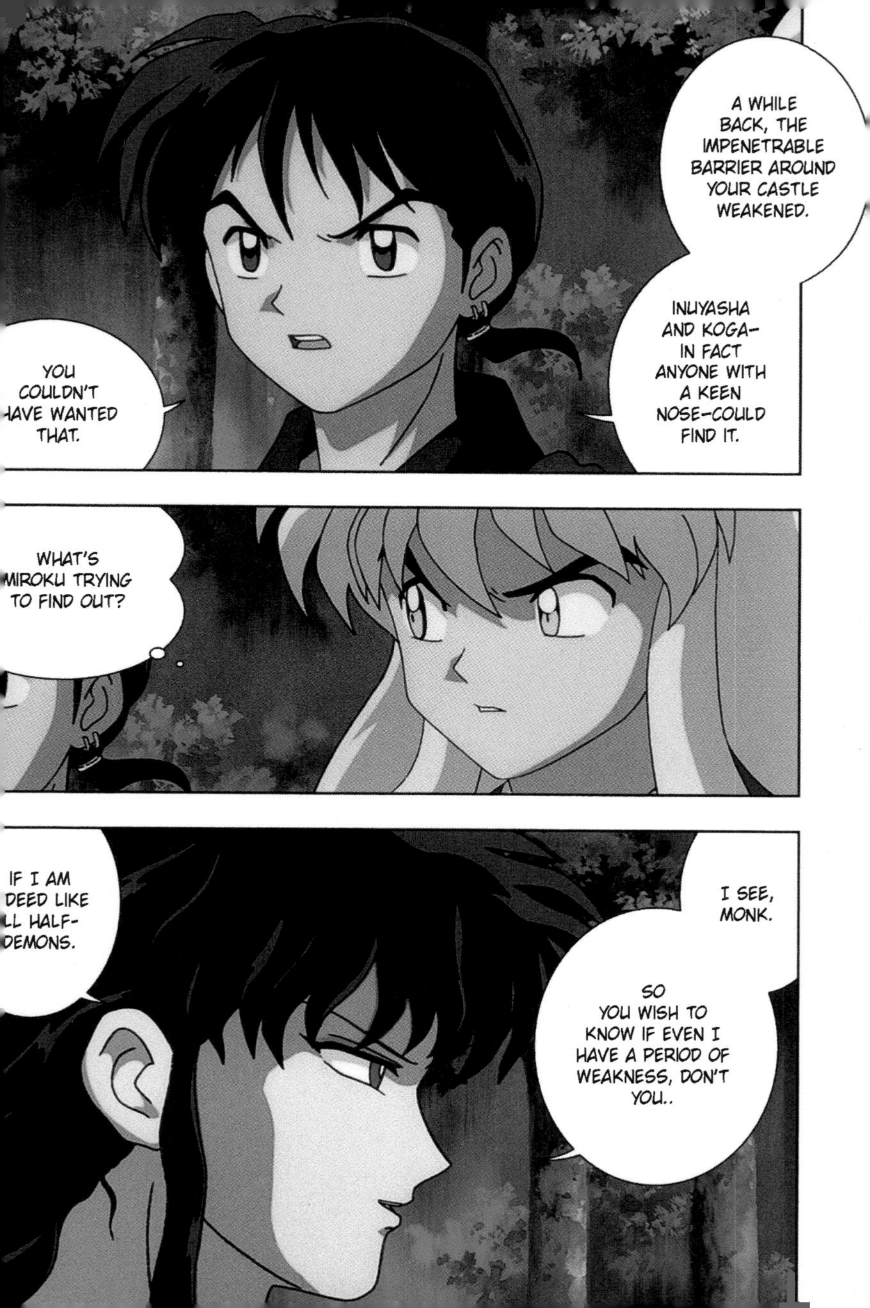
A WHILE BACK, THE IMPENETRABLE BARRIER AROUND YOUR CASTLE WEAKENED.
INUYASHA AND KOGA–IN FACT ANYONE WITH A KEEN NOSE–COULD FIND IT.
YOU COULDN'T HAVE WANTED THAT.
WHAT'S MIROKU TRYING TO FIND OUT?
I SEE, MONK.
SO YOU WISH TO KNOW IF EVEN I HAVE A PERIOD OF WEAKNESS, DON'T YOU..
IF I AM DEED LIKE LL HALF-DEMONS.

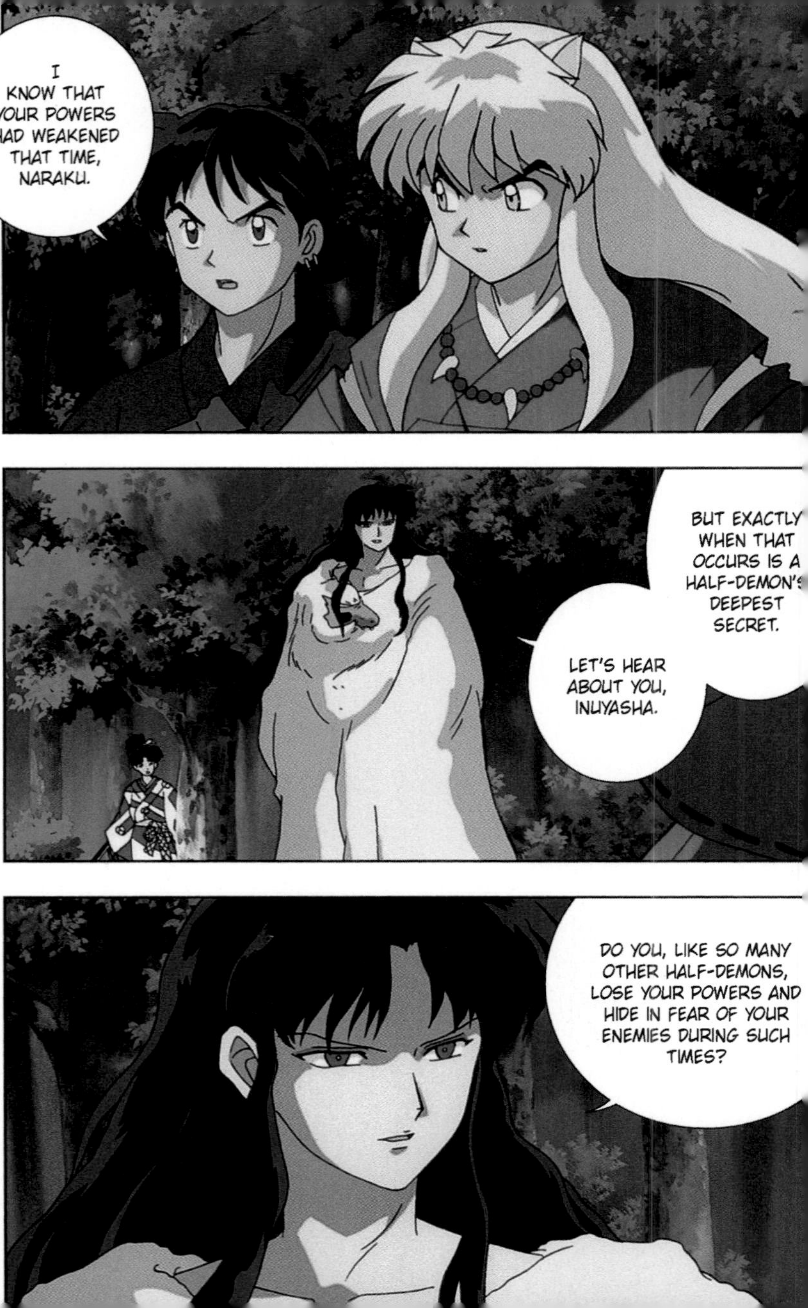
I KNOW THAT YOUR POWERS HAD WEAKENED THAT TIME, NARAKU.
BUT EXACTLY WHEN THAT OCCURS IS A HALF-DEMON'S DEEPEST SECRET.
LET'S HEAR ABOUT YOU, INUYASHA.
DO YOU, LIKE SO MANY OTHER HALF-DEMONS, LOSE YOUR POWERS AND HIDE IN FEAR OF YOUR ENEMIES DURING SUCH TIMES?

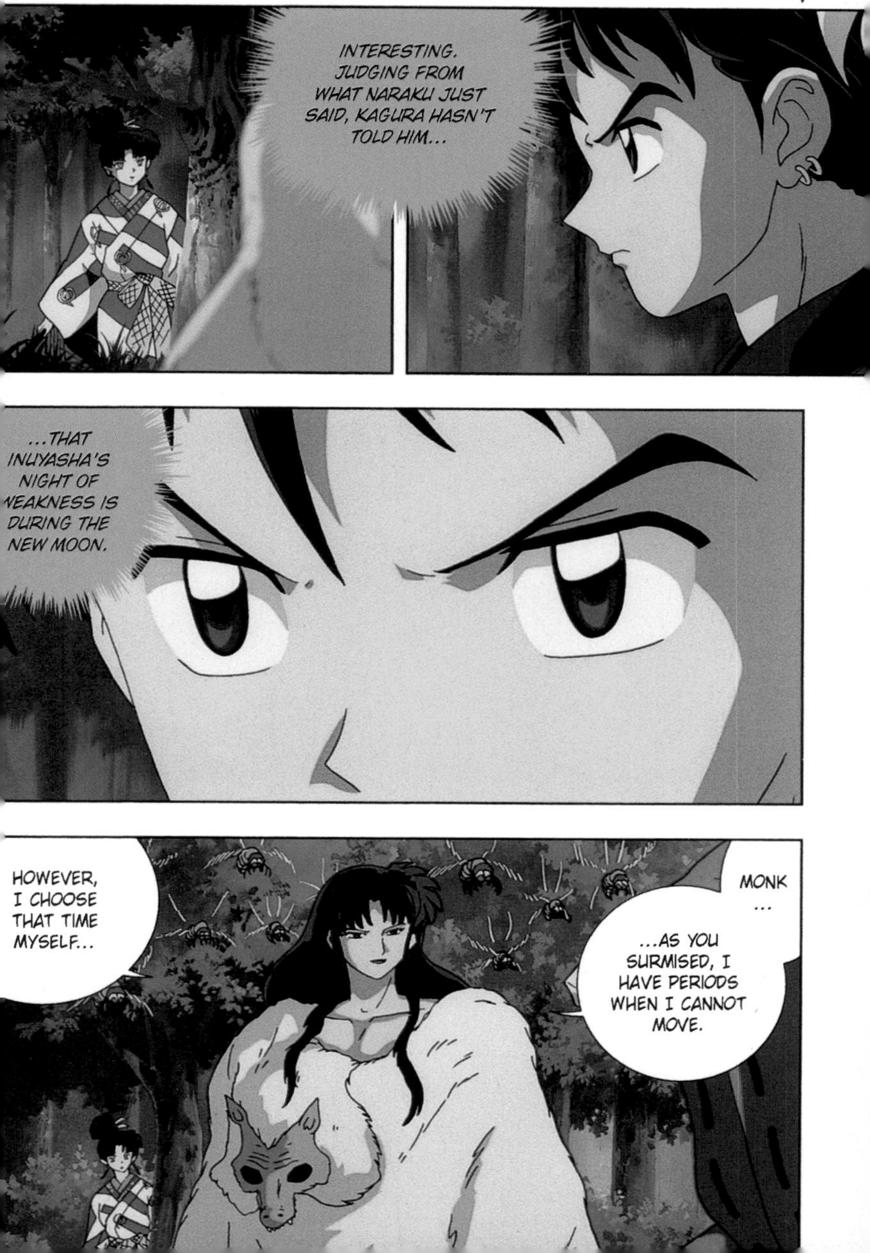
INTERESTING. JUDGING FROM WHAT NARAKU JUST SAID, KAGURA HASN'T TOLD HIM...
...THAT INUYASHA'S NIGHT OF WEAKNESS IS DURING THE NEW MOON.
MONK...
...AS YOU SURMISED, I HAVE PERIODS WHEN I CANNOT MOVE.
HOWEVER, I CHOOSE THAT TIME MYSELF...

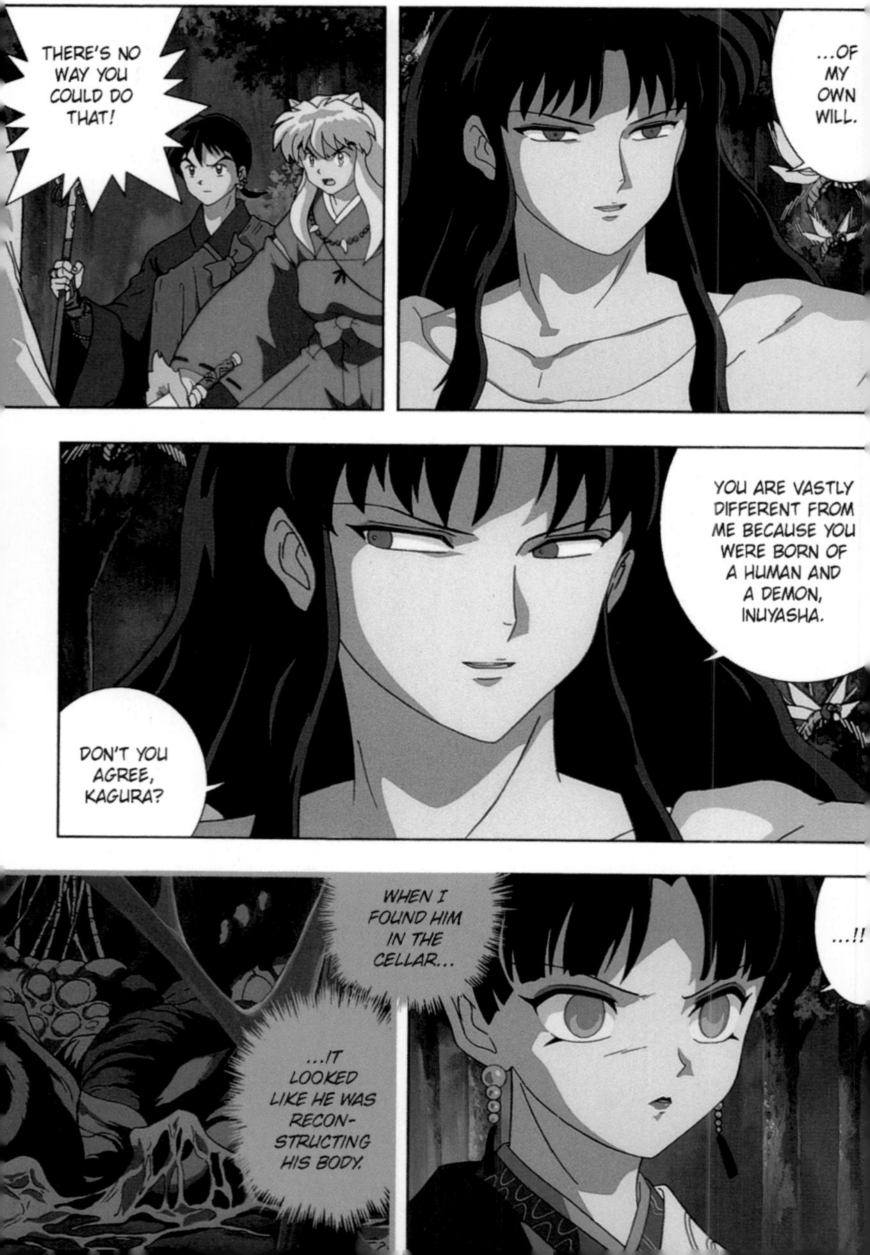
...OF MY OWN WILL.
THERE'S NO WAY YOU COULD DO THAT!
YOU ARE VASTLY DIFFERENT FROM ME BECAUSE YOU WERE BORN OF A HUMAN AND A DEMON, INUYASHA.
DON'T YOU AGREE, KAGURA?
...!!
WHEN I FOUND HIM IN THE CELLAR...
...IT LOOKED LIKE HE WAS RECON-STRUCTING HIS BODY.

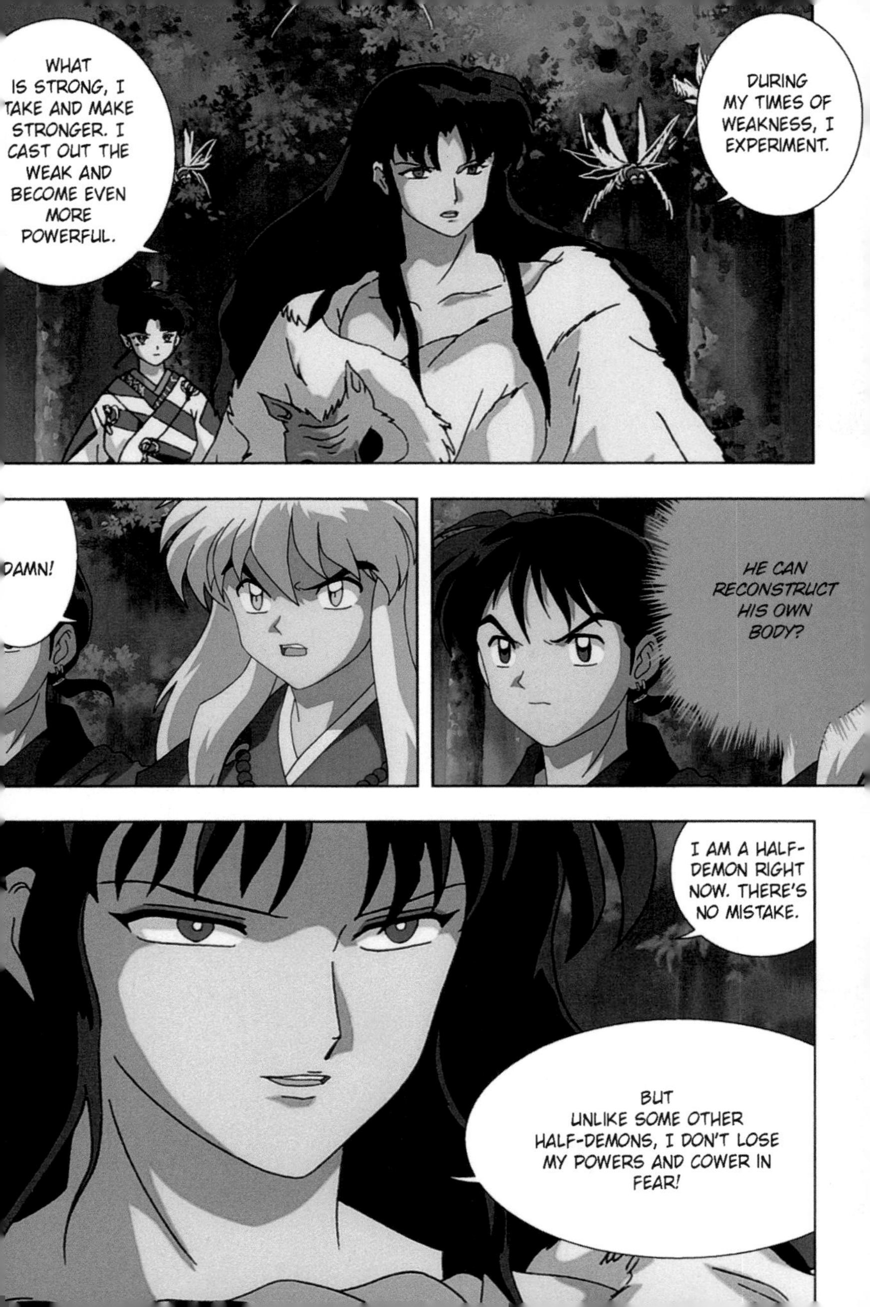
DURING MY TIMES OF WEAKNESS, I EXPERIMENT.
WHAT IS STRONG, I TAKE AND MAKE STRONGER. I CAST OUT THE WEAK AND BECOME EVEN MORE POWERFUL.
HE CAN RECONSTRUCT HIS OWN BODY?
DAMN!
I AM A HALF-DEMON RIGHT NOW. THERE'S NO MISTAKE.
BUT UNLIKE SOME OTHER HALF-DEMONS, I DON'T LOSE MY POWERS AND COWER IN FEAR!

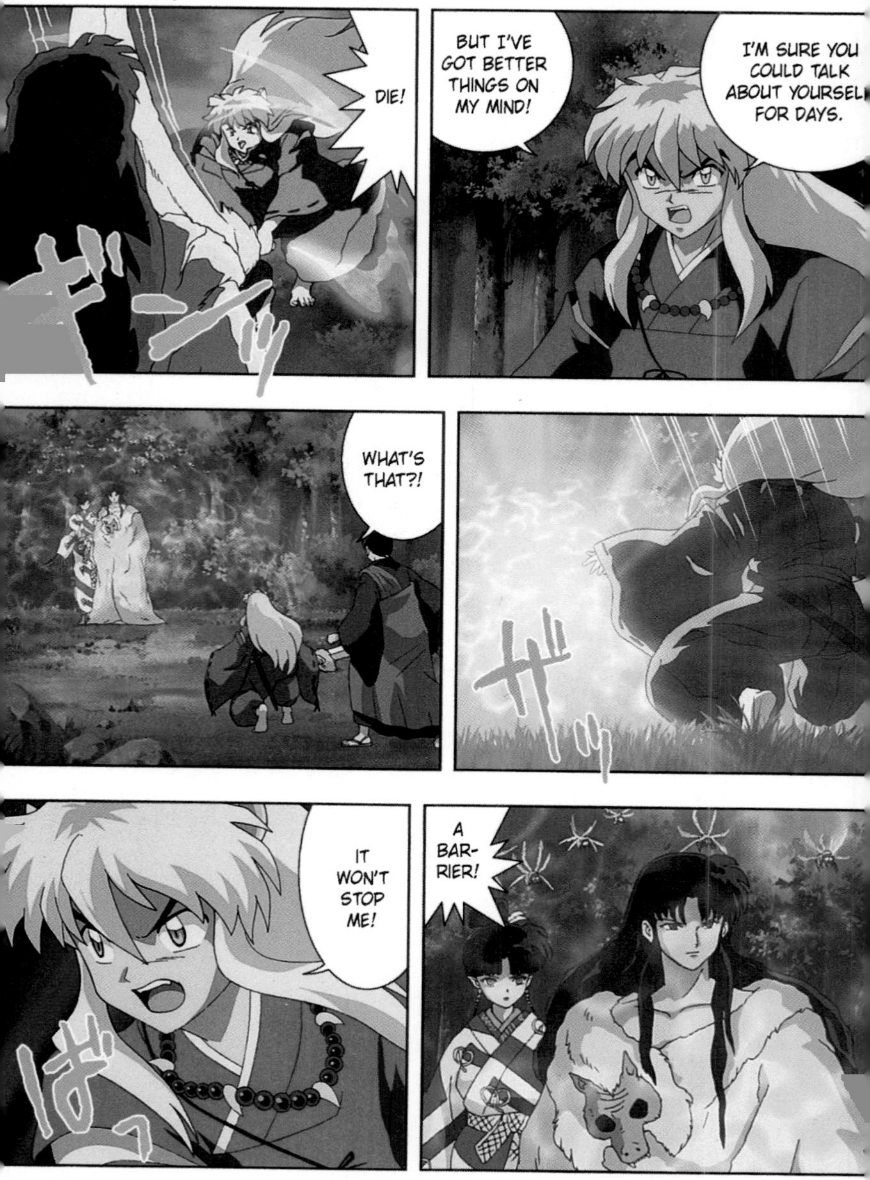
I'M SURE YOU COULD TALK ABOUT YOURSEL FOR DAYS.
BUT I'VE GOT BETTER THINGS ON MY MIND!
DIE!
ザッ
WHAT'S THAT?!
A BAR-RIER!
IT WON'T STOP ME!
ばっ

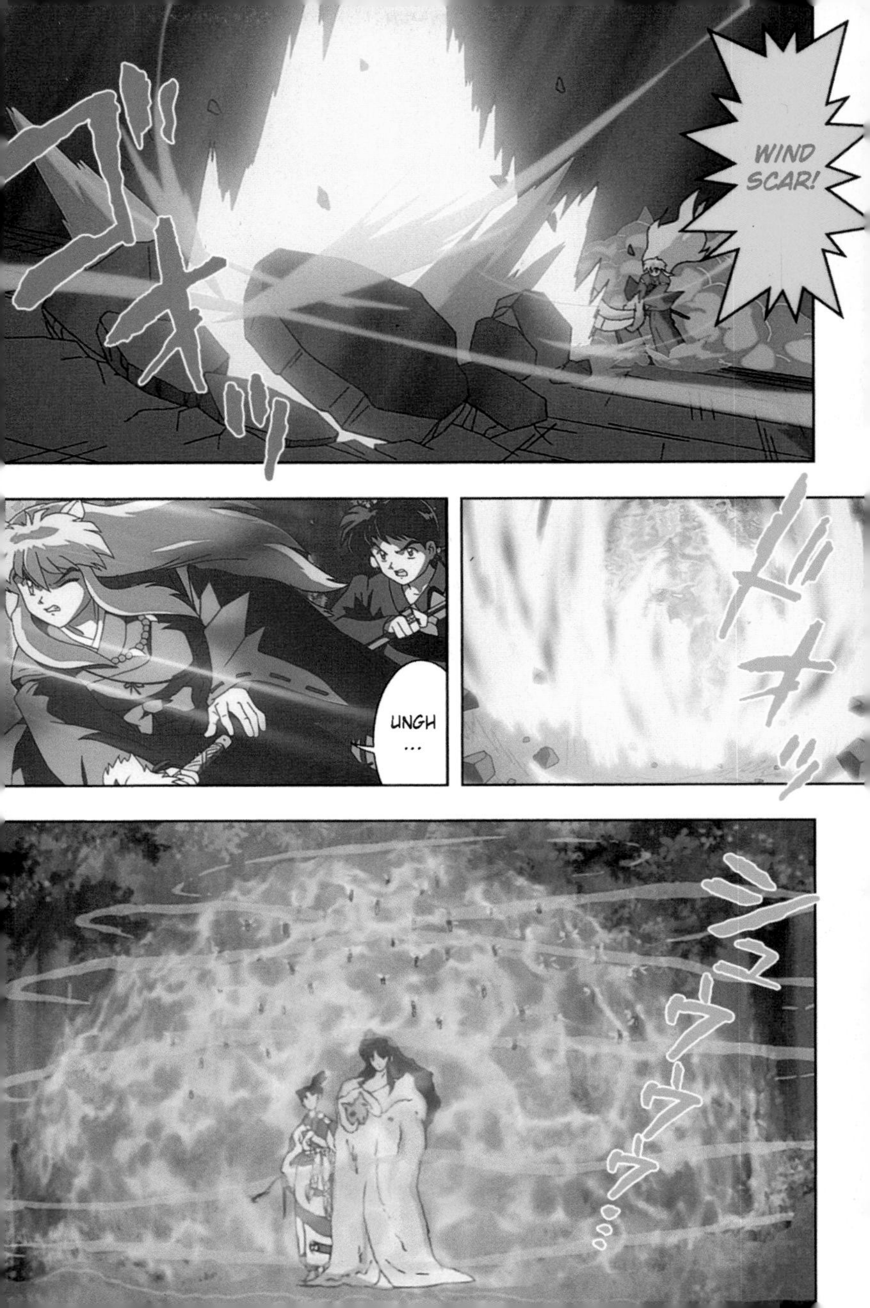
WIND SCAR!
ゴオッ
ドオッ
UNGH ...
シュウウウ...

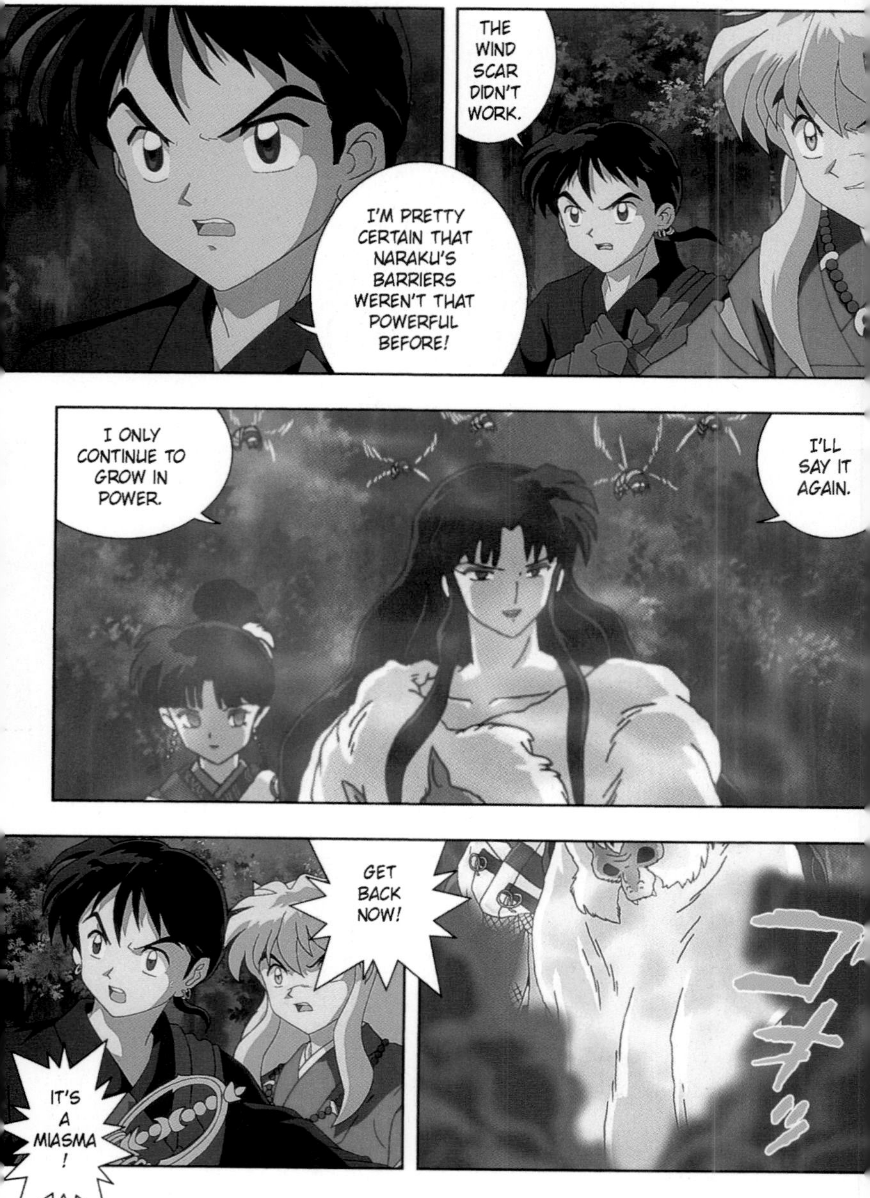
THE WIND SCAR DIDN'T WORK.
I'M PRETTY CERTAIN THAT NARAKU'S BARRIERS WEREN'T THAT POWERFUL BEFORE!
I'LL SAY IT AGAIN.
I ONLY CONTINUE TO GROW IN POWER.
GET BACK NOW!
IT'S A MIASMA!

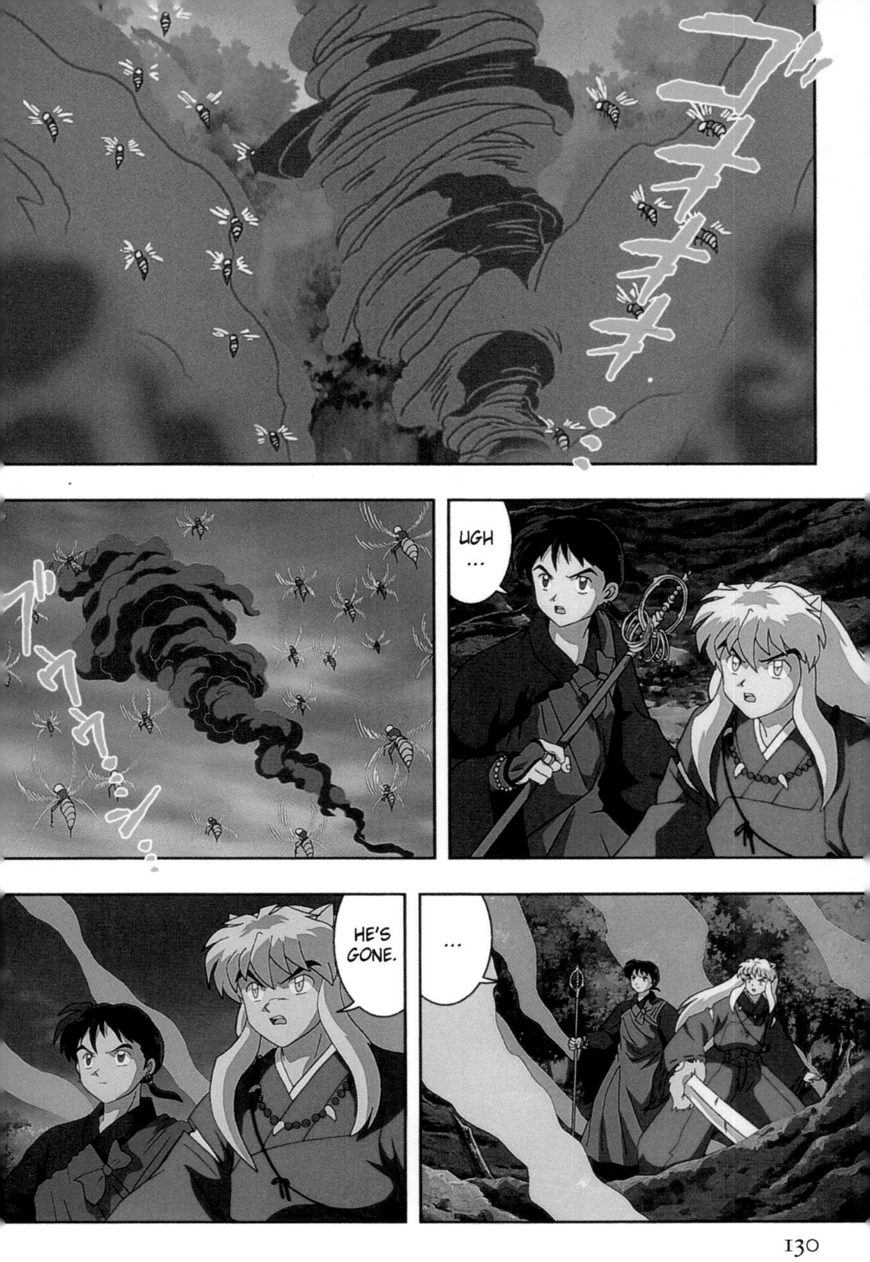
UGH ...
...
HE'S GONE.

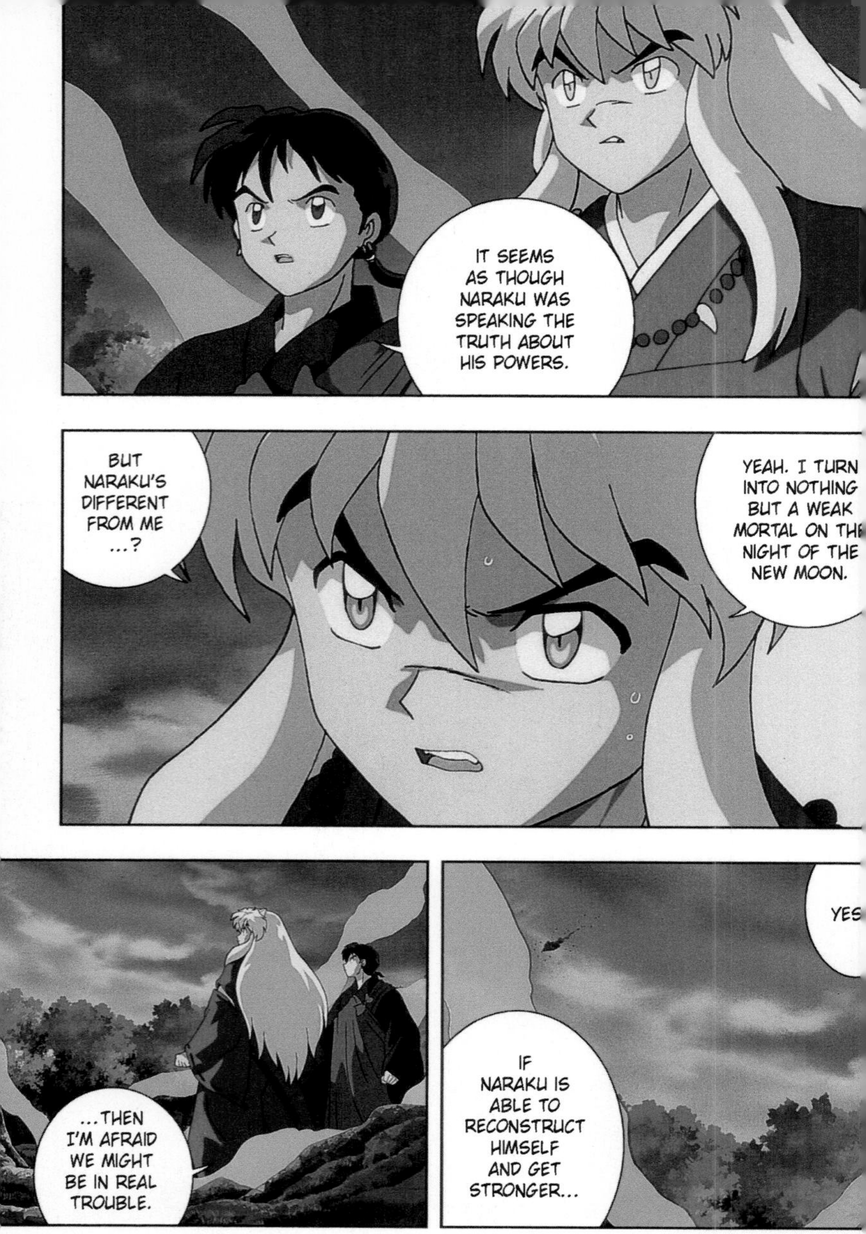
IT SEEMS AS THOUGH NARAKU WAS SPEAKING THE TRUTH ABOUT HIS POWERS.
YEAH. I TURN INTO NOTHING BUT A WEAK MORTAL ON THE NIGHT OF THE NEW MOON.
BUT NARAKU'S DIFFERENT FROM ME ...?
YES
IF NARAKU IS ABLE TO RECONSTRUCT HIMSELF AND GET STRONGER...
...THEN I'M AFRAID WE MIGHT BE IN REAL TROUBLE.

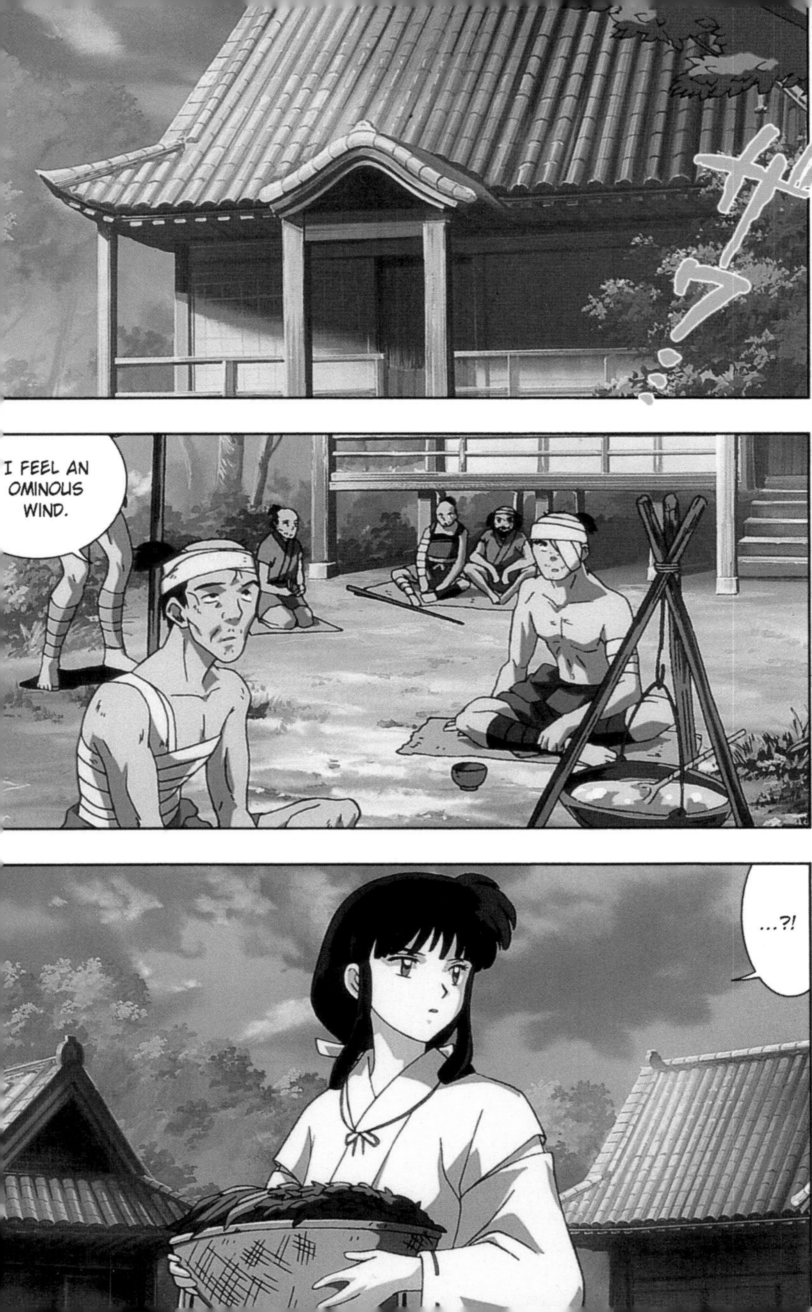
ザワ…
I FEEL AN OMINOUS WIND.
...?!

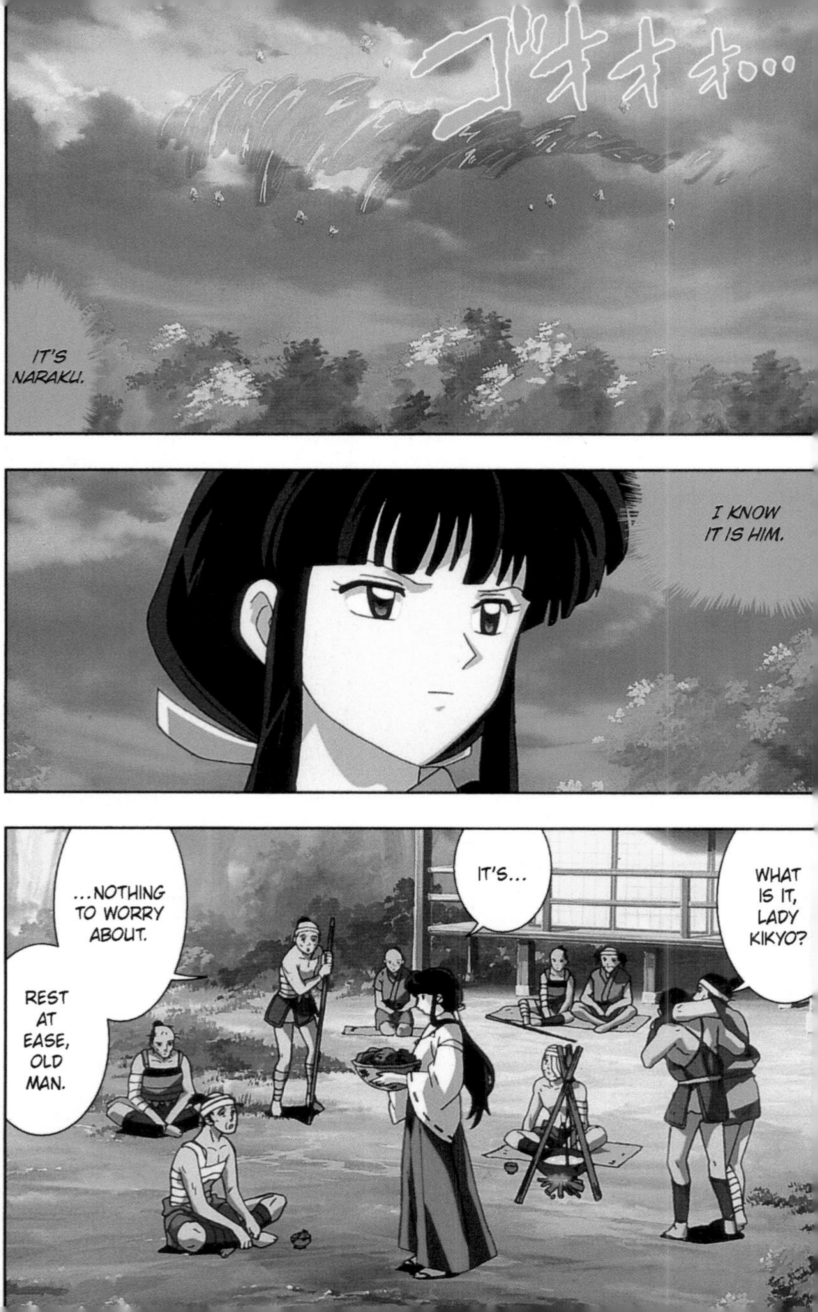
ゴオオオ…
IT'S NARAKU.
I KNOW IT IS HIM.
WHAT IS IT, LADY KIKYO?
IT'S…
…NOTHING TO WORRY ABOUT.
REST AT EASE, OLD MAN.

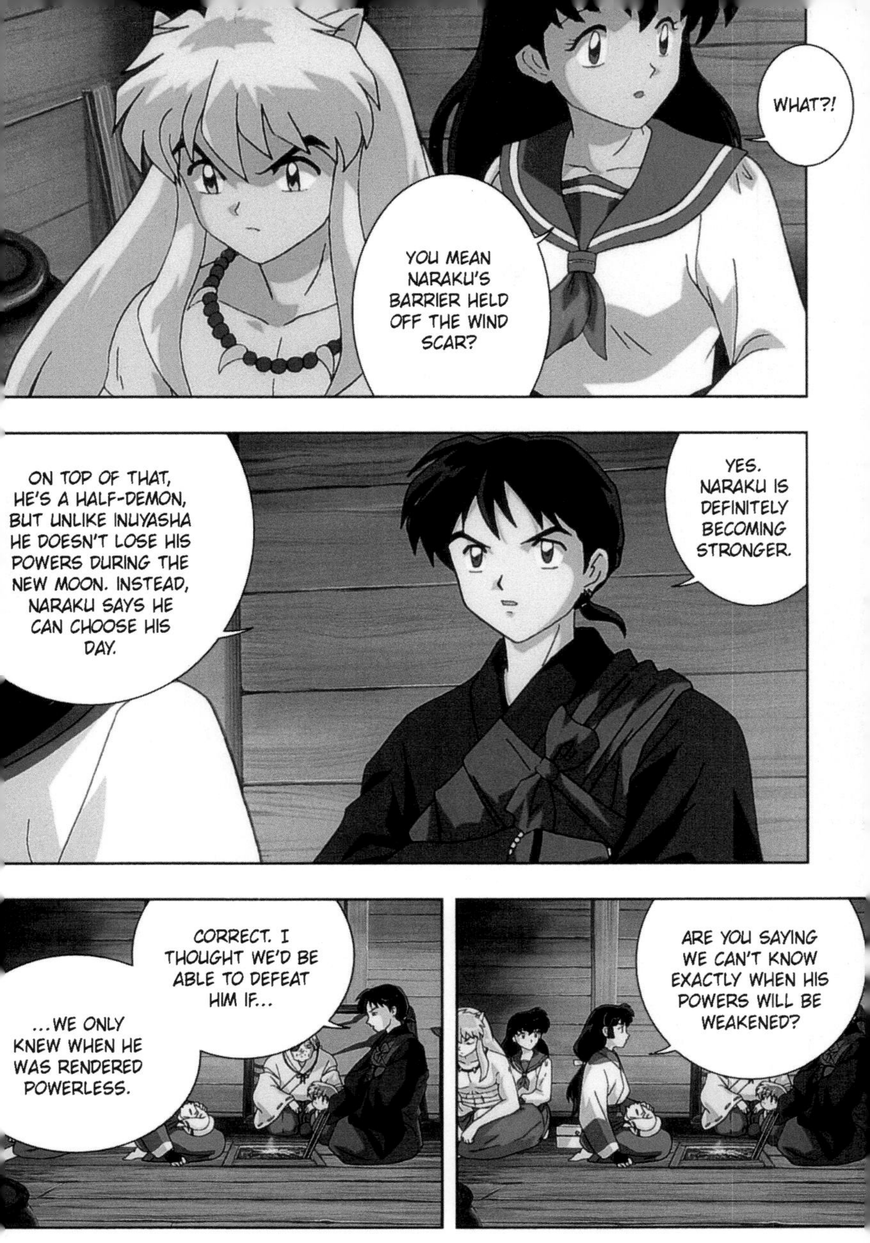
WHAT?!
YOU MEAN NARAKU'S BARRIER HELD OFF THE WIND SCAR?
YES. NARAKU IS DEFINITELY BECOMING STRONGER.
ON TOP OF THAT, HE'S A HALF-DEMON, BUT UNLIKE INUYASHA HE DOESN'T LOSE HIS POWERS DURING THE NEW MOON. INSTEAD, NARAKU SAYS HE CAN CHOOSE HIS DAY.
ARE YOU SAYING WE CAN'T KNOW EXACTLY WHEN HIS POWERS WILL BE WEAKENED?
CORRECT. I THOUGHT WE'D BE ABLE TO DEFEAT HIM IF...
...WE ONLY KNEW WHEN HE WAS RENDERED POWERLESS.

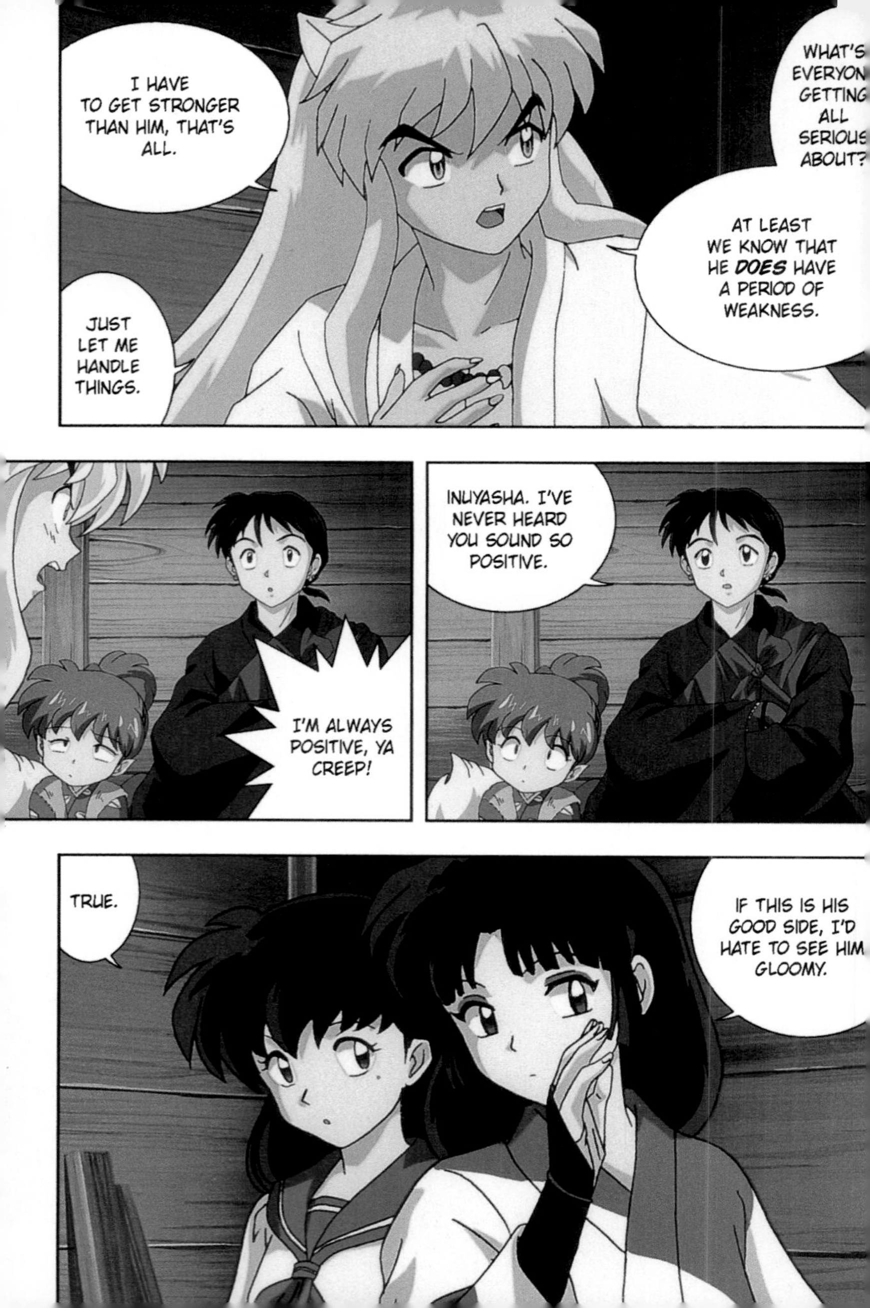
WHAT'S EVERYON GETTING ALL SERIOUS ABOUT?
AT LEAST WE KNOW THAT HE *DOES* HAVE A PERIOD OF WEAKNESS.
I HAVE TO GET STRONGER THAN HIM, THAT'S ALL.
JUST LET ME HANDLE THINGS.
INUYASHA. I'VE NEVER HEARD YOU SOUND SO POSITIVE.
I'M ALWAYS POSITIVE, YA CREEP!
IF THIS IS HIS GOOD SIDE, I'D HATE TO SEE HIM GLOOMY.
TRUE.

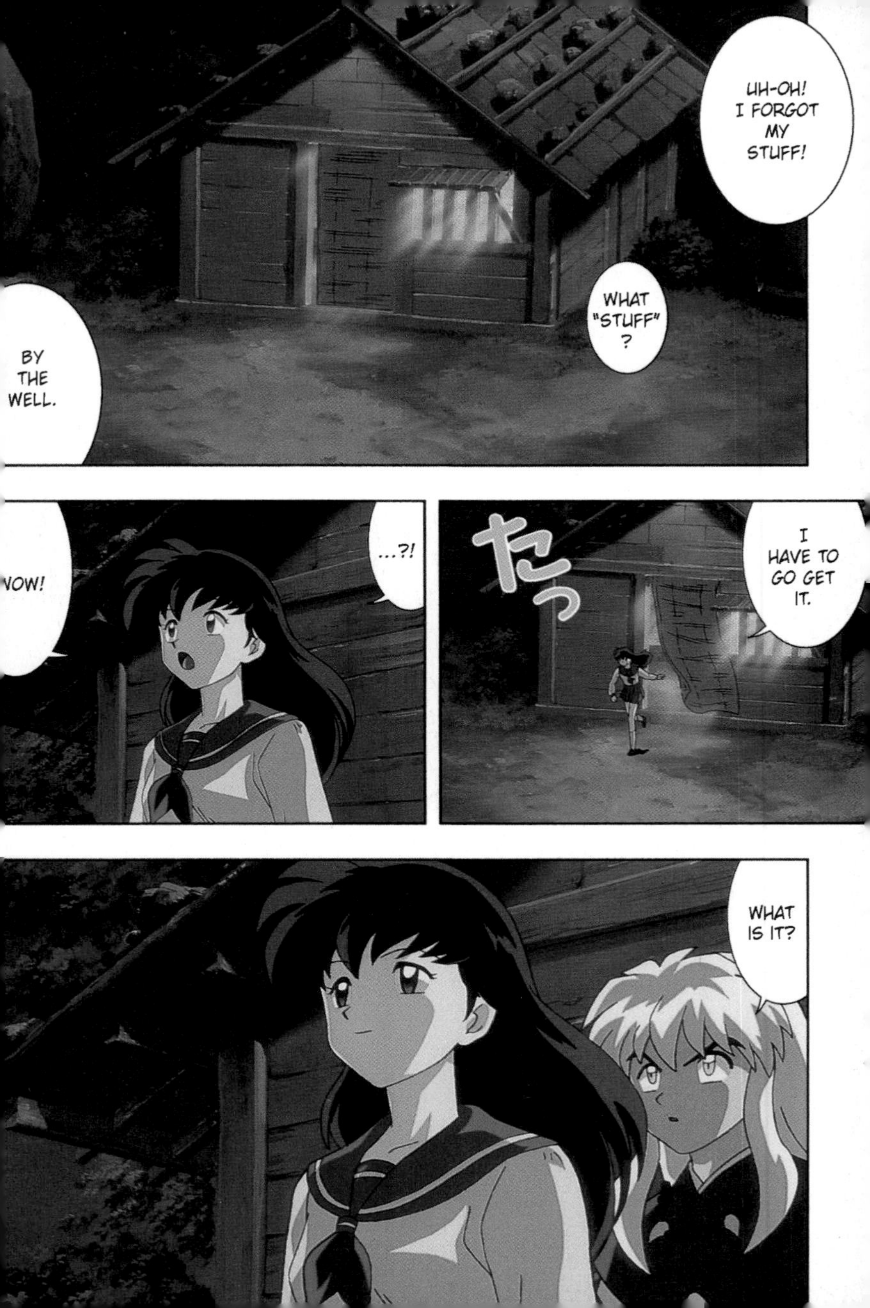

UH-OH! I FORGOT MY STUFF!
WHAT "STUFF"?
BY THE WELL.
I HAVE TO GO GET IT.
たっ
...?!
NOW!
WHAT IS IT?

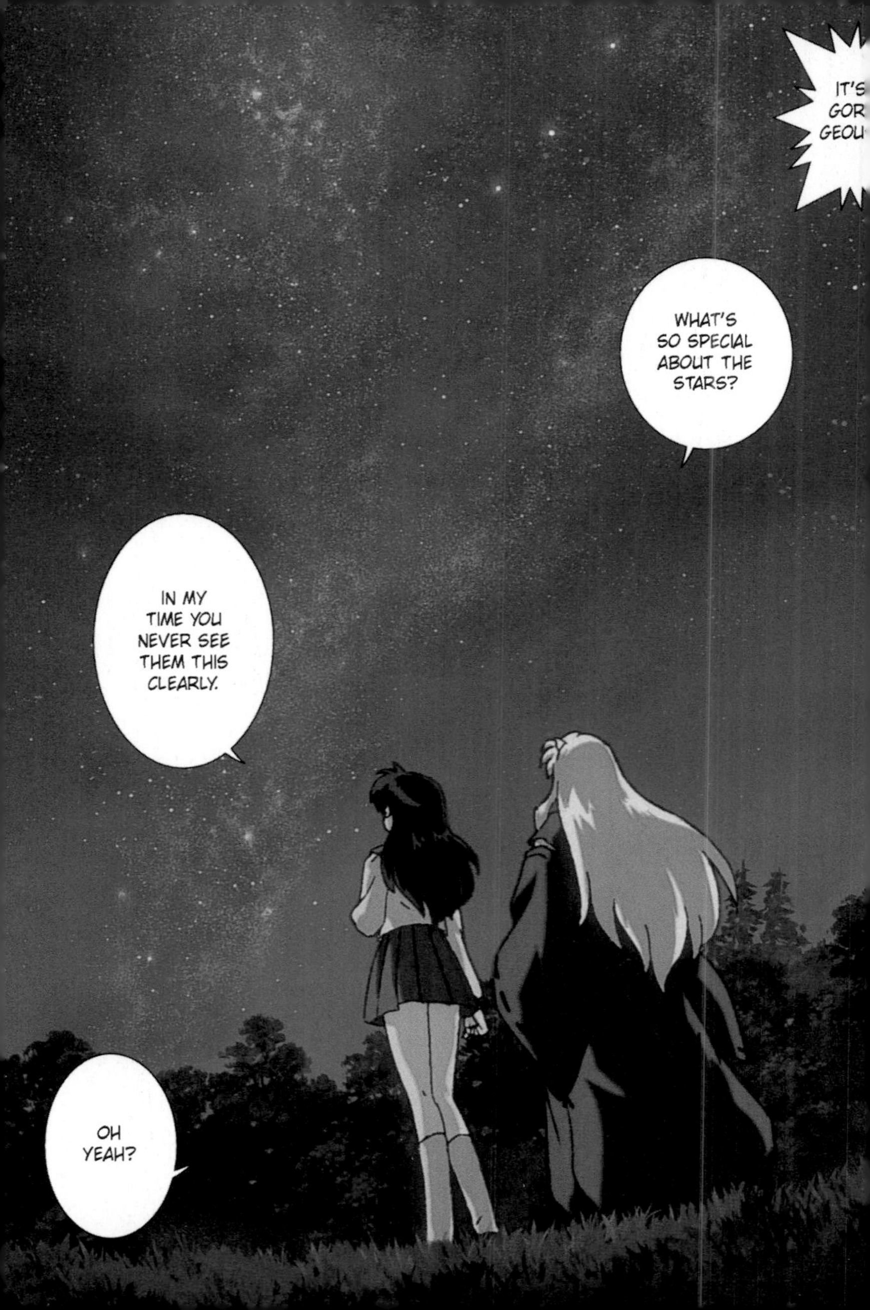
IT'S
WHAT'S SO SPECIAL ABOUT THE STARS?
IN MY TIME YOU NEVER SEE THEM THIS CLEARLY.
OH YEAH?

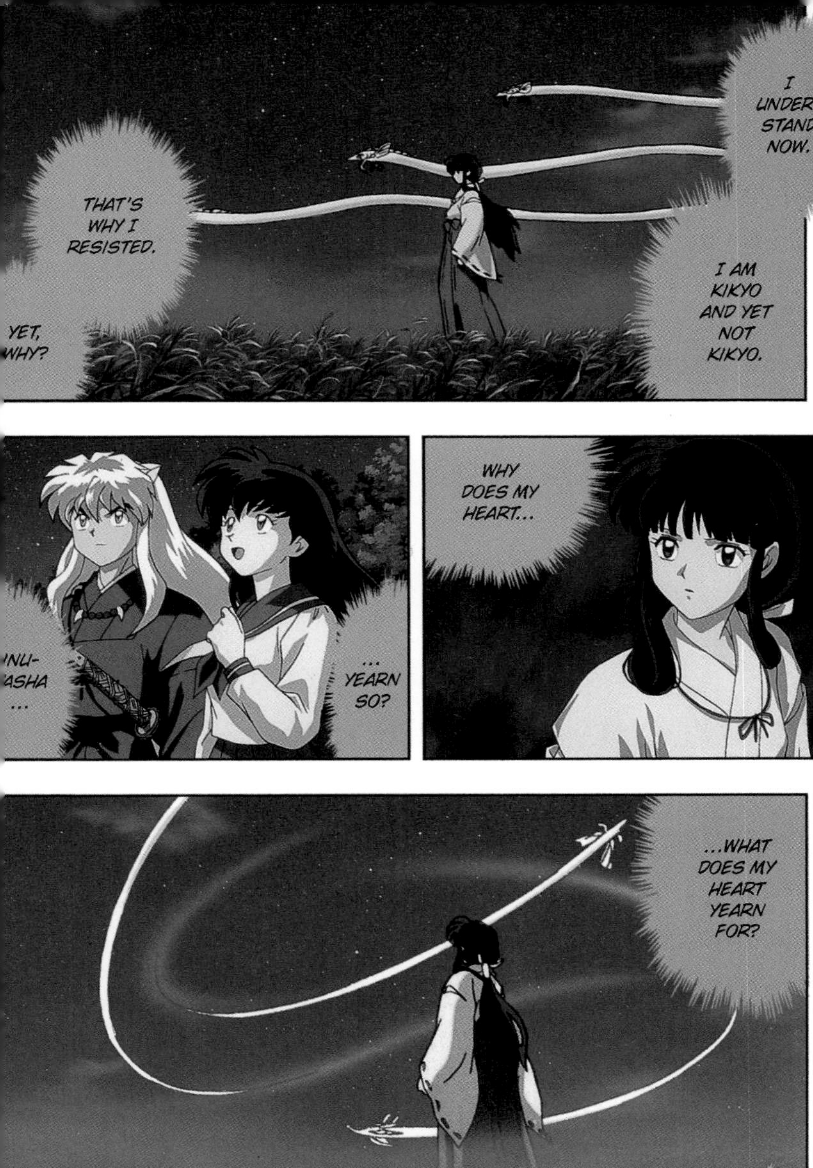
I UNDER-STAND NOW.
I AM KIKYO AND YET NOT KIKYO.
THAT'S WHY I RESISTED.
YET, WHY?
WHY DOES MY HEART...
...YEARN SO?
NU-ASHA ...
...WHAT DOES MY HEART YEARN FOR?

72
Totosai's Strange Training

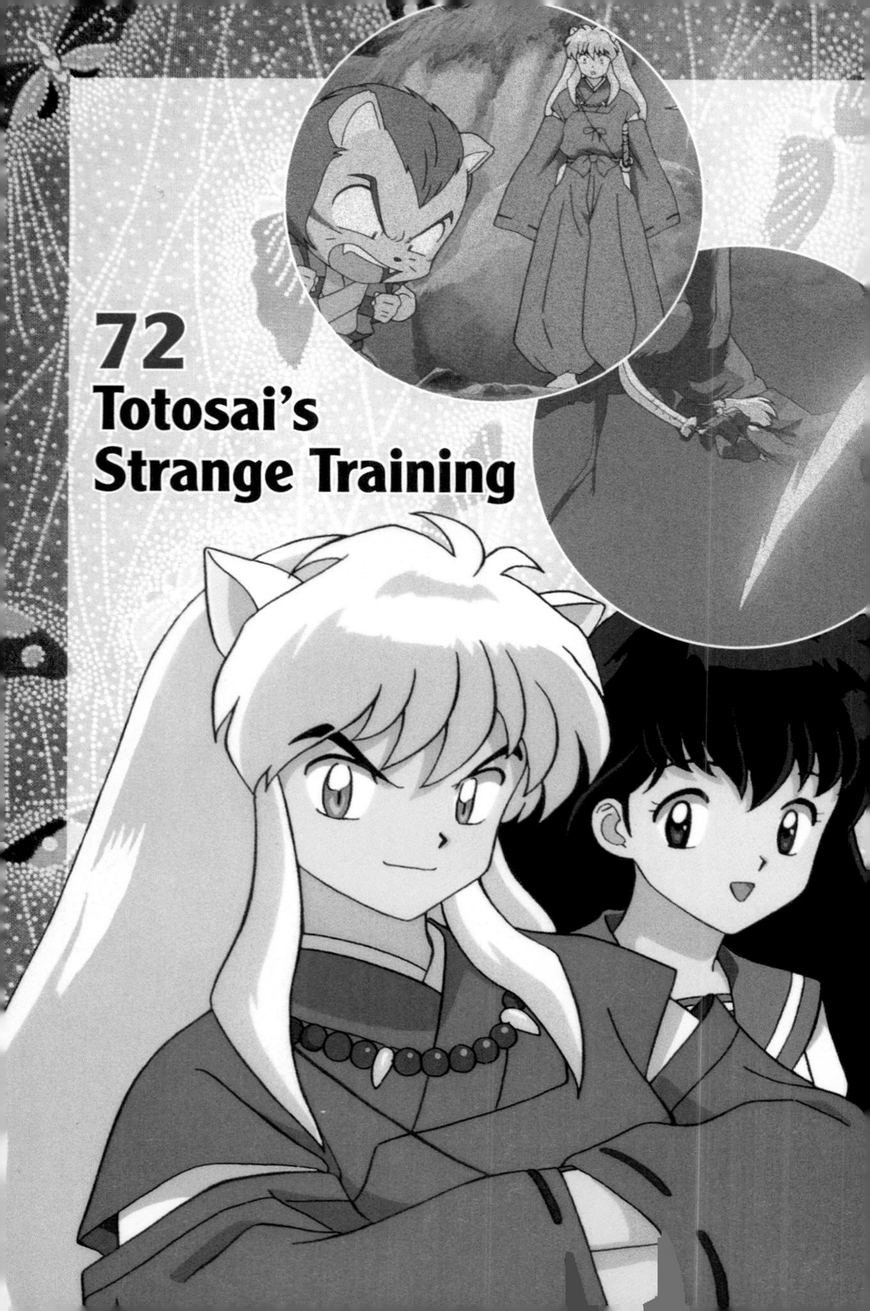

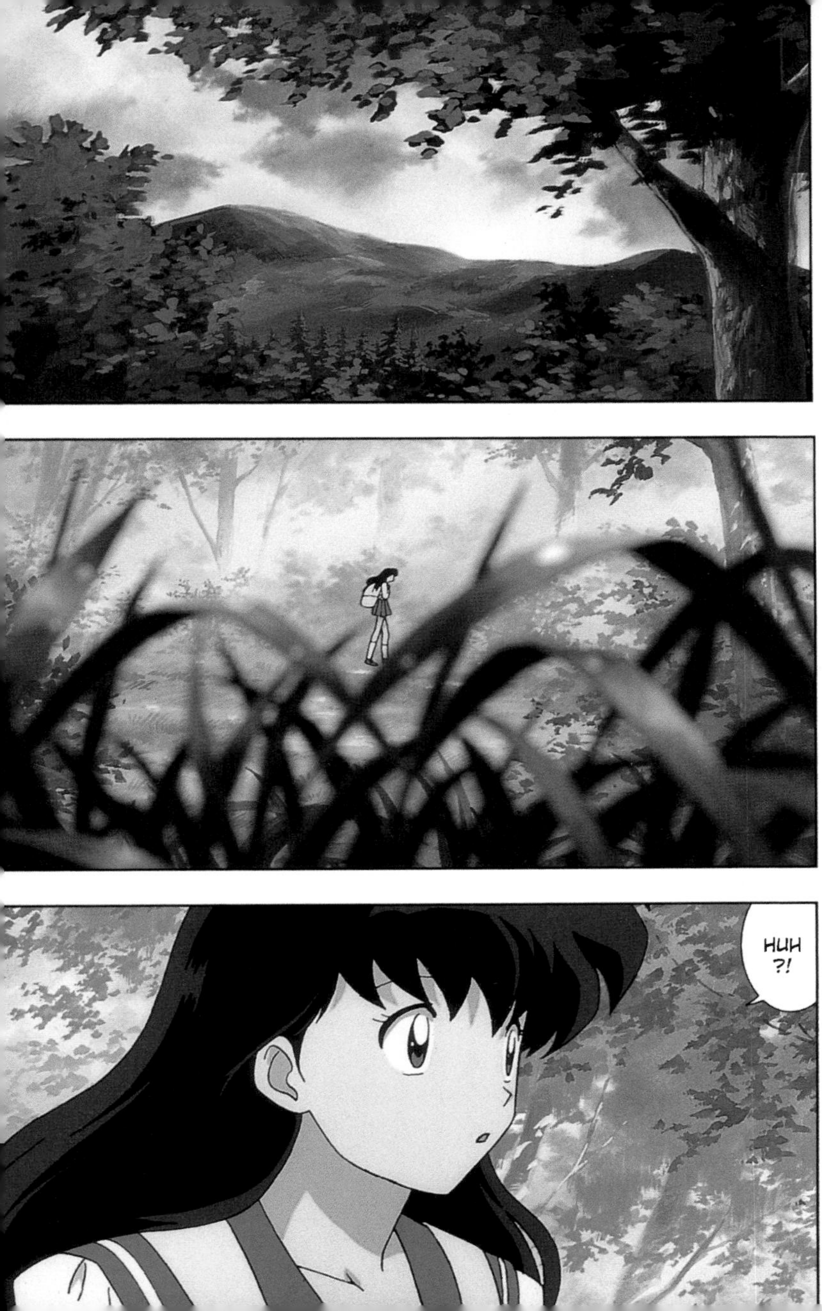
HUH ?!

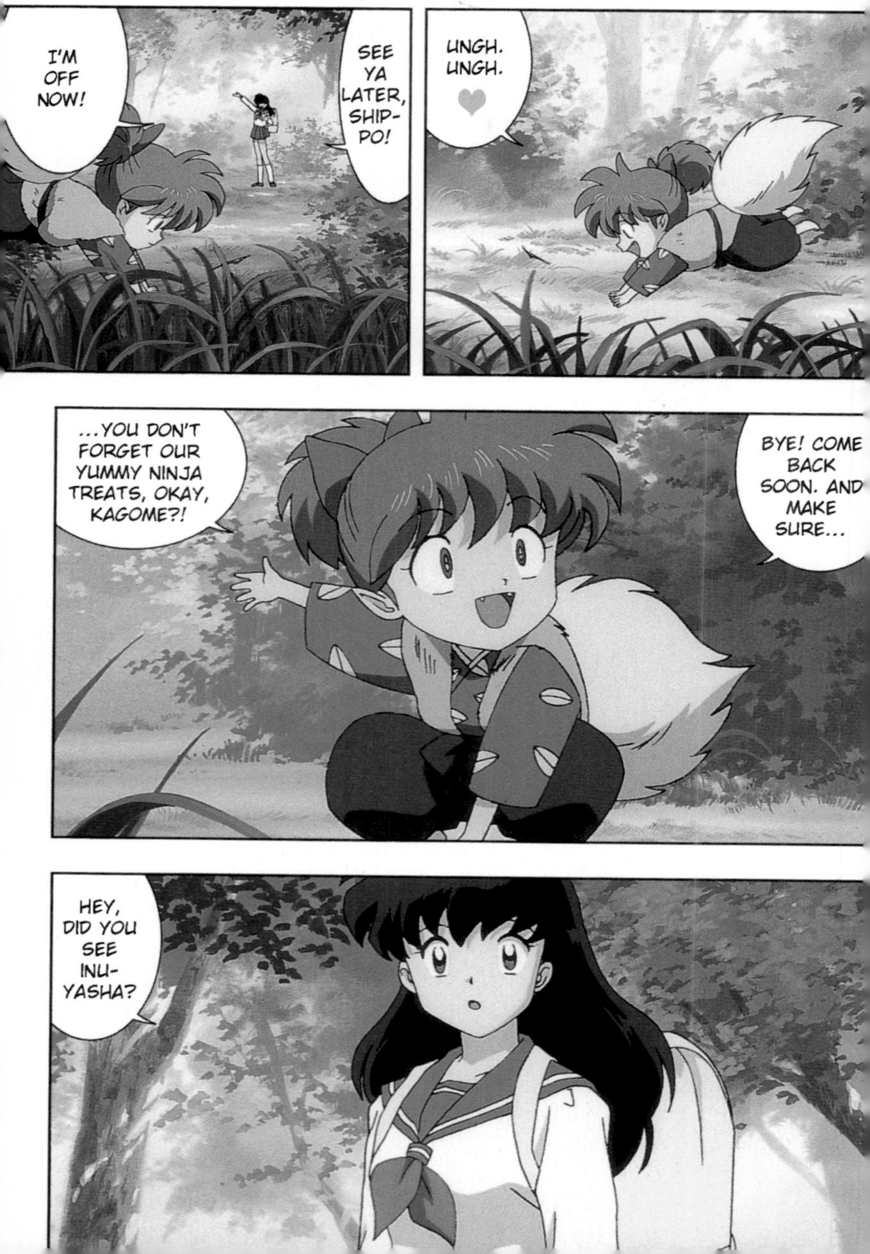
UNGH. UNGH. ♥
SEE YA LATER, SHIP-PO!
I'M OFF NOW!
BYE! COME BACK SOON. AND MAKE SURE...
...YOU DON'T FORGET OUR YUMMY NINJA TREATS, OKAY, KAGOME?!
HEY, DID YOU SEE INU-YASHA?

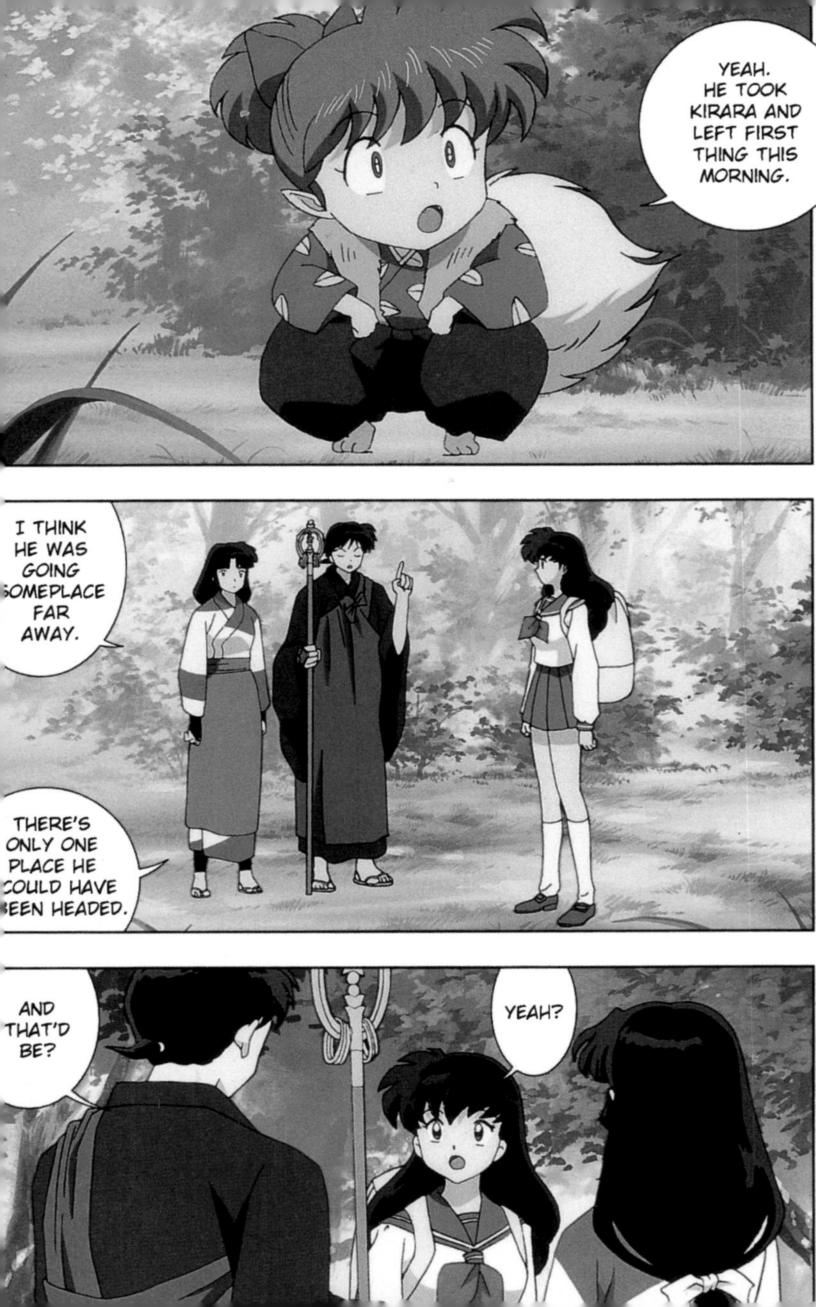
YEAH. HE TOOK KIRARA AND LEFT FIRST THING THIS MORNING.
I THINK HE WAS GOING SOMEPLACE FAR AWAY.
THERE'S ONLY ONE PLACE HE COULD HAVE BEEN HEADED.
YEAH?
AND THAT'D BE?

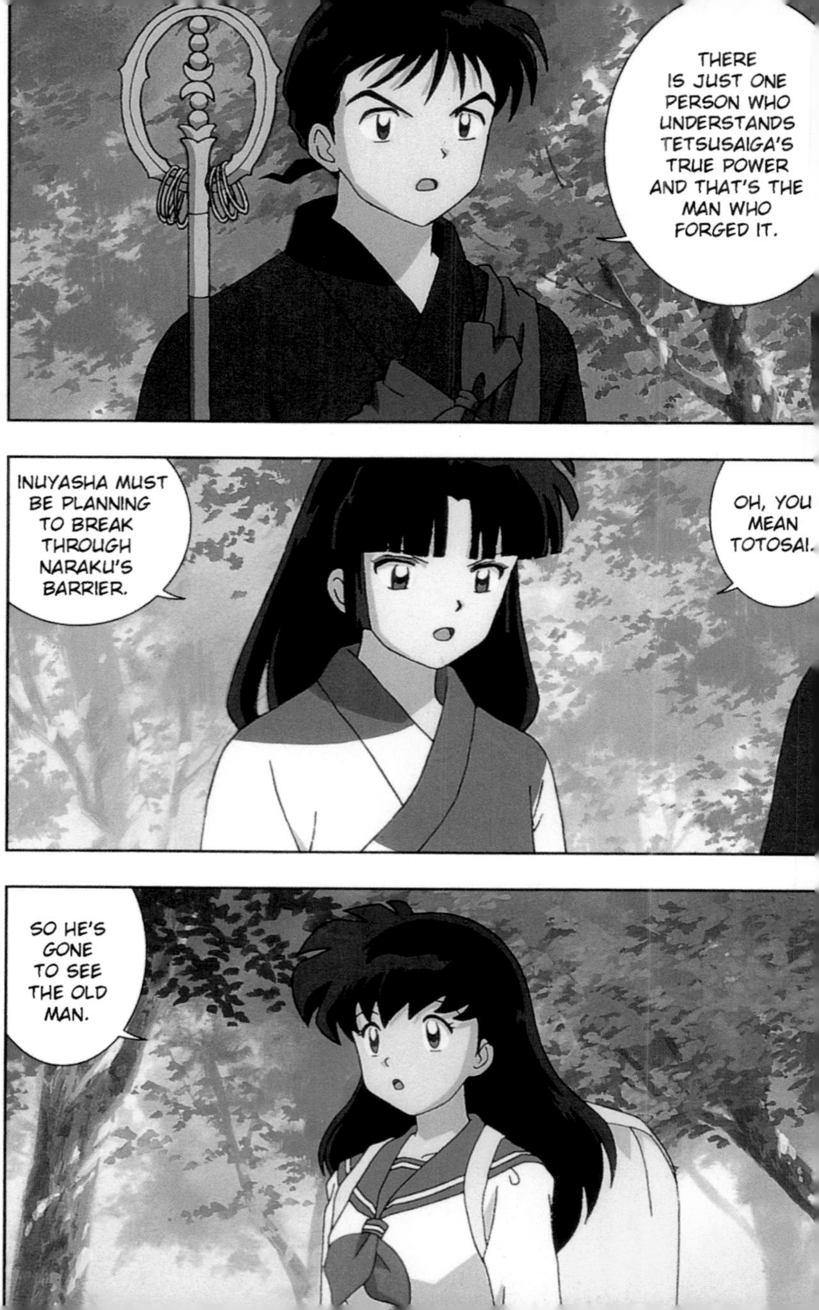
THERE IS JUST ONE PERSON WHO UNDERSTANDS TETSUSAIGA'S TRUE POWER AND THAT'S THE MAN WHO FORGED IT.
OH, YOU MEAN TOTOSAI.
INUYASHA MUST BE PLANNING TO BREAK THROUGH NARAKU'S BARRIER.
SO HE'S GONE TO SEE THE OLD MAN.

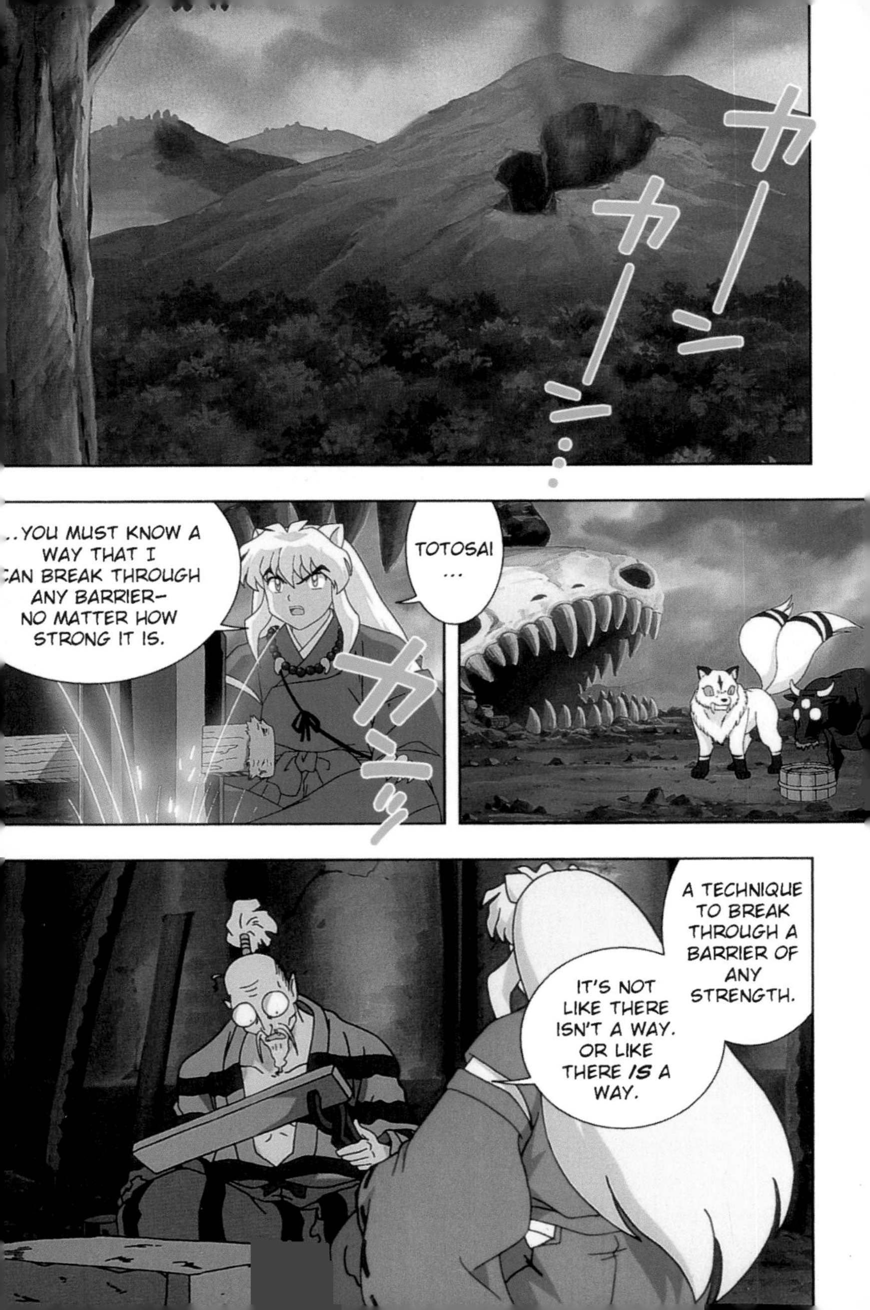

カーン
カーン…
TOTOSAI ...
..YOU MUST KNOW A WAY THAT I CAN BREAK THROUGH ANY BARRIER– NO MATTER HOW STRONG IT IS.
カンッ
A TECHNIQUE TO BREAK THROUGH A BARRIER OF ANY STRENGTH.
IT'S NOT LIKE THERE ISN'T A WAY. OR LIKE THERE *IS* A WAY.

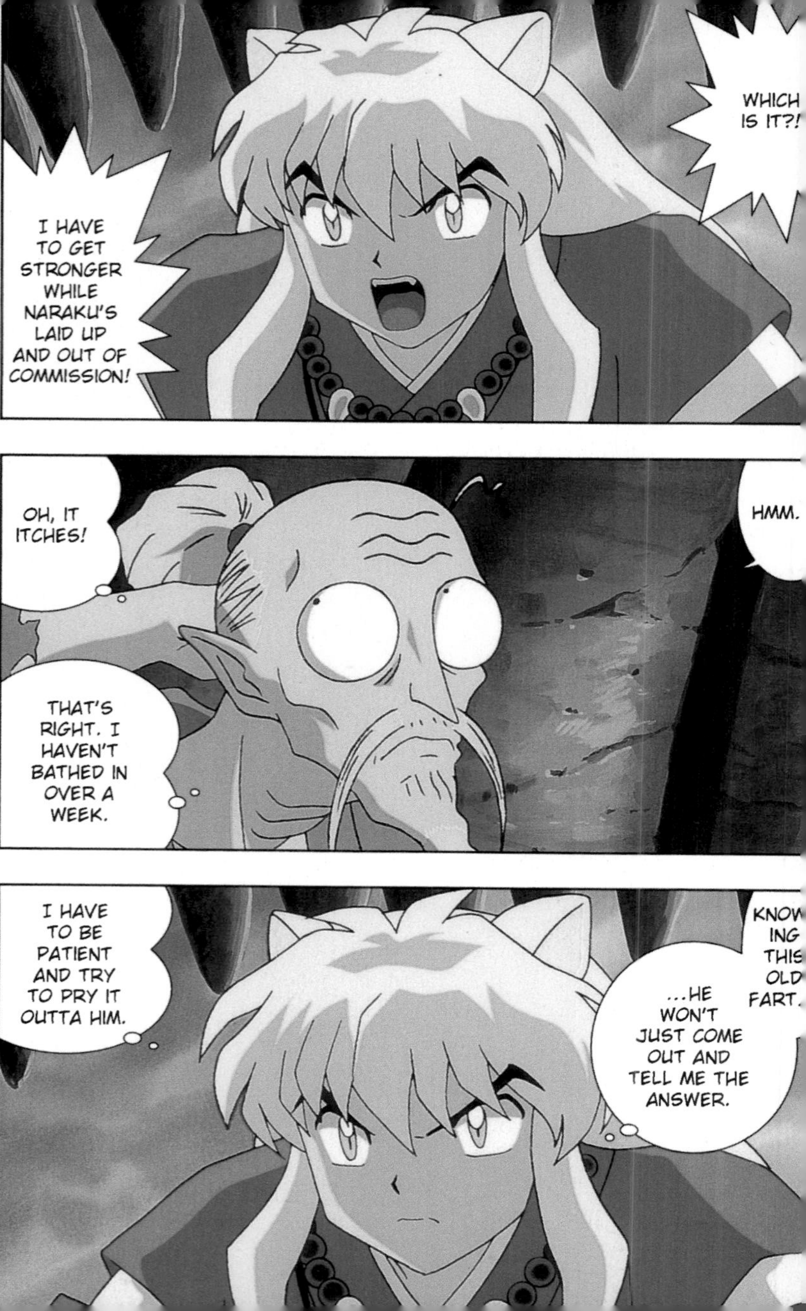
WHICH IS IT?!
I HAVE TO GET STRONGER WHILE NARAKU'S LAID UP AND OUT OF COMMISSION!
HMM.
OH, IT ITCHES!
THAT'S RIGHT. I HAVEN'T BATHED IN OVER A WEEK.
KNOWING THIS OLD FART.
...HE WON'T JUST COME OUT AND TELL ME THE ANSWER.
I HAVE TO BE PATIENT AND TRY TO PRY IT OUTTA HIM.

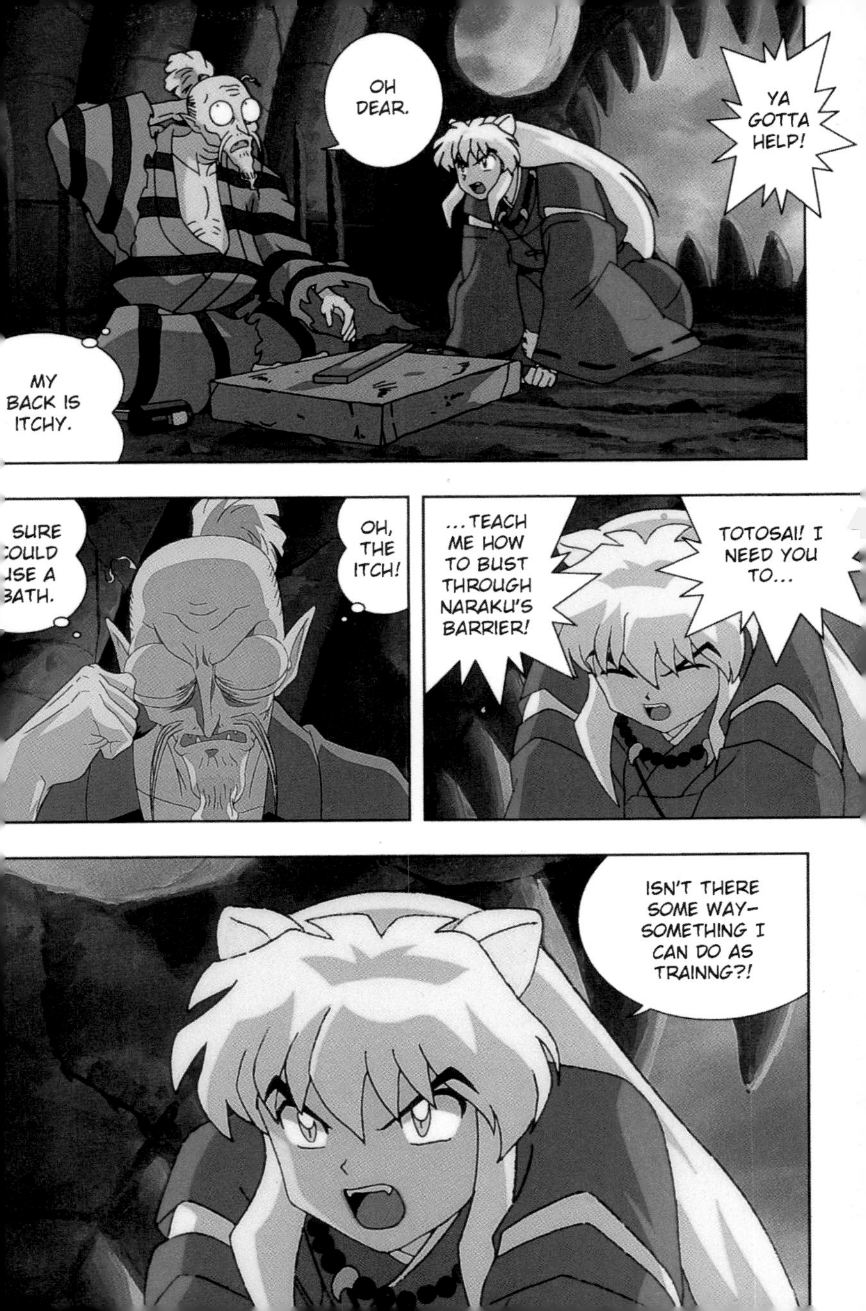
YA GOTTA HELP!
OH DEAR.
MY BACK IS ITCHY.
TOTOSAI! I NEED YOU TO...
...TEACH ME HOW TO BUST THROUGH NARAKU'S BARRIER!
OH, THE ITCH!
SURE COULD USE A BATH.
ISN'T THERE SOME WAY- SOMETHING I CAN DO AS TRAINNG?!

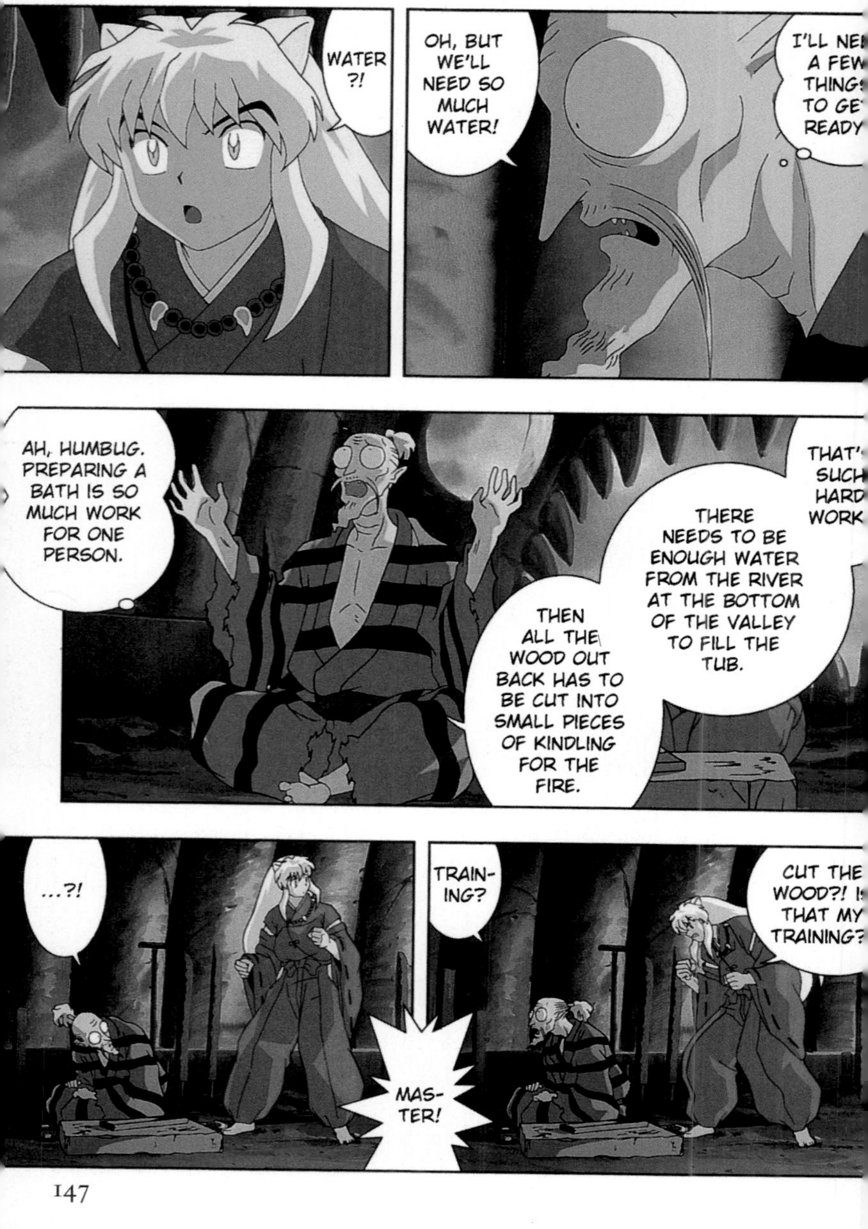
I'LL NE A FEW THING TO GE READY
OH, BUT WE'LL NEED SO MUCH WATER!
WATER ?!
THAT' SUCH HARD WORK
THERE NEEDS TO BE ENOUGH WATER FROM THE RIVER AT THE BOTTOM OF THE VALLEY TO FILL THE TUB.
THEN ALL THE WOOD OUT BACK HAS TO BE CUT INTO SMALL PIECES OF KINDLING FOR THE FIRE.
AH, HUMBUG. PREPARING A BATH IS SO MUCH WORK FOR ONE PERSON.
CUT THE WOOD?! I THAT MY TRAINING?
TRAIN-ING?
MAS-TER!
...?!

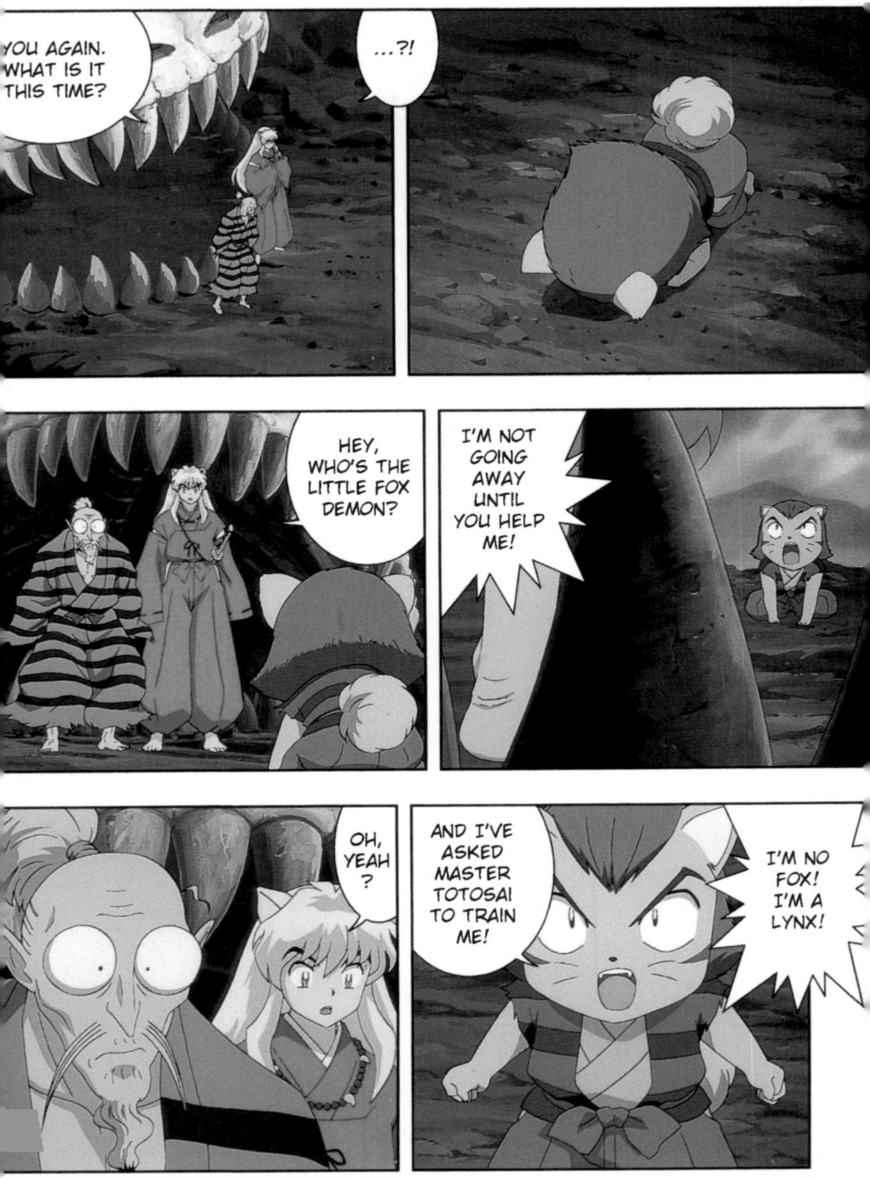

...?!
YOU AGAIN. WHAT IS IT THIS TIME?
I'M NOT GOING AWAY UNTIL YOU HELP ME!
HEY, WHO'S THE LITTLE FOX DEMON?
I'M NO FOX! I'M A LYNX!
AND I'VE ASKED MASTER TOTOSAI TO TRAIN ME!
OH, YEAH?

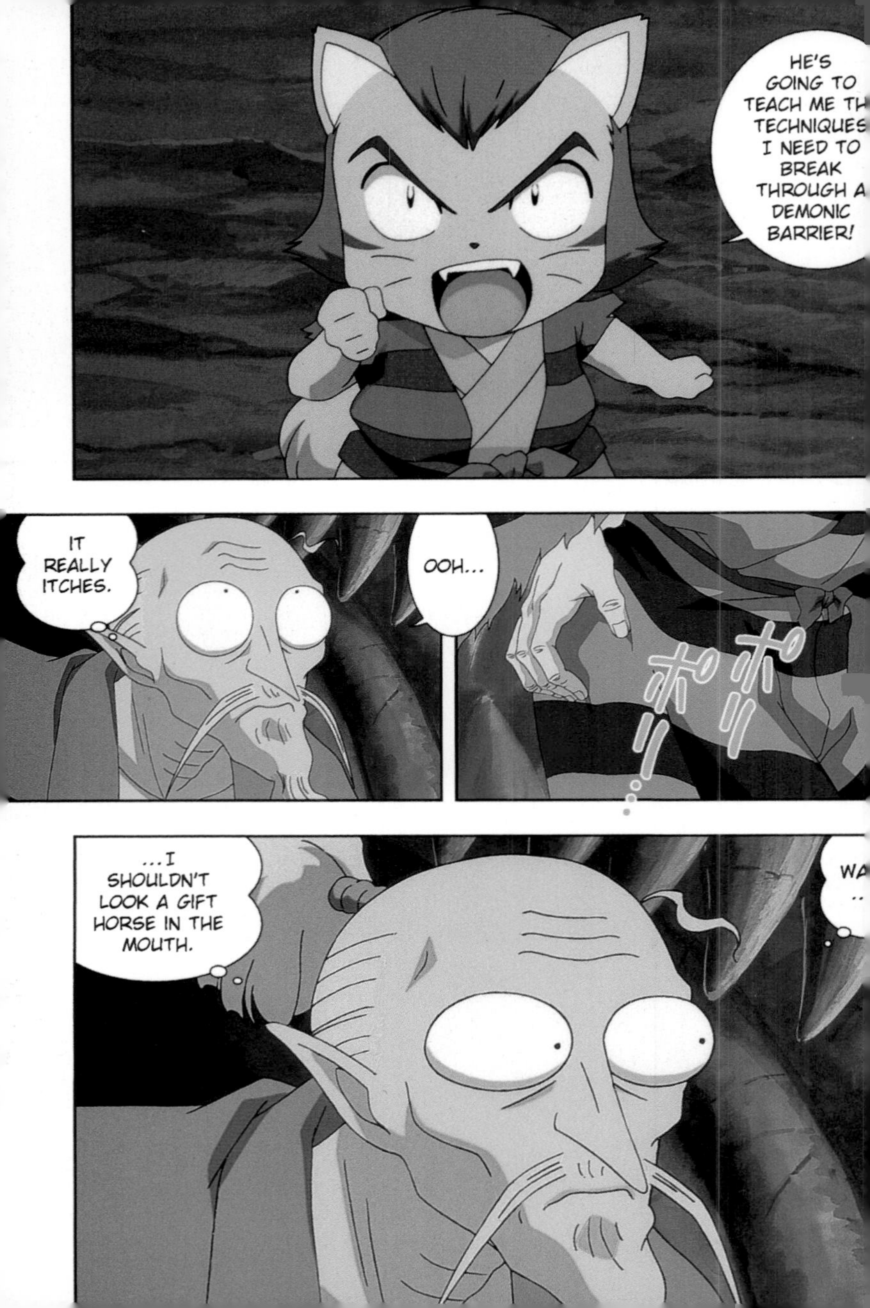
HE'S GOING TO TEACH ME TH TECHNIQUES I NEED TO BREAK THROUGH A DEMONIC BARRIER!
OOH...
ポリポリ...
IT REALLY ITCHES.
WA
...I SHOULDN'T LOOK A GIFT HORSE IN THE MOUTH.

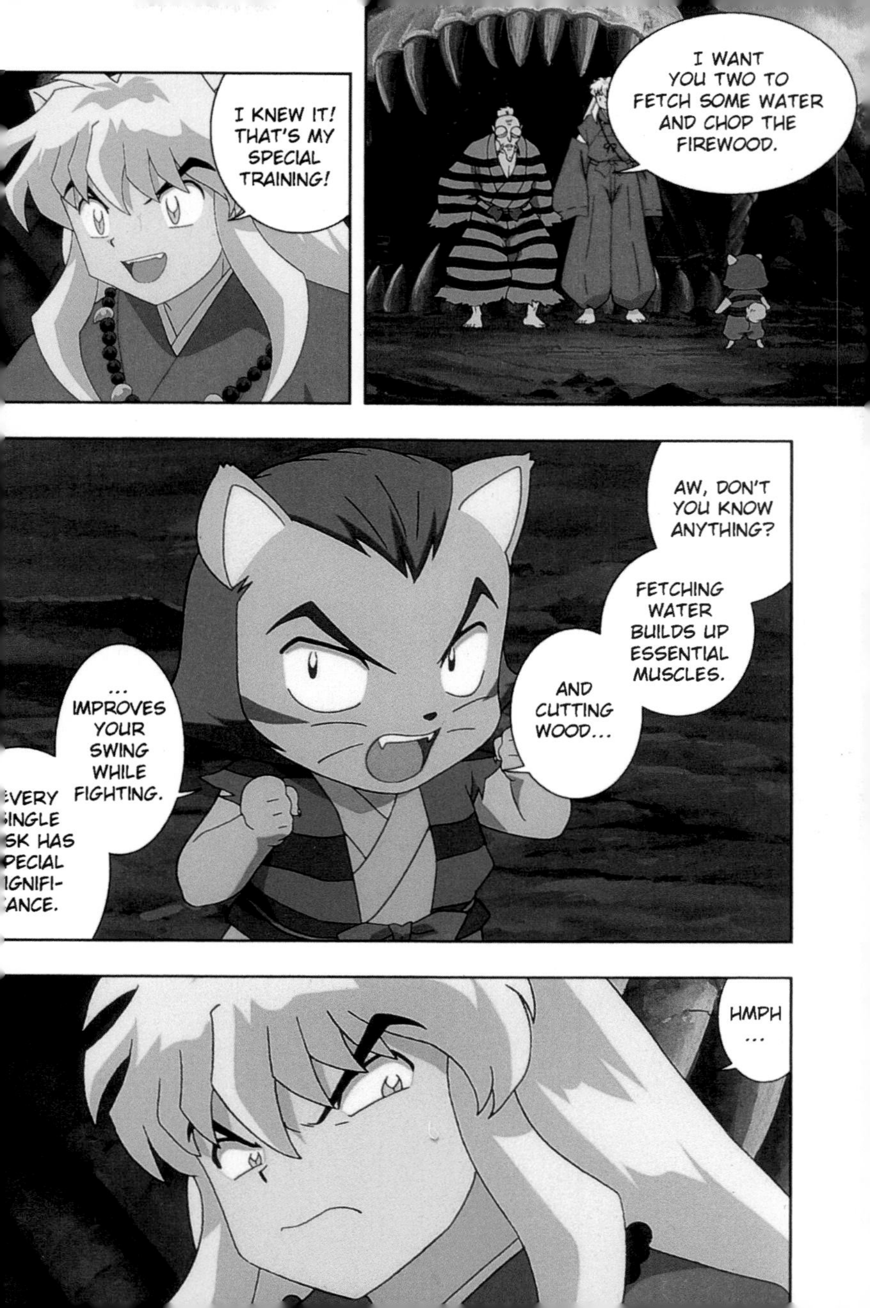
I WANT YOU TWO TO FETCH SOME WATER AND CHOP THE FIREWOOD.
I KNEW IT! THAT'S MY SPECIAL TRAINING!
AW, DON'T YOU KNOW ANYTHING?
FETCHING WATER BUILDS UP ESSENTIAL MUSCLES.
AND CUTTING WOOD...
... IMPROVES YOUR SWING WHILE FIGHTING.
VERY INGLE SK HAS PECIAL IGNIFI- ANCE.
HMPH ...

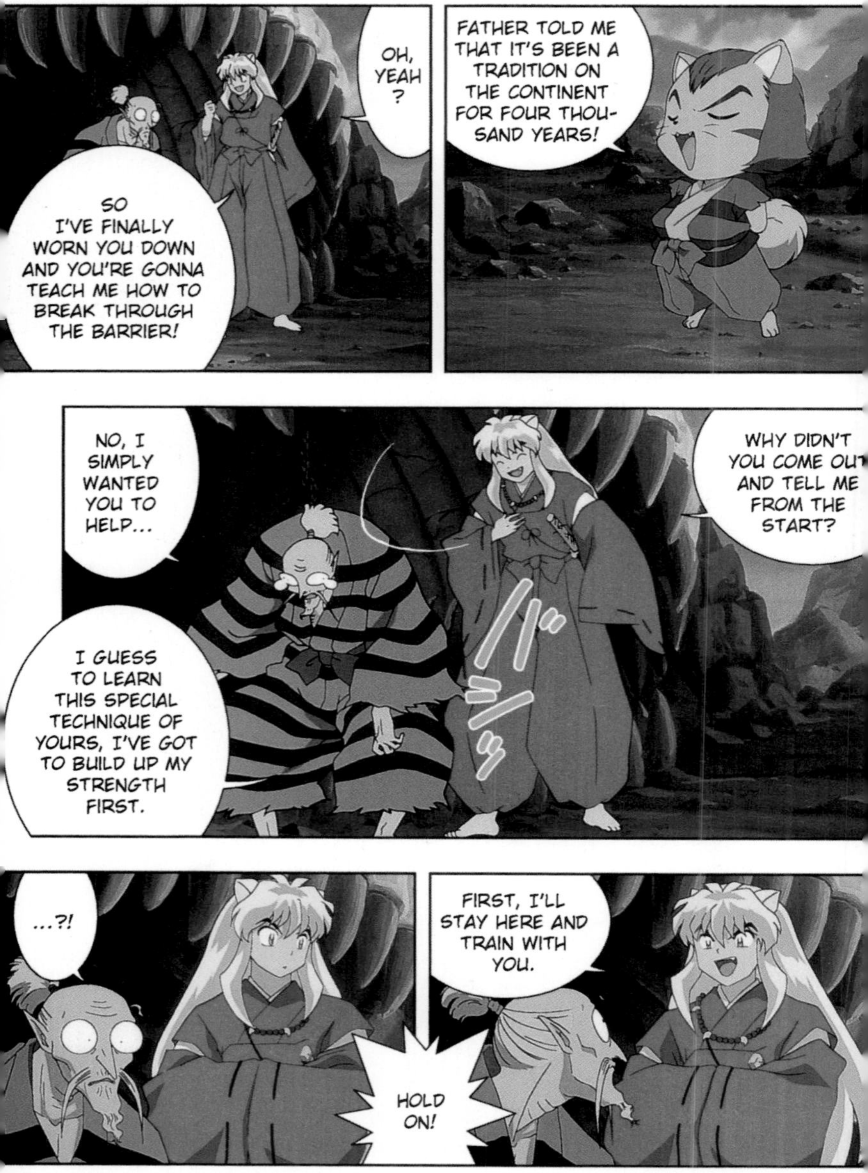

FATHER TOLD ME THAT IT'S BEEN A TRADITION ON THE CONTINENT FOR FOUR THOU-SAND YEARS!
OH, YEAH?
SO I'VE FINALLY WORN YOU DOWN AND YOU'RE GONNA TEACH ME HOW TO BREAK THROUGH THE BARRIER!
WHY DIDN'T YOU COME OUT AND TELL ME FROM THE START?
NO, I SIMPLY WANTED YOU TO HELP...
バシッ
I GUESS TO LEARN THIS SPECIAL TECHNIQUE OF YOURS, I'VE GOT TO BUILD UP MY STRENGTH FIRST.
FIRST, I'LL STAY HERE AND TRAIN WITH YOU.
HOLD ON!
...?!

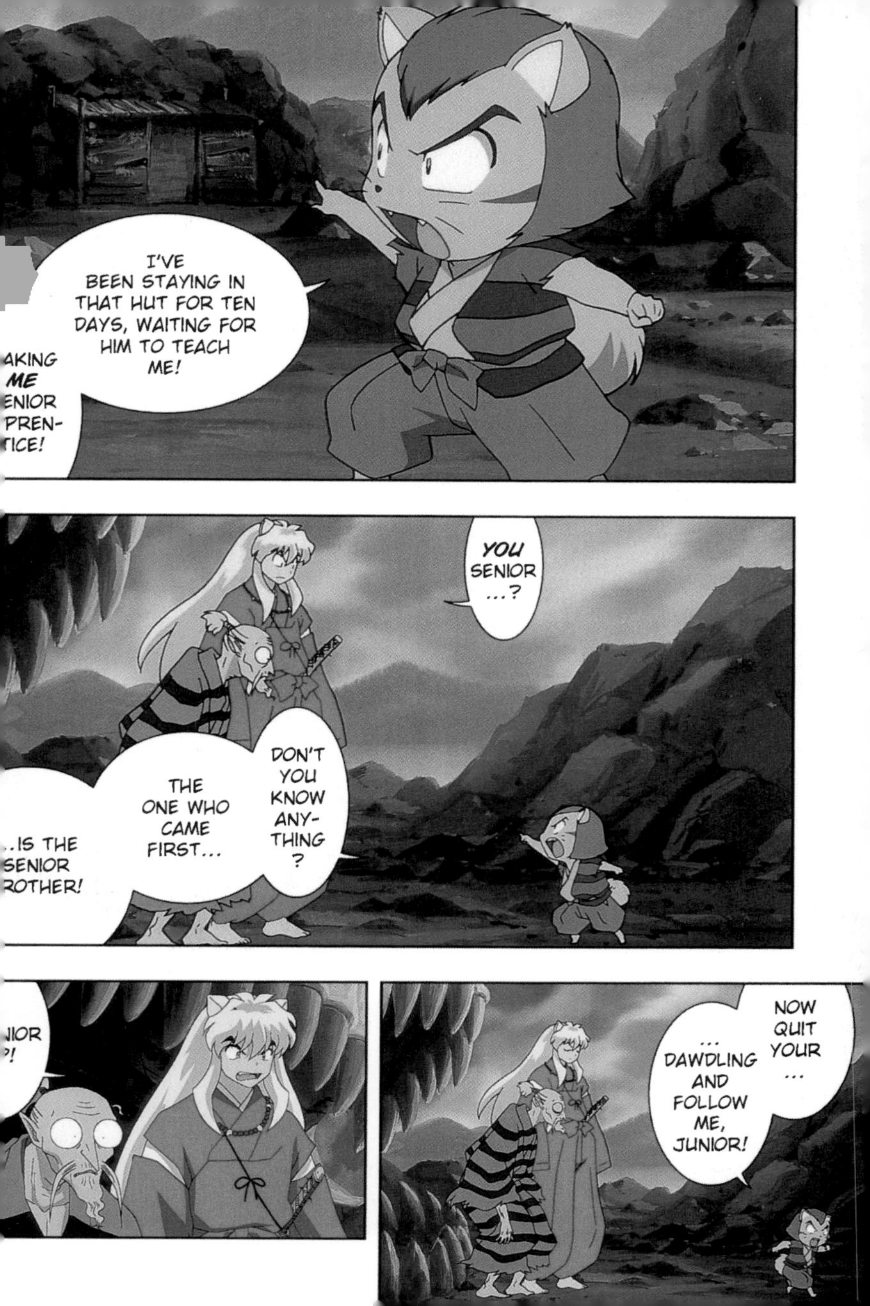
I'VE BEEN STAYING IN THAT HUT FOR TEN DAYS, WAITING FOR HIM TO TEACH ME!
AKING ME ENIOR PREN- TICE!
YOU SENIOR ...?
DON'T YOU KNOW ANY- THING ?
THE ONE WHO CAME FIRST...
..IS THE SENIOR ROTHER!
NOW QUIT YOUR ...
... DAWDLING AND FOLLOW ME, JUNIOR!

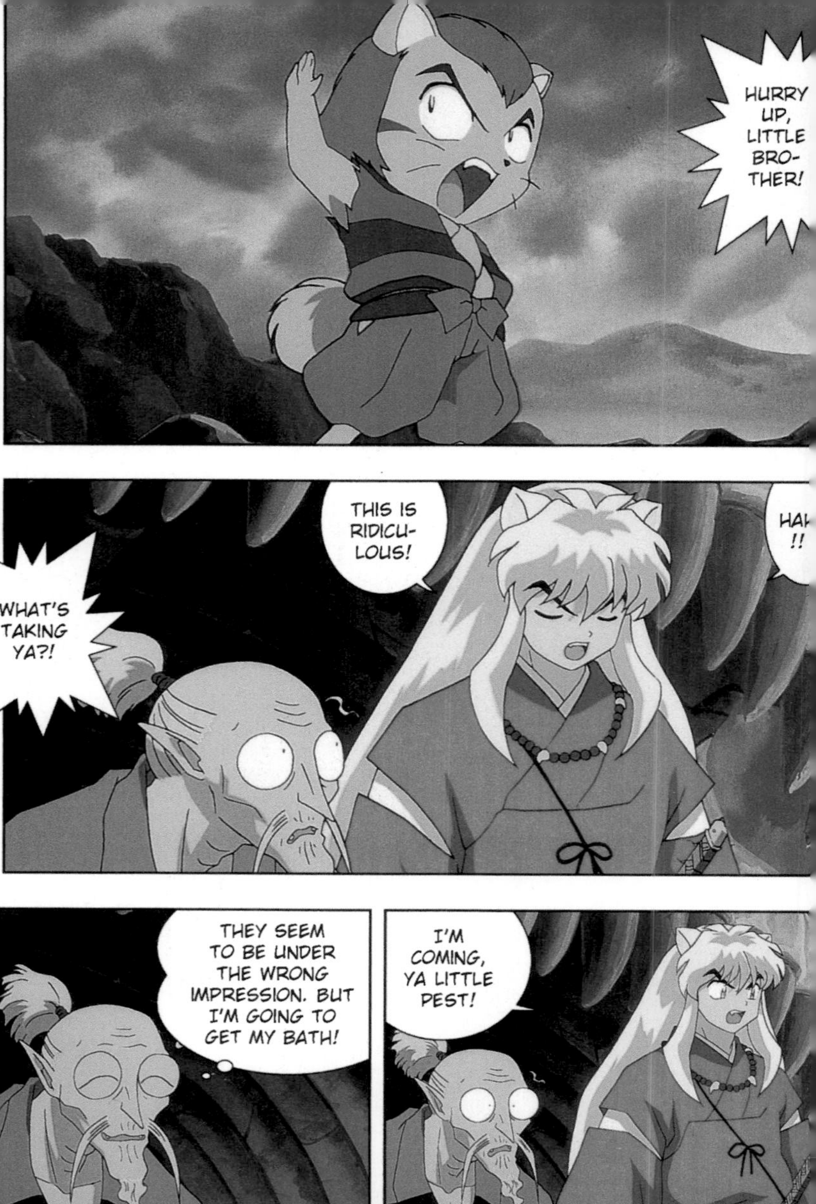

HURRY UP, LITTLE BRO-THER!
HA!!
THIS IS RIDICU-LOUS!
WHAT'S TAKING YA?!
I'M COMING, YA LITTLE PEST!
THEY SEEM TO BE UNDER THE WRONG IMPRESSION. BUT I'M GOING TO GET MY BATH!

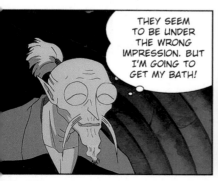

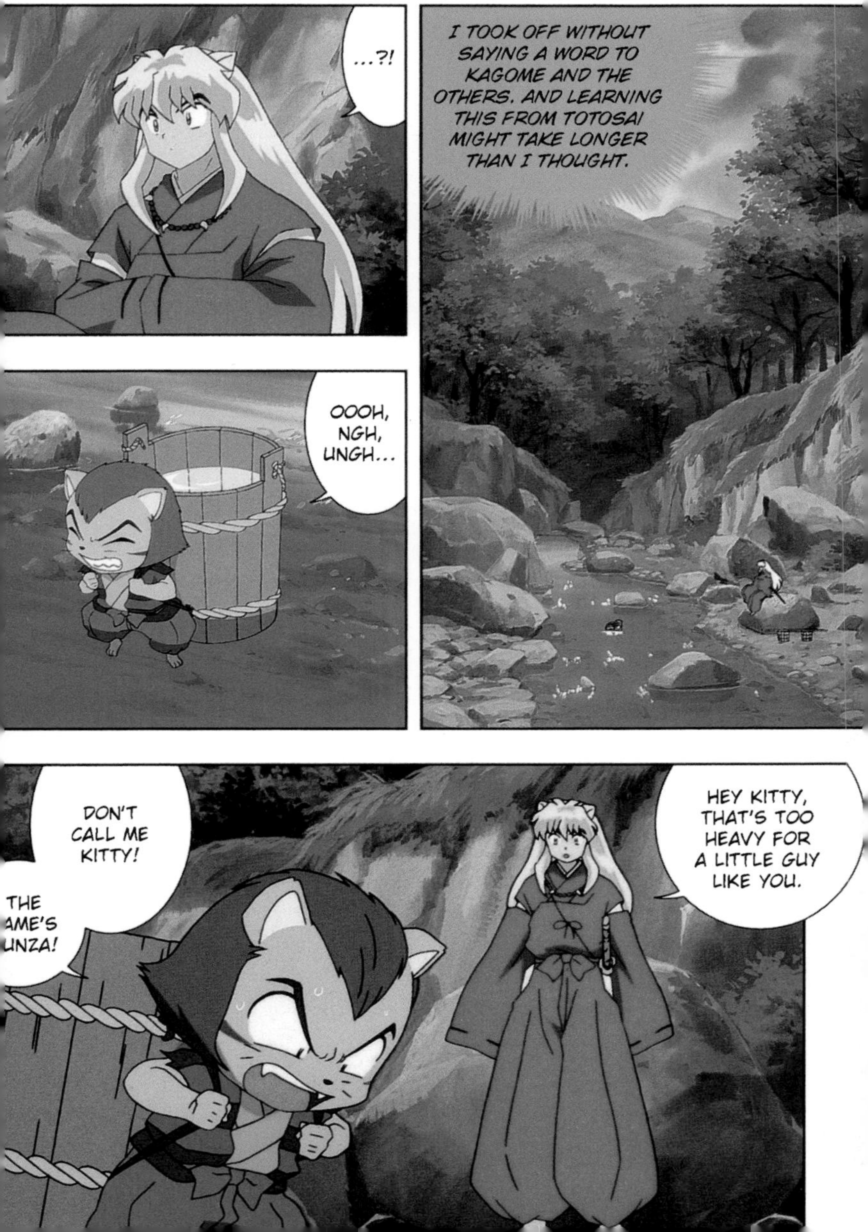
I TOOK OFF WITHOUT SAYING A WORD TO KAGOME AND THE OTHERS. AND LEARNING THIS FROM TOTOSAI MIGHT TAKE LONGER THAN I THOUGHT.
...?!
OOOH, NGH, UNGH...
HEY KITTY, THAT'S TOO HEAVY FOR A LITTLE GUY LIKE YOU.
DON'T CALL ME KITTY!
THE AME'S UNZA!

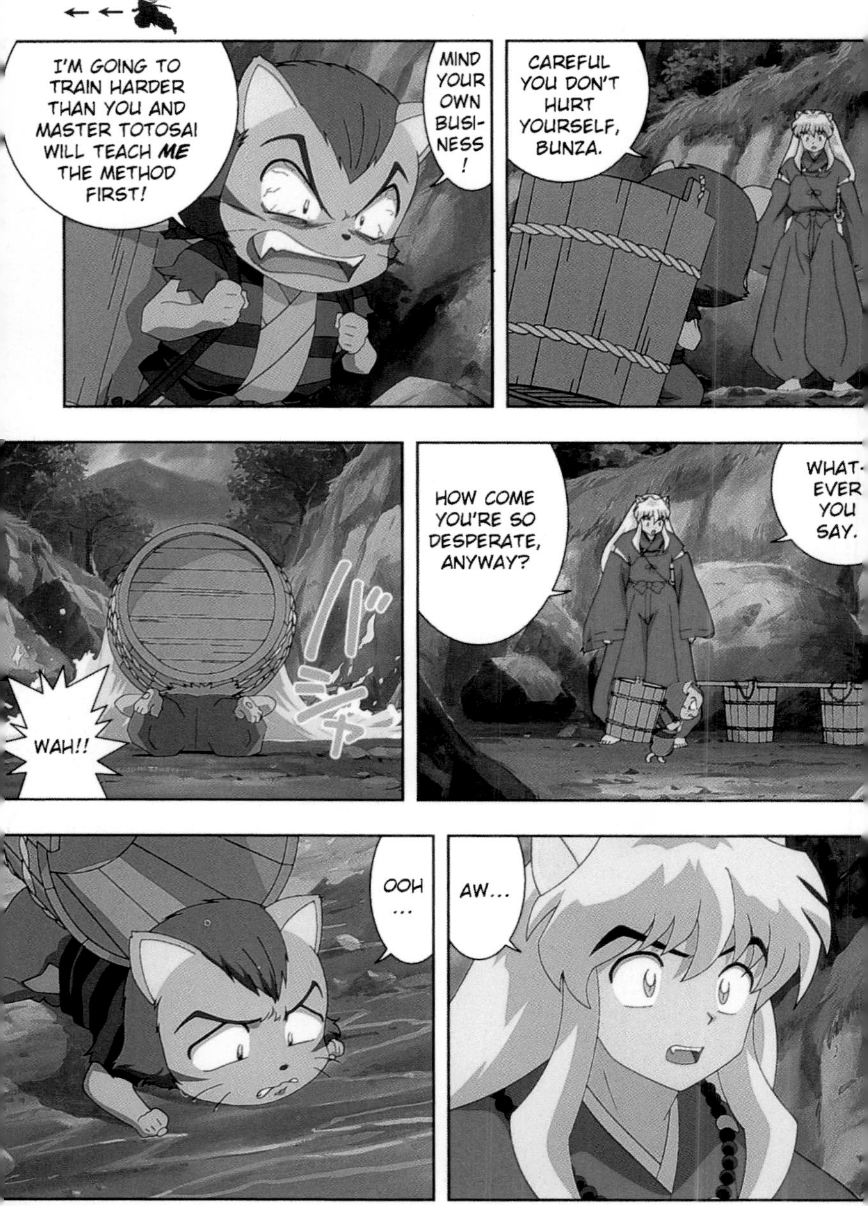
CAREFUL YOU DON'T HURT YOURSELF, BUNZA.
MIND YOUR OWN BUSINESS!
I'M GOING TO TRAIN HARDER THAN YOU AND MASTER TOTOSAI WILL TEACH *ME* THE METHOD FIRST!
WHATEVER YOU SAY.
HOW COME YOU'RE SO DESPERATE, ANYWAY?
WAH!!
AW...
OOH...

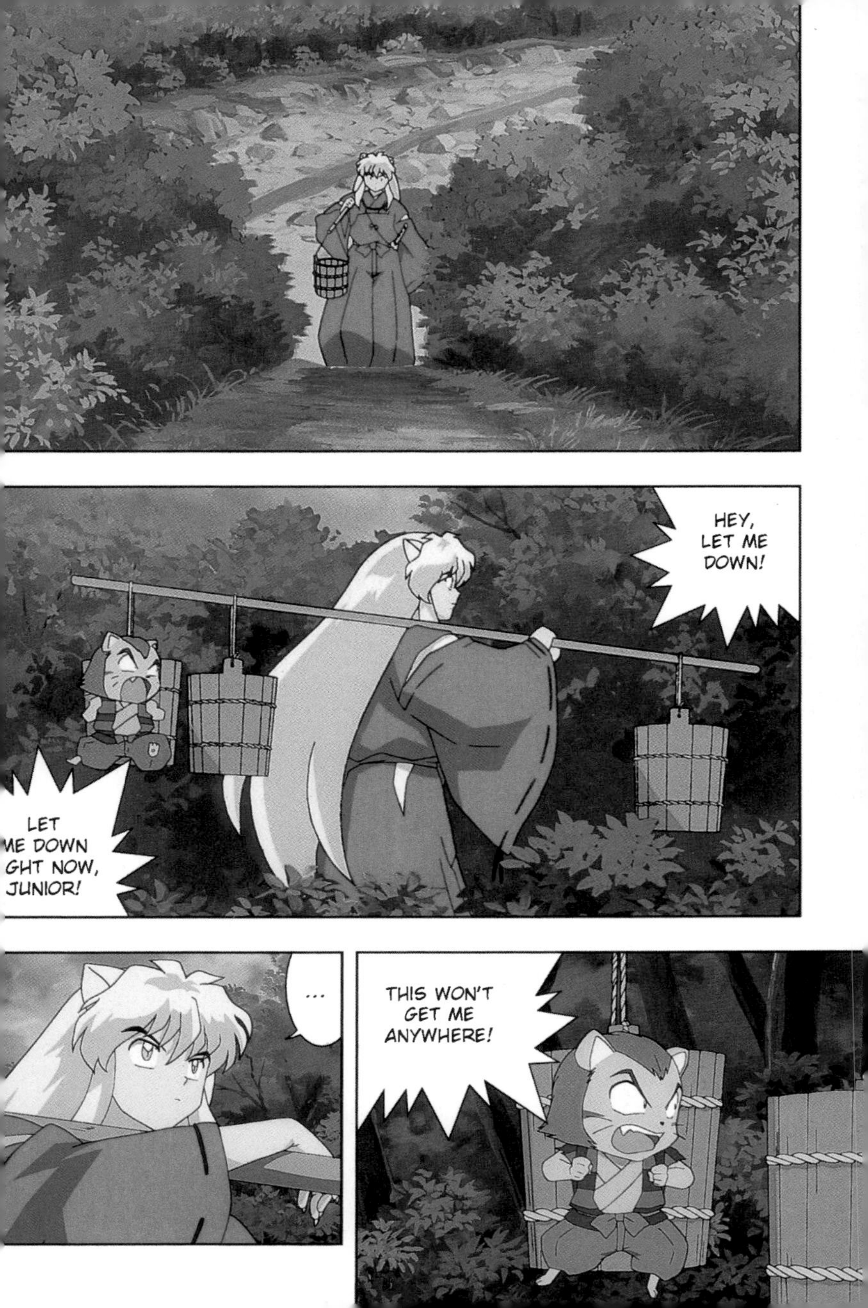
HEY, LET ME DOWN!
LET ME DOWN GHT NOW, JUNIOR!
THIS WON'T GET ME ANYWHERE!
...

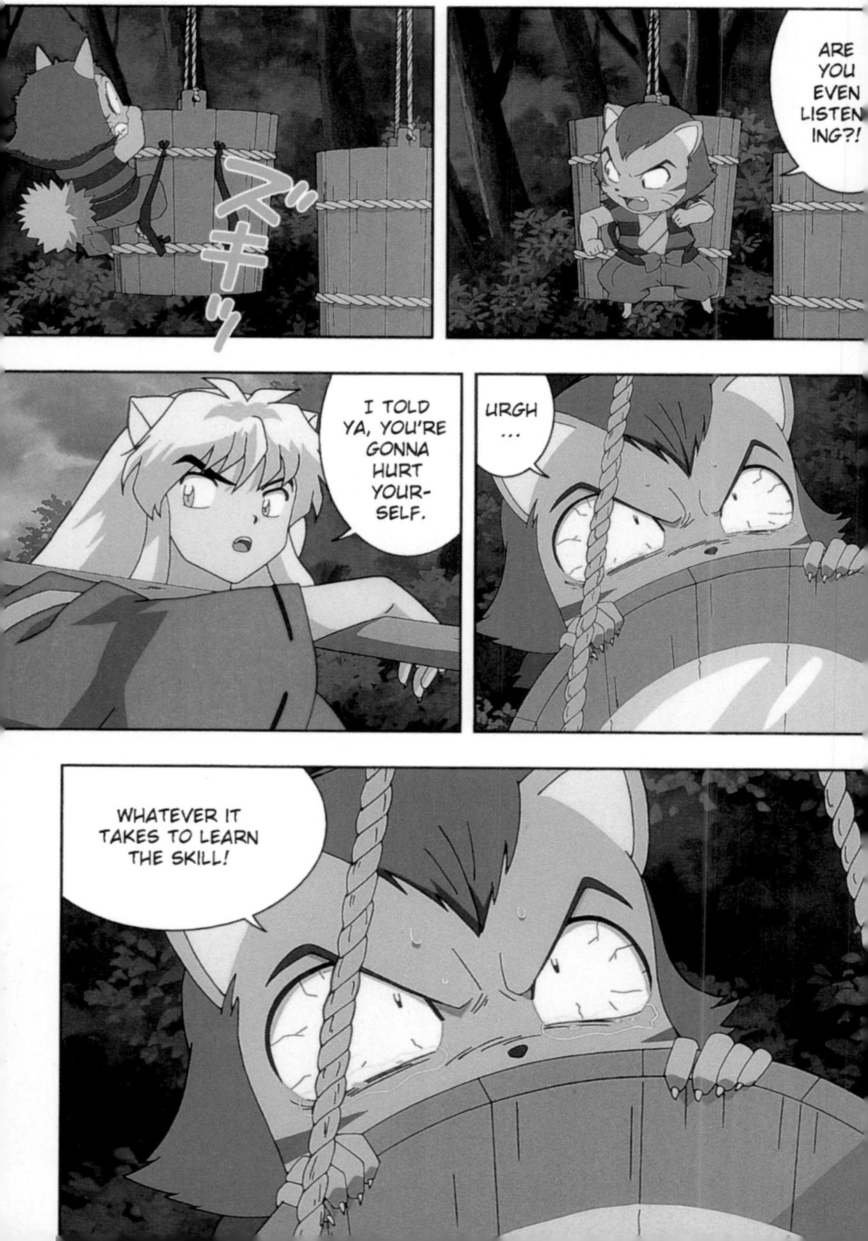
ARE YOU EVEN LISTEN ING?!
ズキッ
URGH ...
I TOLD YA, YOU'RE GONNA HURT YOUR-SELF.
WHATEVER IT TAKES TO LEARN THE SKILL!

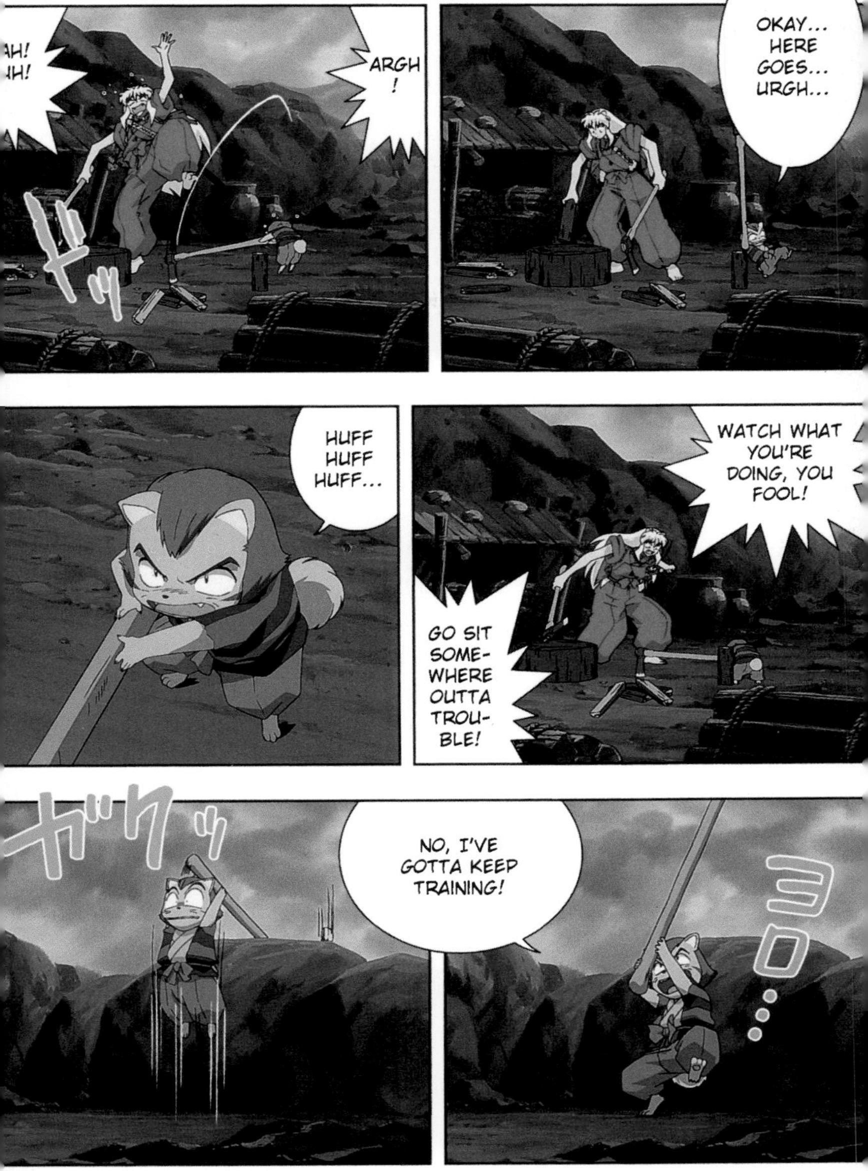
OKAY... HERE GOES... URGH...
ARGH!
AH!
H!
ドッ
WATCH WHAT YOU'RE DOING, YOU FOOL!
GO SIT SOME-WHERE OUTTA TROU-BLE!
HUFF HUFF HUFF...
NO, I'VE GOTTA KEEP TRAINING!
ヨロ...
ガクッ

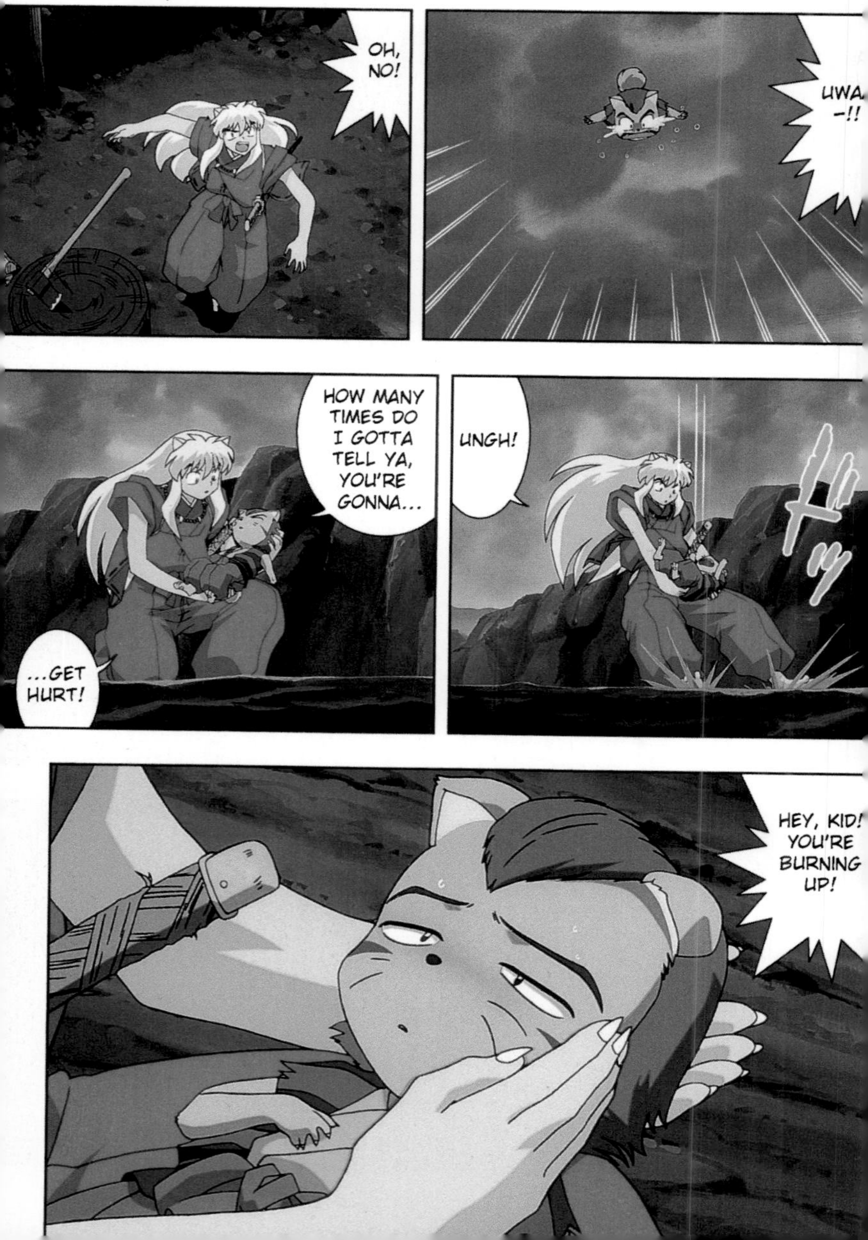
UWA-!!
OH, NO!
UNGH!
HOW MANY TIMES DO I GOTTA TELL YA, YOU'RE GONNA...
...GET HURT!
HEY, KID! YOU'RE BURNING UP!

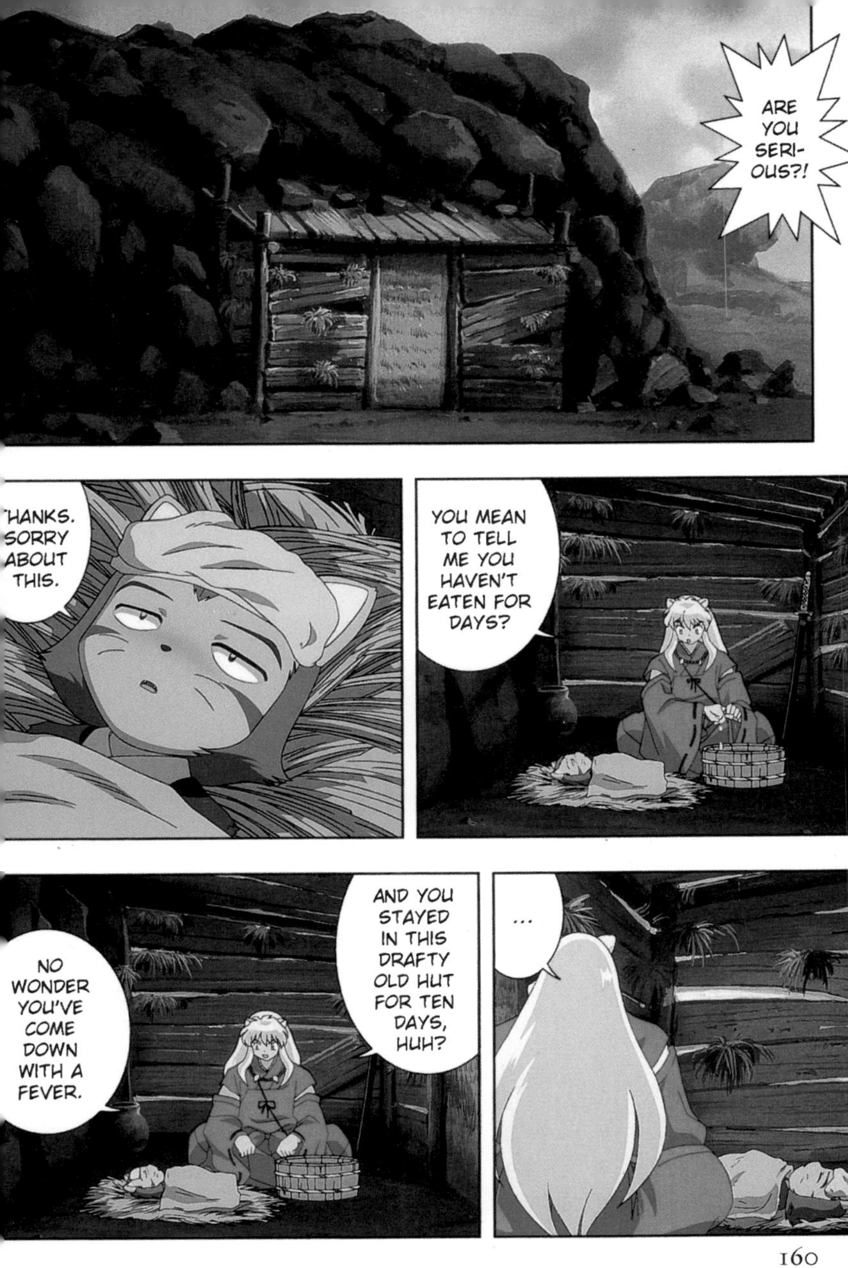
ARE YOU SERI-OUS?!
YOU MEAN TO TELL ME YOU HAVEN'T EATEN FOR DAYS?
THANKS. SORRY ABOUT THIS.
...
AND YOU STAYED IN THIS DRAFTY OLD HUT FOR TEN DAYS, HUH?
NO WONDER YOU'VE COME DOWN WITH A FEVER.

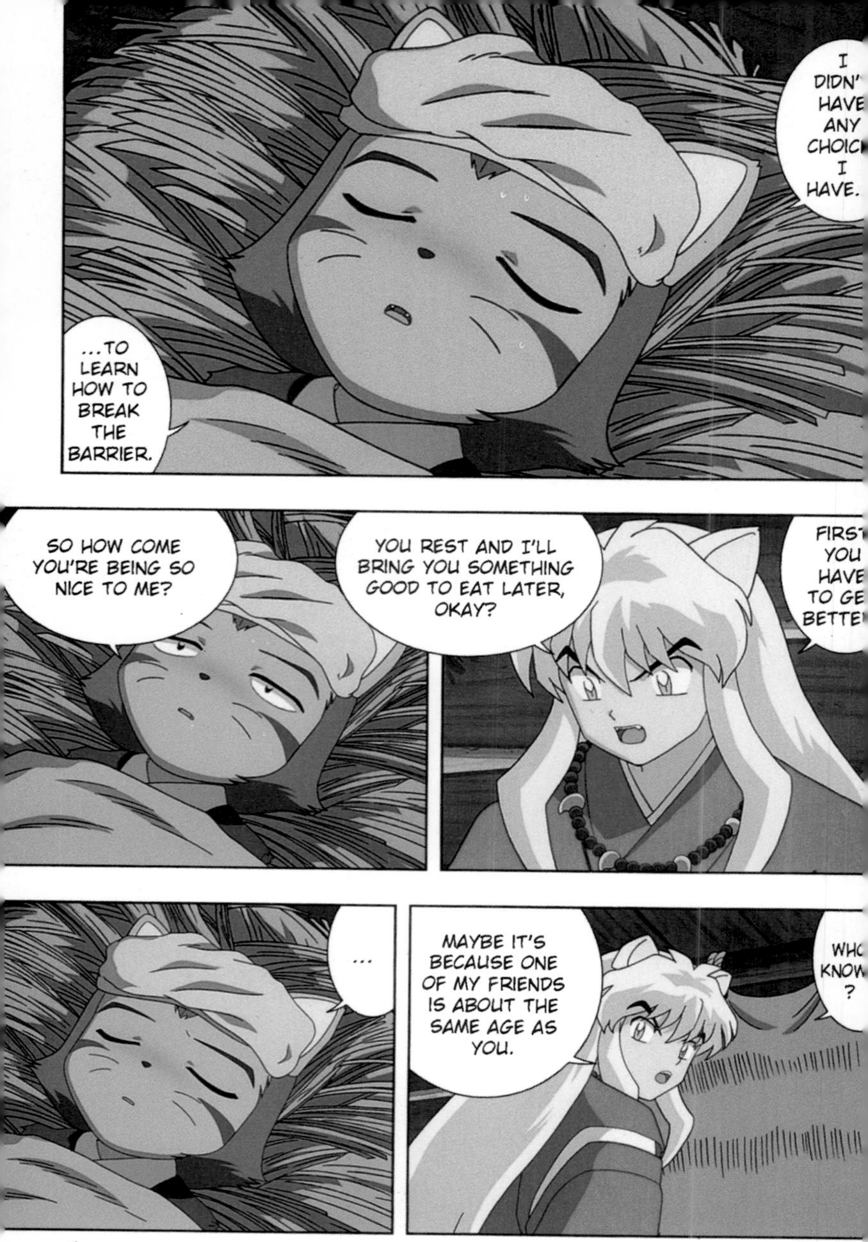
I DIDN' HAVE ANY CHOIC I HAVE.
...TO LEARN HOW TO BREAK THE BARRIER.
FIRST YOU HAVE TO GE BETTE
YOU REST AND I'LL BRING YOU SOMETHING GOOD TO EAT LATER, OKAY?
SO HOW COME YOU'RE BEING SO NICE TO ME?
WHC KNOW ?
MAYBE IT'S BECAUSE ONE OF MY FRIENDS IS ABOUT THE SAME AGE AS YOU.
...

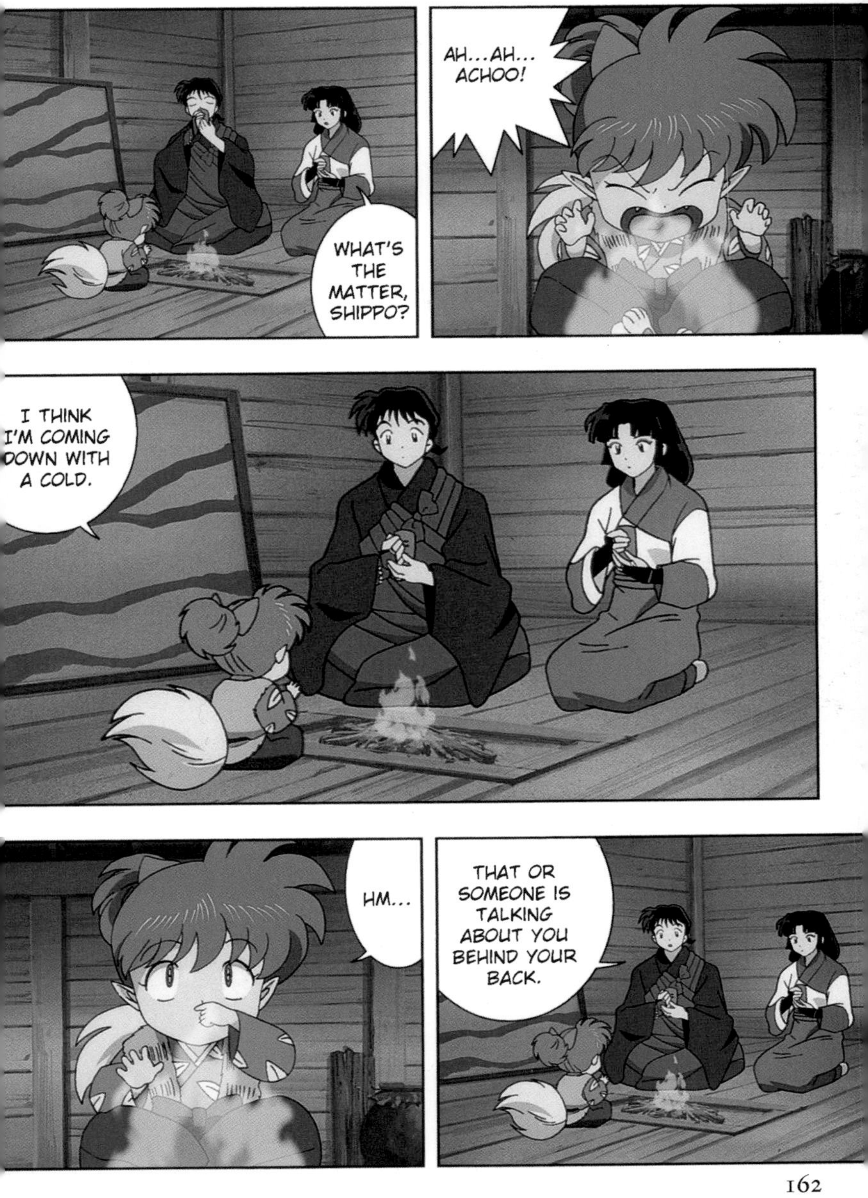

AH...AH... ACHOO!
WHAT'S THE MATTER, SHIPPO?
I THINK I'M COMING DOWN WITH A COLD.
THAT OR SOMEONE IS TALKING ABOUT YOU BEHIND YOUR BACK.
HM...

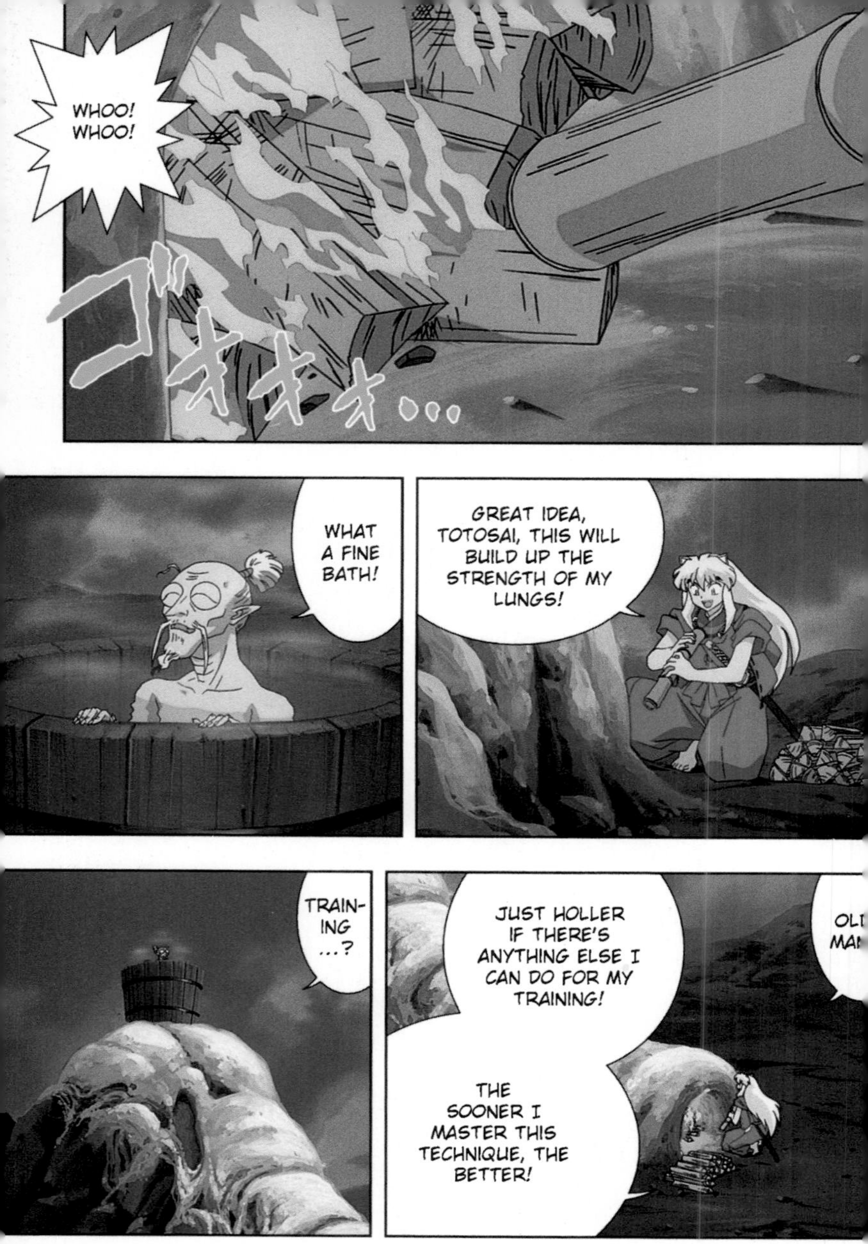
WHOO! WHOO!
ゴオオオ...
GREAT IDEA, TOTOSAI, THIS WILL BUILD UP THE STRENGTH OF MY LUNGS!
WHAT A FINE BATH!
JUST HOLLER IF THERE'S ANYTHING ELSE I CAN DO FOR MY TRAINING!
THE SOONER I MASTER THIS TECHNIQUE, THE BETTER!
TRAIN-ING ...?

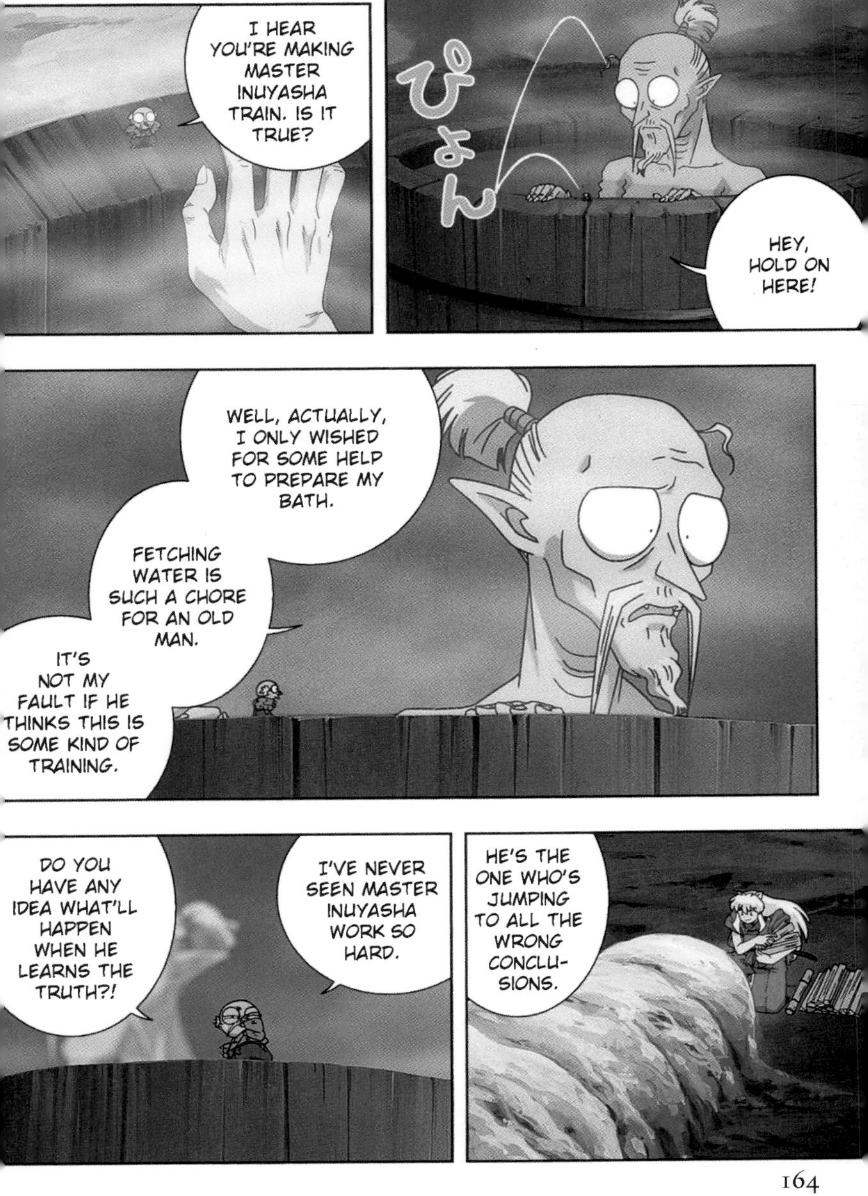
ぴょん
HEY, HOLD ON HERE!
I HEAR YOU'RE MAKING MASTER INUYASHA TRAIN. IS IT TRUE?
WELL, ACTUALLY, I ONLY WISHED FOR SOME HELP TO PREPARE MY BATH.
FETCHING WATER IS SUCH A CHORE FOR AN OLD MAN.
IT'S NOT MY FAULT IF HE THINKS THIS IS SOME KIND OF TRAINING.
HE'S THE ONE WHO'S JUMPING TO ALL THE WRONG CONCLU-SIONS.
I'VE NEVER SEEN MASTER INUYASHA WORK SO HARD.
DO YOU HAVE ANY IDEA WHAT'LL HAPPEN WHEN HE LEARNS THE TRUTH?!

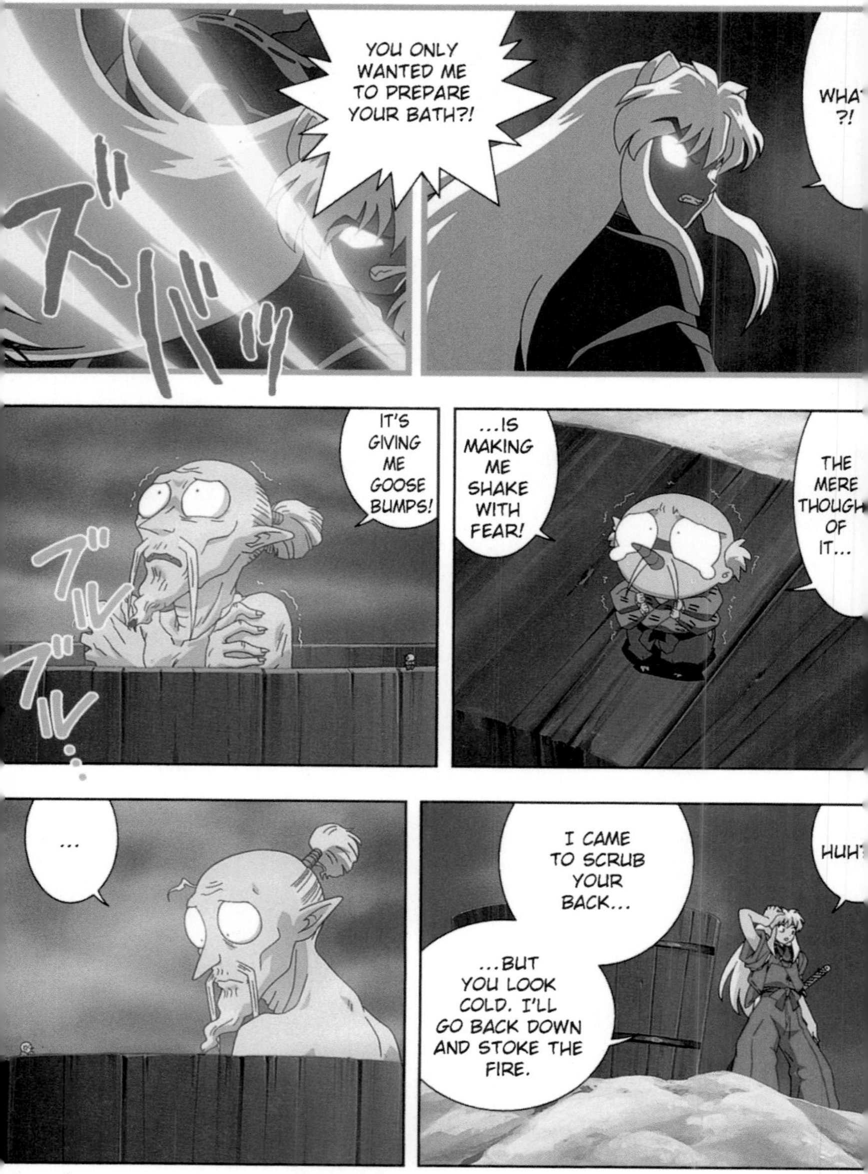
WHA
?!
YOU ONLY WANTED ME TO PREPARE YOUR BATH?!
ズバッ
THE MERE THOUGH OF IT...
...IS MAKING ME SHAKE WITH FEAR!
IT'S GIVING ME GOOSE BUMPS!
ブル ブル...
HUH
I CAME TO SCRUB YOUR BACK...
...BUT YOU LOOK COLD. I'LL GO BACK DOWN AND STOKE THE FIRE.
...

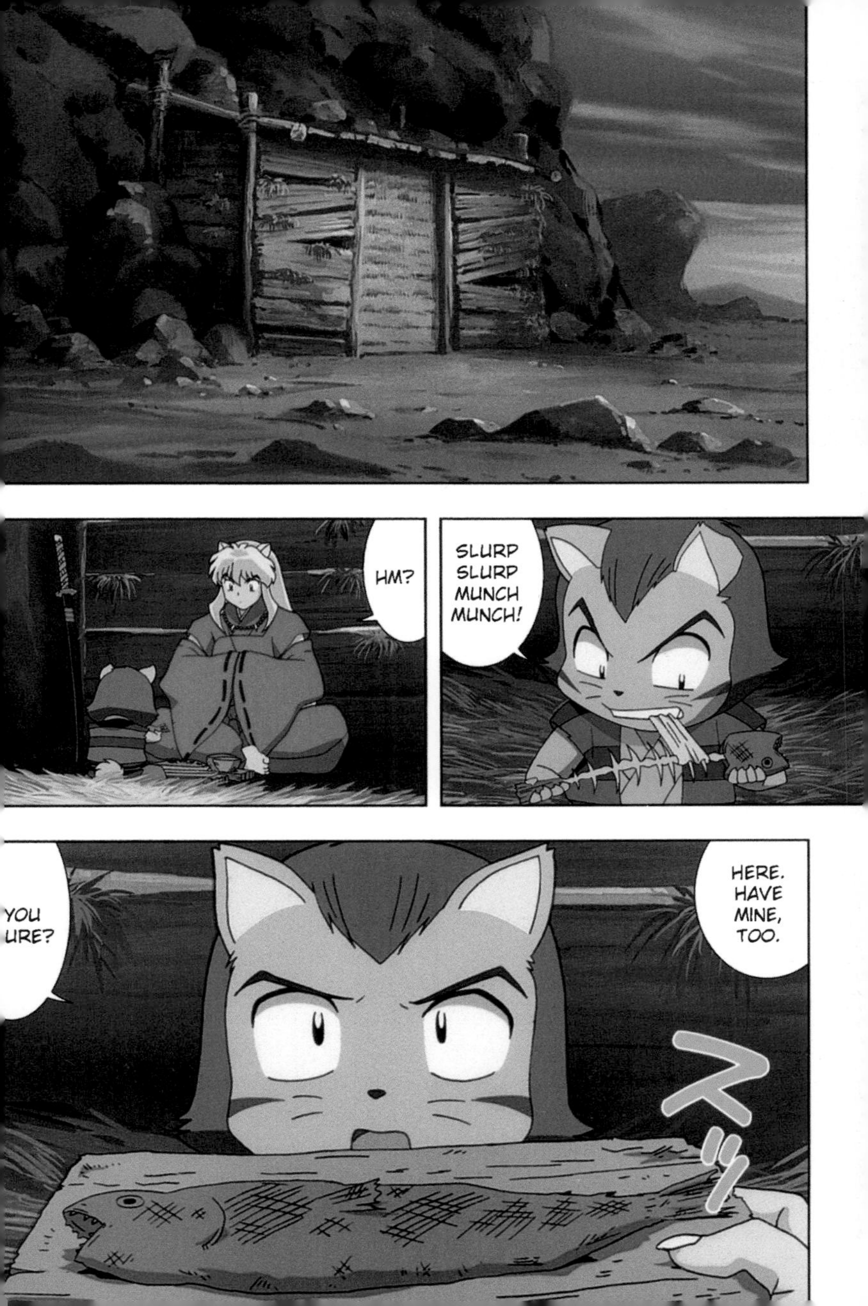
SLURP SLURP MUNCH MUNCH!
HM?
HERE. HAVE MINE, TOO.
スッ
YOU URE?

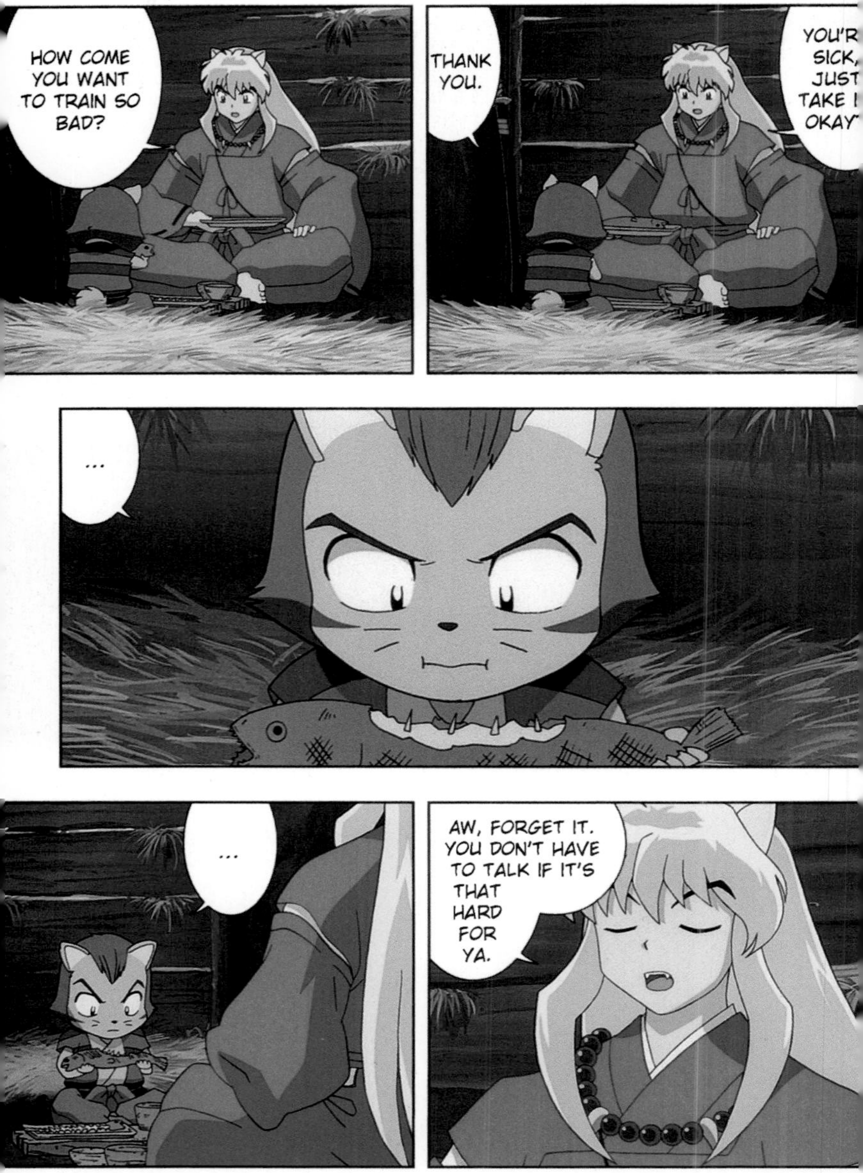
YOU'R SICK, JUST TAKE I OKAY
THANK YOU.
HOW COME YOU WANT TO TRAIN SO BAD?
...
AW, FORGET IT. YOU DON'T HAVE TO TALK IF IT'S THAT HARD FOR YA.
...

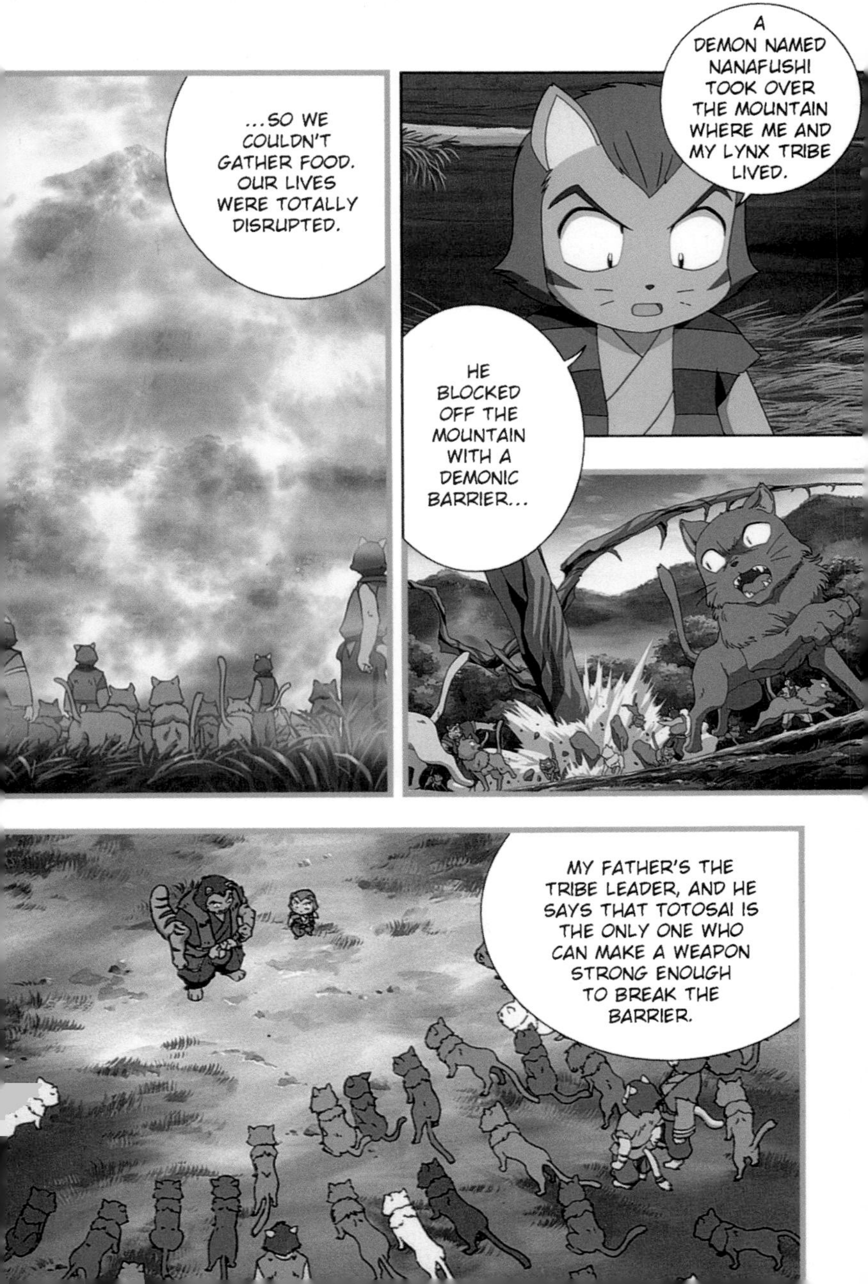
A DEMON NAMED NANAFUSHI TOOK OVER THE MOUNTAIN WHERE ME AND MY LYNX TRIBE LIVED.
HE BLOCKED OFF THE MOUNTAIN WITH A DEMONIC BARRIER...
...SO WE COULDN'T GATHER FOOD. OUR LIVES WERE TOTALLY DISRUPTED.
MY FATHER'S THE TRIBE LEADER, AND HE SAYS THAT TOTOSAI IS THE ONLY ONE WHO CAN MAKE A WEAPON STRONG ENOUGH TO BREAK THE BARRIER.

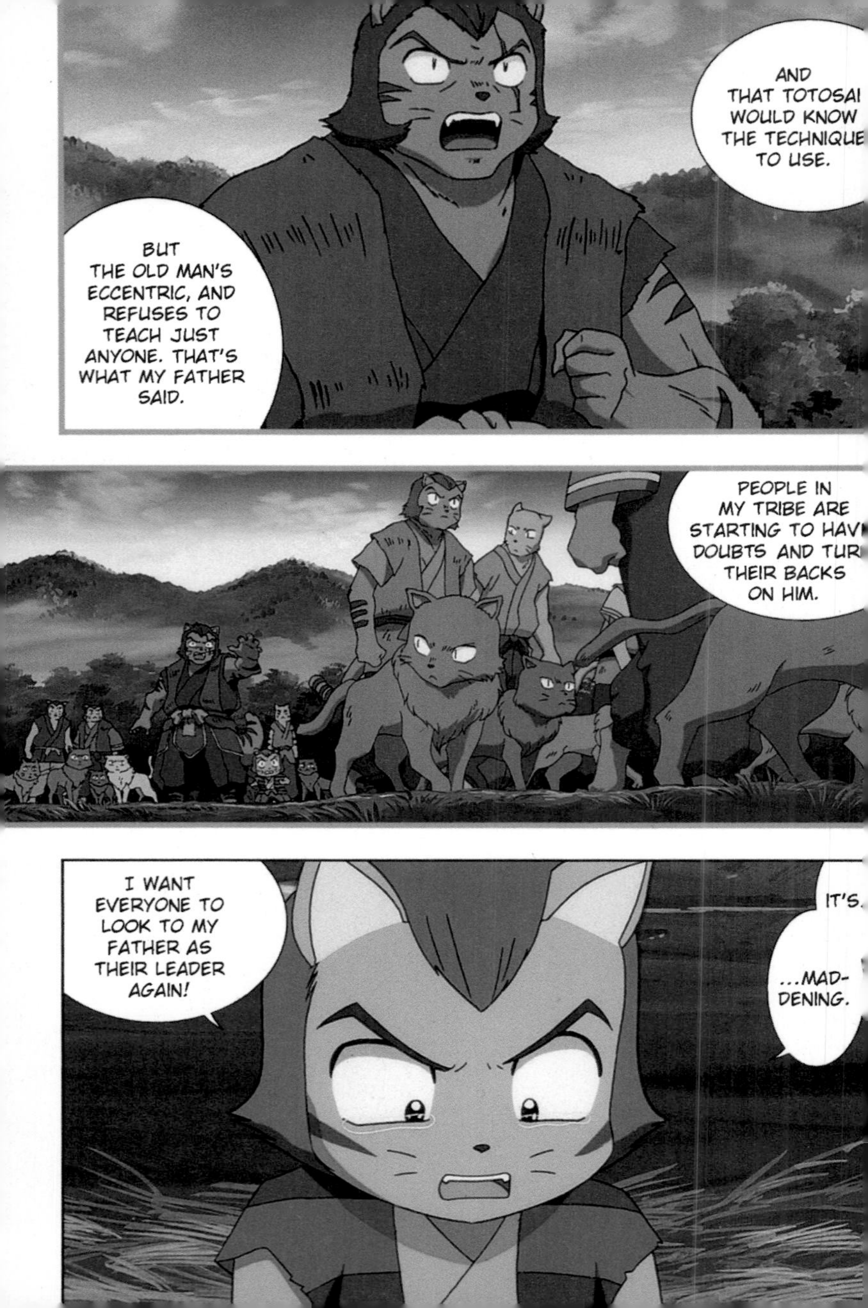
AND THAT TOTOSAI WOULD KNOW THE TECHNIQUE TO USE.
BUT THE OLD MAN'S ECCENTRIC, AND REFUSES TO TEACH JUST ANYONE. THAT'S WHAT MY FATHER SAID.
PEOPLE IN MY TRIBE ARE STARTING TO HAV DOUBTS AND TUR THEIR BACKS ON HIM.
IT'S.
...MAD-DENING.
I WANT EVERYONE TO LOOK TO MY FATHER AS THEIR LEADER AGAIN!

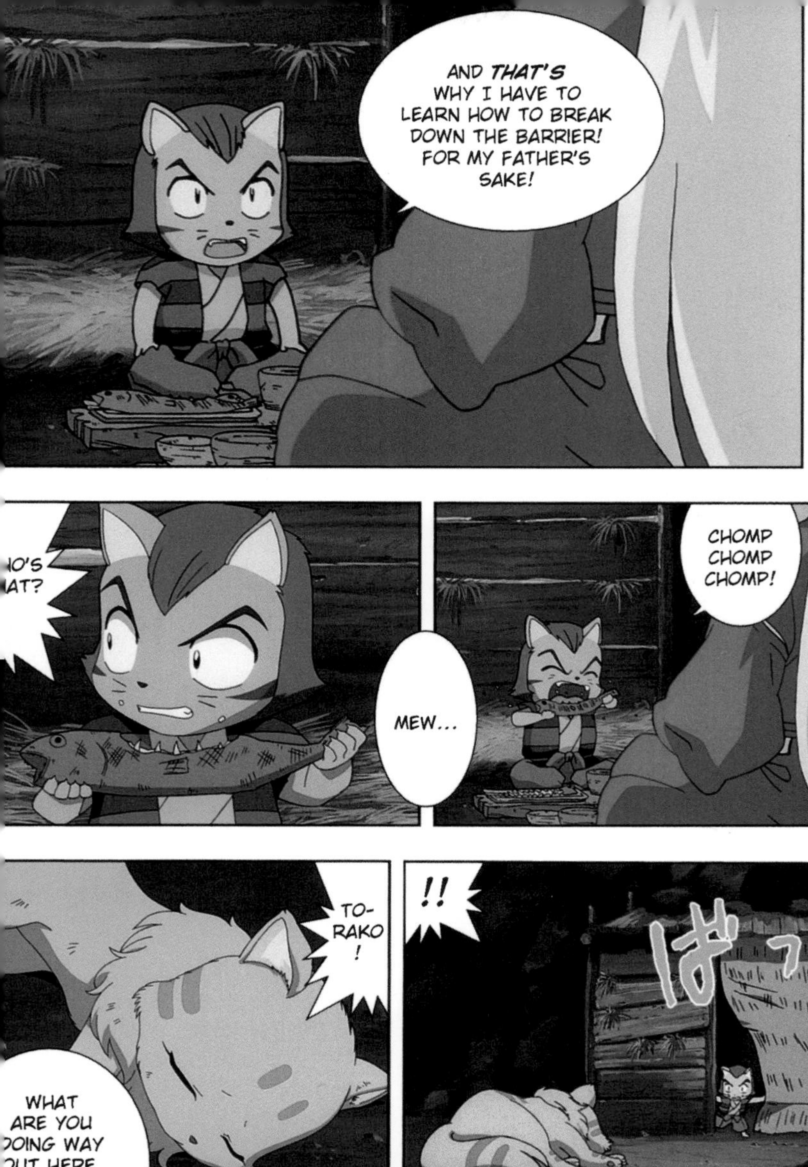
AND THAT'S WHY I HAVE TO LEARN HOW TO BREAK DOWN THE BARRIER! FOR MY FATHER'S SAKE!
CHOMP CHOMP CHOMP!
MEW...
O'S AT?
!!
ぱっ
TO-RAKO!
WHAT ARE YOU OING WAY UT HERE, TORAKO?

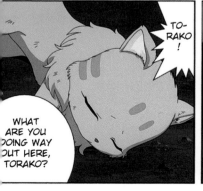

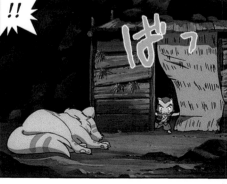

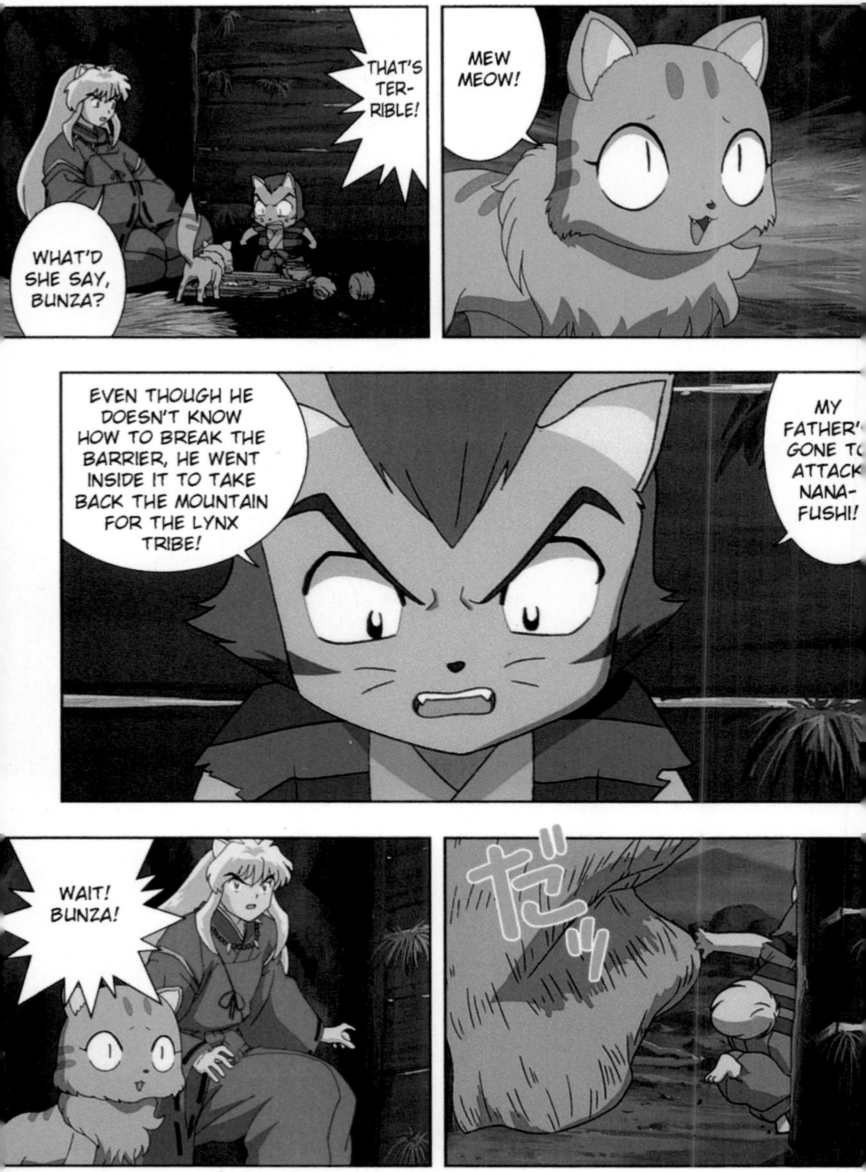
MEW MEOW!
THAT'S TER-RIBLE!
WHAT'D SHE SAY, BUNZA?
MY FATHER' GONE T ATTACK NANA-FUSHI!
EVEN THOUGH HE DOESN'T KNOW HOW TO BREAK THE BARRIER, HE WENT INSIDE IT TO TAKE BACK THE MOUNTAIN FOR THE LYNX TRIBE!
だッ
WAIT! BUNZA!

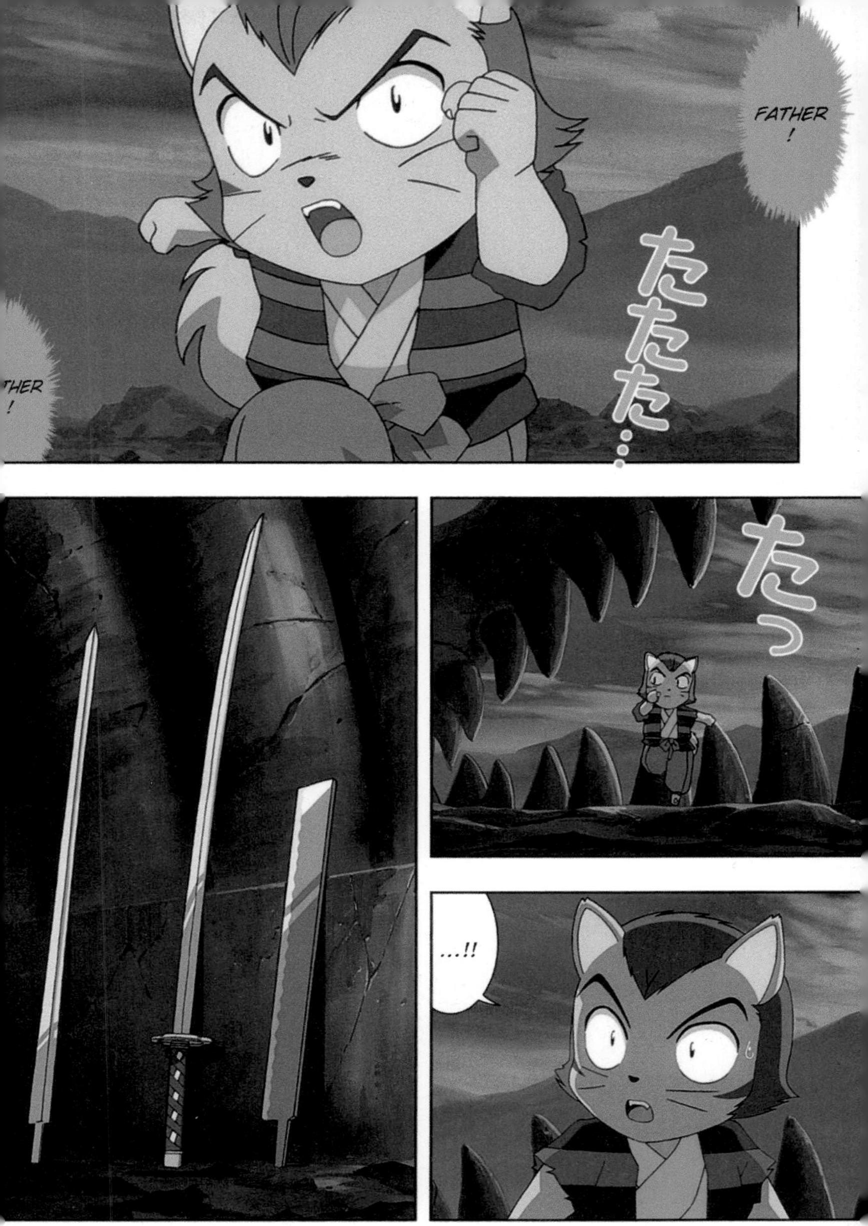
FATHER!
THER!
たたた…
たっ
...!!

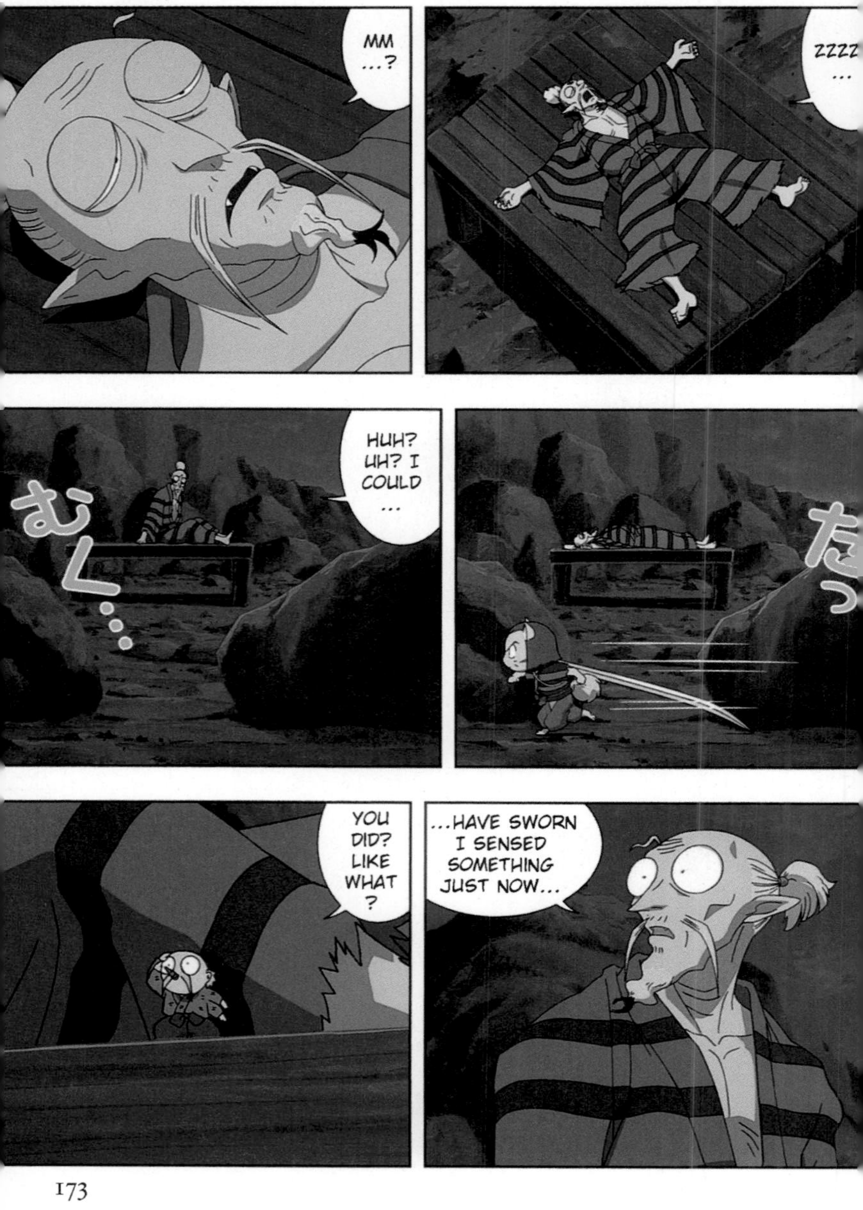
ZZZZ ...
MM ...?
たっ
HUH? UH? I COULD ...
むく…
...HAVE SWORN I SENSED SOMETHING JUST NOW...
YOU DID? LIKE WHAT?

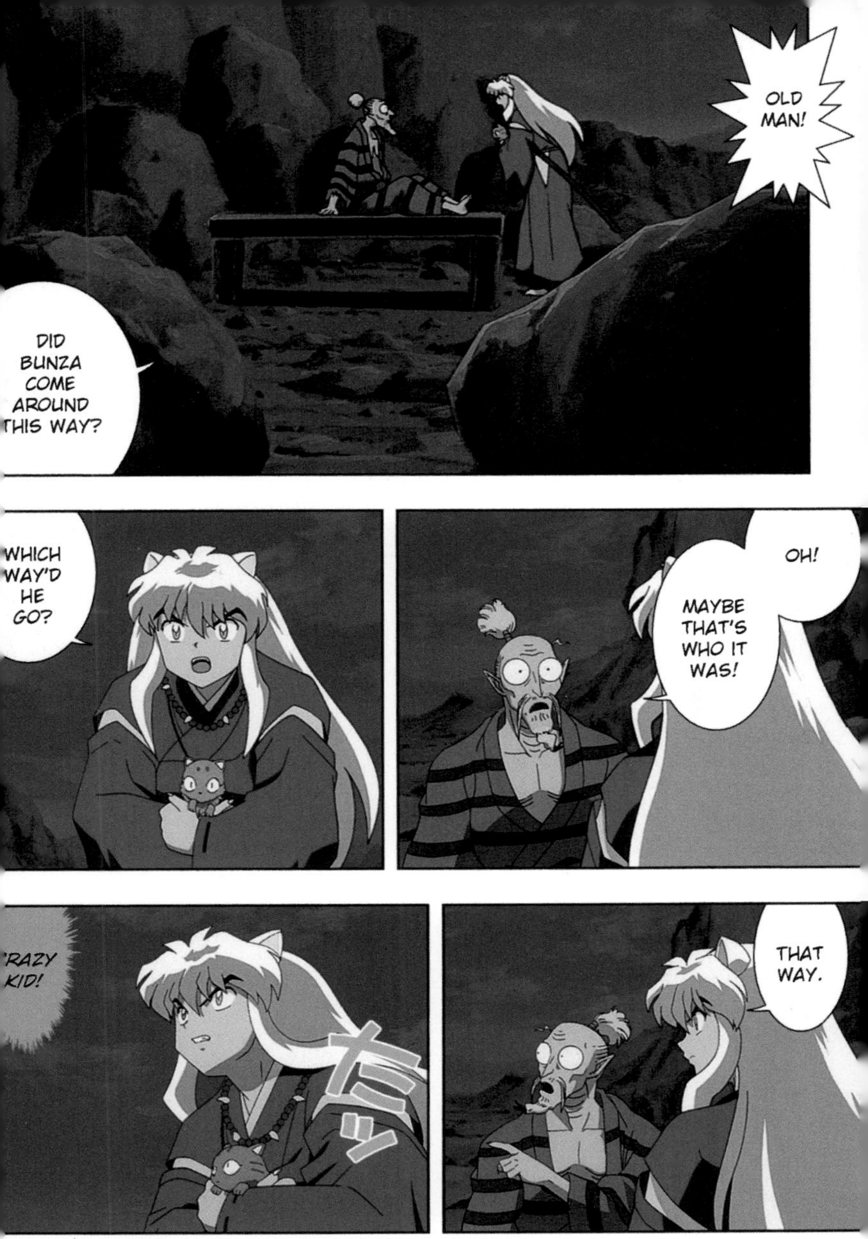
OLD MAN!
DID BUNZA COME AROUND THIS WAY?
OH!
MAYBE THAT'S WHO IT WAS!
WHICH WAY'D HE GO?
THAT WAY.
RAZY KID!
ダッ

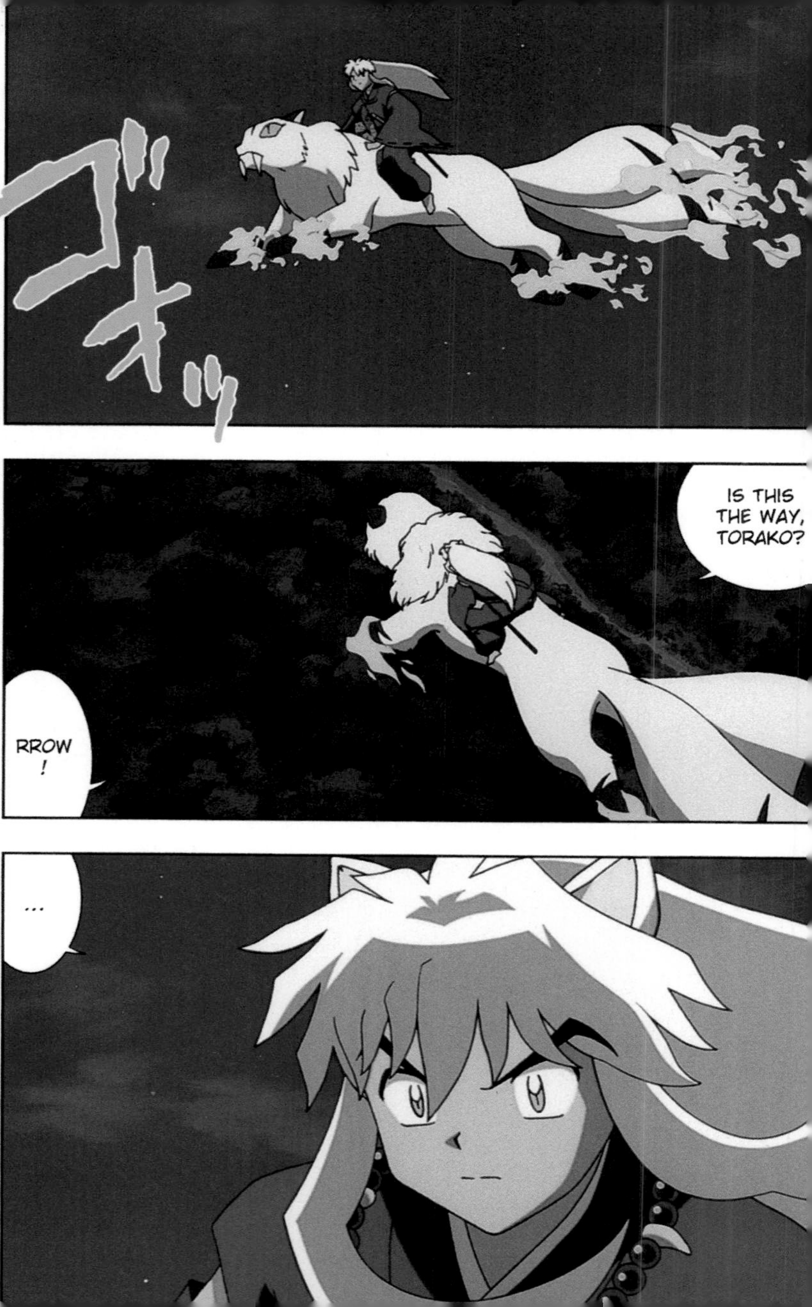
ゴオッ
IS THIS THE WAY, TORAKO?
RROW!
...

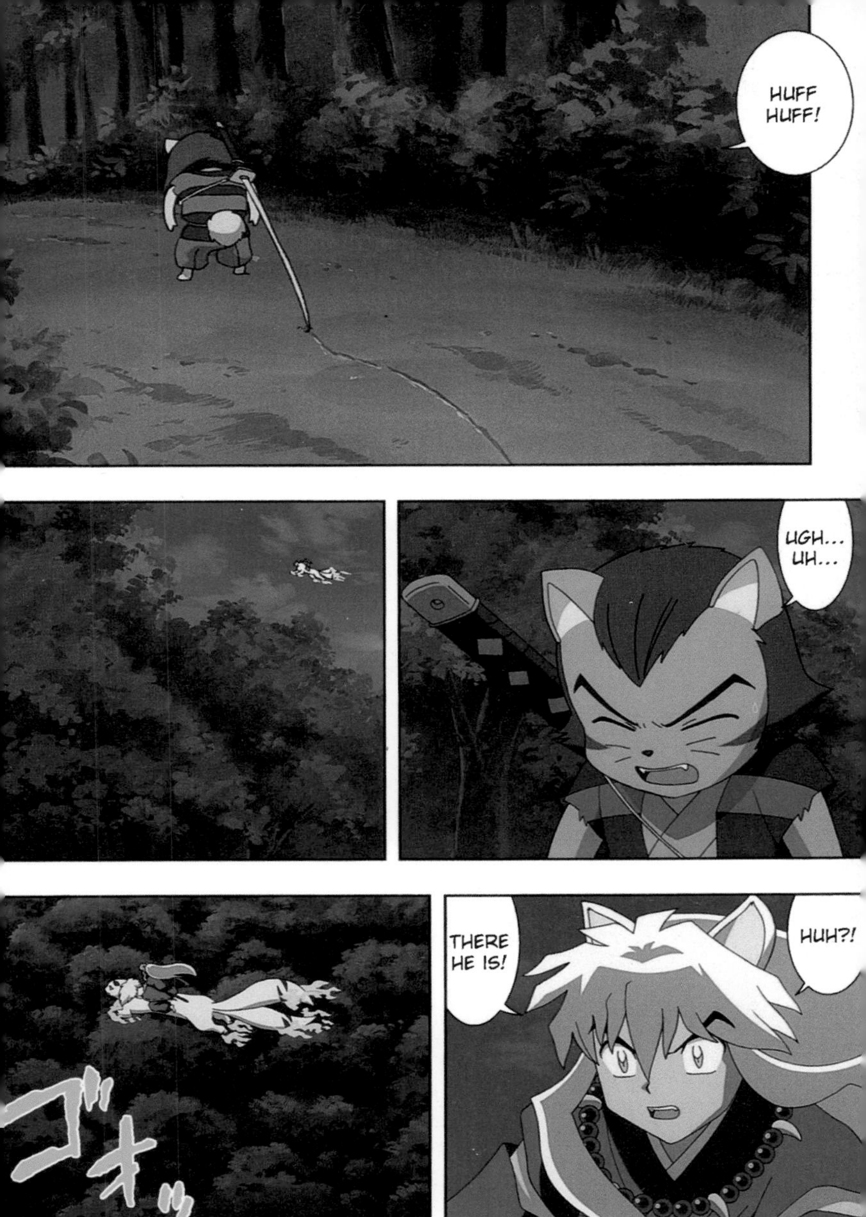
HUFF HUFF!
UGH... UH...
HUH?!
THERE HE IS!
ゴオッ

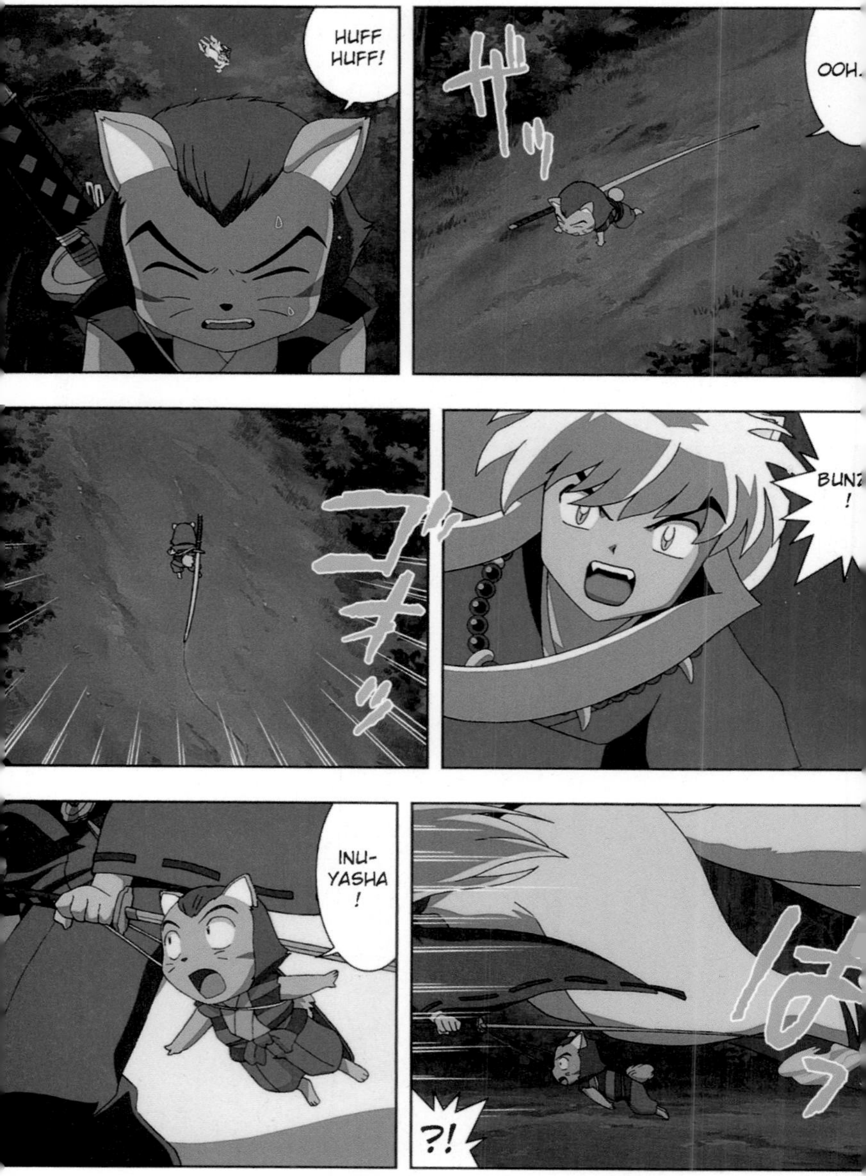
OOH..
HUFF HUFF!
BUNZ !
?!
INU-YASHA!

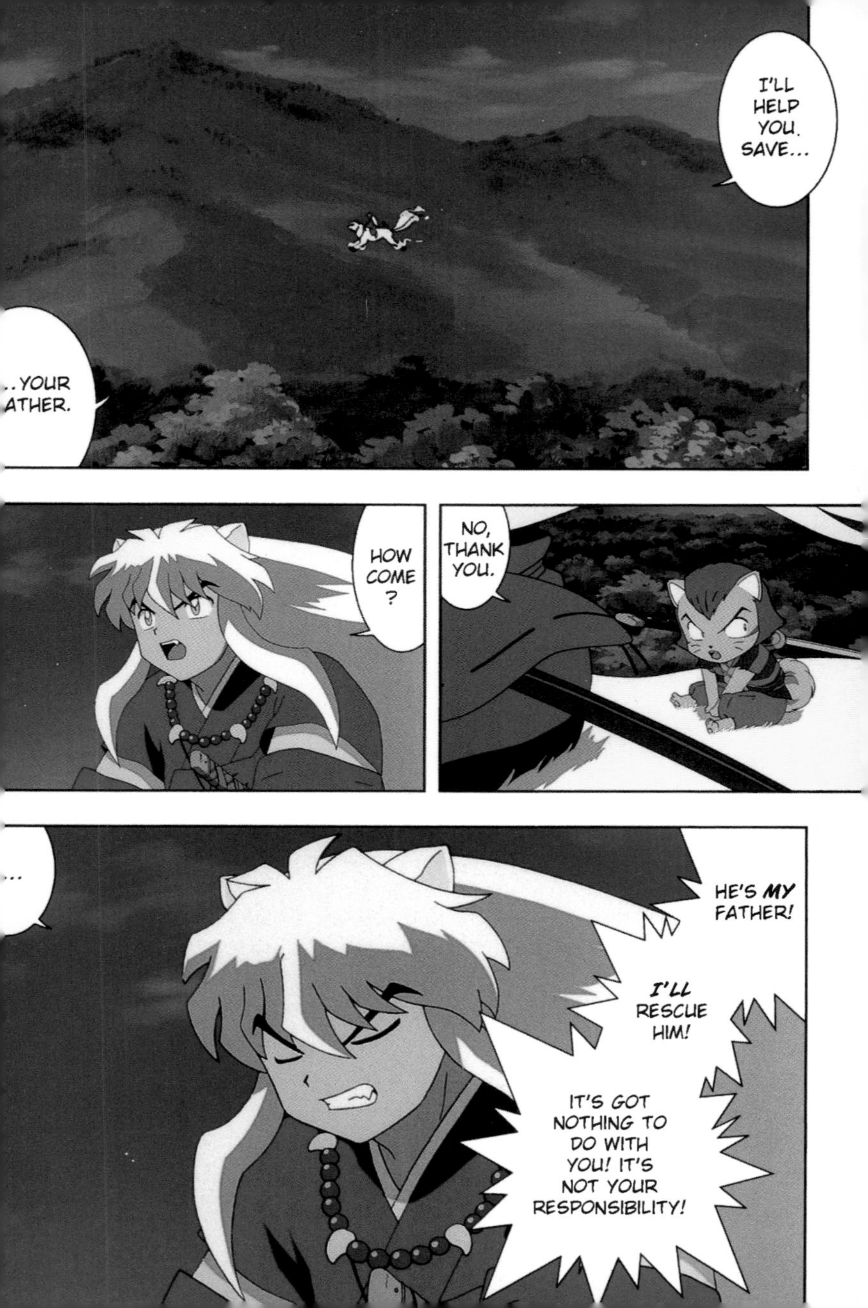
I'LL HELP YOU. SAVE...
..YOUR ATHER.
NO, THANK YOU.
HOW COME?
...
HE'S *MY* FATHER!
I'LL RESCUE HIM!
IT'S GOT NOTHING TO DO WITH YOU! IT'S NOT YOUR RESPONSIBILITY!

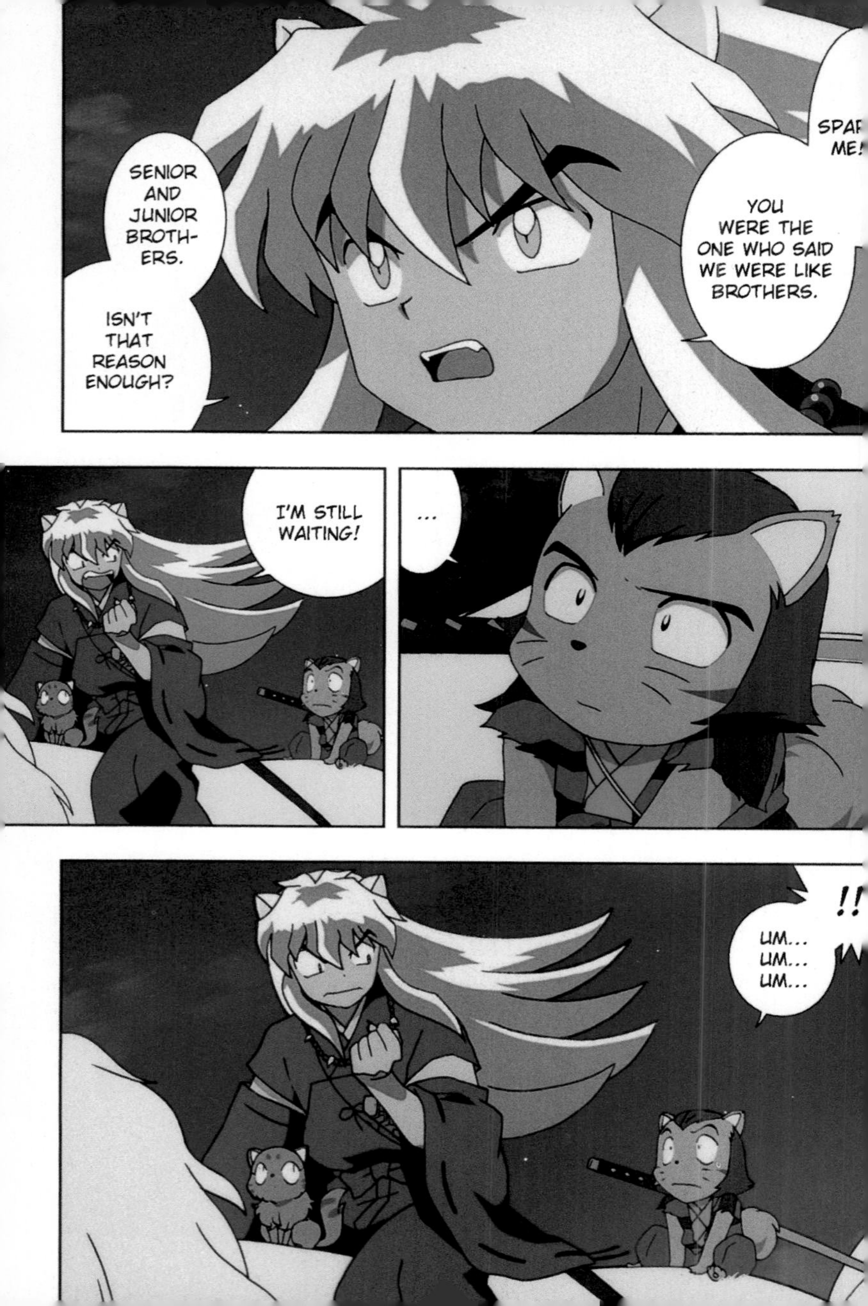
SPAR
ME!
YOU WERE THE ONE WHO SAID WE WERE LIKE BROTHERS.
SENIOR AND JUNIOR BROTH-ERS.
ISN'T THAT REASON ENOUGH?
...
I'M STILL WAITING!
!!
UM... UM... UM...

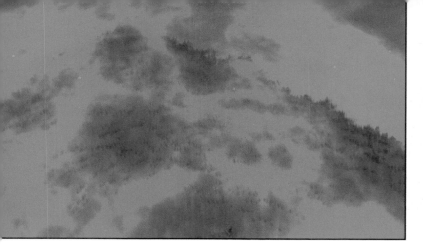

…

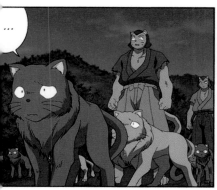

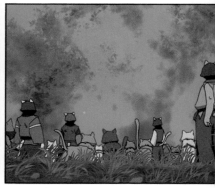

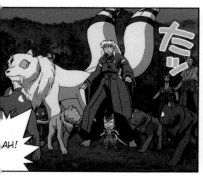

た
ッ

AH!

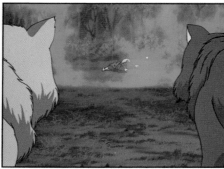

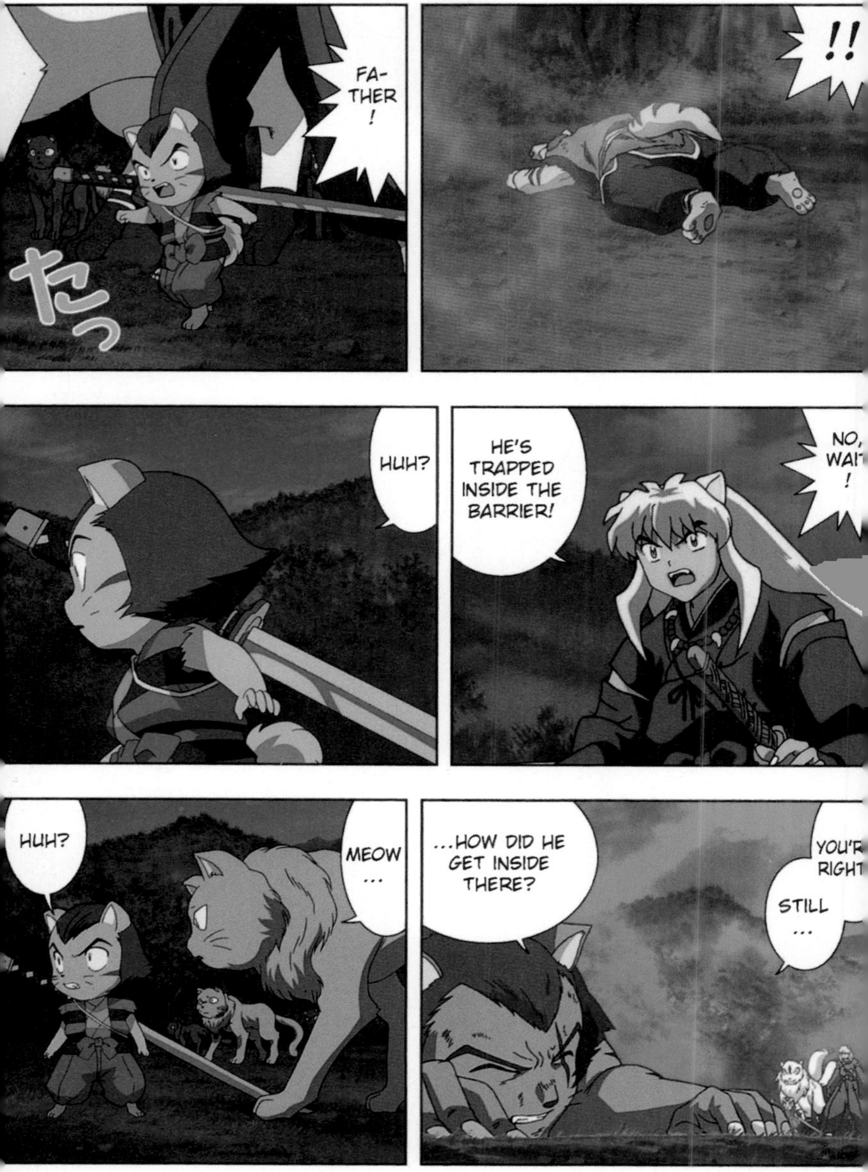
!!
FA-THER!
たっ
NO, WAIT!
HE'S TRAPPED INSIDE THE BARRIER!
HUH?
YOU'R RIGHT
STILL ...
...HOW DID HE GET INSIDE THERE?
MEOW ...
HUH?

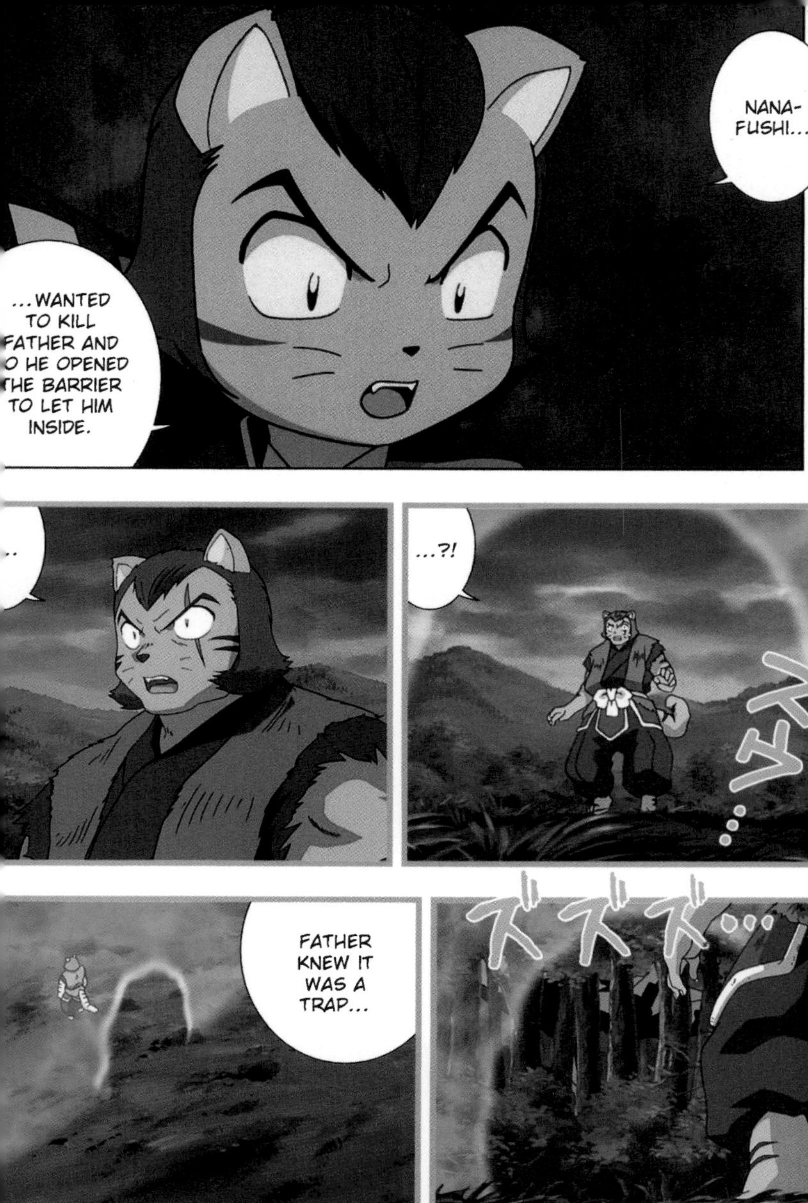
NANA-FUSHI...
...WANTED TO KILL FATHER AND O HE OPENED THE BARRIER TO LET HIM INSIDE.
...?!
..
ズズズ...
FATHER KNEW IT WAS A TRAP...

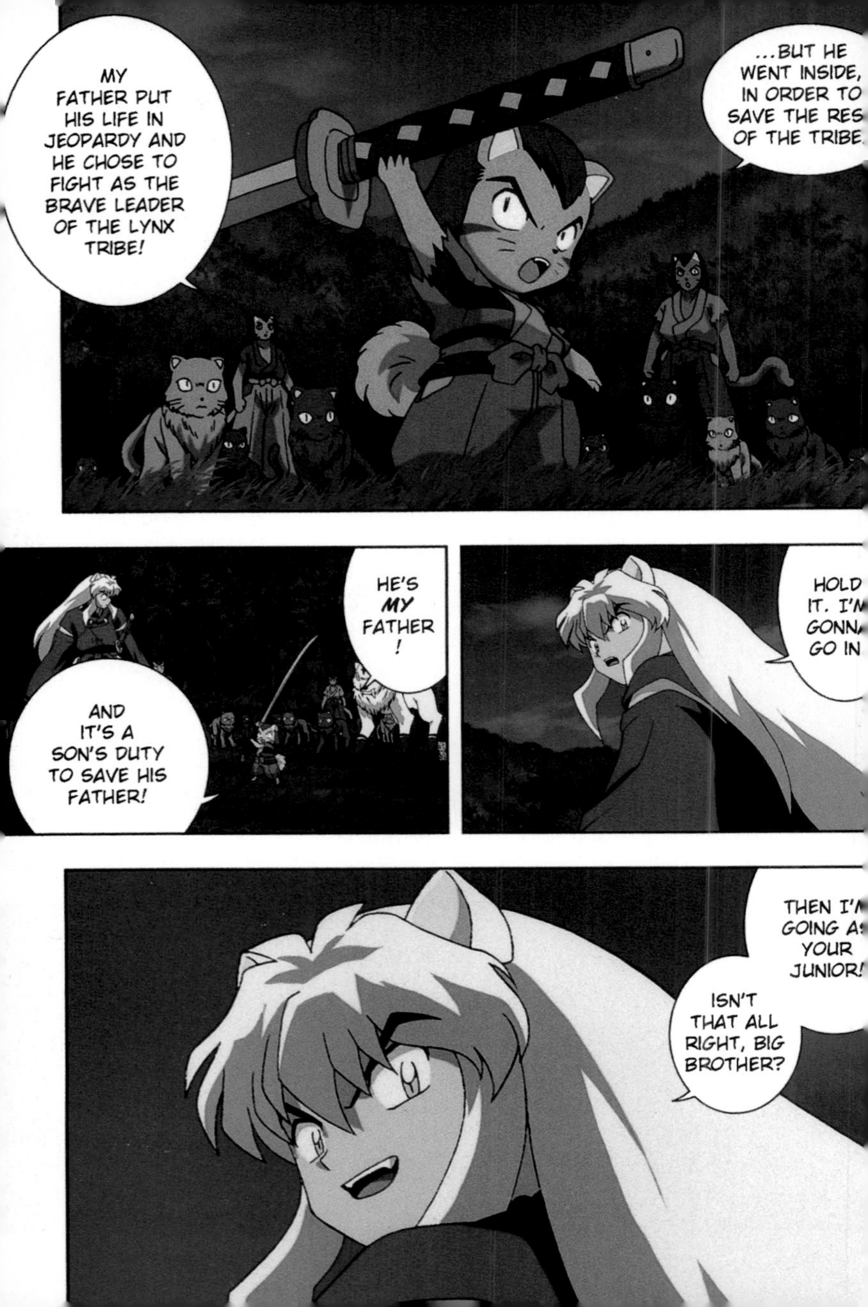
...BUT HE WENT INSIDE, IN ORDER TO SAVE THE RES OF THE TRIBE.
MY FATHER PUT HIS LIFE IN JEOPARDY AND HE CHOSE TO FIGHT AS THE BRAVE LEADER OF THE LYNX TRIBE!
HOLD IT. I'M GONNA GO IN.
HE'S *MY* FATHER!
AND IT'S A SON'S DUTY TO SAVE HIS FATHER!
THEN I'M GOING A YOUR JUNIOR!
ISN'T THAT ALL RIGHT, BIG BROTHER?

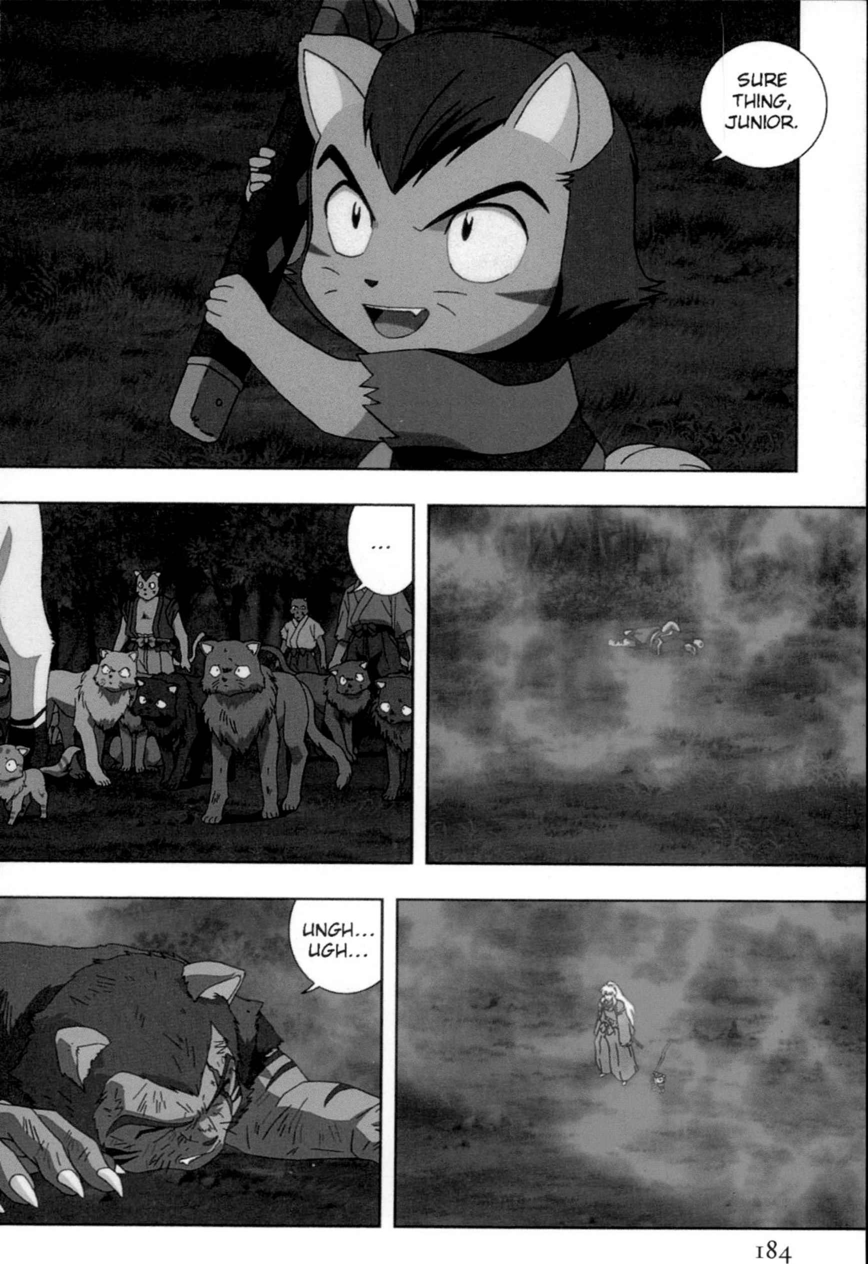
SURE THING, JUNIOR.
...
UNGH... UGH...

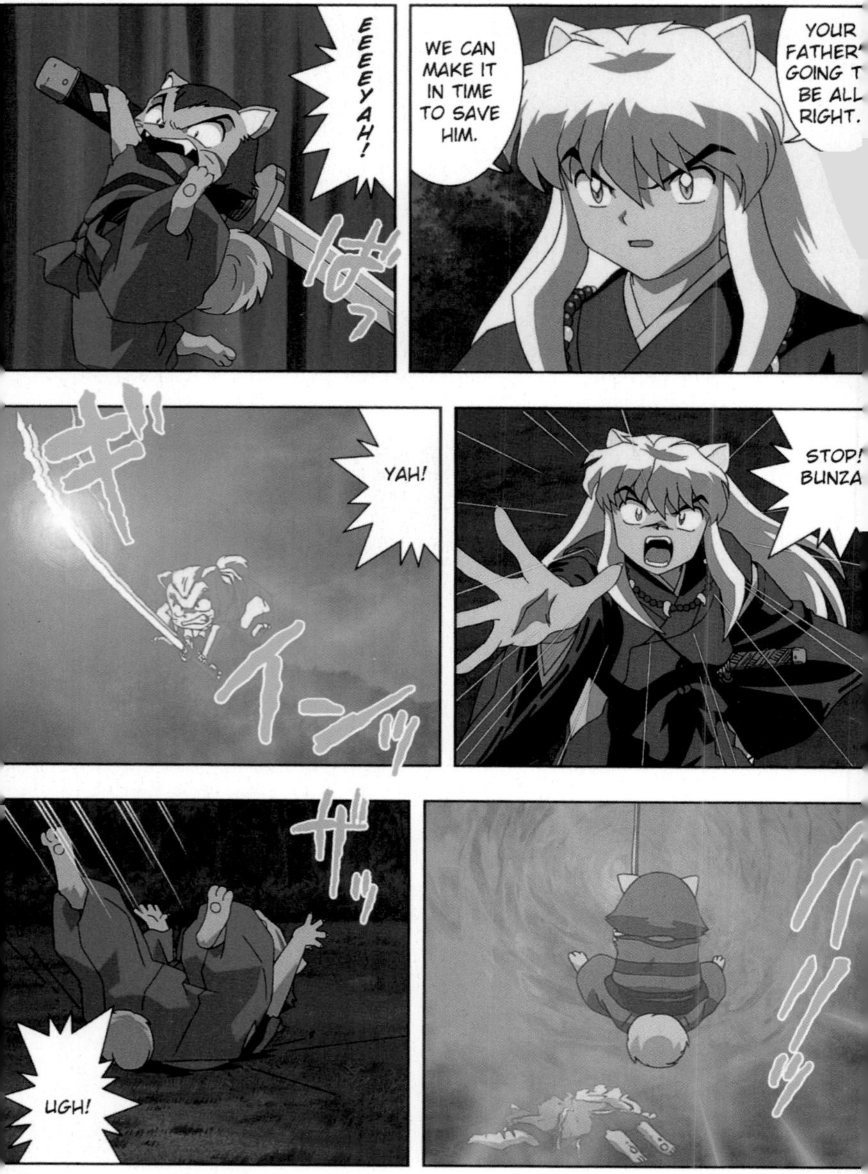
YOUR FATHER' GOING T BE ALL RIGHT.
WE CAN MAKE IT IN TIME TO SAVE HIM.
EEEEYAH!
ぼっ
STOP! BUNZA
YAH!
ギイーンッ
ザッ
UGH!

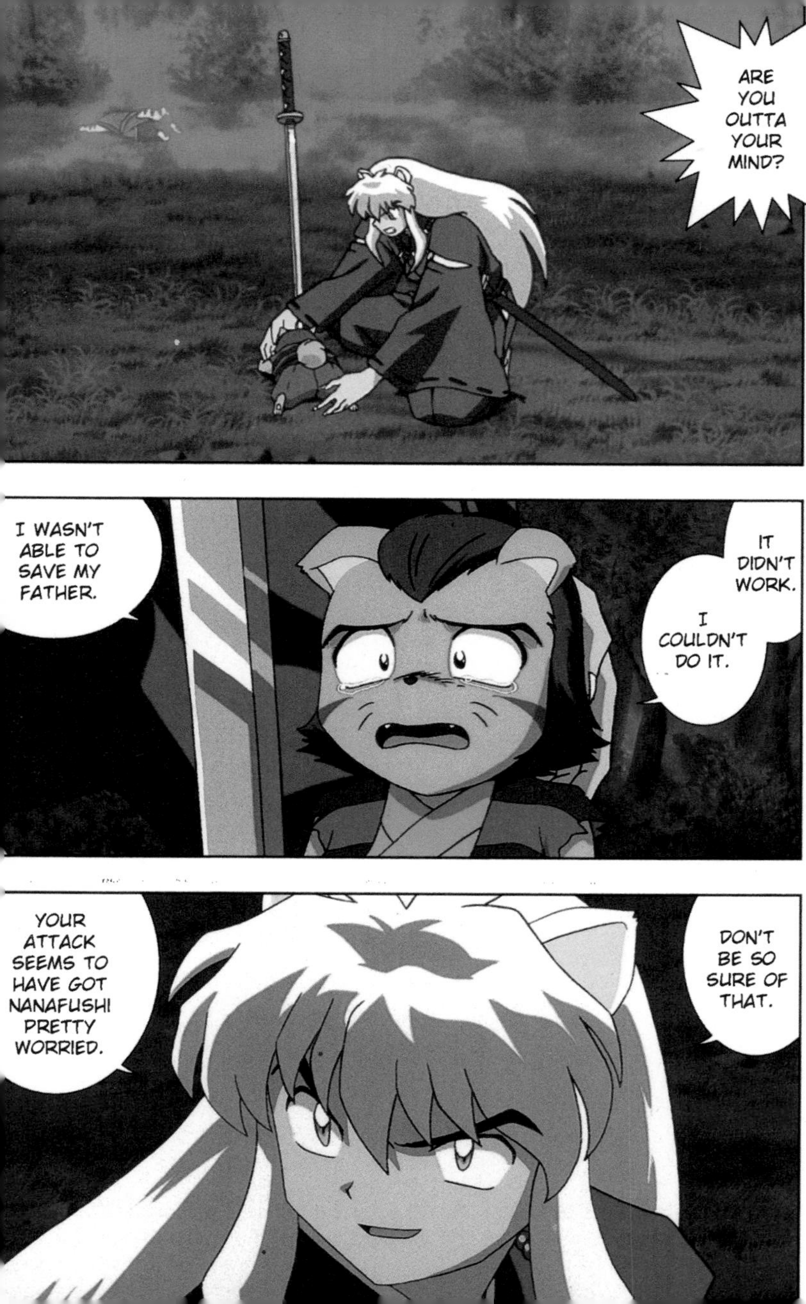
ARE YOU OUTTA YOUR MIND?
IT DIDN'T WORK.
I COULDN'T DO IT.
I WASN'T ABLE TO SAVE MY FATHER.
DON'T BE SO SURE OF THAT.
YOUR ATTACK SEEMS TO HAVE GOT NANAFUSHI PRETTY WORRIED.

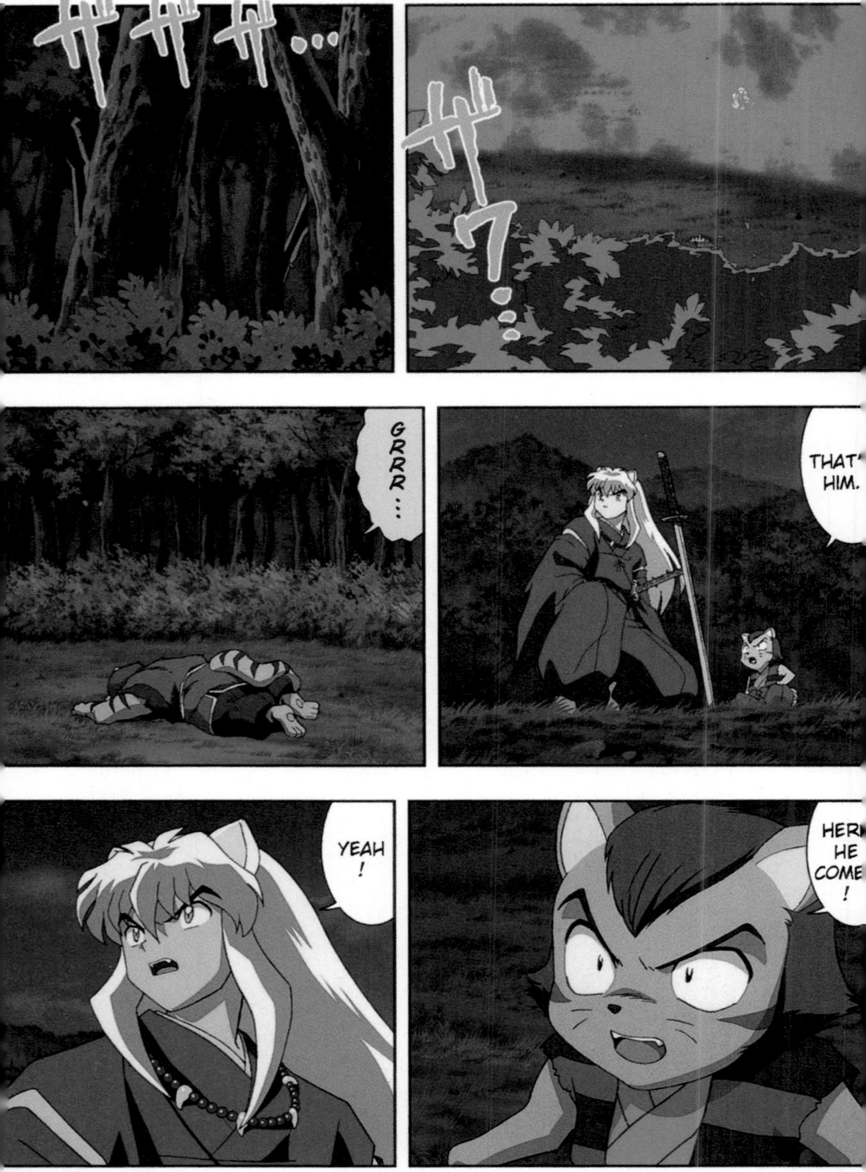
ザワ…
ザザザ…
THAT'
HIM.
GRRR…
HER
HE
COME
!
YEAH
!

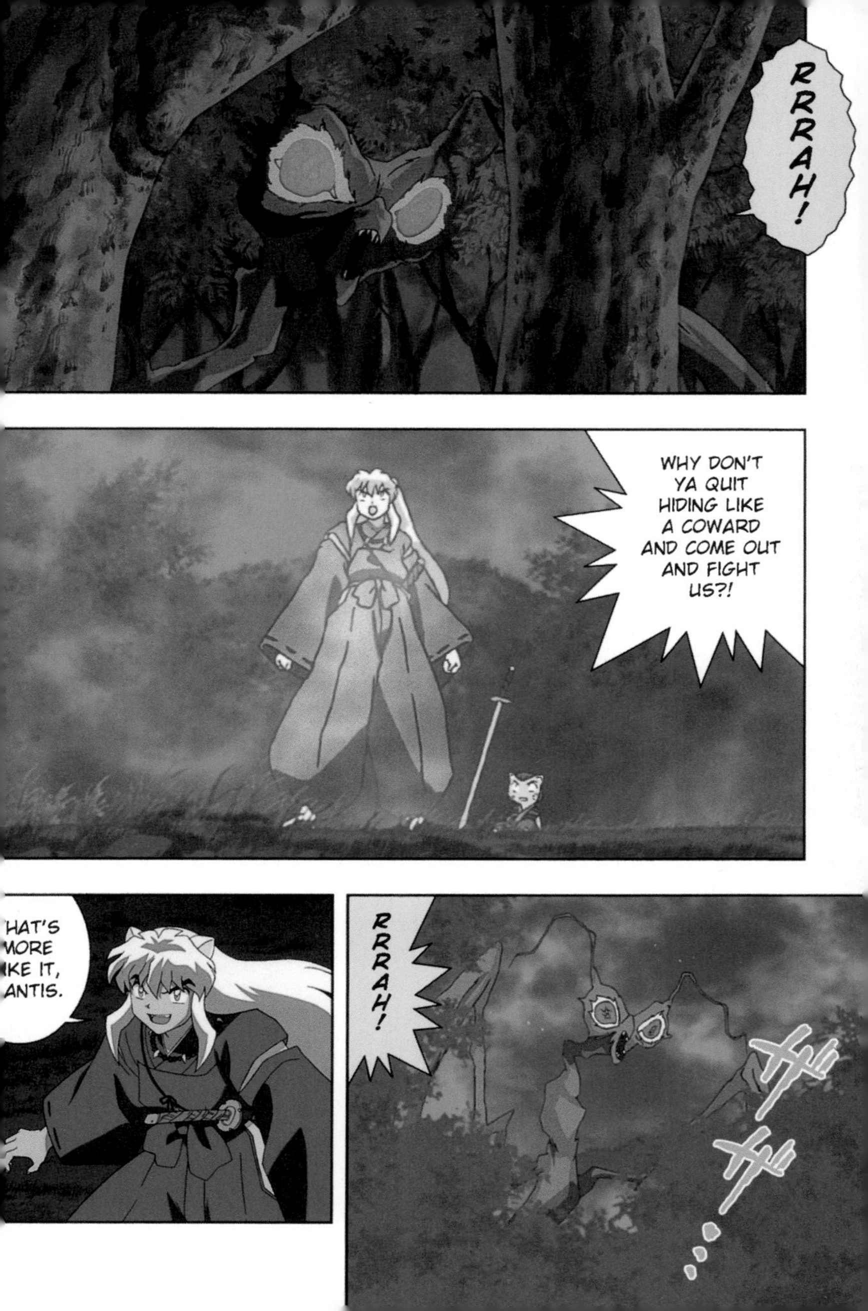
RRRAH!
WHY DON'T YA QUIT HIDING LIKE A COWARD AND COME OUT AND FIGHT US?!
RRRAH!
HAT'S MORE IKE IT, ANTIS.

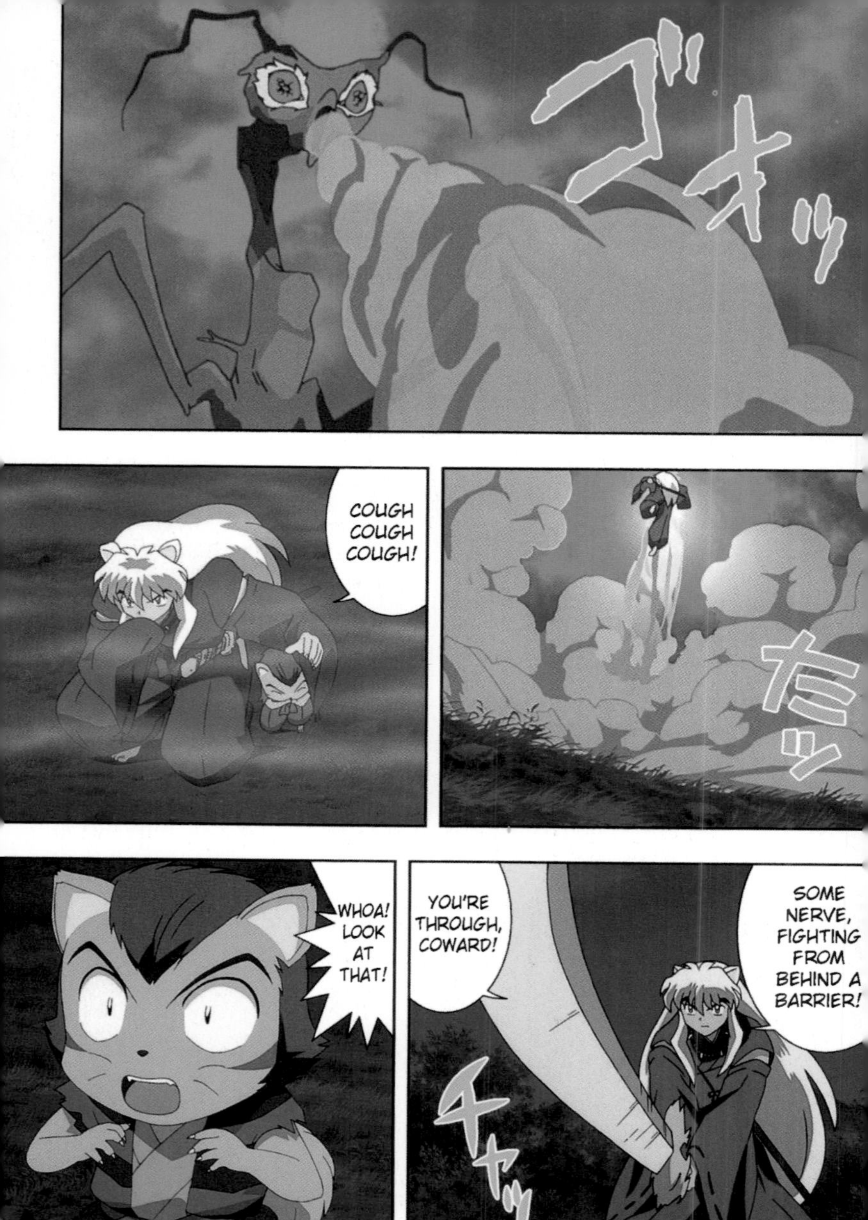
ゴオッ
COUGH COUGH COUGH!
SOME NERVE, FIGHTING FROM BEHIND A BARRIER!
YOU'RE THROUGH, COWARD!
チャッ
WHOA! LOOK AT THAT!

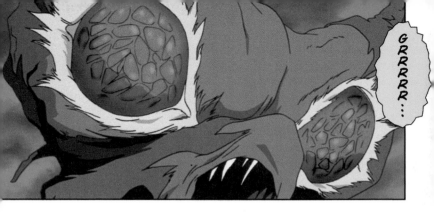

GRRRRR...

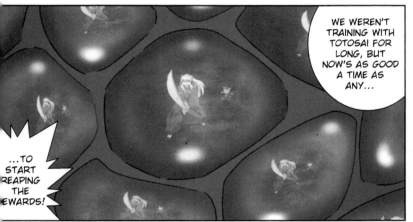

WE WEREN'T TRAINING WITH TOTOSAI FOR LONG, BUT NOW'S AS GOOD A TIME AS ANY...

...TO START REAPING THE EWARDS!

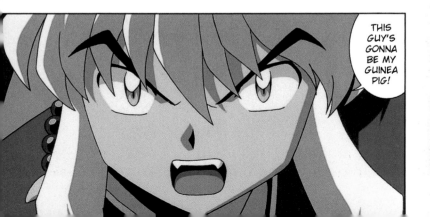

THIS GUY'S GONNA BE MY GUINEA PIG!

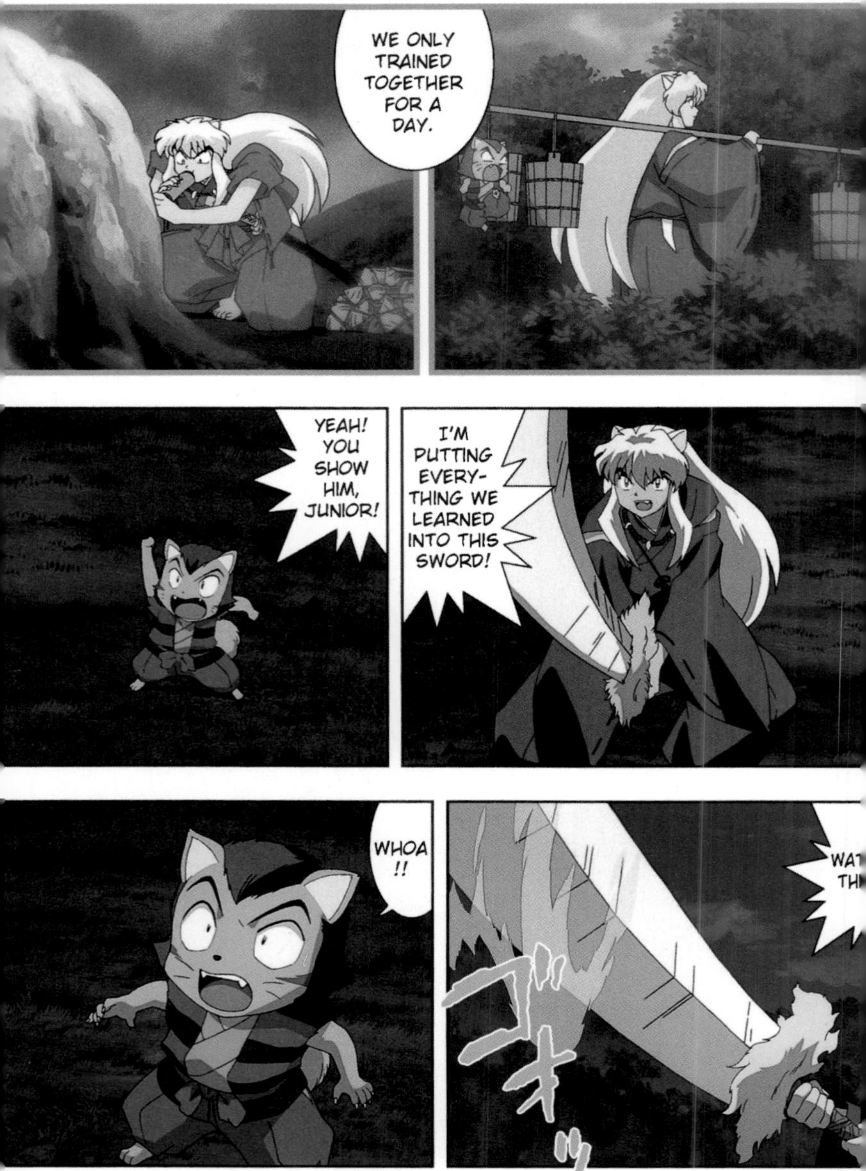
WE ONLY TRAINED TOGETHER FOR A DAY.
I'M PUTTING EVERY-THING WE LEARNED INTO THIS SWORD!
YEAH! YOU SHOW HIM, JUNIOR!
ゴキッ
WHOA !!

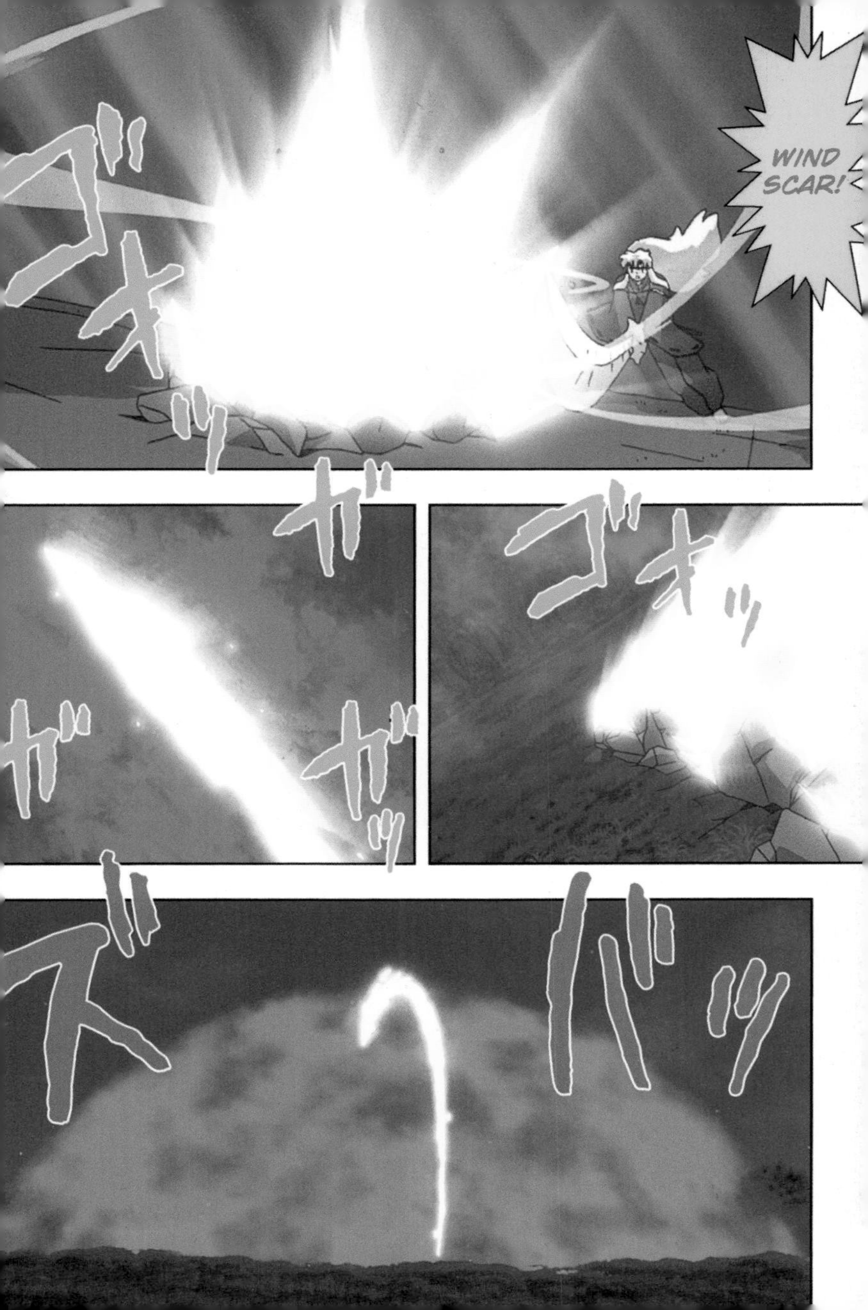
WIND SCAR!
ゴオッ
ゴオッ
ガガガッ
ズバッ

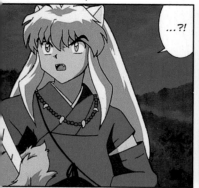

…?!

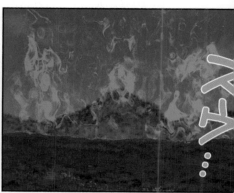

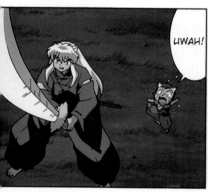

UWAH!

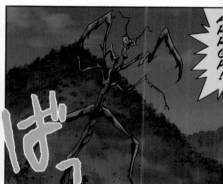

ARRGH!

ばっ

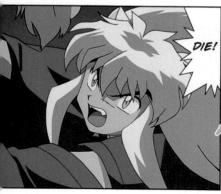

DIE!

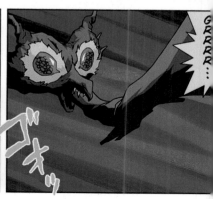

GRRRR…

ゴキッ

193

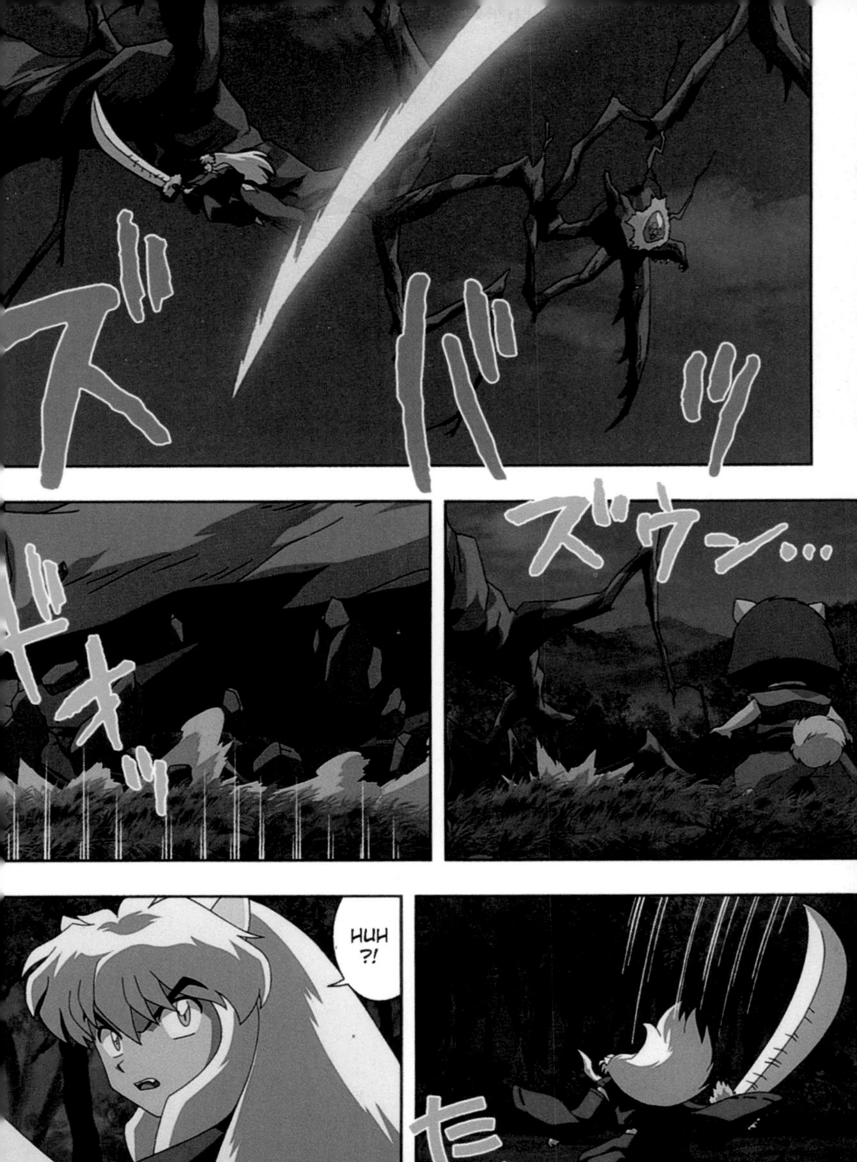
ズバッ
ズウン…
ドオッ
タッ
HUH ?!

ARGH!
ズ…
メキ…
メキ…
YOU WANT ANOTHE GO AT ME?
FINE!
ドガッ

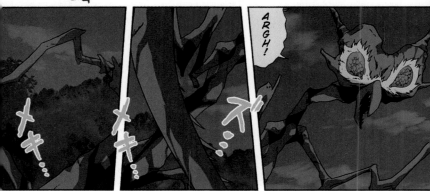

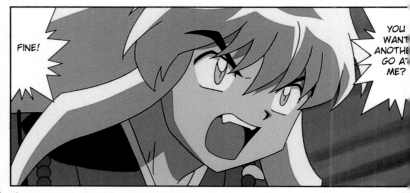

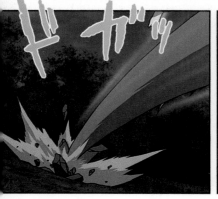

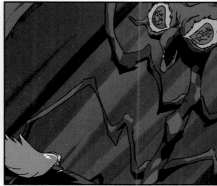

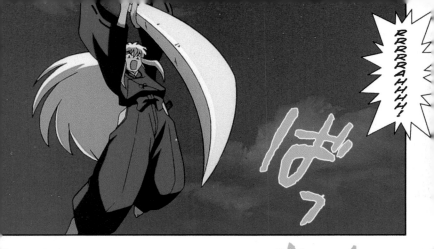

RRRRRAHHHH!

ばっ

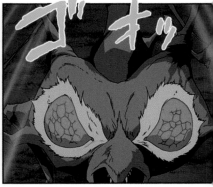

ゴキッ

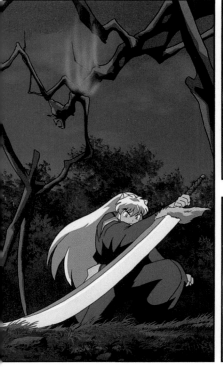

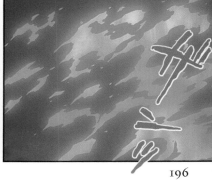

サッ

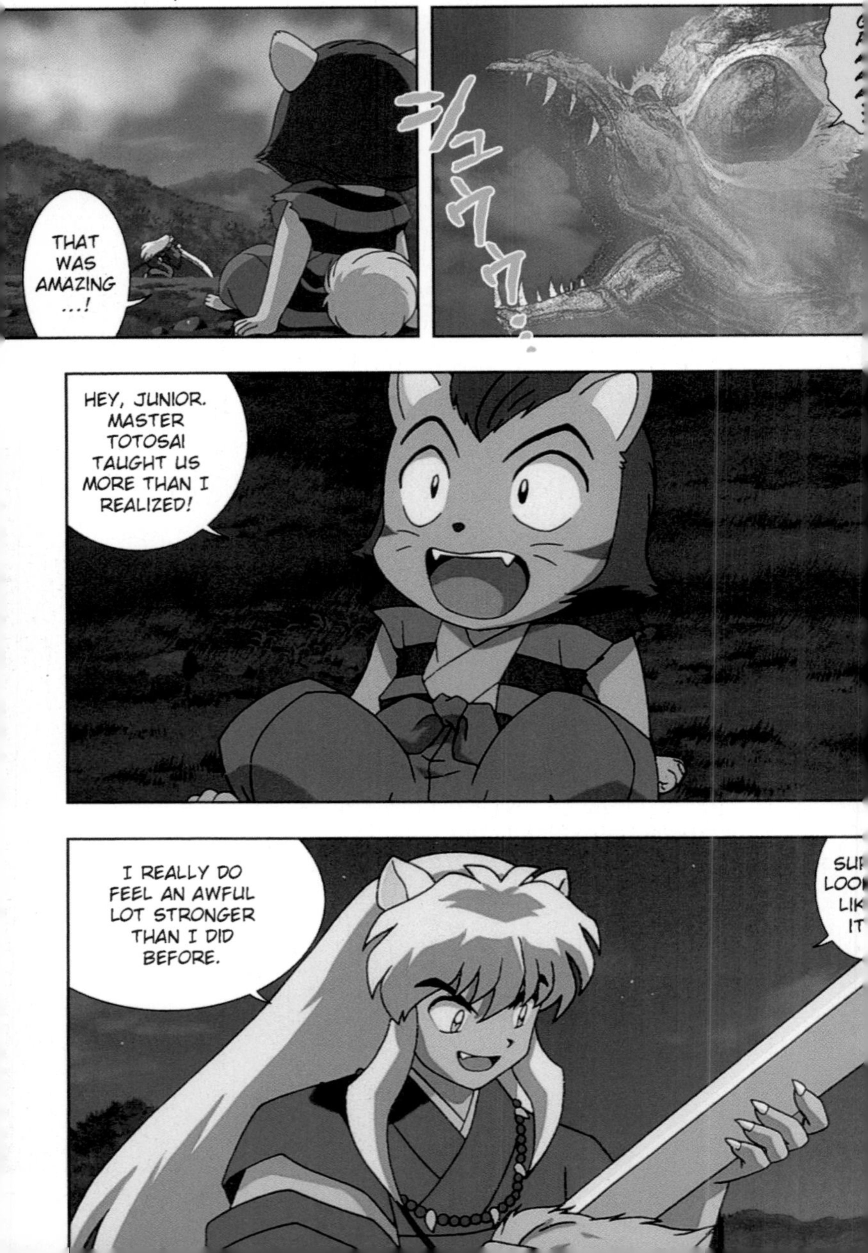
シュウウウ…
THAT WAS AMAZING ...!
HEY, JUNIOR. MASTER TOTOSAI TAUGHT US MORE THAN I REALIZED!
I REALLY DO FEEL AN AWFUL LOT STRONGER THAN I DID BEFORE.

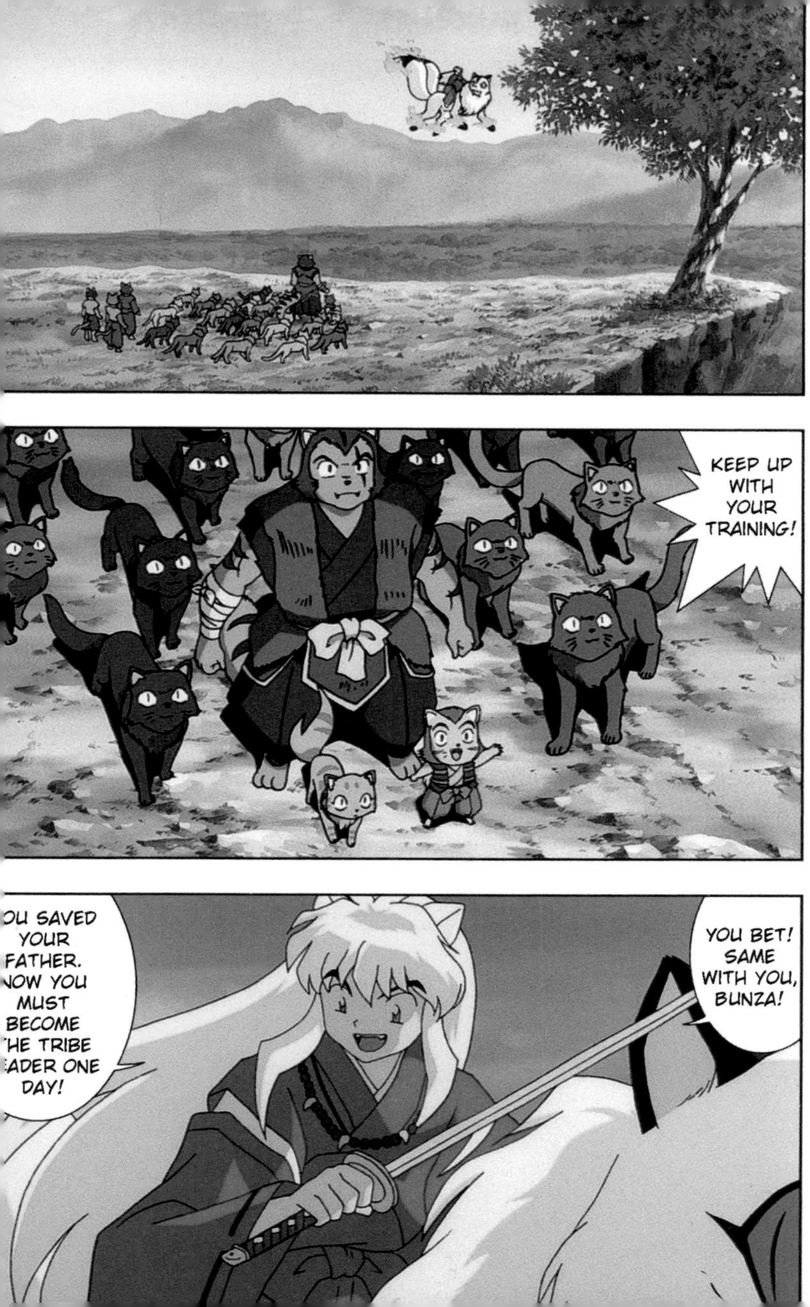
KEEP UP WITH YOUR TRAINING!
YOU BET! SAME WITH YOU, BUNZA!
OU SAVED YOUR FATHER. NOW YOU MUST BECOME THE TRIBE EADER ONE DAY!

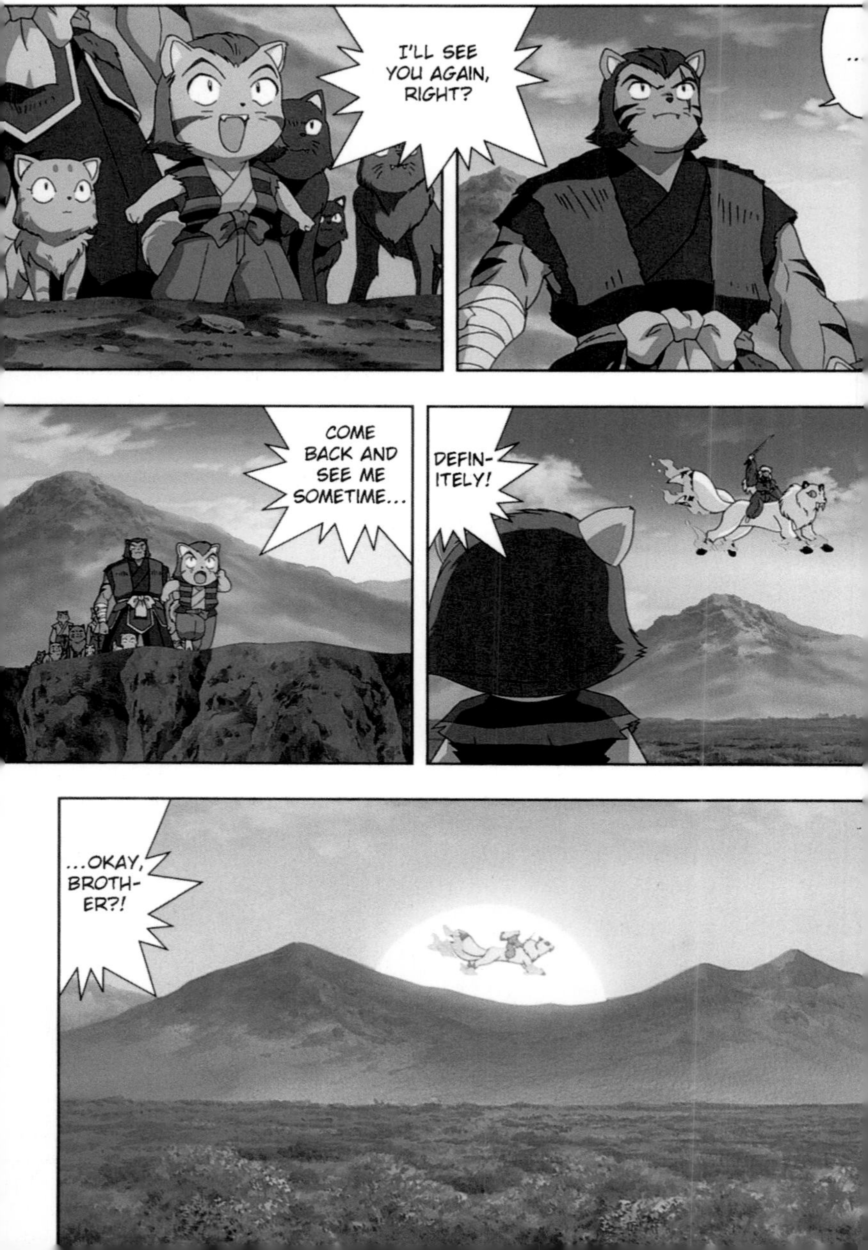
..
I'LL SEE YOU AGAIN, RIGHT?
DEFIN-ITELY!
COME BACK AND SEE ME SOMETIME...
...OKAY, BROTH-ER?!

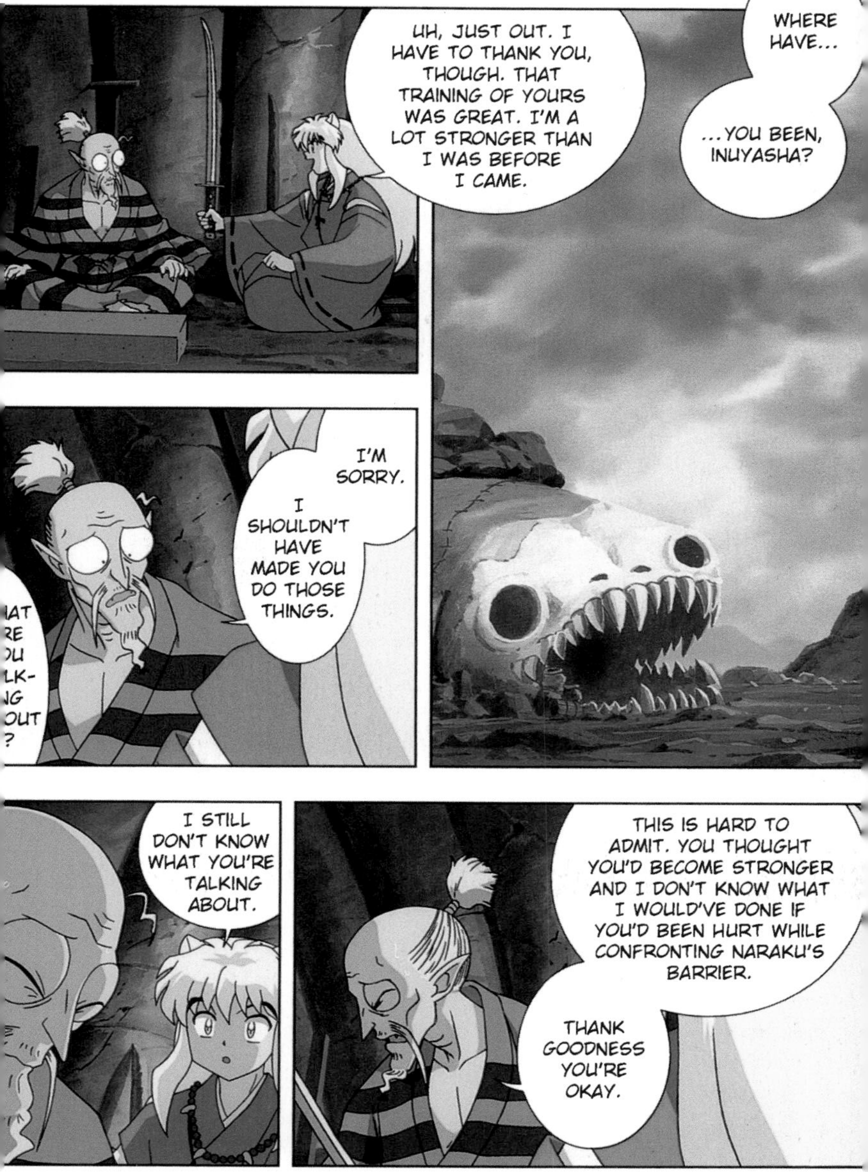
WHERE HAVE...
...YOU BEEN, INUYASHA?
UH, JUST OUT. I HAVE TO THANK YOU, THOUGH. THAT TRAINING OF YOURS WAS GREAT. I'M A LOT STRONGER THAN I WAS BEFORE I CAME.
I'M SORRY.
I SHOULDN'T HAVE MADE YOU DO THOSE THINGS.
THIS IS HARD TO ADMIT. YOU THOUGHT YOU'D BECOME STRONGER AND I DON'T KNOW WHAT I WOULD'VE DONE IF YOU'D BEEN HURT WHILE CONFRONTING NARAKU'S BARRIER.
THANK GOODNESS YOU'RE OKAY.
I STILL DON'T KNOW WHAT YOU'RE TALKING ABOUT.

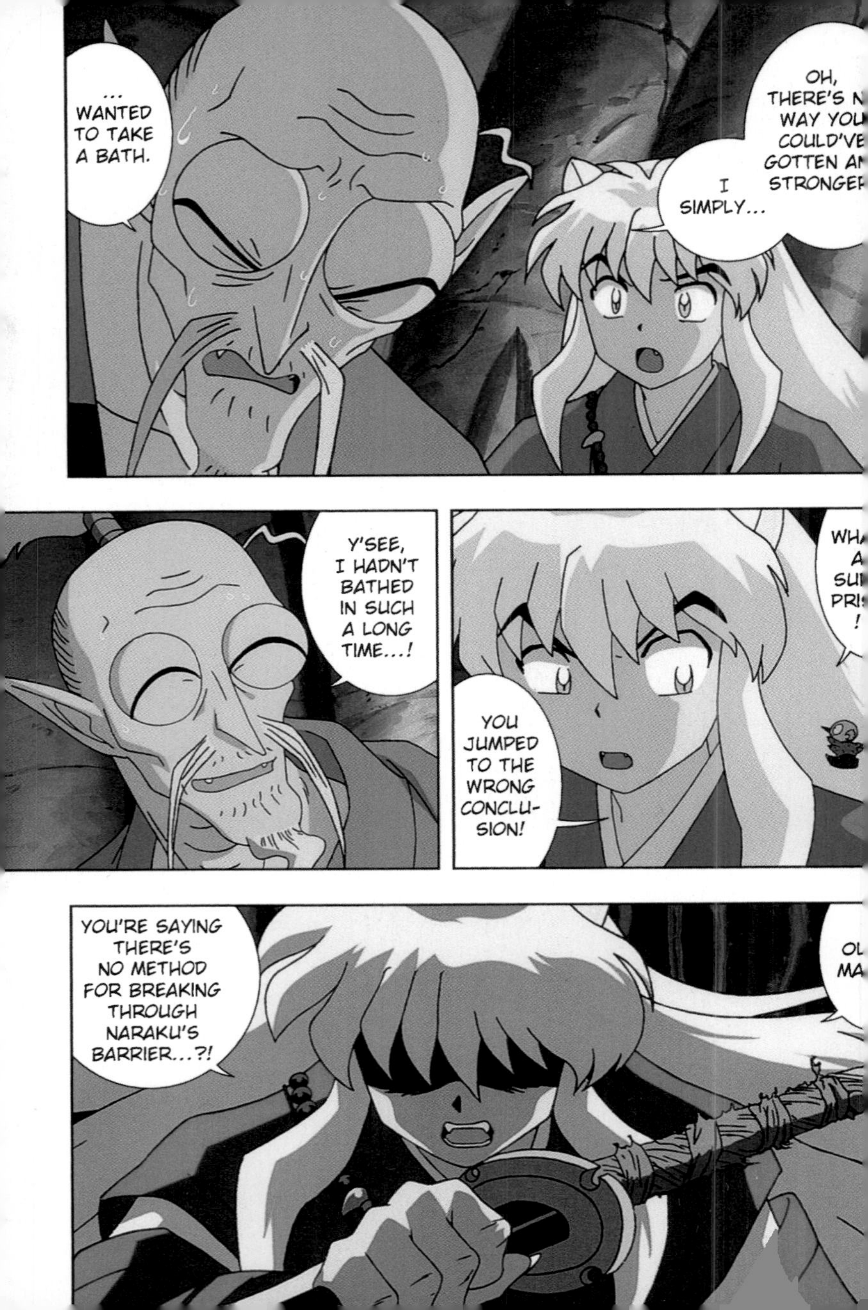

OH, THERE'S N WAY YOU COULD'VE GOTTEN AN STRONGEF
I SIMPLY...
... WANTED TO TAKE A BATH.
WHA A SU PRIS !
YOU JUMPED TO THE WRONG CONCLU-SION!
Y'SEE, I HADN'T BATHED IN SUCH A LONG TIME...!
OL MA
YOU'RE SAYING THERE'S NO METHOD FOR BREAKING THROUGH NARAKU'S BARRIER...?!

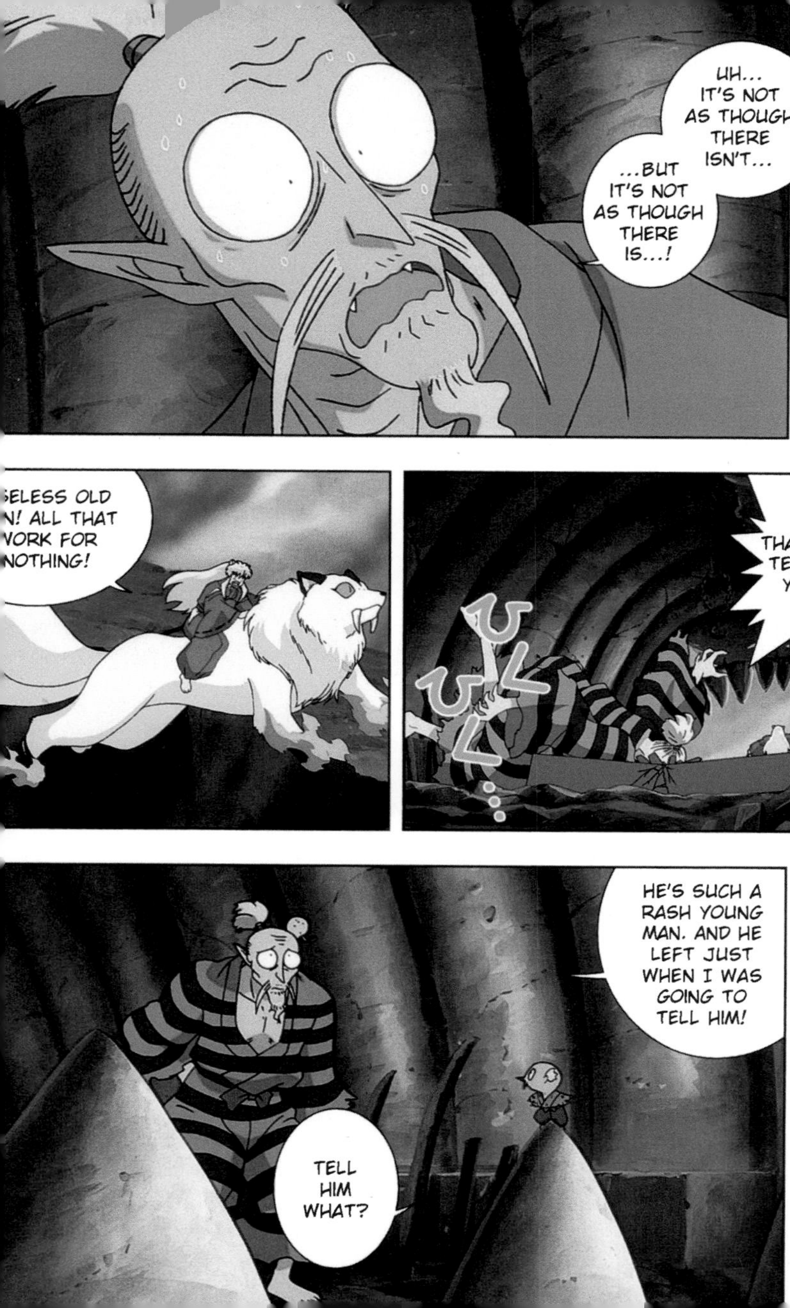
UH... IT'S NOT AS THOUGH THERE ISN'T...
...BUT IT'S NOT AS THOUGH THERE IS...!
THAT'LL TEACH YA!
SELESS OLD N! ALL THAT WORK FOR NOTHING!
HE'S SUCH A RASH YOUNG MAN. AND HE LEFT JUST WHEN I WAS GOING TO TELL HIM!
TELL HIM WHAT?

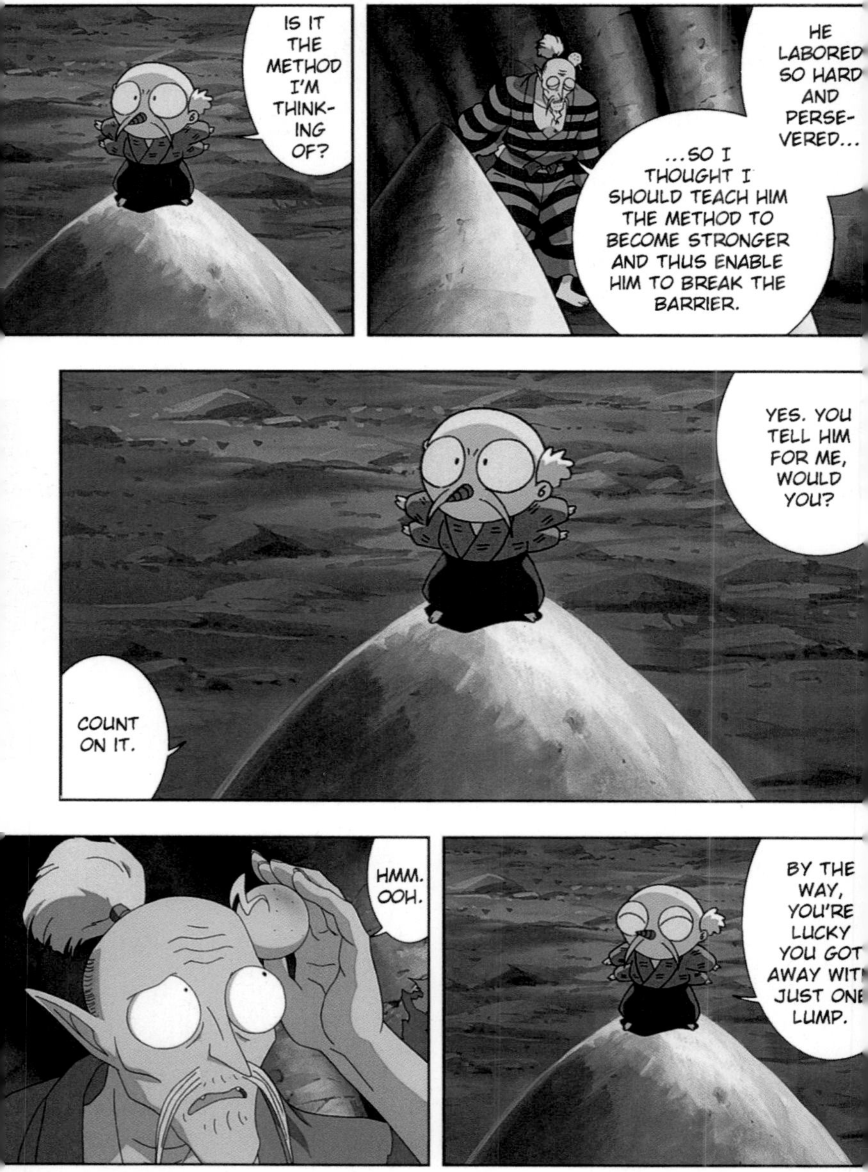
HE LABORED SO HARD AND PERSE-VERED...
...SO I THOUGHT I SHOULD TEACH HIM THE METHOD TO BECOME STRONGER AND THUS ENABLE HIM TO BREAK THE BARRIER.
IS IT THE METHOD I'M THINK-ING OF?
YES. YOU TELL HIM FOR ME, WOULD YOU?
COUNT ON IT.
BY THE WAY, YOU'RE LUCKY YOU GOT AWAY WIT JUST ONE LUMP.
HMM. OOH.

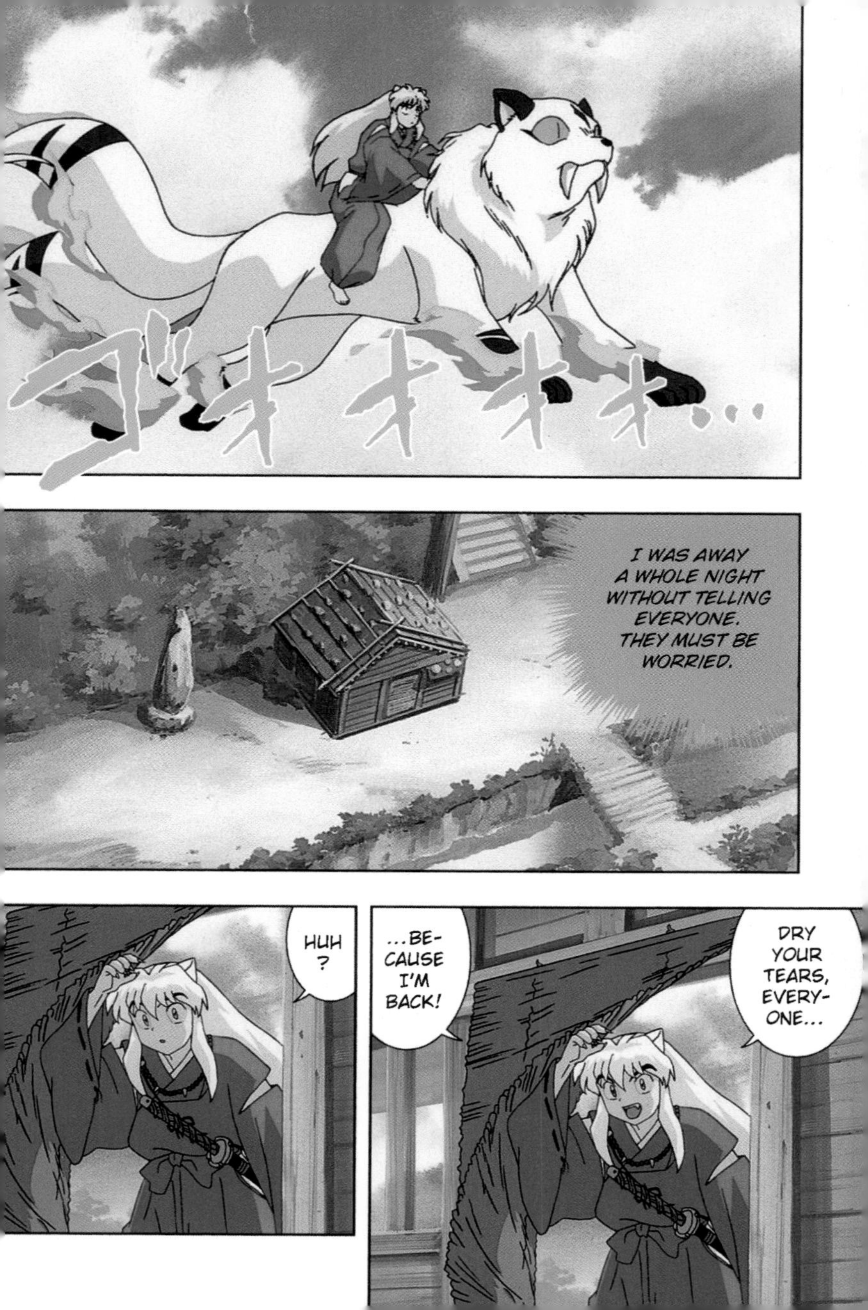
ゴオオオ…
I WAS AWAY A WHOLE NIGHT WITHOUT TELLING EVERYONE. THEY MUST BE WORRIED.
DRY YOUR TEARS, EVERY-ONE...
...BE-CAUSE I'M BACK!
HUH?

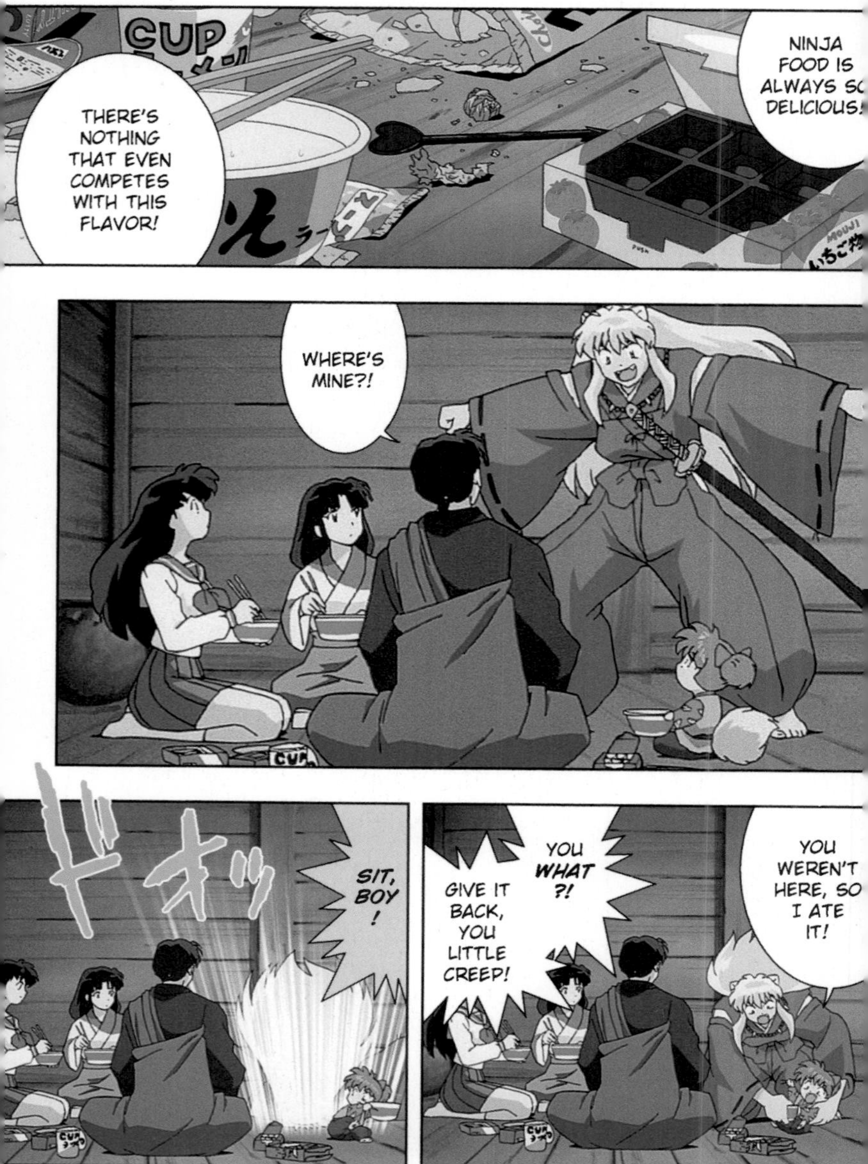
NINJA FOOD IS ALWAYS SO DELICIOUS!
THERE'S NOTHING THAT EVEN COMPETES WITH THIS FLAVOR!
CUP
WHERE'S MINE?!
YOU WEREN'T HERE, SO I ATE IT!
YOU WHAT?!
GIVE IT BACK, YOU LITTLE CREEP!
SIT, BOY!
ドオッ

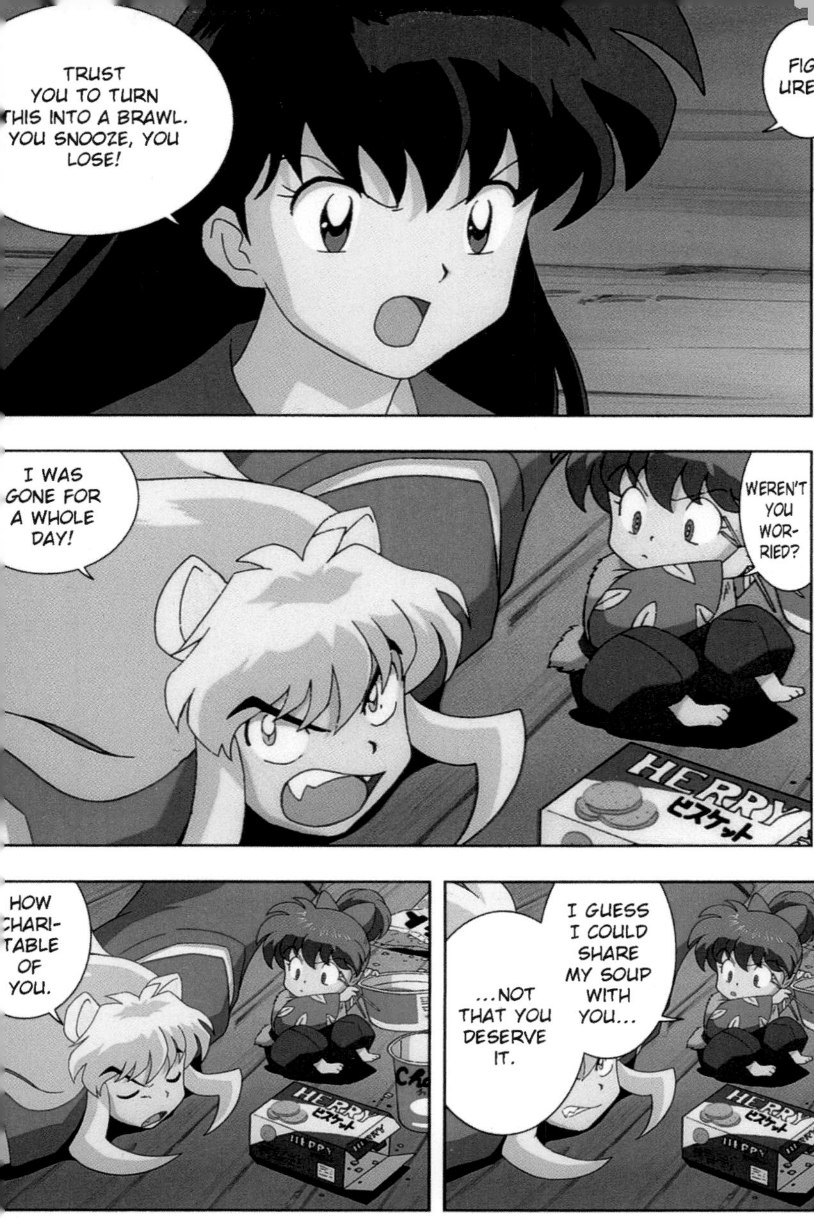
FIG- URES!
TRUST YOU TO TURN THIS INTO A BRAWL. YOU SNOOZE, YOU LOSE!
WEREN'T YOU WOR- RIED?
I WAS GONE FOR A WHOLE DAY!
HERRY
ビスケット
I GUESS I COULD SHARE MY SOUP WITH YOU...
...NOT THAT YOU DESERVE IT.
HOW CHARI- TABLE OF YOU.

Glossary of Sound Effects

Each entry includes: the location, indicated by page number and panel number (so 3.1 means page 3, panel number 1); the phonetic romanization of the original Japanese; and our English "translation"—we offer as close an English equivalent as we can.

11.2 FX: BA (Inuyasha strikes)
11.3 FX: Doga (a wicked slash)
11.4 FX: Goh (whoosh)
11.5 FX: Ka (shining of Wind Scar strike)

12.2 FX: Whooooosh... (Wind Scar consumes Faceless Man)
12.3 FX: Shuuuu... (hissing)

16.4 FX: Gata gata... (trembling)

21.3 FX: Cha (clank as chains release)

22.1 FX: Poh... (reconstituting)
22.2 FX: Zu zu zu... (body parts gravitate back together)
22.3 FX: Zu zu... (more body parts gravitate)
22.4 FX: Zu zu zu (more body parts gravitate)

23.2/3 FX: Suu... (spider burn mark forms)

26.1 FX: Za za... (rustling)
26.2 FX: Za (Muso emerges from bushes)

27.1 FX: Za (footsteps on grass)

35.4 FX: Goh (Kagura whooshes off)

39.3 FX: Goh (Kagura whooshes away)

43.4 FX: Da (running)

44.3 FX: Shururu... (tentacle snakes out)

Chapter 70
Terror of the Faceless Man

6.1 FX: Da (running)
6.2 FX: Shurururu... (tentacle snakes out)
6.4 FX: Shurururu... (more tentacles)

7.5 FX: Ba (Inuyasha reaches for sword)

8.1 FX: Zan (sword strike)
8.2 FX: Ba (Inuyasha cuts the tentacles around Kagome)
8.3 FX: Shurururu... (tentacle severed)
8.4 FX: Buuu...n... (poison insects buzz)

9.1 FX: Bu bu bu bu (buzzing as insects reattach arm)
9.2 FX: Poh... (arm turns back to flesh)
9.3 FX: Shu (Faceless Man's arm snakes out)
9.4 FX: Zuba (slash)
9.5 FX: Da (Faceless Man reaches out, runs)
9.6 FX: Cha (Inuyasha raises his sword to protect Kagome)

10.2 FX: Shuru... (tentacles reach out again)
10.3 FX: Doga (and grab Inuyasha)
10.4 FX: Shururururu... (tentacle sound)
10.5 FX: Doh (tentacle strikes ground in front of Kagome)

11.1 FX: Da (Inuyasha runs toward Faceless Man)

64.1 FX: Dokun dokun (pulsing)
64.2 FX: Zu zu...
(Naraku's hand transforms)

66.1 FX: Ba
(Muso reaches out with tentacle)
66.2 FX: Zan (slash)

67.2 FX: Ba (slash)
67.3 FX: Goh (whoosh)
67.4 FX: Za (Inuyasha thrown to grass)
67.5 FX: Ga (tentacle slams into ground)
67.5 FX: Zu zu zu (dust clears)
67.6 FX: Doga
(Inuyasha impaled on tentacle)

68.1 FX: Bun (Sango throws Hiraikotsu)
68.2 FX: Zan
(tentacle snakes out at Inuyasha)
68.4 FX: Goh (Whoosh)
68.5 FX: Zuba (slash)

70.4 FX: Zu zu zu... (Muso transforms)

71.1 FX: Zu zu zu (more transforming)
71.3 FX: Ba (claw reaches out)
71.4 FX: Ta (Inuyasha leaps)

72.2 FX: ShururuShururuu... (tentacle unfurls)
72.5 FX: Doh
(Inuyasha impaled on tentacle)

Chapter 71
Three-sided Battle to the Death

74.2 FX: Bun
(Muso flings Inuyasha all about)
74.3 FX: Doh (Inuyasha thrown down)

75.1 FX: Zu... (Inuyasha pulls out Muso's
tentacle from his body)
75.2 FX: Goh (tentacle hand whooshes
through the air)
75.3 FX: Ga (tentacle hand grabs Inuyasha)

44.4 FX: Shurururururu...
(tentacle snakes out of cave)
44.5 FX: Doga (tentacle strikes rock)

45.2 FX: Shu (Kaede lets arrow fly)
45.3 FX: Pashi (Muso deflects arrow)

46.2 FX: Shururu...
(tentacle moves toward Kaede)
46.3 FX: Da (running)
46.4 FX: Ta ta ta... (Kagome runs off)
46.5 FX: Doga (tentacle slams in front
of Kagome)

47.1 FX: Bun (Muso leaps)
47.5 FX: Zuba (slash)

54.1 FX: Zu zu... (glowing)

55.2 FX: Buuu...n... (Buzzzzzzz)

56.2 FX: Ba (Muso reaches out)
56.3 FX: Ba ba ba
(tentacles getting hacked)
56.4 FX: Gishi (squeeze)
56.4 FX: Bun (tentacle picks up Inuyasha)

57.2 FX: Ba (Inuyasha breaks tentacle)
57.3 FX: Ta (Inuyasha lands)

59.2 FX: Da
(Inuyasha lunges with Tetsusaiga)

60.2 FX: Buuu...n... (Bzzz)

62.1 FX: Su...
(Naraku reaches toward Kikyo)

63.1 FX: Ga (Naraku chokes Kikyo)
63.2 FX: Ba (Naraku loosens his grip)
63.3 FX: Doh (Inuyasha gets knocked out
of the way)
63.4 FX: Giri
(Kikyo nocks an arrow at Naraku)

76.3 FX: Ga (tentacles slam out at Inuyasha)

77.2 FX: Goh… (whooshing)
77.3 FX: Goh (whoosh)
77.4 FX: Ka (shining)

78.2 FX: Piku… (discarded hand hits ground)
78.4 FX: Zuru zuru… (dragging sound)

79.1 FX: Dokun… (pulsation)
79.2 FX: Dokun dokun (spider scar pulsates)
79.4 FX: Zu zu (pieces inch back toward spider scar piece)
79.5 FX: Meki (spikes pop out)

80.1 FX: Zu zu zu (pieces reconstitute into a scorpion)

82.4 FX: Da (Inuyasha lunges for Muso)

83.1 FX: Baki (smack)
83.2 FX: Zuzaza… (skidding)

85.2 FX: Za (Muso takes a step toward Inuyasha)

86.2 FX: Ba (Inuyasha prepares to strike)
86.3 FX: Doh doh doh (Muso rushes Inuyasha)
86.4 FX: Goh (Whoosh!)

87.1 FX: Ga ga ga (smashing sounds)
87.3 FX: Ga ga ga (smashing sounds)
87.4 FX: Dokun… (pulsating)
87.5 FX: Hyun hyun (pieces of Muso fly through the air)

88.1 FX: Zu zu… (body parts scrape toward spider scar piece)

90.4 FX: Ba (Muso lunges for Inuyasha)

91.1 FX: Goh (whoosh)
91.2 FX: Gohhhh… (whoosh)
91.4 FX: Goh (whoosh as Kagura flips fan)

92.1 FX: Goh (whoosh of blade)
92.2 FX: Ga ga ga (wind blades strike)
92.3 FX: Doh (blades deflect Wind Scar)

93.2 FX: Goh (Kagura flies off)

94.1 FX: Buuu…n… (buzzing)
94.2 FX: Goh (body parts whoosh up into the sky)

95.1 FX: Ta ta ta… (Miroku runs off)

96.1 FX: Ta ta ta… (running)

102.3 FX: Shuru… (tentacles snake out of Naraku)
102.4 FX: Shu (tentacles reach for Faceless Man)

103.1 FX: Da (Muso runs off)
103.4 FX: Su (Naraku appears at Muso's side)
103.5 FX: Shu (here comes the tentacle!)
103.5 FX: Baki (crackling)

104.2 FX: Ga ga (Muso swats at Naraku with tentacle)

105.1 FX: Doh (tentacles slam into Muso's back)

106.6 FX: Zuru (Naraku lets Muso down)

107.2 FX: Da (Inuyasha lunges for Naraku)
107.3 FX: Bun (Inuyasha swings Tetsusaiga at Naraku)
107.4 FX: Gin (Tetsusaiga clangs off Naraku's tentacle)
107.5 FX: Ga (Inuyasha swings at tentacle)
107.5 FX: Gin (sword clangs off tentacle)

108.1 FX: Ga ga... (energy from tentacles)
108.3 FX: Ta (Muso steals away)
108.5 FX: Ba (Inuyasha leaps to take a big swing at Naraku)

109.1 FX: Gin (clang)

110.1 FX: Ta ta ta... (running)

111.3 FX: Pita... (Muso comes to a stop)
111.5 FX: Ta (Muso turns and starts back the other way)

112.2 FX: Goh (tentacles whoosh out)
112.3 FX: Zan (Inuyasha slashes off tentacles)
112.4 FX: Bu shuuuu... (tentacles go flying)
112.6 FX: Ta (Inuyasha dodges)

113.1 FX: Toh (Naraku appears)
113.3 FX: Ta ta ta... (running)

114.1 FX: Ba (tentacles snake out from Naraku)
114.3 FX: Doga (Inuyasha smacks Tetsusaiga into the ground for an attack)
114.4 FX: Ta (Naraku dodges)

115.2 FX: Shururu... (tentacle snakes out)
115.3 FX: Doh (Naraku pierced by tentacles)

118.3 FX: Ba (tentacles envelop Muso)
118.4 FX: Baki beki... (Muso is sucked in)

119.5 FX: Zu zu (Muso is absorbed)

120.2 FX: Kaaaa... (shining)

127.2 FX: Gin (clang)
127.3 FX: Za (rustling)
127.6 FX: Ba (Inuyasha lunges)

128.1 FX: Goh (Wind Scar whooshes)
128.2 FX: Doh (Wind Scar strikes)

128.4 FX: Shuuuu... (barrier sound)
129.4 FX: Goh (whoosh)

130.1 FX: Gohhhh... (whooshing)
130.3 FX: Buuu...n... (buzzing)

132.1 FX: Zawa... (rustling of wind)

133.1 FX: Gohhh... (Naraku's whirlwind whooshing)

136.2 FX: Ta (Kagome runs out of house)

Chapter 72
Totosai's Strange Training

144.1 FX: Ka—n ka—n (clang clang)
144.3 FX: Kan (clang)

149.2 FX: Pori pori (scratching)

150.3 FX: Bashi (Inuyasha smacks Totosai on the shoulder)

155.4 FX: Basha (splash)

157.2 FX: Zuki (struggling)

158.2 FX: Doh (chomp)
158.5 FX: Yoro... (stagger)
158.6 FX: Gaku (Bunza's ax pulls him over backwards)

159.3 FX: Doh (plop)

163.1 FX: Gohhhh... (whoosh)

164.1 FX: Pyon (hop)

165.2 FX: Zuba (slash)
165.4 FX: Buru buru... (shivering)

166.4 FX: Su (Inuyasha proffers his own dinner)

191.6 FX: Goh (Inuyasha conjures up Tetsusaiga's power)

192.1 FX: Goh (whoosh of Wind Scar)
192.2 FX: Goh (whoosh)
192.3 FX: Ga ga ga (Wind Scar heads toward barrier)
192.4 FX: Zuba (Wind Scar slashes barrier)
193.1 FX: Suu... (barrier disintegrates)
193.3 FX: Ba (mantis demon lunges)
193.5 FX: Go (mantis demon lunges)

194.1 FX: Zuba (a big slash)
194.2 FX: Zuun... (mantis demon gets sliced like sashimi)
194.3 FX: Dosa (mantis demon crashes lifeless to the ground, hopefully dead)
194.4 FX: Ta (Inuyahsa touches down to safety)

195.2 FX: Zu... (mantis gets up)
195.2/3 FX: Meki (crackling)
195.3 FX: Meki (crackling)
195.6 FX: Doga (demon slashes where Inuyasha just was)

196.1 FX: Ba (Inuyasha slashes)
196.2 FX: Goh (whoosh)
196.3 FX: Zan (demon's power destroyed)

197.1 FX: Shuuu... (demon fades away)

202.2 FX: Hiku hiku... (twitching)

204.1 FX: Gohhhh... (Kirara whooshes through the air)

205.4 FX: Doh (Inuyasha does face plant)

170.4 FX: Ba (Bunza moves door mat aside)

171.4 FX: Da (Bunza dashes off to help)

172.1 FX: Ta ta ta... (running)
172.2 FX: Ta (running)

173.3 FX: Ta (running)

174.4 FX: Muku (Totosai sits up)
174.5 FX: Ta (running)

175.1 FX: Goh (Kirara whooshes off)

176.5 FX: Goh (Kirara whooshes overhead)

177.1 FX: Za (Bunza falls)
177.4 FX: Goh (Kirara dives)
177.5 FX: Ba (Inuyasha grabs Bunza)

180.5 FX: Ta (Inuyasha and Bunza alight)

181.2 FX: Ta (running)

182.2 FX: Suu... (barrier opens)
182.4 FX: Zu zu zu... (hole opens in barrier)

185.2 FX: Ba (Bunza charges toward barrier)
185.4 FX: Giin (clang)
185.5 FX: Bari (crackling as Bunza is repulsed by barrier)
185.6 FX: Za (Bunza lands on ground)

187.1 FX: Zawa... (rustling in the underbrush)
187.2 FX: Za za za... (the demon approaches)

188.3 FX: Za za... (mantis demon emerges)

189.1 FX: Grrrr!
189.2 FX: Ta (Inuyasha leaps upwards)
189.4 FX: Cha (Inuyasha whips out Tetsusaiga)

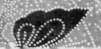

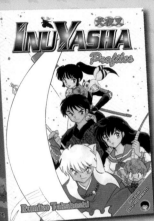
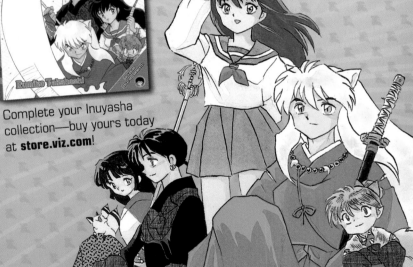

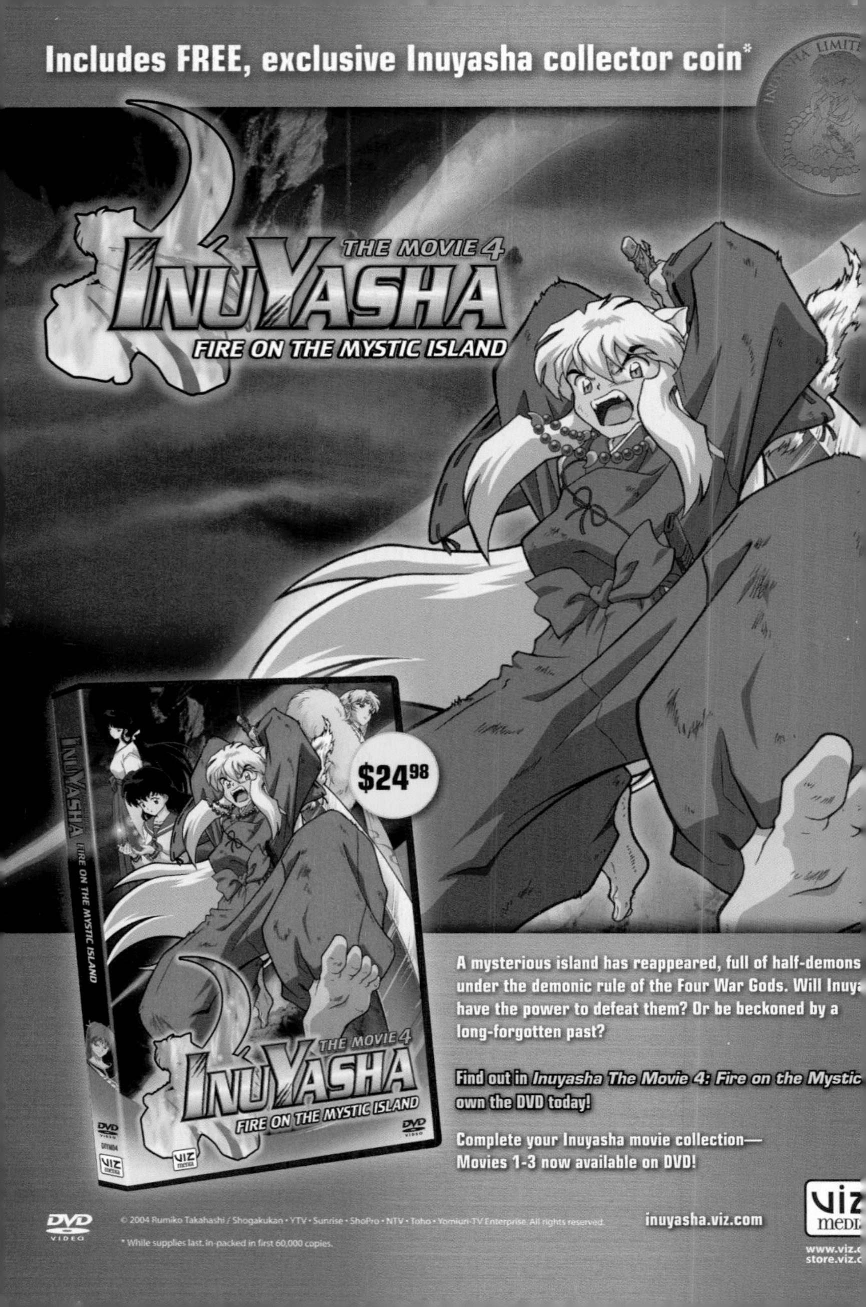

Includes FREE, exclusive Inuyasha collector coin*
INUYASHA THE MOVIE 4
FIRE ON THE MYSTIC ISLAND
$24.98
A mysterious island has reappeared, full of half-demons under the demonic rule of the Four War Gods. Will Inuy
have the power to defeat them? Or be beckoned by a long-forgotten past?
Find out in Inuyasha The Movie 4: Fire on the Mystic
own the DVD today!
Complete your Inuyasha movie collection—
Movies 1-3 now available on DVD!
© 2004 Rumiko Takahashi / Shogakukan • YTV • Sunrise • ShoPro • NTV • Toho • Yomiuri-TV Enterprise. All rights reserved.
* While supplies last. in-packed in first 60,000 copies.
inuyasha.viz.com

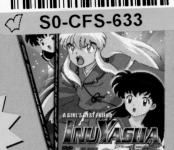
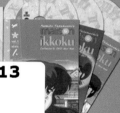
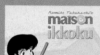
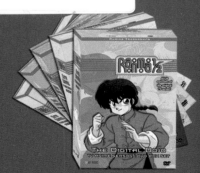